The COMPLETE ENCYCLICALS, BULLS, and APOSTOLIC EXHORTATIONS

Volume II

"If you don't feel challenged by his words, then you're not paying attention. With the passion of a pastor and the wisdom of a bishop, Pope Francis addresses urgent, global events including the pandemic, the Amazon, young people, and family life. In word and deed, the Holy Father brings the Gospel message to comfort the afflicted and afflict the comfortable."

Fr. Joseph Laramie, S.J.

National director of the Pope's Worldwide Prayer Network

"With *Fratelli Tutti,* Francis has moved opposition to the death penalty into the foreground of Catholic social teaching, completing the Church's long journey of mercy and reconciliation."

Fr. James Martin, S.J.

"*Christus Vivit* is a wonderful summons to the whole Church to more vigorously invest in youth and young adults, especially those on the peripheries and those who are disconnected from the Church."

The United States Conference of Catholic Bishops

POPE FRANCIS

The COMPLETE ENCYCLICALS, BULLS, and APOSTOLIC EXHORTATIONS

VOLUME II

AVE MARIA PRESS AVE Notre Dame, Indiana

Founded in 1865, Ave Maria Press is a ministry of the United States Province of Holy Cross.

www.avemariapress.com

Paperback: ISBN-13 978-1-64680-113-8

E-book: ISBN-13 978-1-64680-114-5

Cover and text design by K. H. Bonelli and David Scholtes.

Printed and bound in the United States of America.

Contents

Publisher's Note

The writings contained in this second volume of Pope Francis's major works were promulgated between 2018 and 2020. As such, they take up where the first volume left off. These teachings are presented in various categories of papal instruction: encyclicals, apostolic exhortations, apostolic letters. Despite the title, this volume does not contain any papal bulls because none were released by the Holy Father during this time period. The appendix, however, includes a document signed in Abu Dhabi by Pope Francis and the Grand Imam of Al-Azhar Ahmad Al-Tayyeb. This document is of particular importance, as it was the impetus for Pope Francis's most recent encyclical, *Fratelli Tutti*.

It may be useful to review what these various terms mean. *Encyclical* comes from the Latin word *encyclicus*, meaning "circular." In the ancient Church, encyclicals were actual circulating letters. Today, they are book-length reflections by the Holy Father on significant issues—usually matters of faith or morals—of vital importance to the worldwide Church and beyond. Papal bulls are formal legal declarations, named for the *bulla* or traditional leaden "seal" on the document. Similarly, a document issued *motu proprio* is a legal act, but one that is at the pope's initiative and not covered by the Code of Canon Law. An apostolic letter is generally addressed to particular groups, often on the occasion of a milestone anniversary, for the purpose of clarifying or communicating a concern. Lastly, apostolic exhortations are intended to encourage the faithful to greater virtue or deeper conversion.

Each of the six writings collected here could be books in themselves. They are presented in this volume, as in the first, in the order in which they were promulgated:

Gaudete et Exultate, March 19, 2018: In his apostolic exhortation *Rejoice and Be Glad: On the Call of Holiness in Today's World,* Pope

Francis reissues the universal call to holiness, challenges us to recognize the "saints next door" whom we encounter in daily life, and provides a practical meditation on how we can respond to the Lord's invitation to become his disciples.

Christus Vivit, March 25, 2019: *Christ Is Alive* is the post-synodal apostolic exhortation to young people framed on three key principles: God loves you, Jesus saves and suffers with you, and Jesus is alive. In it, Pope Francis reflects on Jesus as a young man and encourages the whole Church to reclaim a spirit of youthful vitality.

Aperuit Illis, September 30, 2019: This apostolic letter, *Instituting the Sunday of the Word of God*, was issued *motu proprio* on the Feast of St. Jerome, the Church's first biblical translator. While brief, the letter reflects on Vatican II's teaching on the importance of the scriptures and encourages all Catholics to embrace the Bible as part of their rich spiritual heritage.

Querida Amazonia, February 12, 2020: The 2020 post-synodal apostolic exhortation *Beloved Amazon* addresses injustice and exploitation in the Amazon region, outlines challenges to caring for creation and respecting the cultures of indigenous peoples, and renews consideration of how the Church's mission can and should take shape in the twenty-first century.

Fratelli Tutti, October 4, 2020: *All Brothers and Sisters: On Fraternity and Social Friendship* is Pope Francis's third encyclical and the only one written between 2017 and 2020. This seminal work challenges us to take a fresh look at the great ideals of the Church's social teaching and put them into practice on a new—and more personal—level.

Patris Corde, December 8, 2020: In this unexpected apostolic letter, *With a Father's Heart*, Pope Francis marks the 150th anniversary of Bl. Pope Pius IX's designation of St. Joseph as Patron of the Universal

Church, declares a Year of St. Joseph, and provides a beautiful extended meditation on the various facets of Joseph's fatherhood.

Apostolic Journey to the United Arab Emirates, February 4, 2019: The *Document on Human Fraternity for World Peace and Living Together* was cosigned in Abu Dhabi by Pope Francis and the Grand Imam of Al-Azhar Ahmad Al-Tayyeb. *Fratelli Tutti* has been called an extension of this document and cites it frequently; therefore, this document is included in this volume's appendix.

Abbreviations

The following abbreviations for texts referenced in many papal documents appear in the endnotes. They are listed below for the convenience of readers who desire to explore the pope's ideas in greater detail.

AAS *Acta Apostolicae Sedis*: Latin for "Acts of the Apostolic See." An official journal of the Holy See first established by Pope Pius X in 1908.

GS *Gaudium et Spes*: Pastoral Constitution on the Church in the Modern World. A constitution of the Second Vatican Council, first promulgated by Pope Paul VI in 1965.

PG *Patrologia Graeca*, edited by J. P. Migne. One hundred sixty-one volumes of the works of early Christian writers in Greek, published in Paris between 1857 and 1866.

PL *Patrologia Latina*, edited by J. P. Migne. Two hundred seventeen volumes of early Christian writers in Latin, plus additional indices, published in Paris between 1878 and 1890.

SC *Sacrosanctum Concilium*: Constitution on Sacred Liturgy. A constitution of the Second Vatican Council, first promulgated by Pope Paul VI in 1963.

Gaudete et Exsultate
Rejoice and Be Glad

Apostolic Exhortation on the Call of Holiness in Today's World

March 19, 2018

GAUDETE ET EXSULTATE
APOSTOLIC EXHORTATION OF THE HOLY FATHER **FRANCIS** ON THE CALL OF HOLINESS IN TODAY'S WORLD

1. "Rejoice and be glad" (Mt 5:12), Jesus tells those persecuted or humiliated for his sake. The Lord asks everything of us, and in return he offers us true life, the happiness for which we were created. He wants us to be saints and not to settle for a bland and mediocre existence. The call to holiness is present in various ways from the very first pages of the Bible. We see it expressed in the Lord's words to Abraham: "Walk before me, and be blameless" (Gn 17:1).

2. What follows is not meant to be a treatise on holiness, containing definitions and distinctions helpful for understanding this important subject, or a discussion of the various means of sanctification. My modest goal is to repropose the call to holiness in a practical way for our own time, with all its risks, challenges, and opportunities. For the Lord has chosen each one of us "to be holy and blameless before him in love" (Eph 1:4).

CHAPTER ONE

THE CALL TO HOLINESS

The Saints Who Encourage and Accompany Us

3. The Letter to the Hebrews presents a number of testimonies that encourage us to "run with perseverance the race that is set before us" (12:1). It speaks of Abraham, Sarah, Moses, Gideon, and others (cf. 11:1–12:3). Above all, it invites us to realize that "a great cloud of witnesses" (12:1) impels us to advance constantly toward the goal. These witnesses may include our own mothers, grandmothers, or other loved ones (cf. 2 Tm 1:5). Their lives may not always have been perfect, yet even amid their faults and failings they kept moving forward and proved pleasing to the Lord.

4. The saints now in God's presence preserve their bonds of love and communion with us. The Book of Revelation attests to this when it speaks of the intercession of the martyrs: "I saw under the altar the souls of those who had been slain for the word of God and for the witness they had borne; they cried out with a loud voice, 'O sovereign Lord, holy and true, how long will it be before you judge?'" (6:9–10). Each of us can say: "Surrounded, led, and guided by the friends of God. . . . I do not have to carry alone what, in truth, I could never carry alone. All the saints of God are there to protect me, to sustain me, and to carry me."[1]

5. The processes of beatification and canonization recognize the signs of heroic virtue, the sacrifice of one's life in martyrdom, and certain cases where a life is constantly offered for others, even until death. This shows an exemplary imitation of Christ, one worthy of the admiration of the faithful.[2] We can think, for example, of Blessed Maria Gabriella Sagheddu, who offered her life for the unity of Christians.

The Saints "Next Door"

6. Nor need we think only of those already beatified and canonized. The Holy Spirit bestows holiness in abundance among God's holy and

faithful people, for "it has pleased God to make men and women holy and to save them, not as individuals without any bond between them, but rather as a people who might acknowledge him in truth and serve him in holiness."[3] In salvation history, the Lord saved one people. We are never completely ourselves unless we belong to a people. That is why no one is saved alone, as an isolated individual. Rather, God draws us to himself, taking into account the complex fabric of interpersonal relationships present in a human community. God wanted to enter into the life and history of a people.

7. I like to contemplate the holiness present in the patience of God's people: in those parents who raise their children with immense love, in those men and women who work hard to support their families, in the sick, in elderly religious who never lose their smile. In their daily perseverance I see the holiness of the Church militant. Very often it is a holiness found in our next-door neighbors, those who, living in our midst, reflect God's presence. We might call them "the middle class of holiness."[4]

8. Let us be spurred on by the signs of holiness that the Lord shows us through the humblest members of that people which "shares also in Christ's prophetic office, spreading abroad a living witness to him, especially by means of a life of faith and charity."[5] We should consider the fact that, as Saint Teresa Benedicta of the Cross suggests, real history is made by so many of them. As she writes: "The greatest figures of prophecy and sanctity step forth out of the darkest night. But for the most part, the formative stream of the mystical life remains invisible. Certainly the most decisive turning points in world history are substantially co-determined by souls whom no history book ever mentions. And we will only find out about those souls to whom we owe the decisive turning points in our personal lives on the day when all that is hidden is revealed."[6]

9. Holiness is the most attractive face of the Church. But even outside the Catholic Church and in very different contexts, the Holy Spirit raises up "signs of his presence which help Christ's followers."[7] Saint John Paul

II reminded us that "the witness to Christ borne even to the shedding of blood has become a common inheritance of Catholics, Orthodox, Anglicans and Protestants."[8] In the moving ecumenical commemoration held in the Colosseum during the Great Jubilee of the Year 2000, he stated that the martyrs are "a heritage which speaks more powerfully than all the causes of division."[9]

The Lord Calls

10. All this is important. Yet with this Exhortation I would like to insist primarily on the call to holiness that the Lord addresses to each of us, the call that he also addresses, personally, to you: "Be holy, for I am holy" (Lv 11:44; cf. 1 Pt 1:16). The Second Vatican Council stated this clearly: "Strengthened by so many and such great means of salvation, all the faithful, whatever their condition or state, are called by the Lord—each in his or her own way—to that perfect holiness by which the Father himself is perfect."[10]

11. "Each in his or her own way," the Council says. We should not grow discouraged before examples of holiness that appear unattainable. There are some testimonies that may prove helpful and inspiring, but that we are not meant to copy, for that could even lead us astray from the one specific path that the Lord has in mind for us. The important thing is that each believer discern his or her own path, that they bring out the very best of themselves, the most personal gifts that God has placed in their hearts (cf. 1 Cor 12:7), rather than hopelessly trying to imitate something not meant for them. We are all called to be witnesses, but there are many actual ways of bearing witness.[11] Indeed, when the great mystic, Saint John of the Cross, wrote his *Spiritual Canticle*, he preferred to avoid hard and fast rules for all. He explained that his verses were composed so that everyone could benefit from them "in his or her own way."[12] For God's life is communicated "to some in one way and to others in another."[13]

12. Within these various forms, I would stress too that the "genius of woman" is seen in feminine styles of holiness, which are an essential

means of reflecting God's holiness in this world. Indeed, in times when women tended to be most ignored or overlooked, the Holy Spirit raised up saints whose attractiveness produced new spiritual vigor and important reforms in the Church. We can mention Saint Hildegard of Bingen, Saint Bridget, Saint Catherine of Siena, Saint Teresa of Avila, and Saint Thérèse of Lisieux. But I think too of all those unknown or forgotten women who, each in her own way, sustained and transformed families and communities by the power of their witness.

13. This should excite and encourage us to give our all and to embrace that unique plan that God willed for each of us from eternity: "Before I formed you in the womb I knew you, and before you were born I consecrated you" (Jer 1:5).

For You Too

14. To be holy does not require being a bishop, a priest, or a religious. We are frequently tempted to think that holiness is only for those who can withdraw from ordinary affairs to spend much time in prayer. That is not the case. We are all called to be holy by living our lives with love and by bearing witness in everything we do, wherever we find ourselves. Are you called to the consecrated life? Be holy by living out your commitment with joy. Are you married? Be holy by loving and caring for your husband or wife, as Christ does for the Church. Do you work for a living? Be holy by laboring with integrity and skill in the service of your brothers and sisters. Are you a parent or grandparent? Be holy by patiently teaching the little ones how to follow Jesus. Are you in a position of authority? Be holy by working for the common good and renouncing personal gain.[14]

15. Let the grace of your baptism bear fruit in a path of holiness. Let everything be open to God; turn to him in every situation. Do not be dismayed, for the power of the Holy Spirit enables you to do this, and holiness, in the end, is the fruit of the Holy Spirit in your life (cf. Gal 5:22–23). When you feel the temptation to dwell on your own weakness,

raise your eyes to Christ crucified and say: "Lord, I am a poor sinner, but you can work the miracle of making me a little bit better." In the Church, holy yet made up of sinners, you will find everything you need to grow toward holiness. The Lord has bestowed on the Church the gifts of scripture, the sacraments, holy places, living communities, the witness of the saints, and a multifaceted beauty that proceeds from God's love, "like a bride bedecked with jewels" (Is 61:10).

16. This holiness to which the Lord calls you will grow through small gestures. Here is an example: a woman goes shopping, she meets a neighbor and they begin to speak, and the gossip starts. But she says in her heart: "No, I will not speak badly of anyone." This is a step forward in holiness. Later, at home, one of her children wants to talk to her about his hopes and dreams, and even though she is tired, she sits down and listens with patience and love. That is another sacrifice that brings holiness. Later she experiences some anxiety, but recalling the love of the Virgin Mary, she takes her rosary and prays with faith. Yet another path of holiness. Later still, she goes out onto the street, encounters a poor person, and stops to say a kind word to him. One more step.

17. At times, life presents great challenges. Through them, the Lord calls us anew to a conversion that can make his grace more evident in our lives, "in order that we may share his holiness" (Heb 12:10). At other times, we need only find a more perfect way of doing what we are already doing: "There are inspirations that tend solely to perfect in an extraordinary way the ordinary things we do in life."[15] When Cardinal François-Xavier Nguyên van Thuân was imprisoned, he refused to waste time waiting for the day he would be set free. Instead, he chose "to live the present moment, filling it to the brim with love." He decided: "I will seize the occasions that present themselves every day; I will accomplish ordinary actions in an extraordinary way."[16]

18. In this way, led by God's grace, we shape by many small gestures the holiness God has willed for us, not as men and women sufficient unto

ourselves but rather "as good stewards of the manifold grace of God" (1 Pt 4:10). The New Zealand bishops rightly teach us that we are capable of loving with the Lord's unconditional love, because the risen Lord shares his powerful life with our fragile lives: "His love set no limits and, once given, was never taken back. It was unconditional and remained faithful. To love like that is not easy because we are often so weak. But just to try to love as Christ loved us shows that Christ shares his own risen life with us. In this way, our lives demonstrate his power at work—even in the midst of human weakness."[17]

Your Mission in Christ

19. A Christian cannot think of his or her mission on earth without seeing it as a path of holiness, for "this is the will of God, your sanctification" (1 Thes 4:3). Each saint is a mission, planned by the Father to reflect and embody, at a specific moment in history, a certain aspect of the Gospel.

20. That mission has its fullest meaning in Christ, and can only be understood through him. At its core, holiness is experiencing, in union with Christ, the mysteries of his life. It consists in uniting ourselves to the Lord's death and resurrection in a unique and personal way, constantly dying and rising anew with him. But it can also entail reproducing in our own lives various aspects of Jesus' earthly life: his hidden life, his life in community, his closeness to the outcast, his poverty, and other ways in which he showed his self-sacrificing love. The contemplation of these mysteries, as Saint Ignatius of Loyola pointed out, leads us to incarnate them in our choices and attitudes.[18] Because "everything in Jesus' life was a sign of his mystery,"[19] "Christ's whole life is a revelation of the Father,"[20] "Christ's whole life is a mystery of redemption,"[21] "Christ's whole life is a mystery of recapitulation."[22] "Christ enables us to live in him all that he himself lived, and he lives it in us."[23]

21. The Father's plan is Christ, and ourselves in him. In the end, it is Christ who loves in us, for "holiness is nothing other than charity lived to the full."[24] As a result, "the measure of our holiness stems from the

stature that Christ achieves in us, to the extent that, by the power of the Holy Spirit, we model our whole life on his."[25] Every saint is a message which the Holy Spirit takes from the riches of Jesus Christ and gives to his people.

22. To recognize the word that the Lord wishes to speak to us through one of his saints, we do not need to get caught up in details, for there we might also encounter mistakes and failures. Not everything a saint says is completely faithful to the Gospel; not everything he or she does is authentic or perfect. What we need to contemplate is the totality of their life, their entire journey of growth in holiness, the reflection of Jesus Christ that emerges when we grasp their overall meaning as a person.[26]

23. This is a powerful summons to all of us. You too need to see the entirety of your life as a mission. Try to do so by listening to God in prayer and recognizing the signs that he gives you. Always ask the Spirit what Jesus expects from you at every moment of your life and in every decision you must make, so as to discern its place in the mission you have received. Allow the Spirit to forge in you the personal mystery that can reflect Jesus Christ in today's world.

24. May you come to realize what that word is, the message of Jesus that God wants to speak to the world by your life. Let yourself be transformed. Let yourself be renewed by the Spirit, so that this can happen, lest you fail in your precious mission. The Lord will bring it to fulfillment despite your mistakes and missteps, provided that you do not abandon the path of love but remain ever open to his supernatural grace, which purifies and enlightens.

Activity That Sanctifies

25. Just as you cannot understand Christ apart from the kingdom he came to bring, so too your personal mission is inseparable from the building of that kingdom: "Strive first for the kingdom of God and his righteousness" (Mt 6:33). Your identification with Christ and his will involves a commitment to build with him that kingdom of love, justice,

and universal peace. Christ himself wants to experience this with you, in all the efforts and sacrifices that it entails, but also in all the joy and enrichment it brings. You cannot grow in holiness without committing yourself, body and soul, to giving your best to this endeavor.

26. It is not healthy to love silence while fleeing interaction with others, to want peace and quiet while avoiding activity, to seek prayer while disdaining service. Everything can be accepted and integrated into our life in this world, and become a part of our path to holiness. We are called to be contemplatives even in the midst of action, and to grow in holiness by responsibly and generously carrying out our proper mission.

27. Could the Holy Spirit urge us to carry out a mission and then ask us to abandon it, or not fully engage in it, so as to preserve our inner peace? Yet there are times when we are tempted to relegate pastoral engagement or commitment in the world to second place, as if these were "distractions" along the path to growth in holiness and interior peace. We can forget that "life does not have a mission, but is a mission."[27]

28. Needless to say, anything done out of anxiety, pride, or the need to impress others will not lead to holiness. We are challenged to show our commitment in such a way that everything we do has evangelical meaning and identifies us all the more with Jesus Christ. We often speak, for example, of the spirituality of the catechist, the spirituality of the diocesan priesthood, the spirituality of work. For the same reason, in *Evangelii Gaudium* I concluded by speaking of a spirituality of mission, in *Laudato Si'* of an ecological spirituality, and in *Amoris Laetitia* of a spirituality of family life.

29. This does not mean ignoring the need for moments of quiet, solitude, and silence before God. Quite the contrary. The presence of constantly new gadgets, the excitement of travel, and an endless array of consumer goods at times leave no room for God's voice to be heard. We are overwhelmed by words, by superficial pleasures, and by an increasing din, filled not by joy but rather by the discontent of those whose lives have lost meaning. How can we fail to realize the need to stop this rat race

and to recover the personal space needed to carry on a heartfelt dialogue with God? Finding that space may prove painful but it is always fruitful. Sooner or later, we have to face our true selves and let the Lord enter. This may not happen unless "we see ourselves staring into the abyss of a frightful temptation, or have the dizzying sensation of standing on the precipice of utter despair, or find ourselves completely alone and abandoned."[28] In such situations, we find the deepest motivation for living fully our commitment to our work.

30. The same distractions that are omnipresent in today's world also make us tend to absolutize our free time, so that we can give ourselves over completely to the devices that provide us with entertainment or ephemeral pleasures.[29] As a result, we come to resent our mission, our commitment grows slack, and our generous and ready spirit of service begins to flag. This denatures our spiritual experience. Can any spiritual fervor be sound when it dwells alongside sloth in evangelization or in service to others?

31. We need a spirit of holiness capable of filling both our solitude and our service, our personal life and our evangelizing efforts, so that every moment can be an expression of self-sacrificing love in the Lord's eyes. In this way, every minute of our lives can be a step along the path to growth in holiness.

More Alive, More Human

32. Do not be afraid of holiness. It will take away none of your energy, vitality, or joy. On the contrary, you will become what the Father had in mind when he created you, and you will be faithful to your deepest self. To depend on God sets us free from every form of enslavement and leads us to recognize our great dignity. We see this in Saint Josephine Bakhita: "Abducted and sold into slavery at the tender age of seven, she suffered much at the hands of cruel masters. But she came to understand the profound truth that God, and not man, is the true Master of every human being, of every human life. This experience became a source of great wisdom for this humble daughter of Africa."[30]

33. To the extent that each Christian grows in holiness, he or she will bear greater fruit for our world. The bishops of West Africa have observed that "we are being called in the spirit of the New Evangelization to be evangelized and to evangelize through the empowering of all you, the baptized, to take up your roles as salt of the earth and light of the world wherever you find yourselves."[31]

34. Do not be afraid to set your sights higher, to allow yourself to be loved and liberated by God. Do not be afraid to let yourself be guided by the Holy Spirit. Holiness does not make you less human, since it is an encounter between your weakness and the power of God's grace. For in the words of León Bloy, when all is said and done, "the only great tragedy in life, is not to become a saint."[32]

CHAPTER TWO

TWO SUBTLE ENEMIES OF HOLINESS

35. Here I would like to mention two false forms of holiness that can lead us astray: gnosticism and pelagianism. They are two heresies from early Christian times, yet they continue to plague us. In our times too, many Christians, perhaps without realizing it, can be seduced by these deceptive ideas, which reflect an anthropocentric immanentism disguised as Catholic truth.[33] Let us take a look at these two forms of doctrinal or disciplinary security that give rise "to a narcissistic and authoritarian elitism, whereby instead of evangelizing, one analyses and classifies others, and instead of opening the door to grace, one exhausts his or her energies in inspecting and verifying. In neither case is one really concerned about Jesus Christ or others."[34]

Contemporary Gnosticism

36. Gnosticism presumes "a purely subjective faith whose only interest is a certain experience or a set of ideas and bits of information which are meant to console and enlighten, but which ultimately keep one imprisoned in his or her own thoughts and feelings."[35]

An Intellect without God and without Flesh

37. Thanks be to God, throughout the history of the Church it has always been clear that a person's perfection is measured not by the information or knowledge they possess, but by the depth of their charity. "Gnostics" do not understand this, because they judge others based on their ability to understand the complexity of certain doctrines. They think of the intellect as separate from the flesh, and thus become incapable of touching Christ's suffering flesh in others, locked up as they are in an encyclopedia of abstractions. In the end, by disembodying the mystery, they prefer "a God without Christ, a Christ without the Church, a Church without her people."[36]

38. Certainly this is a superficial conceit: there is much movement on the surface, but the mind is neither deeply moved nor affected. Still, gnosticism exercises a deceptive attraction for some people, since the gnostic approach is strict and allegedly pure, and can appear to possess a certain harmony or order that encompasses everything.

39. Here we have to be careful. I am not referring to a rationalism inimical to Christian faith. It can be present within the Church, both among the laity in parishes and teachers of philosophy and theology in centers of formation. Gnostics think that their explanations can make the entirety of the faith and the Gospel perfectly comprehensible. They absolutize their own theories and force others to submit to their way of thinking. A healthy and humble use of reason in order to reflect on the theological and moral teaching of the Gospel is one thing. It is another to reduce Jesus' teaching to a cold and harsh logic that seeks to dominate everything.[37]

A Doctrine without Mystery

40. Gnosticism is one of the most sinister ideologies because, while unduly exalting knowledge or a specific experience, it considers its own vision of reality to be perfect. Thus, perhaps without even realizing it, this ideology feeds on itself and becomes even more myopic. It can become all the more illusory when it masks itself as a disembodied spirituality. For gnosticism "by its very nature seeks to domesticate the mystery,"[38] whether the mystery of God and his grace, or the mystery of others' lives.

41. When somebody has an answer for every question, it is a sign that they are not on the right road. They may well be false prophets, who use religion for their own purposes, to promote their own psychological or intellectual theories. God infinitely transcends us; he is full of surprises. We are not the ones to determine when and how we will encounter him; the exact times and places of that encounter are not up to us. Someone who wants everything to be clear and sure presumes to control God's transcendence.

42. Nor can we claim to say where God is not, because God is mysteriously present in the life of every person, in a way that he himself chooses, and we cannot exclude this by our presumed certainties. Even when someone's life appears completely wrecked, even when we see it devastated by vices or addictions, God is present there. If we let ourselves be guided by the Spirit rather than our own preconceptions, we can and must try to find the Lord in every human life. This is part of the mystery that a gnostic mentality cannot accept, since it is beyond its control.

The Limits of Reason

43. It is not easy to grasp the truth that we have received from the Lord. And it is even more difficult to express it. So we cannot claim that our way of understanding this truth authorizes us to exercise a strict supervision over others' lives. Here I would note that in the Church there legitimately coexist different ways of interpreting many aspects of doctrine and Christian life; in their variety, they "help to express more clearly the immense riches of God's word." It is true that "for those who long for a monolithic body of doctrine guarded by all and leaving no room for nuance, this might appear as undesirable and leading to confusion."[39] Indeed, some currents of gnosticism scorned the concrete simplicity of the Gospel and attempted to replace the trinitarian and incarnate God with a superior Unity, wherein the rich diversity of our history disappeared.

44. In effect, doctrine, or better, our understanding and expression of it, "is not a closed system, devoid of the dynamic capacity to pose questions, doubts, inquiries. . . . The questions of our people, their suffering, their struggles, their dreams, their trials and their worries, all possess an interpretational value that we cannot ignore if we want to take the principle of the incarnation seriously. Their wondering helps us to wonder, their questions question us."[40]

45. A dangerous confusion can arise. We can think that because we know something, or are able to explain it in certain terms, we are already saints, perfect and better than the "ignorant masses." Saint John Paul II warned

of the temptation on the part of those in the Church who are more highly educated "to feel somehow superior to other members of the faithful."[41] In point of fact, what we think we know should always motivate us to respond more fully to God's love. Indeed, "you learn so as to live: theology and holiness are inseparable."[42]

46. When Saint Francis of Assisi saw that some of his disciples were engaged in teaching, he wanted to avoid the temptation to gnosticism. He wrote to Saint Anthony of Padua: "I am pleased that you teach sacred theology to the brothers, provided that . . . you do not extinguish the spirit of prayer and devotion during study of this kind."[43] Francis recognized the temptation to turn the Christian experience into a set of intellectual exercises that distance us from the freshness of the Gospel. Saint Bonaventure, on the other hand, pointed out that true Christian wisdom can never be separated from mercy toward our neighbor: "The greatest possible wisdom is to share fruitfully what we have to give. . . . Even as mercy is the companion of wisdom, avarice is its enemy."[44] "There are activities that, united to contemplation, do not prevent the latter, but rather facilitate it, such as works of mercy and devotion."[45]

Contemporary Pelagianism

47. Gnosticism gave way to another heresy, likewise present in our day. As time passed, many came to realize that it is not knowledge that betters us or makes us saints, but the kind of life we lead. But this subtly led back to the old error of the gnostics, which was simply transformed rather than eliminated.

48. The same power that the gnostics attributed to the intellect, others now began to attribute to the human will, to personal effort. This was the case with the pelagians and semi-pelagians. Now it was not intelligence that took the place of mystery and grace, but our human will. It was forgotten that everything "depends not on human will or exertion, but on God who shows mercy" (Rom 9:16) and that "he first loved us" (cf. 1 Jn 4:19).

A Will Lacking Humility

49. Those who yield to this pelagian or semi-pelagian mindset, even though they speak warmly of God's grace, "ultimately trust only in their own powers and feel superior to others because they observe certain rules or remain intransigently faithful to a particular Catholic style."[46] When some of them tell the weak that all things can be accomplished with God's grace, deep down they tend to give the idea that all things are possible by the human will, as if it were something pure, perfect, all-powerful, to which grace is then added. They fail to realize that "not everyone can do everything,"[47] and that in this life human weaknesses are not healed completely and once for all by grace.[48] In every case, as Saint Augustine taught, God commands you to do what you can and to ask for what you cannot,[49] and indeed to pray to him humbly: "Grant what you command, and command what you will."[50]

50. Ultimately, the lack of a heartfelt and prayerful acknowledgment of our limitations prevents grace from working more effectively within us, for no room is left for bringing about the potential good that is part of a sincere and genuine journey of growth.[51] Grace, precisely because it builds on nature, does not make us superhuman all at once. That kind of thinking would show too much confidence in our own abilities. Underneath our orthodoxy, our attitudes might not correspond to our talk about the need for grace, and in specific situations we can end up putting little trust in it. Unless we can acknowledge our concrete and limited situation, we will not be able to see the real and possible steps that the Lord demands of us at every moment, once we are attracted and empowered by his gift. Grace acts in history; ordinarily it takes hold of us and transforms us progressively.[52] If we reject this historical and progressive reality, we can actually refuse and block grace, even as we extol it by our words.

51. When God speaks to Abraham, he tells him: "I am God Almighty, walk before me, and be blameless" (Gn 17:1). In order to be blameless,

as he would have us, we need to live humbly in his presence, cloaked in his glory; we need to walk in union with him, recognizing his constant love in our lives. We need to lose our fear before that presence which can only be for our good. God is the Father who gave us life and loves us greatly. Once we accept him, and stop trying to live our lives without him, the anguish of loneliness will disappear (cf. Ps 139:23–24). In this way we will know the pleasing and perfect will of the Lord (cf. Rom 12:1–2) and allow him to mold us like a potter (cf. Is 29:16). So often we say that God dwells in us, but it is better to say that we dwell in him, that he enables us to dwell in his light and love. He is our temple; we ask to dwell in the house of the Lord all the days of our life (cf. Ps 27:4). "For one day in your courts is better than a thousand elsewhere" (Ps 84:10). In him is our holiness.

An Often Overlooked Church Teaching

52. The Church has repeatedly taught that we are justified not by our own works or efforts, but by the grace of the Lord, who always takes the initiative. The Fathers of the Church, even before Saint Augustine, clearly expressed this fundamental belief. Saint John Chrysostom said that God pours into us the very source of all his gifts even before we enter into battle.[53] Saint Basil the Great remarked that the faithful glory in God alone, for "they realize that they lack true justice and are justified only through faith in Christ."[54]

53. The Second Synod of Orange taught with firm authority that nothing human can demand, merit, or buy the gift of divine grace, and that all cooperation with it is a prior gift of that same grace: "Even the desire to be cleansed comes about in us through the outpouring and working of the Holy Spirit."[55] Subsequently, the Council of Trent, while emphasizing the importance of our cooperation for spiritual growth, reaffirmed that dogmatic teaching: "We are said to be justified gratuitously because nothing that precedes justification, neither faith nor works, merits the

grace of justification; for 'if it is by grace, it is no longer on the basis of works; otherwise, grace would no longer be grace'" (Rom 11:6).[56]

54. The Catechism of the Catholic Church also reminds us that the gift of grace "surpasses the power of human intellect and will"[57] and that "with regard to God, there is no strict right to any merit on the part of man. Between God and us there is an immeasurable inequality."[58] His friendship infinitely transcends us; we cannot buy it with our works, it can only be a gift born of his loving initiative. This invites us to live in joyful gratitude for this completely unmerited gift, since "after one has grace, the grace already possessed cannot come under merit."[59] The saints avoided putting trust in their own works: "In the evening of this life, I shall appear before you empty-handed, for I do not ask you, Lord, to count my works. All our justices have stains in your sight."[60]

55. This is one of the great convictions that the Church has come firmly to hold. It is so clearly expressed in the word of God that there can be no question of it. Like the supreme commandment of love, this truth should affect the way we live, for it flows from the heart of the Gospel and demands that we not only accept it intellectually but also make it a source of contagious joy. Yet we cannot celebrate this free gift of the Lord's friendship unless we realize that our earthly life and our natural abilities are his gift. We need "to acknowledge jubilantly that our life is essentially a gift, and recognize that our freedom is a grace. This is not easy today, in a world that thinks it can keep something for itself, the fruits of its own creativity or freedom."[61]

56. Only on the basis of God's gift, freely accepted and humbly received, can we cooperate by our own efforts in our progressive transformation.[62] We must first belong to God, offering ourselves to him who was there first, and entrusting to him our abilities, our efforts, our struggle against evil and our creativity, so that his free gift may grow and develop within us: "I appeal to you, therefore, brethren, by the mercies of God, to present your bodies as a living sacrifice, holy and acceptable to God" (Rom

12:1). For that matter, the Church has always taught that charity alone makes growth in the life of grace possible, for "if I do not have love, I am nothing" (1 Cor 13:2).

New Pelagians

57. Still, some Christians insist on taking another path, that of justification by their own efforts, the worship of the human will and their own abilities. The result is a self-centered and elitist complacency, bereft of true love. This finds expression in a variety of apparently unconnected ways of thinking and acting: an obsession with the law, an absorption with social and political advantages, a punctilious concern for the Church's liturgy, doctrine, and prestige, a vanity about the ability to manage practical matters, and an excessive concern with programs of self-help and personal fulfillment. Some Christians spend their time and energy on these things, rather than letting themselves be led by the Spirit in the way of love, rather than being passionate about communicating the beauty and the joy of the Gospel and seeking out the lost among the immense crowds that thirst for Christ.[63]

58. Not infrequently, contrary to the promptings of the Spirit, the life of the Church can become a museum piece or the possession of a select few. This can occur when some groups of Christians give excessive importance to certain rules, customs, or ways of acting. The Gospel then tends to be reduced and constricted, deprived of its simplicity, allure, and savor. This may well be a subtle form of pelagianism, for it appears to subject the life of grace to certain human structures. It can affect groups, movements, and communities, and it explains why so often they begin with an intense life in the Spirit, only to end up fossilized . . . or corrupt.

59. Once we believe that everything depends on human effort as channeled by ecclesial rules and structures, we unconsciously complicate the Gospel and become enslaved to a blueprint that leaves few openings for the working of grace. Saint Thomas Aquinas reminded us that the precepts added to the Gospel by the Church should be imposed with

moderation "lest the conduct of the faithful become burdensome," for then our religion would become a form of servitude.[64]

The Summation of the Law

60. To avoid this, we do well to keep reminding ourselves that there is a hierarchy of virtues that bids us seek what is essential. The primacy belongs to the theological virtues, which have God as their object and motive. At the center is charity. Saint Paul says that what truly counts is "faith working through love" (Gal 5:6). We are called to make every effort to preserve charity: "The one who loves another has fulfilled the law . . . for love is the fulfillment of the law" (Rom 13:8.10). "For the whole law is summed up in a single commandment, 'You shall love your neighbor as yourself'" (Gal 5:14).

61. In other words, amid the thicket of precepts and prescriptions, Jesus clears a way to seeing two faces, that of the Father and that of our brother. He does not give us two more formulas or two more commands. He gives us two faces, or better yet, one alone: the face of God reflected in so many other faces. For in every one of our brothers and sisters, especially the least, the most vulnerable, the defenseless, and those in need, God's very image is found. Indeed, with the scraps of this frail humanity, the Lord will shape his final work of art. For "what endures, what has value in life, what riches do not disappear? Surely these two: the Lord and our neighbor. These two riches do not disappear!"[65]

62. May the Lord set the Church free from these new forms of gnosticism and pelagianism that weigh her down and block her progress along the path to holiness! These aberrations take various shapes, according to the temperament and character of each person. So I encourage everyone to reflect and discern before God whether they may be present in their lives.

CHAPTER THREE

IN THE LIGHT OF THE MASTER

63. There can be any number of theories about what constitutes holiness, with various explanations and distinctions. Such reflection may be useful, but nothing is more enlightening than turning to Jesus' words and seeing his way of teaching the truth. Jesus explained with great simplicity what it means to be holy when he gave us the Beatitudes (cf. Mt 5:3–12; Lk 6:20–23). The Beatitudes are like a Christian's identity card. So if anyone asks: "What must one do to be a good Christian?" the answer is clear. We have to do, each in our own way, what Jesus told us in the Sermon on the Mount.[66] In the Beatitudes, we find a portrait of the Master, which we are called to reflect in our daily lives.

64. The word *happy* or *blessed* thus becomes a synonym for "holy." It expresses the fact that those faithful to God and his word, by their self-giving, gain true happiness.

Going against the Flow

65. Although Jesus' words may strike us as poetic, they clearly run counter to the way things are usually done in our world. Even if we find Jesus' message attractive, the world pushes us toward another way of living. The Beatitudes are in no way trite or undemanding, quite the opposite. We can only practice them if the Holy Spirit fills us with his power and frees us from our weakness, our selfishness, our complacency, and our pride.

66. Let us listen once more to Jesus, with all the love and respect that the Master deserves. Let us allow his words to unsettle us, to challenge us, and to demand a real change in the way we live. Otherwise, holiness will remain no more than an empty word. We turn now to the individual Beatitudes in the Gospel of Matthew (cf. Mt 5:3–12).[67]

"Blessed are the poor in spirit, for theirs is the kingdom of heaven"

67. The Gospel invites us to peer into the depths of our heart, to see where we find our security in life. Usually the rich feel secure in their wealth, and think that, if that wealth is threatened, the whole meaning of their earthly life can collapse. Jesus himself tells us this in the parable of the rich fool: he speaks of a man who was sure of himself, yet foolish, for it did not dawn on him that he might die that very day (cf. Lk 12:16–21).

68. Wealth ensures nothing. Indeed, once we think we are rich, we can become so self-satisfied that we leave no room for God's word, for the love of our brothers and sisters, or for the enjoyment of the most important things in life. In this way, we miss out on the greatest treasure of all. That is why Jesus calls blessed those who are poor in spirit, those who have a poor heart, for there the Lord can enter with his perennial newness.

69. This spiritual poverty is closely linked to what Saint Ignatius of Loyola calls "holy indifference," which brings us to a radiant interior freedom: "We need to train ourselves to be indifferent in our attitude to all created things, in all that is permitted to our free will and not forbidden; so that on our part, we do not set our hearts on good health rather than bad, riches rather than poverty, honor rather than dishonor, a long life rather than a short one, and so in all the rest."[68]

70. Luke does not speak of poverty "of spirit" but simply of those who are "poor" (cf. Lk 6:20). In this way, he too invites us to live a plain and austere life. He calls us to share in the life of those most in need, the life lived by the Apostles, and ultimately to configure ourselves to Jesus who, though rich, "made himself poor" (2 Cor 8:9).

Being poor of heart: that is holiness.

"Blessed are the meek, for they will inherit the earth"

71. These are strong words in a world that from the beginning has been a place of conflict, disputes, and enmity on all sides, where we constantly pigeonhole others on the basis of their ideas, their customs, and even their way of speaking or dressing. Ultimately, it is the reign of pride and

vanity, where each person thinks he or she has the right to dominate others. Nonetheless, impossible as it may seem, Jesus proposes a different way of doing things: the way of meekness. This is what we see him doing with his disciples. It is what we contemplate on his entrance to Jerusalem: "Behold, your king is coming to you, humble, and mounted on a donkey" (Mt 21:5; Zec 9:9).

72. Christ says: "Learn from me; for I am gentle and humble of heart, and you will find rest for your souls" (Mt 11:29). If we are constantly upset and impatient with others, we will end up drained and weary. But if we regard the faults and limitations of others with tenderness and meekness, without an air of superiority, we can actually help them and stop wasting our energy on useless complaining. Saint Thérèse of Lisieux tells us that "perfect charity consists in putting up with others' mistakes, and not being scandalized by their faults."[69]

73. Paul speaks of meekness as one of the fruits of the Holy Spirit (cf. Gal 5:23). He suggests that, if a wrongful action of one of our brothers or sisters troubles us, we should try to correct them, but "with a spirit of meekness," since "you too could be tempted" (Gal 6:1). Even when we defend our faith and convictions, we are to do so "with meekness" (cf. 1 Pt 3:16). Our enemies too are to be treated "with meekness" (2 Tm 2:25). In the Church we have often erred by not embracing this demand of God's word.

74. Meekness is yet another expression of the interior poverty of those who put their trust in God alone. Indeed, in the Bible the same word—*anawim*—usually refers both to the poor and to the meek. Someone might object: "If I am that meek, they will think that I am an idiot, a fool, or a weakling." At times they may, but so be it. It is always better to be meek, for then our deepest desires will be fulfilled. The meek "shall inherit the earth," for they will see God's promises accomplished in their lives. In every situation, the meek put their hope in the Lord, and those who hope for him shall possess the land . . . and enjoy the fullness of peace (cf. Ps 37:9.11). For his part, the

Lord trusts in them: "This is the one to whom I will look, to the humble and contrite in spirit, who trembles at my word" (Is 66:2).

Reacting with meekness and humility: that is holiness.

"Blessed are those who mourn, for they will be comforted"

75. The world tells us exactly the opposite: entertainment, pleasure, diversion, and escape make for the good life. The worldly person ignores problems of sickness or sorrow in the family or all around him; he averts his gaze. The world has no desire to mourn; it would rather disregard painful situations, cover them up, or hide them. Much energy is expended on fleeing from situations of suffering in the belief that reality can be concealed. But the cross can never be absent.

76. A person who sees things as they truly are and sympathizes with pain and sorrow is capable of touching life's depths and finding authentic happiness.[70] He or she is consoled, not by the world but by Jesus. Such persons are unafraid to share in the suffering of others; they do not flee from painful situations. They discover the meaning of life by coming to the aid of those who suffer, understanding their anguish and bringing relief. They sense that the other is flesh of our flesh, and are not afraid to draw near, even to touch their wounds. They feel compassion for others in such a way that all distance vanishes. In this way they can embrace Saint Paul's exhortation: "Weep with those who weep" (Rom 12:15).

Knowing how to mourn with others: that is holiness.

"Blessed are those who hunger and thirst for righteousness, for they will be filled"

77. Hunger and thirst are intense experiences, since they involve basic needs and our instinct for survival. There are those who desire justice and yearn for righteousness with similar intensity. Jesus says that they will be satisfied, for sooner or later justice will come. We can cooperate to make that possible, even if we may not always see the fruit of our efforts.

78. Jesus offers a justice other than that of the world, so often marred by petty interests and manipulated in various ways. Experience shows how

easy it is to become mired in corruption, ensnared in the daily politics of *quid pro quo*, where everything becomes business. How many people suffer injustice, standing by powerlessly while others divvy up the good things of this life. Some give up fighting for real justice and opt to follow in the train of the winners. This has nothing to do with the hunger and thirst for justice that Jesus praises.

79. True justice comes about in people's lives when they themselves are just in their decisions; it is expressed in their pursuit of justice for the poor and the weak. While it is true that the word *justice* can be a synonym for faithfulness to God's will in every aspect of our life, if we give the word too general a meaning, we forget that it is shown especially in justice toward those who are most vulnerable: "Seek justice, correct oppression; defend the fatherless, plead for the widow" (Is 1:17).

Hungering and thirsting for righteousness: that is holiness.

"Blessed are the merciful, for they will receive mercy"

80. Mercy has two aspects. It involves giving, helping, and serving others, but it also includes forgiveness and understanding. Matthew sums it up in one golden rule: "In everything, do to others as you would have them do to you" (7:12). The Catechism reminds us that this law is to be applied "in every case,"[71] especially when we are "confronted by situations that make moral judgments less assured and decision difficult."[72]

81. Giving and forgiving means reproducing in our lives some small measure of God's perfection, which gives and forgives superabundantly. For this reason, in the Gospel of Luke we do not hear the words, "Be perfect" (Mt 5:48), but rather, "Be merciful, even as your Father is merciful. Judge not, and you will not be judged; condemn not, and you will not be condemned; forgive, and you will be forgiven; give, and it will be given to you" (6:36–38). Luke then adds something not to be overlooked: "The measure you give will be the measure you get back" (6:38). The yardstick we use for understanding and forgiving others will measure

the forgiveness we receive. The yardstick we use for giving will measure what we receive. We should never forget this.

82. Jesus does not say, "Blessed are those who plot revenge." He calls "blessed" those who forgive and do so "seventy times seven" (Mt 18:22). We need to think of ourselves as an army of the forgiven. All of us have been looked upon with divine compassion. If we approach the Lord with sincerity and listen carefully, there may well be times when we hear his reproach: "Should not you have had mercy on your fellow servant, as I had mercy on you?" (Mt 18:33).

Seeing and acting with mercy: that is holiness.

"Blessed are the pure in heart, for they will see God"

83. This Beatitude speaks of those whose hearts are simple, pure, and undefiled, for a heart capable of love admits nothing that might harm, weaken, or endanger that love. The Bible uses the heart to describe our real intentions, the things we truly seek and desire, apart from all appearances. "Man sees the appearance, but the Lord looks into the heart" (1 Sm 16:7). God wants to speak to our hearts (cf. Hos 2:16); there he desires to write his law (cf. Jer 31:33). In a word, he wants to give us a new heart (cf. Ez 36:26).

84. "Guard your heart with all vigilance" (Prv 4:23). Nothing stained by falsehood has any real worth in the Lord's eyes. He "flees from deceit, and rises and departs from foolish thoughts" (Ws 1:5). The Father, "who sees in secret" (Mt 6:6), recognizes what is impure and insincere, mere display or appearance, as does the Son, who knows "what is in man" (cf. Jn 2:25).

85. Certainly there can be no love without works of love, but this Beatitude reminds us that the Lord expects a commitment to our brothers and sisters that comes from the heart. For "if I give away all I have, and if I deliver my body to be burned, but have no love, I gain nothing" (1 Cor 13:3). In Matthew's Gospel too, we see that what proceeds from the heart is what defiles a person (cf. 15:18), for from the heart come murder, theft,

false witness, and other evil deeds (cf. 15:19). From the heart's intentions come the desires and the deepest decisions that determine our actions.

86. A heart that loves God and neighbor (cf. Mt 22:36–40), genuinely and not merely in words, is a pure heart; it can see God. In his hymn to charity, Saint Paul says that "now we see in a mirror, dimly" (1 Cor 13:12), but to the extent that truth and love prevail, we will then be able to see "face to face." Jesus promises that those who are pure in heart "will see God."

Keeping a heart free of all that tarnishes love: that is holiness.

"Blessed are the peacemakers, for they will be called children of God"

87. This Beatitude makes us think of the many endless situations of war in our world. Yet we ourselves are often a cause of conflict or at least of misunderstanding. For example, I may hear something about someone and I go off and repeat it. I may even embellish it the second time around and keep spreading it. . . . And the more harm it does, the more satisfaction I seem to derive from it. The world of gossip, inhabited by negative and destructive people, does not bring peace. Such people are really the enemies of peace; in no way are they "blessed."[73]

88. Peacemakers truly "make" peace; they build peace and friendship in society. To those who sow peace Jesus makes this magnificent promise: "They will be called children of God" (Mt 5:9). He told his disciples that, wherever they went, they were to say: "Peace to this house!" (Lk 10:5). The word of God exhorts every believer to work for peace, "along with all who call upon the Lord with a pure heart" (cf. 2 Tm 2:22), for "the harvest of righteousness is sown in peace by those who make peace" (Jas 3:18). And if there are times in our community when we question what ought to be done, "let us pursue what makes for peace" (Rom 14:19), for unity is preferable to conflict.[74]

89. It is not easy to "make" this evangelical peace, which excludes no one but embraces even those who are a bit odd, troublesome or difficult, demanding, different, beaten down by life, or simply uninterested. It is hard work; it calls for great openness of mind and heart, since it is not about creating "a consensus on paper or a transient peace for a contented minority,"[75] or

a project "by a few for the few."[76] Nor can it attempt to ignore or disregard conflict; instead, it must "face conflict head on, resolve it and make it a link in the chain of a new process."[77] We need to be artisans of peace, for building peace is a craft that demands serenity, creativity, sensitivity, and skill.

Sowing peace all around us: that is holiness.

"Blessed are those who are persecuted for righteousness' sake, for theirs is the kingdom of heaven"

90. Jesus himself warns us that the path he proposes goes against the flow, even making us challenge society by the way we live and, as a result, becoming a nuisance. He reminds us how many people have been, and still are, persecuted simply because they struggle for justice, because they take seriously their commitment to God and to others. Unless we wish to sink into an obscure mediocrity, let us not long for an easy life, for "whoever would save his life will lose it" (Mt 16:25).

91. In living the Gospel, we cannot expect that everything will be easy, for the thirst for power and worldly interests often stands in our way. Saint John Paul II noted that "a society is alienated if its forms of social organization, production and consumption make it more difficult to offer this gift of self and to establish this solidarity between people."[78] In such a society, politics, mass communications, and economic, cultural, and even religious institutions become so entangled as to become an obstacle to authentic human and social development. As a result, the Beatitudes are not easy to live out; any attempt to do so will be viewed negatively, regarded with suspicion, and met with ridicule.

92. Whatever weariness and pain we may experience in living the commandment of love and following the way of justice, the cross remains the source of our growth and sanctification. We must never forget that when the New Testament tells us that we will have to endure suffering for the Gospel's sake, it speaks precisely of persecution (cf. Acts 5:41; Phil 1:29; Col 1:24; 2 Tm 1:12; 1 Pt 2:20; 4:14–16; Rv 2:10).

93. Here we are speaking about inevitable persecution, not the kind of persecution we might bring upon ourselves by our mistreatment of others. The saints are not odd and aloof, unbearable because of their vanity, negativity, and bitterness. The Apostles of Christ were not like that. The Book of Acts states repeatedly that they enjoyed favor "with all the people" (2:47; cf. 4:21–33; 5:13), even as some authorities harassed and persecuted them (cf. 4:1–3; 5:17–18).

94. Persecutions are not a reality of the past, for today too we experience them, whether by the shedding of blood, as is the case with so many contemporary martyrs, or by more subtle means, by slander and lies. Jesus calls us blessed when people "utter all kinds of evil against you falsely on my account" (Mt 5:11). At other times, persecution can take the form of gibes that try to caricature our faith and make us seem ridiculous. Accepting daily the path of the Gospel, even though it may cause us problems: that is holiness.

The Great Criterion

95. In the twenty-fifth chapter of Matthew's Gospel (vv. 31–46), Jesus expands on the Beatitude that calls the merciful blessed. If we seek the holiness pleasing to God's eyes, this text offers us one clear criterion on which we will be judged. "I was hungry and you gave me food, I was thirsty and you gave me drink, I was a stranger and you welcomed me, I was naked and you clothed me, I was sick and you took care of me, I was in prison and you visited me" (vv. 35–36).

In Fidelity to the Master

96. Holiness, then, is not about swooning in mystic rapture. As Saint John Paul II said: "If we truly start out anew from the contemplation of Christ, we must learn to see him especially in the faces of those with whom he himself wished to be identified."[79] The text of Matthew 25:35–36 is "not a simple invitation to charity: it is a page of Christology which sheds a ray of light on the mystery of Christ."[80] In this call to recognize him in

the poor and the suffering, we see revealed the very heart of Christ, his deepest feelings and choices, which every saint seeks to imitate.

97. Given these uncompromising demands of Jesus, it is my duty to ask Christians to acknowledge and accept them in a spirit of genuine openness, *sine glossa*. In other words, without any "ifs or buts" that could lessen their force. Our Lord made it very clear that holiness cannot be understood or lived apart from these demands, for mercy is "the beating heart of the Gospel."[81]

98. If I encounter a person sleeping outdoors on a cold night, I can view him or her as an annoyance, an idler, an obstacle in my path, a troubling sight, a problem for politicians to sort out, or even a piece of refuse cluttering a public space. Or I can respond with faith and charity, and see in this person a human being with a dignity identical to my own, a creature infinitely loved by the Father, an image of God, a brother or sister redeemed by Jesus Christ. That is what it is to be a Christian! Can holiness somehow be understood apart from this lively recognition of the dignity of each human being?[82]

99. For Christians, this involves a constant and healthy unease. Even if helping one person alone could justify all our efforts, it would not be enough. The bishops of Canada made this clear when they noted, for example, that the biblical understanding of the jubilee year was about more than simply performing certain good works. It also meant seeking social change: "For later generations to also be released, clearly the goal had to be the restoration of just social and economic systems, so there could no longer be exclusion."[83]

Ideologies Striking at the Heart of the Gospel

100. I regret that ideologies lead us at times to two harmful errors. On the one hand, there is the error of those Christians who separate these Gospel demands from their personal relationship with the Lord, from their interior union with him, from openness to his grace. Christianity thus

becomes a sort of NGO stripped of the luminous mysticism so evident in the lives of Saint Francis of Assisi, Saint Vincent de Paul, Saint Teresa of Calcutta, and many others. For these great saints, mental prayer, the love of God, and the reading of the Gospel in no way detracted from their passionate and effective commitment to their neighbors; quite the opposite.

101. The other harmful ideological error is found in those who find suspect the social engagement of others, seeing it as superficial, worldly, secular, materialist, communist, or populist. Or they relativize it, as if there are other more important matters, or the only thing that counts is one particular ethical issue or cause that they themselves defend. Our defense of the innocent unborn, for example, needs to be clear, firm, and passionate, for at stake is the dignity of a human life, which is always sacred and demands love for each person, regardless of his or her stage of development. Equally sacred, however, are the lives of the poor, those already born, the destitute, the abandoned, and the underprivileged, the vulnerable infirm and elderly exposed to covert euthanasia, the victims of human trafficking, new forms of slavery, and every form of rejection.[84] We cannot uphold an ideal of holiness that would ignore injustice in a world where some revel, spend with abandon, and live only for the latest consumer goods, even as others look on from afar, living their entire lives in abject poverty.

102. We often hear it said that, with respect to relativism and the flaws of our present world, the situation of migrants, for example, is a lesser issue. Some Catholics consider it a secondary issue compared to the "grave" bioethical questions. That a politician looking for votes might say such a thing is understandable, but not a Christian, for whom the only proper attitude is to stand in the shoes of those brothers and sisters of ours who risk their lives to offer a future to their children. Can we not realize that this is exactly what Jesus demands of us, when he tells us that in welcoming the stranger we welcome him (cf. Mt 25:35)? Saint Benedict did so readily, and though it might have "complicated" the life of his monks, he ordered that all guests who knocked at the monastery

door be welcomed "like Christ,"[85] with a gesture of veneration;[86] the poor and pilgrims were to be met with "the greatest care and solicitude."[87]

103. A similar approach is found in the Old Testament: "You shall not wrong a stranger or oppress him, for you yourselves were strangers in the land of Egypt" (Ex 22:21). "When a stranger resides with you in your land, you shall not oppress him. The stranger who resides with you shall be to you as the citizen among you; and you shall love him as yourself; for you were strangers in the land of Egypt" (Lv 19:33–34). This is not a notion invented by some Pope, or a momentary fad. In today's world too, we are called to follow the path of spiritual wisdom proposed by the prophet Isaiah to show what is pleasing to God. "Is it not to share your bread with the hungry and bring the homeless poor into your house; when you see the naked, to cover him, and not to hide yourself from your own kin? Then your light shall break forth like the dawn" (58:7–8).

The Worship Most Acceptable to God

104. We may think that we give glory to God only by our worship and prayer, or simply by following certain ethical norms. It is true that the primacy belongs to our relationship with God, but we cannot forget that the ultimate criterion on which our lives will be judged is what we have done for others. Prayer is most precious, for it nourishes a daily commitment to love. Our worship becomes pleasing to God when we devote ourselves to living generously, and allow God's gift, granted in prayer, to be shown in our concern for our brothers and sisters.

105. Similarly, the best way to discern if our prayer is authentic is to judge to what extent our life is being transformed in the light of mercy. For "mercy is not only an action of the Father; it becomes a criterion for ascertaining who his true children are."[88] Mercy "is the very foundation of the Church's life."[89] In this regard, I would like to reiterate that mercy does not exclude justice and truth; indeed, "we have to say that mercy is the fullness of justice and the most radiant manifestation of God's truth."[90] It is "the key to heaven."[91]

106. Here I think of Saint Thomas Aquinas, who asked which actions of ours are noblest, which external works best show our love for God. Thomas answered unhesitatingly that they are the works of mercy toward our neighbor,[92] even more than our acts of worship: "We worship God by outward sacrifices and gifts, not for his own benefit, but for that of ourselves and our neighbor. For he does not need our sacrifices, but wishes them to be offered to him, in order to stir our devotion and to profit our neighbor. Hence mercy, whereby we supply others' defects, is a sacrifice more acceptable to him, as conducing more directly to our neighbor's well-being."[93]

107. Those who really wish to give glory to God by their lives, who truly long to grow in holiness, are called to be single-minded and tenacious in their practice of the works of mercy. Saint Teresa of Calcutta clearly realized this: "Yes, I have many human faults and failures. . . . But God bends down and uses us, you and me, to be his love and his compassion in the world; he bears our sins, our troubles and our faults. He depends on us to love the world and to show how much he loves it. If we are too concerned with ourselves, we will have no time left for others."[94]

108. Hedonism and consumerism can prove our downfall, for when we are obsessed with our own pleasure, we end up being all too concerned about ourselves and our rights, and we feel a desperate need for free time to enjoy ourselves. We will find it hard to feel and show any real concern for those in need, unless we are able to cultivate a certain simplicity of life, resisting the feverish demands of a consumer society, which leave us impoverished and unsatisfied, anxious to have it all now. Similarly, when we allow ourselves to be caught up in superficial information, instant communication, and virtual reality, we can waste precious time and become indifferent to the suffering flesh of our brothers and sisters. Yet even amid this whirlwind of activity, the Gospel continues to resound, offering us the promise of a different life, a healthier and happier life.

•••

109. The powerful witness of the saints is revealed in their lives, shaped by the Beatitudes and the criterion of the final judgement. Jesus' words are few and straightforward, yet practical and valid for everyone, for Christianity is meant above all to be put into practice. It can also be an object of study and reflection, but only to help us better live the Gospel in our daily lives. I recommend rereading these great biblical texts frequently, referring back to them, praying with them, trying to embody them. They will benefit us; they will make us genuinely happy.

CHAPTER FOUR

SIGNS OF HOLINESS IN TODAY'S WORLD

110. Within the framework of holiness offered by the Beatitudes and Matthew 25:31–46, I would like to mention a few signs or spiritual attitudes that, in my opinion, are necessary if we are to understand the way of life to which the Lord calls us. I will not pause to explain the means of sanctification already known to us: the various methods of prayer, the inestimable sacraments of the Eucharist and Reconciliation, the offering of personal sacrifices, different forms of devotion, spiritual direction, and many others as well. Here I will speak only of certain aspects of the call to holiness that I hope will prove especially meaningful.

111. The signs I wish to highlight are not the sum total of a model of holiness, but they are five great expressions of love for God and neighbor that I consider of particular importance in the light of certain dangers and limitations present in today's culture. There we see a sense of anxiety, sometimes violent, that distracts and debilitates; negativity and sullenness; the self-content bred by consumerism; individualism; and all those forms of ersatz spirituality—having nothing to do with God—that dominate the current religious marketplace.

Perseverance, Patience, and Meekness

112. The first of these great signs is solid grounding in the God who loves and sustains us. This source of inner strength enables us to persevere amid life's ups and downs, but also to endure hostility, betrayal, and failings on the part of others. "If God is for us, who is against us?" (Rom 8:31): this is the source of the peace found in the saints. Such inner strength makes it possible for us, in our fast-paced, noisy, and aggressive world, to give a witness of holiness through patience and constancy in doing good. It is a sign of the fidelity born of love, for those who put their faith in God (*pístis*) can also be faithful to others (*pistós*). They do

not desert others in bad times; they accompany them in their anxiety and distress, even though doing so may not bring immediate satisfaction.

113. Saint Paul bade the Romans not to repay evil for evil (cf. Rom 12:17), not to seek revenge (v. 19), and not to be overcome by evil, but instead to "overcome evil with good" (v. 21). This attitude is not a sign of weakness but of true strength, because God himself "is slow to anger but great in power" (Na 1:3). The word of God exhorts us to "put away all bitterness and wrath and wrangling and slander, together with all malice" (Eph 4:31).

114. We need to recognize and combat our aggressive and selfish inclinations, and not let them take root. "Be angry but do not sin; do not let the sun go down on your anger" (Eph 4:26). When we feel overwhelmed, we can always cling to the anchor of prayer, which puts us back in God's hands and the source of our peace. "Have no anxiety about anything, but in everything, by prayer and supplication with thanksgiving, let your requests be made known to God. And the peace of God, which surpasses all understanding, will guard your hearts . . ." (Phil 4:6–7).

115. Christians too can be caught up in networks of verbal violence through the internet and the various forums of digital communication. Even in Catholic media, limits can be overstepped, defamation and slander can become commonplace, and all ethical standards and respect for the good name of others can be abandoned. The result is a dangerous dichotomy, since things can be said there that would be unacceptable in public discourse, and people look to compensate for their own discontent by lashing out at others. It is striking that at times, in claiming to uphold the other commandments, they completely ignore the eighth, which forbids bearing false witness or lying, and ruthlessly vilify others. Here we see how the unguarded tongue, set on fire by hell, sets all things ablaze (cf. Jas 3:6).

116. Inner strength, as the work of grace, prevents us from becoming carried away by the violence that is so much a part of life today, because grace defuses vanity and makes possible meekness of heart. The saints do

not waste energy complaining about the failings of others; they can hold their tongue before the faults of their brothers and sisters, and avoid the verbal violence that demeans and mistreats others. Saints hesitate to treat others harshly; they consider others better than themselves (cf. Phil 2:3).

117. It is not good when we look down on others like heartless judges, lording it over them and always trying to teach them lessons. That is itself a subtle form of violence.[95] Saint John of the Cross proposed a different path: "Always prefer to be taught by all, rather than to desire teaching even the least of all."[96] And he added advice on how to keep the devil at bay: "Rejoice in the good of others as if it were your own, and desire that they be given precedence over you in all things; this you should do wholeheartedly. You will thereby overcome evil with good, banish the devil, and possess a happy heart. Try to practice this all the more with those who least attract you. Realize that if you do not train yourself in this way, you will not attain real charity or make any progress in it."[97]

118. Humility can only take root in the heart through humiliations. Without them, there is no humility or holiness. If you are unable to suffer and offer up a few humiliations, you are not humble and you are not on the path to holiness. The holiness that God bestows on his Church comes through the humiliation of his Son. He is the way. Humiliation makes you resemble Jesus; it is an unavoidable aspect of the imitation of Christ. For "Christ suffered for you, leaving you an example, so that you might follow in his steps" (1 Pt 2:21). In turn, he reveals the humility of the Father, who condescends to journey with his people, enduring their infidelities and complaints (cf. Ex 34:6–9; Wis 11:23–12:2; Lk 6:36). For this reason, the Apostles, after suffering humiliation, rejoiced "that they were counted worthy to suffer dishonor for [Jesus'] name" (Acts 5:41).

119. Here I am not speaking only about stark situations of martyrdom, but about the daily humiliations of those who keep silent to save their families, who prefer to praise others rather than boast about themselves, or who choose the less welcome tasks, at times even choosing to bear

an injustice so as to offer it to the Lord. "If when you do right and suffer for it, you have God's approval" (1 Pt 2:20). This does not mean walking around with eyes lowered, not saying a word, and fleeing the company of others. At times, precisely because someone is free of selfishness, he or she can dare to disagree gently, to demand justice, or to defend the weak before the powerful, even if it may harm his or her reputation.

120. I am not saying that such humiliation is pleasant, for that would be masochism, but that it is a way of imitating Jesus and growing in union with him. This is incomprehensible on a purely natural level, and the world mocks any such notion. Instead, it is a grace to be sought in prayer: "Lord, when humiliations come, help me to know that I am following in your footsteps."

121. To act in this way presumes a heart set at peace by Christ, freed from the aggressiveness born of overweening egotism. That same peacefulness, the fruit of grace, makes it possible to preserve our inner trust and persevere in goodness, "though I walk through the valley of the shadow of death" (Ps 23:4) or "a host encamp against me" (Ps 27:3). Standing firm in the Lord, the Rock, we can sing: "In peace I will both lie down and sleep; for you alone, O Lord, make me dwell in safety" (Ps 4:8). Christ, in a word, "is our peace" (Eph 2:14); he came "to guide our feet into the way of peace" (Lk 1:79). As he told Saint Faustina Kowalska, "Mankind will not have peace until it turns with trust to my mercy."[98] So let us not fall into the temptation of looking for security in success, vain pleasures, possessions, power over others, or social status. Jesus says: "My peace I give to you; I do not give it to you as the world gives peace" (Jn 14:27).

Joy and a Sense of Humor

122. Far from being timid, morose, acerbic, or melancholy, or putting on a dreary face, the saints are joyful and full of good humor. Though completely realistic, they radiate a positive and hopeful spirit. The Christian life is "joy in the Holy Spirit" (Rom 14:17), for "the necessary result of the love of charity is joy; since every lover rejoices at being united to the

beloved . . . the effect of charity is joy."[99] Having received the beautiful gift of God's word, we embrace it "in much affliction, with joy inspired by the Holy Spirit" (1 Thes 1:6). If we allow the Lord to draw us out of our shell and change our lives, then we can do as Saint Paul tells us: "Rejoice in the Lord always; I say it again, rejoice!" (Phil 4:4).

123. The prophets proclaimed the times of Jesus, in which we now live, as a revelation of joy. "Shout and sing for joy!" (Is 12:6). "Get you up to a high mountain, O herald of good tidings to Zion; lift up your voice with strength, O herald of good tidings to Jerusalem!" (Is 40:9). "Break forth, O mountains, into singing! For the Lord has comforted his people, and he will have compassion on his afflicted" (Is 49:13). "Rejoice greatly, O daughter of Zion! Shout aloud, O daughter of Jerusalem! Behold, your king comes to you; triumphant and victorious is he" (Zec 9:9). Nor should we forget Nehemiah's exhortation: "Do not be grieved, for the joy of the Lord is your strength!" (8:10).

124. Mary, recognizing the newness that Jesus brought, sang: "My spirit rejoices" (Lk 1:47), and Jesus himself "rejoiced in the Holy Spirit" (Lk 10:21). As he passed by, "all the people rejoiced" (Lk 13:17). After his resurrection, wherever the disciples went, there was "much joy" (Acts 8:8). Jesus assures us: "You will be sorrowful, but your sorrow will turn into joy. . . . I will see you again and your hearts will rejoice, and no one will take your joy from you" (Jn 16:20, 22). "These things I have spoken to you, that my joy may be in you, and that your joy may be full" (Jn 15:11).

125. Hard times may come, when the cross casts its shadow, yet nothing can destroy the supernatural joy that "adapts and changes, but always endures, even as a flicker of light born of our personal certainty that, when everything is said and done, we are infinitely loved."[100] That joy brings deep security, serene hope, and a spiritual fulfillment that the world cannot understand or appreciate.

126. Christian joy is usually accompanied by a sense of humor. We see this clearly, for example, in Saint Thomas More, Saint Vincent de Paul,

and Saint Philip Neri. Ill humor is no sign of holiness. "Remove vexation from your mind" (Eccl 11:10). We receive so much from the Lord "for our enjoyment" (1 Tm 6:17), that sadness can be a sign of ingratitude. We can get so caught up in ourselves that we are unable to recognize God's gifts.[101]

127. With the love of a father, God tells us: "My son, treat yourself well. . . . Do not deprive yourself of a happy day" (Sir 14:11, 14). He wants us to be positive, grateful, and uncomplicated: "In the day of prosperity, be joyful. . . . God created human beings straightforward, but they have devised many schemes" (Eccl 7:14, 29). Whatever the case, we should remain resilient and imitate Saint Paul: "I have learned to be content with what I have" (Phil 4:11). Saint Francis of Assisi lived by this; he could be overwhelmed with gratitude before a piece of hard bread, or joyfully praise God simply for the breeze that caressed his face.

128. This is not the joy held out by today's individualistic and consumerist culture. Consumerism only bloats the heart. It can offer occasional and passing pleasures, but not joy. Here I am speaking of a joy lived in communion, which shares and is shared, since "there is more happiness in giving than in receiving" (Acts 20:35) and "God loves a cheerful giver" (2 Cor 9:7). Fraternal love increases our capacity for joy, since it makes us capable of rejoicing in the good of others: "Rejoice with those who rejoice" (Rom 12:15). "We rejoice when we are weak and you are strong" (2 Cor 13:9). On the other hand, when we "focus primarily on our own needs, we condemn ourselves to a joyless existence."[102]

Boldness and Passion

129. Holiness is also *parrhesía*: it is boldness, an impulse to evangelize and to leave a mark in this world. To allow us to do this, Jesus himself comes and tells us once more, serenely yet firmly: "Do not be afraid" (Mk 6:50). "I am with you always, to the end of the world" (Mt 28:20). These words enable us to go forth and serve with the same courage that the Holy Spirit stirred up in the Apostles, impelling them to proclaim

Jesus Christ. Boldness, enthusiasm, the freedom to speak out, apostolic fervor, all these are included in the word *parrhesía*. The Bible also uses this word to describe the freedom of a life open to God and to others (cf. Acts 4:29; 9:28; 28:31; 2 Cor 3:12; Eph 3:12; Heb 3:6; 10:19).

130. Blessed Paul VI, in referring to obstacles to evangelization, spoke of a lack of fervor (*parrhesía*) that is "all the more serious because it comes from within."[103] How often we are tempted to keep close to the shore! Yet the Lord calls us to put out into the deep and let down our nets (cf. Lk 5:4). He bids us spend our lives in his service. Clinging to him, we are inspired to put all our charisms at the service of others. May we always feel compelled by his love (2 Cor 5:14) and say with Saint Paul: "Woe to me if I do not preach the Gospel" (1 Cor 9:16).

131. Look at Jesus. His deep compassion reached out to others. It did not make him hesitant, timid, or self-conscious, as often happens with us. Quite the opposite. His compassion made him go out actively to preach and to send others on a mission of healing and liberation. Let us acknowledge our weakness, but allow Jesus to lay hold of it and send us too on mission. We are weak, yet we hold a treasure that can enlarge us and make those who receive it better and happier. Boldness and apostolic courage are an essential part of mission.

132. *Parrhesía* is a seal of the Spirit; it testifies to the authenticity of our preaching. It is a joyful assurance that leads us to glory in the Gospel we proclaim. It is an unshakeable trust in the faithful Witness who gives us the certainty that nothing can "separate us from the love of God" (Rom 8:39).

133. We need the Spirit's prompting, lest we be paralyzed by fear and excessive caution, lest we grow used to keeping within safe bounds. Let us remember that closed spaces grow musty and unhealthy. When the Apostles were tempted to let themselves be crippled by danger and threats, they joined in prayer to implore *parrhesía*: "And now, Lord, look upon their threats, and grant to your servants to speak your word

with all boldness" (Acts 4:29). As a result, "when they had prayed, the place in which they were gathered together was shaken; and they were all filled with the Holy Spirit and spoke the word of God with boldness" (Acts 4:31).

134. Like the prophet Jonah, we are constantly tempted to flee to a safe haven. It can have many names: individualism, spiritualism, living in a little world, addiction, intransigence, the rejection of new ideas and approaches, dogmatism, nostalgia, pessimism, hiding behind rules and regulations. We can resist leaving behind a familiar and easy way of doing things. Yet the challenges involved can be like the storm, the whale, the worm that dried the gourd plant, or the wind and sun that burned Jonah's head. For us, as for him, they can serve to bring us back to the God of tenderness, who invites us to set out ever anew on our journey.

135. God is eternal newness. He impels us constantly to set out anew, to pass beyond what is familiar, to the fringes and beyond. He takes us to where humanity is most wounded, where men and women, beneath the appearance of a shallow conformity, continue to seek an answer to the question of life's meaning. God is not afraid! He is fearless! He is always greater than our plans and schemes. Unafraid of the fringes, he himself became a fringe (cf. Phil 2:6–8; Jn 1:14). So if we dare to go to the fringes, we will find him there; indeed, he is already there. Jesus is already there, in the hearts of our brothers and sisters, in their wounded flesh, in their troubles, and in their profound desolation. He is already there.

136. True enough, we need to open the door of our hearts to Jesus, who stands and knocks (cf. Rv 3:20). Sometimes I wonder, though, if perhaps Jesus is already inside us and knocking on the door for us to let him escape from our stale self-centeredness. In the Gospel, we see how Jesus "went through the cities and villages, preaching and bringing the good news of the kingdom of God" (Lk 8:1). After the resurrection, when the disciples went forth in all directions, the Lord accompanied them (cf. Mk 16:20). This is what happens as the result of true encounter.

137. Complacency is seductive; it tells us that there is no point in trying to change things, that there is nothing we can do, because this is the way things have always been and yet we always manage to survive. By force of habit we no longer stand up to evil. We "let things be," or as others have decided they ought to be. Yet let us allow the Lord to rouse us from our torpor, to free us from our inertia. Let us rethink our usual way of doing things; let us open our eyes and ears, and above all our hearts, so as not to be complacent about things as they are, but unsettled by the living and effective word of the risen Lord.

138. We are inspired to act by the example of all those priests, religious, and laity who devote themselves to proclamation and to serving others with great fidelity, often at the risk of their lives and certainly at the cost of their comfort. Their testimony reminds us that, more than bureaucrats and functionaries, the Church needs passionate missionaries, enthusiastic about sharing true life. The saints surprise us, they confound us, because by their lives they urge us to abandon a dull and dreary mediocrity.

139. Let us ask the Lord for the grace not to hesitate when the Spirit calls us to take a step forward. Let us ask for the apostolic courage to share the Gospel with others and to stop trying to make our Christian life a museum of memories. In every situation, may the Holy Spirit cause us to contemplate history in the light of the risen Jesus. In this way, the Church will not stand still, but constantly welcome the Lord's surprises.

In Community

140. When we live apart from others, it is very difficult to fight against concupiscence, the snares and temptations of the devil, and the selfishness of the world. Bombarded as we are by so many enticements, we can grow too isolated, lose our sense of reality and inner clarity, and easily succumb.

141. Growth in holiness is a journey in community, side by side with others. We see this in some holy communities. From time to time, the

Church has canonized entire communities that lived the Gospel heroically or offered to God the lives of all their members. We can think, for example, of the seven holy founders of the Order of the Servants of Mary, the seven blessed sisters of the first monastery of the Visitation in Madrid, the Japanese martyrs Saint Paul Miki and companions, the Korean martyrs Saint Andrew Taegon and companions, or the South American martyrs Saint Roque González, Saint Alonso Rodríguez, and companions. We should also remember the more recent witness borne by the Trappists of Tibhirine, Algeria, who prepared as a community for martyrdom. In many holy marriages too, each spouse becomes a means used by Christ for the sanctification of the other. Living or working alongside others is surely a path of spiritual growth. Saint John of the Cross told one of his followers: "You are living with others in order to be fashioned and tried."[104]

142. Each community is called to create a "God-enlightened space in which to experience the hidden presence of the risen Lord."[105] Sharing the word and celebrating the Eucharist together fosters fraternity and makes us a holy and missionary community. It also gives rise to authentic and shared mystical experiences. Such was the case with Saints Benedict and Scholastica. We can also think of the sublime spiritual experience shared by Saint Augustine and his mother, Saint Monica. "As the day now approached on which she was to depart this life, a day known to you but not to us, it came about, as I believe by your secret arrangement, that she and I stood alone leaning in a window that looked onto a garden, . . . We opened wide our hearts to drink in the streams of your fountain, the source of life that is in you. . . . And as we spoke of that wisdom and strained after it, we touched it in some measure by the impetus of our hearts . . . eternal life might be like that one moment of knowledge which we now sighed after."[106]

143. Such experiences, however, are neither the most frequent nor the most important. The common life, whether in the family, the parish, the religious community, or any other, is made up of small everyday things. This was true of the holy community formed by Jesus, Mary, and Joseph,

which reflected in an exemplary way the beauty of the Trinitarian communion. It was also true of the life that Jesus shared with his disciples and with ordinary people.

144. Let us not forget that Jesus asked his disciples to pay attention to details.

The little detail that wine was running out at a party.

The little detail that one sheep was missing.

The little detail of noticing the widow who offered her two small coins.

The little detail of having spare oil for the lamps, should the bridegroom delay.

The little detail of asking the disciples how many loaves of bread they had.

The little detail of having a fire burning and a fish cooking as he waited for the disciples at daybreak.

145. A community that cherishes the little details of love,[107] whose members care for one another and create an open and evangelizing environment, is a place where the risen Lord is present, sanctifying it in accordance with the Father's plan. There are times when, by a gift of the Lord's love, we are granted, amid these little details, consoling experiences of God. "One winter night I was carrying out my little duty as usual. . . . Suddenly, I heard off in the distance the harmonious sound of a musical instrument. I then pictured a well-lighted drawing room, brilliantly gilded, filled with elegantly dressed young ladies conversing together and conferring upon each other all sorts of compliments and other worldly remarks. Then my glance fell upon the poor invalid whom I was supporting. Instead of the beautiful strains of music I heard only her occasional complaints. . . . I cannot express in words what happened in my soul; what I know is that the Lord illumined it with rays of truth which so surpassed the dark brilliance of earthly feasts that I could not believe my happiness."[108]

146. Contrary to the growing consumerist individualism that tends to isolate us in a quest for well-being apart from others, our path to holiness

can only make us identify all the more with Jesus' prayer "that all may be one; even as you, Father, are in me, and I in you" (Jn 17:21).

In Constant Prayer

147. Finally, though it may seem obvious, we should remember that holiness consists in a habitual openness to the transcendent, expressed in prayer and adoration. The saints are distinguished by a spirit of prayer and a need for communion with God. They find an exclusive concern with this world to be narrow and stifling, and, amid their own concerns and commitments, they long for God, losing themselves in praise and contemplation of the Lord. I do not believe in holiness without prayer, even though that prayer need not be lengthy or involve intense emotions.

148. Saint John of the Cross tells us: "Endeavor to remain always in the presence of God, either real, imaginative, or unitive, insofar as is permitted by your works."[109] In the end, our desire for God will surely find expression in our daily lives: "Try to be continuous in prayer, and in the midst of bodily exercises do not leave it. Whether you eat, drink, talk with others, or do anything, always go to God and attach your heart to him."[110]

149. For this to happen, however, some moments spent alone with God are also necessary. For Saint Teresa of Avila, prayer "is nothing but friendly intercourse, and frequent solitary converse, with him who we know loves us."[111] I would insist that this is true not only for a privileged few, but for all of us, for "we all have need of this silence, filled with the presence of him who is adored."[112] Trust-filled prayer is a response of a heart open to encountering God face to face, where all is peaceful and the quiet voice of the Lord can be heard in the midst of silence.

150. In that silence, we can discern, in the light of the Spirit, the paths of holiness to which the Lord is calling us. Otherwise, any decisions we make may only be window-dressing that, rather than exalting the Gospel in our lives, will mask or submerge it. For each disciple, it is essential to spend time with the Master, to listen to his words, and to

learn from him always. Unless we listen, all our words will be nothing but useless chatter.

151. We need to remember that "contemplation of the face of Jesus, died and risen, restores our humanity, even when it has been broken by the troubles of this life or marred by sin. We must not domesticate the power of the face of Christ."[113] So let me ask you: Are there moments when you place yourself quietly in the Lord's presence, when you calmly spend time with him, when you bask in his gaze? Do you let his fire inflame your heart? Unless you let him warm you more and more with his love and tenderness, you will not catch fire. How will you then be able to set the hearts of others on fire by your words and witness? If, gazing on the face of Christ, you feel unable to let yourself be healed and transformed, then enter into the Lord's heart, into his wounds, for that is the abode of divine mercy.[114]

152. I ask that we never regard prayerful silence as a form of escape and rejection of the world around us. The Russian pilgrim, who prayed constantly, says that such prayer did not separate him from what was happening all around him. "Everybody was kind to me; it was as though everyone loved me. . . . Not only did I feel [happiness and consolation] in my own soul, but the whole outside world also seemed to me full of charm and delight."[115]

153. Nor does history vanish. Prayer, because it is nourished by the gift of God present and at work in our lives, must always be marked by remembrance. The memory of God's works is central to the experience of the covenant between God and his people. God wished to enter history, and so our prayer is interwoven with memories. We think back not only on his revealed Word, but also on our own lives, the lives of others, and all that the Lord has done in his Church. This is the grateful memory that Saint Ignatius of Loyola refers to in his *Contemplation for Attaining Love*,[116] when he asks us to be mindful of all the blessings we have received from the Lord. Think of your own history when you pray, and there you will find much mercy. This will also increase your awareness that the Lord

is ever mindful of you; he never forgets you. So it makes sense to ask him to shed light on the smallest details of your life, for he sees them all.

154. Prayer of supplication is an expression of a heart that trusts in God and realizes that of itself it can do nothing. The life of God's faithful people is marked by constant supplication born of faith-filled love and great confidence. Let us not downplay prayer of petition, which so often calms our hearts and helps us persevere in hope. Prayer of intercession has particular value, for it is an act of trust in God and, at the same time, an expression of love for our neighbor. There are those who think, based on a one-sided spirituality, that prayer should be unalloyed contemplation of God, free of all distraction, as if the names and faces of others were somehow an intrusion to be avoided. Yet in reality, our prayer will be all the more pleasing to God and more effective for our growth in holiness if, through intercession, we attempt to practice the twofold commandment that Jesus left us. Intercessory prayer is an expression of our fraternal concern for others, since we are able to embrace their lives, their deepest troubles, and their loftiest dreams. Of those who commit themselves generously to intercessory prayer we can apply the words of Scripture: "This is a man who loves the brethren and prays much for the people" (2 Mc 15:14).

155. If we realize that God exists, we cannot help but worship him, at times in quiet wonder, and praise him in festive song. We thus share in the experience of Blessed Charles de Foucauld, who said: "As soon as I believed that there was a God, I understood that I could do nothing other than to live for him."[117] In the life of God's pilgrim people, there can be many simple gestures of pure adoration, as when "the gaze of a pilgrim rests on an image that symbolizes God's affection and closeness. Love pauses, contemplates the mystery, and enjoys it in silence."[118]

156. The prayerful reading of God's word, which is "sweeter than honey" (Ps 119:103) yet a "two-edged sword" (Heb 4:12), enables us to pause and listen to the voice of the Master. It becomes a lamp for our steps and a

light for our path (cf. Ps 119:105). As the bishops of India have reminded us, "Devotion to the word of God is not simply one of many devotions, beautiful but somewhat optional. It goes to the very heart and identity of Christian life. The word has the power to transform lives."[119]

157. Meeting Jesus in the Scriptures leads us to the Eucharist, where the written word attains its greatest efficacy, for there the living Word is truly present. In the Eucharist, the one true God receives the greatest worship the world can give him, for it is Christ himself who is offered. When we receive him in Holy Communion, we renew our covenant with him and allow him to carry out ever more fully his work of transforming our lives.

CHAPTER FIVE

SPIRITUAL COMBAT, VIGILANCE, AND DISCERNMENT

158. The Christian life is a constant battle. We need strength and courage to withstand the temptations of the devil and to proclaim the Gospel. This battle is sweet, for it allows us to rejoice each time the Lord triumphs in our lives.

Combat and Violence

159. We are not dealing merely with a battle against the world and a worldly mentality that would deceive us and leave us dull and mediocre, lacking in enthusiasm and joy. Nor can this battle be reduced to the struggle against our human weaknesses and proclivities (be they laziness, lust, envy, jealousy, or any others). It is also a constant struggle against the devil, the prince of evil. Jesus himself celebrates our victories. He rejoiced when his disciples made progress in preaching the Gospel and overcoming the opposition of the evil one: "I saw Satan fall like lightning from heaven" (Lk 10:18).

More Than a Myth

160. We will not admit the existence of the devil if we insist on regarding life by empirical standards alone, without a supernatural understanding. It is precisely the conviction that this malign power is present in our midst that enables us to understand how evil can at times have so much destructive force. True enough, the biblical authors had limited conceptual resources for expressing certain realities, and in Jesus' time epilepsy, for example, could easily be confused with demonic possession. Yet this should not lead us to an oversimplification that would conclude that all the cases related in the Gospel had to do with psychological disorders and hence that the devil does not exist or is not at work. He is present in the very first pages of the Scriptures, which end with God's victory

over the devil.[120] Indeed, in leaving us the Our Father, Jesus wanted us to conclude by asking the Father to "deliver us from evil." That final word does not refer to evil in the abstract; a more exact translation would be "the evil one." It indicates a personal being who assails us. Jesus taught us to ask daily for deliverance from him, lest his power prevail over us.

161. Hence, we should not think of the devil as a myth, a representation, a symbol, a figure of speech, or an idea.[121] This mistake would lead us to let down our guard, to grow careless and end up more vulnerable. The devil does not need to possess us. He poisons us with the venom of hatred, desolation, envy, and vice. When we let down our guard, he takes advantage of it to destroy our lives, our families, and our communities. "Like a roaring lion, he prowls around, looking for someone to devour" (1 Pt 5:8).

Alert and Trustful

162. God's word invites us clearly to "stand against the wiles of the devil" (Eph 6:11) and to "quench all the flaming darts of the evil one" (Eph 6:16). These expressions are not melodramatic, precisely because our path toward holiness is a constant battle. Those who do not realize this will be prey to failure or mediocrity. For this spiritual combat, we can count on the powerful weapons that the Lord has given us: faith-filled prayer, meditation on the word of God, the celebration of Mass, Eucharistic adoration, sacramental Reconciliation, works of charity, community life, missionary outreach. If we become careless, the false promises of evil will easily seduce us. As the sainted Cura Brochero observed: "What good is it when Lucifer promises you freedom and showers you with all his benefits, if those benefits are false, deceptive and poisonous?"[122]

163. Along this journey, the cultivation of all that is good, progress in the spiritual life and growth in love are the best counterbalance to evil. Those who choose to remain neutral, who are satisfied with little, who renounce the ideal of giving themselves generously to the Lord, will never hold out. Even less if they fall into defeatism, for "if we start

without confidence, we have already lost half the battle and we bury our talents. . . . Christian triumph is always a cross, yet a cross which is at the same time a victorious banner, borne with aggressive tenderness against the assaults of evil."[123]

Spiritual Corruption

164. The path of holiness is a source of peace and joy, given to us by the Spirit. At the same time, it demands that we keep "our lamps lit" (Lk 12:35) and be attentive. "Abstain from every form of evil" (1 Thes 5:22). "Keep awake" (Mt 24:42; Mk 13:35). "Let us not fall asleep" (1 Thes 5:6). Those who think they commit no grievous sins against God's law can fall into a state of dull lethargy. Since they see nothing serious to reproach themselves with, they fail to realize that their spiritual life has gradually turned lukewarm. They end up weakened and corrupted.

165. Spiritual corruption is worse than the fall of a sinner, for it is a comfortable and self-satisfied form of blindness. Everything then appears acceptable: deception, slander, egotism, and other subtle forms of self-centeredness, for "even Satan disguises himself as an angel of light" (2 Cor 11:14). So Solomon ended his days, whereas David, who sinned greatly, was able to make up for disgrace. Jesus warned us against this self-deception that easily leads to corruption. He spoke of a person freed from the devil who, convinced that his life was now in order, ended up being possessed by seven other evil spirits (cf. Lk 11:24–26). Another biblical text puts it bluntly: "The dog turns back to his own vomit" (2 Pt 2:22; cf. Prv 26:11).

Discernment

166. How can we know if something comes from the Holy Spirit or if it stems from the spirit of the world or the spirit of the devil? The only way is through discernment, which calls for something more than intelligence or common sense. It is a gift which we must implore. If we ask with confidence that the Holy Spirit grant us this gift, and then seek to

develop it through prayer, reflection, reading, and good counsel, then surely we will grow in this spiritual endowment.

An Urgent Need

167. The gift of discernment has become all the more necessary today, since contemporary life offers immense possibilities for action and distraction, and the world presents all of them as valid and good. All of us, but especially the young, are immersed in a culture of zapping. We can navigate simultaneously on two or more screens and interact at the same time with two or three virtual scenarios. Without the wisdom of discernment, we can easily become prey to every passing trend.

168. This is all the more important when some novelty presents itself in our lives. Then we have to decide whether it is new wine brought by God or an illusion created by the spirit of this world or the spirit of the devil. At other times, the opposite can happen, when the forces of evil induce us not to change, to leave things as they are, to opt for a rigid resistance to change. Yet that would be to block the working of the Spirit. We are free, with the freedom of Christ. Still, he asks us to examine what is within us—our desires, anxieties, fears, and questions—and what takes place all around us—"the signs of the times"—and thus to recognize the paths that lead to complete freedom. "Test everything; hold fast to what is good" (1 Thes 5:21).

Always in the Light of the Lord

169. Discernment is necessary not only at extraordinary times, when we need to resolve grave problems and make crucial decisions. It is a means of spiritual combat for helping us to follow the Lord more faithfully. We need it at all times, to help us recognize God's timetable, lest we fail to heed the promptings of his grace and disregard his invitation to grow. Often discernment is exercised in small and apparently irrelevant things, since greatness of spirit is manifested in simple everyday realities.[124] It involves striving untrammeled for all that is great, better and more

beautiful, while at the same time being concerned for the little things, for each day's responsibilities and commitments. For this reason, I ask all Christians not to omit, in dialogue with the Lord, a sincere daily "examination of conscience." Discernment also enables us to recognize the concrete means that the Lord provides in his mysterious and loving plan, to make us move beyond mere good intentions.

A Supernatural Gift

170. Certainly, spiritual discernment does not exclude existential, psychological, sociological, or moral insights drawn from the human sciences. At the same time, it transcends them. Nor are the Church's sound norms sufficient. We should always remember that discernment is a grace. Even though it includes reason and prudence, it goes beyond them, for it seeks a glimpse of that unique and mysterious plan that God has for each of us, which takes shape amid so many varied situations and limitations. It involves more than my temporal well-being, my satisfaction at having accomplished something useful, or even my desire for peace of mind. It has to do with the meaning of my life before the Father who knows and loves me, with the real purpose of my life, which nobody knows better than he. Ultimately, discernment leads to the wellspring of undying life: to know the Father, the only true God, and the one whom he has sent, Jesus Christ (cf. Jn 17:3). It requires no special abilities, nor is it only for the more intelligent or better educated. The Father readily reveals himself to the lowly (cf. Mt 11:25).

171. The Lord speaks to us in a variety of ways, at work, through others, and at every moment. Yet we simply cannot do without the silence of prolonged prayer, which enables us better to perceive God's language, to interpret the real meaning of the inspirations we believe we have received, to calm our anxieties, and to see the whole of our existence afresh in his own light. In this way, we allow the birth of a new synthesis that springs from a life inspired by the Spirit.

Speak, Lord

172. Nonetheless, it is possible that, even in prayer itself, we could refuse to let ourselves be confronted by the freedom of the Spirit, who acts as he wills. We must remember that prayerful discernment must be born of a readiness to listen: to the Lord and to others, and to reality itself, which always challenges us in new ways. Only if we are prepared to listen, do we have the freedom to set aside our own partial or insufficient ideas, our usual habits and ways of seeing things. In this way, we become truly open to accepting a call that can shatter our security, but lead us to a better life. It is not enough that everything be calm and peaceful. God may be offering us something more, but in our comfortable inadvertence, we do not recognize it.

173. Naturally, this attitude of listening entails obedience to the Gospel as the ultimate standard, but also to the Magisterium that guards it, as we seek to find in the treasury of the Church whatever is most fruitful for the "today" of salvation. It is not a matter of applying rules or repeating what was done in the past, since the same solutions are not valid in all circumstances and what was useful in one context may not prove so in another. The discernment of spirits liberates us from rigidity, which has no place before the perennial "today" of the risen Lord. The Spirit alone can penetrate what is obscure and hidden in every situation, and grasp its every nuance, so that the newness of the Gospel can emerge in another light.

The Logic of Gift and of the Cross

174. An essential condition for progress in discernment is a growing understanding of God's patience and his timetable, which are never our own. God does not pour down fire upon those who are unfaithful (cf. Lk 9:54), or allow the zealous to uproot the tares growing among the wheat (cf. Mt 13:29). Generosity too is demanded, for "it is more blessed to give than to receive" (Acts 20:35). Discernment is not about discovering what more we can get out of this life, but about recognizing how we can better accomplish the mission entrusted to us at our baptism. This

entails a readiness to make sacrifices, even to sacrificing everything. For happiness is a paradox. We experience it most when we accept the mysterious logic that is not of this world: "This is our logic," says Saint Bonaventure,[125] pointing to the cross. Once we enter into this dynamic, we will not let our consciences be numbed and we will open ourselves generously to discernment.

175. When, in God's presence, we examine our life's journey, no areas can be off limits. In all aspects of life we can continue to grow and offer something greater to God, even in those areas we find most difficult. We need, though, to ask the Holy Spirit to liberate us and to expel the fear that makes us ban him from certain parts of our lives. God asks everything of us, yet he also gives everything to us. He does not want to enter our lives to cripple or diminish them, but to bring them to fulfillment. Discernment, then, is not a solipsistic self-analysis or a form of egotistical introspection, but an authentic process of leaving ourselves behind in order to approach the mystery of God, who helps us to carry out the mission to which he has called us, for the good of our brothers and sisters.

•••

176. I would like these reflections to be crowned by Mary, because she lived the Beatitudes of Jesus as none other. She is that woman who rejoiced in the presence of God, who treasured everything in her heart, and who let herself be pierced by the sword. Mary is the saint among the saints, blessed above all others. She teaches us the way of holiness and she walks ever at our side. She does not let us remain fallen and at times she takes us into her arms without judging us. Our converse with her consoles, frees, and sanctifies us. Mary our Mother does not need a flood of words. She does not need us to tell her what is happening in our lives. All we need do is whisper, time and time again: "Hail Mary . . ."

177. It is my hope that these pages will prove helpful by enabling the whole Church to devote herself anew to promoting the desire for holiness. Let us ask the Holy Spirit to pour out upon us a fervent longing

to be saints for God's greater glory, and let us encourage one another in this effort. In this way, we will share a happiness that the world will not be able to take from us.

Given in Rome, at Saint Peter's, on 19 March, the Solemnity of Saint Joseph, in the year 2018, the sixth of my Pontificate.

FRANCISCUS

Notes

1. Benedict XVI, *Homily for the Solemn Inauguration of the Petrine Ministry* (24 April 2005): AAS 97 (2005), 708.

2. This always presumes a reputation of holiness and the exercise, at least to an ordinary degree, of the Christian virtues: cf. Motu Proprio *Maiorem Hac Dilectionem* (11 July 2017), Art. 2c: *L'Osservatore Romano*, 12 July 2017, p. 8.

3. Second Vatican Ecumenical Council, Dogmatic Constitution on the Church *Lumen Gentium*, 9.

4. Cf. Joseph Malegue, *Pierres noires. Les classes moyennes du Salut*, Paris, 1958.

5. Second Vatican Ecumenical Council, Dogmatic Constitution on the Church *Lumen Gentium*, 12.

6. *Verborgenes Leben und Epiphanie:* GW XI, 145.

7. John Paul II, Encyclical Letter *Novo Millennio Ineunte* (6 January 2001), 56: AAS 93 (2001), 307.

8. Encyclical Letter *Tertio Millennio Adveniente* (10 November 1994), 37: AAS 87 (1995), 29.

9. *Homily for the Ecumenical Commemoration of Witnesses to the Faith in the Twentieth Century* (7 May 2000), 5: AAS 92 (2000), 680–81.

10. Dogmatic Constitution on the Church *Lumen Gentium*, 11.

11. Cf. Hans Urs von Balthasar, "Theology and Holiness," in *Communio* 14/4 (1987), 345.

12. *Spiritual Canticle*, Red. B, Prologue, 2.

13. Cf. ibid., 14–15, 2.

14. Cf. *Catechesis*, General Audience of 19 November 2014: *Insegnamenti* II/2 (2014), 555.

15. Francis de Sales, *Treatise on the Love of God*, VIII, 11.

16. *Five Loaves and Two Fish*, Pauline Books and Media, 2003, pp. 9, 13.

17. New Zealand Catholic Bishops' Conference, *Healing Love*, 1 January 1988.

18. *Spiritual Exercises*, 102–312.

19. Catechism of the Catholic Church, 515.

20. Ibid., 516.

21. Ibid., 517.

22. Ibid., 518.

23. Ibid., 521.

24. Benedict XVI, *Catechesis*, General Audience of 13 April 2011: *Insegnamenti* VII (2011), 451.

25. Ibid., 450.

26. Cf. Hans Urs von Balthasar, "Theology and Holiness," in *Communio* 14/4 (1987), 341–50.

27. Xavier Zubiri, *Naturaleza, historia, Dios*, Madrid, 1993[3], 427.

28. Carlo M. Martini, *Le confessioni di Pietro*, Cinisello Balsamo, 2017, 69.

29. We need to distinguish between this kind of superficial entertainment and a healthy culture of leisure, which opens us to others and to reality itself in a spirit of openness and contemplation.

30. John Paul II, *Homily at the Mass of Canonization* (1 October 2000), 5: AAS 92 (2000), 852.

31. Regional Episcopal Conference of West Africa, *Pastoral Message at the End of the Second Plenary Assembly*, 29 February 2016, 2.

32. *La femme pauvre*, Paris, II, 27.

33. Cf. Congregation for the Doctrine of the Faith, Letter *Placuit Deo* on Certain Aspects of Christian Salvation (22 February 2018), 4, in *L'Osservatore Romano*, 2 March 2018, pp. 4–5: "Both neo-Pelagian individualism and the neo-Gnostic disregard of the body deface the confession of faith in Christ, the one, universal Savior." This document provides the doctrinal bases for understanding Christian salvation in reference to contemporary neo-gnostic and neo-pelagian tendencies.

34. Apostolic Exhortation *Evangelii Gaudium* (24 November 2013), 94: AAS 105 (2013), 1060.

35. Ibid.: AAS 105 (2013), 1059.

36. *Homily at Mass in Casa Santa Marta*, 11 November 2016: *L'Osservatore Romano*, 12 November 2016, p. 8.

37. As Saint Bonaventure teaches, "We must suspend all the operations of the mind and we must transform the peak of our affections, directing them to God alone. . . . Since nature can achieve nothing and personal effort very little, it is necessary to give little importance to investigation and much to unction, little to speech and much to interior joy, little to words or writing but all to the gift of God, namely the Holy Spirit, little or no importance should be given to the creature, but all to the Creator, the Father and the Son and the Holy Spirit": Bonaventure, *Itinerarium Mentis in Deum*, VII, 4–5.

38. Cf. *Letter to the Grand Chancellor of the Pontifical Catholic University of Argentina for the Centenary of the Founding of the Faculty of Theology* (3 March 2015): *L'Osservatore Romano*, 9–10 March 2015, p. 6.

39. Apostolic Exhortation *Evangelii Gaudium* (24 November 2013), 40: AAS 105 (2013), 1037.

40. *Video Message to Participants in an International Theological Congress held at the Pontifical Catholic University of Argentina* (1-3 September 2015): AAS 107 (2015), 980.

41. Post-Synodal Apostolic Exhortation *Vita Consecrata* (25 March 1996), 38: AAS 88 (1996), 412.

42. *Letter to the Grand Chancellor of the Pontifical Catholic University of Argentina for the Centenary of the Founding of the Faculty of Theology* (3 March 2015): *L'Osservatore Romano*, 9–10 March 2015, p. 6.

43. *Letter to Brother Anthony*, 2: FF 251.

44. *De septem donis*, 9, 15.

45. *In IV Sent.* 37, 1, 3, ad 6.

46. Apostolic Exhortation *Evangelii Gaudium* (24 November 2013), 94: AAS 105 (2013), 1059.

47. Cf. Bonaventure, *De sex alis Seraphim*, 3, 8: "*Non omnes omnia possunt.*" The phrase is to be understood along the lines of the Catechism of the Catholic Church, 1735.

48. Cf. Thomas Aquinas, *Summa Theologiae* II-II, q. 109, a. 9, ad 1: "But here grace is to some extent imperfect, inasmuch as it does not completely heal man, as we have said."

49. Cf. *De natura et gratia*, 43, 50: PL 44, 271.

50. *Confessiones*, X, 29, 40: PL 32, 796.

51. Cf. Apostolic Exhortation *Evangelii Gaudium* (24 November 2013), 44: AAS 105 (2013), 1038.

52. In the understanding of Christian faith, grace precedes, accompanies and follows all our actions (cf. Ecumenical Council of Trent, Session VI, *Decree on Justification*, ch. 5: DH 1525).

53. Cf. *In Ep. ad Romanos*, 9, 11: PG 60, 470.

54. *Homilia de Humilitate*: PG 31, 530.

55. Canon 4: DH 374.

56. Session VI, *Decree on Justification*, ch. 8: DH 1532.

57. No. 1998.

58. Ibid., 2007.

59. Thomas Aquinas, *Summa Theologiae*, I-II, q. 114, a. 5.

60. Thérèse of the Child Jesus, "Act of Offering to Merciful Love" (Prayers, 6).

61. Lucio Gera, *Sobre el misterio del pobre*, in P. GRELOT-L. GERA-A. DUMAS, *El Pobre*, Buenos Aires, 1962, 103.

62 .This is, in a word, the Catholic doctrine on "merit" subsequent to justification: it has to do with the cooperation of the justified for growth in the life of grace (cf. Catechism of the Catholic Church, 2010). Yet this cooperation in no way makes justification itself or friendship with God the object of human merit.

63. Cf. Apostolic Exhortation *Evangelii Gaudium* (24 November 2013), 95: AAS 105 (2013), 1060.

64. *Summa Theologiae* I-II, q. 107, art. 4.

65. Francis, *Homily at Mass for the Jubilee of Socially Excluded People* (13 November 2016): *L'Osservatore Romano*, 14–15 November 2016, p. 8.

66. Cf. *Homily at Mass in Casa Santa Marta*, 9 June 2014: *L'Osservatore Romano*, 10 June 2014, p. 8.

67. The order of the second and third Beatitudes varies in accordance with the different textual traditions.

68. *Spiritual Exercises*, 23d.

69. *Manuscript* C, 12r.

70. From the patristic era, the Church has valued the gift of tears, as seen in the fine prayer "*Ad petendam compunctionem cordis.*" It reads: "Almighty and most

merciful God, who brought forth from the rock a spring of living water for your thirsting people: bring forth tears of compunction from our hardness of heart, that we may grieve for our sins, and, by your mercy, obtain their forgiveness" (cf. *Missale Romanum*, ed. typ. 1962, p. 110).

71. Catechism of the Catholic Church, 1789; cf. 1970.

72. Ibid., 1787.

73. Detraction and calumny are acts of terrorism: a bomb is thrown, it explodes, and the attacker walks away calm and contented. This is completely different from the nobility of those who speak to others face to face, serenely and frankly, out of genuine concern for their good.

74. At times, it may be necessary to speak of the difficulties of a particular brother or sister. In such cases, it can happen that an interpretation is passed on in place of an objective fact. Emotions can misconstrue and alter the facts of a matter, and end up passing them on laced with subjective elements. In this way, neither the facts themselves nor the truth of the other person are respected.

75. Apostolic Exhortation, *Evangelii Gaudium* (24 November 2013), 218: AAS 105 (2013), 1110.

76. Ibid., 239: 1116.

77. Ibid., 227: 1112.

78. Encyclical Letter *Centesimus Annus* (1 May 1991), 41c: AAS 81 (1993), 844–45.

79. Apostolic Letter *Novo Millennio Ineunte* (6 January 2001), 49: AAS 93 (2001), 302.

80. Ibid.

81. Bull *Misericordiae Vultus* (11 April 2015), 12: AAS 107 (2015), 407.

82. We can recall the Good Samaritan's reaction upon meeting the man attacked by robbers and left for dead (cf. Lk 10:30–37).

83. Social Affairs Commission of the Canadian Conference of Catholic Bishops, Open Letter to the Members of Parliament, *The Common Good or Exclusion: A Choice for Canadians* (1 February 2001), 9.

84. The Fifth General Conference of the Latin American and Caribbean Bishops, echoing the Church's constant teaching, stated that human beings "are always sacred, from their conception, at all stages of existence, until their natural death, and after death," and that life must be safeguarded "starting at conception, *in all its stages*, until natural death" (*Aparecida Document*, 29 June 2007, 388; 464).

85. *Rule*, 53, 1: PL 66, 749.

86. Cf. ibid., 53, 7: PL 66, 750.

87. Ibid., 53, 15: PL 66, 751.

88. Bull *Misericordiae Vultus* (11 April 2015), 9: AAS 107 (2015), 405.

89. Ibid., 10, 406.

90. Post-Synodal Apostolic Exhortation *Amoris Laetitia* (19 March 2016), 311: AAS 108 (2016), 439.

91. Apostolic Exhortation *Evangelii Gaudium* (24 November 2013), 197: AAS 105 (2013), 1103.

92. Cf. *Summa Theologiae*, II-II, q. 30, a. 4.

93. Ibid., ad 1.

94. Cited (in Spanish translation) in: *Cristo en los Pobres*, Madrid, 1981, 37–38.

95. There are some forms of bullying that, while seeming delicate or respectful and even quite spiritual, cause great damage to others' self-esteem.

96. *Precautions*, 13.

97. Ibid., 13.

98. Cf. *Diary. Divine Mercy in My Soul*, Stockbridge, 2000, p. 139 (300).

99. Thomas Aquinas, *Summa Theologiae*, I-II, q. 70, a. 3.

100. Apostolic Exhortation *Evangelii Gaudium* (24 November 2013), 6: AAS 105 (2013), 1221.

101. I recommend praying the prayer attributed to Saint Thomas More: "Grant me, O Lord, good digestion, and also something to digest. Grant me a healthy body, and the necessary good humor to maintain it. Grant me a simple soul that knows to treasure all that is good and that doesn't frighten easily at the sight of evil, but rather finds the means to put things back in their place. Give me a soul that knows not boredom, grumbling, sighs and laments, nor excess of stress, because of that obstructing thing called 'I.' Grant me, O Lord, a sense of good humor. Allow me the grace to be able to take a joke and to discover in life a bit of joy, and to be able to share it with others."

102. Post-Synodal Apostolic Exhortation *Amoris Laetitia* (19 March 2016), 110: AAS 108 (2016), 354.

103. Apostolic Exhortation *Evangelii Nuntiandi* (8 December 1975), 80: AAS 68 (1976), 73. It is worth noting that in this text Blessed Paul VI closely links joy and *parrhesía*. While lamenting a "lack of joy and hope" as an obstacle to evangelization, he extols the "delightful and comforting joy of evangelizing," linked to "an interior enthusiasm that nobody and nothing can quench." This ensures that the world does not receive the Gospel "from evangelizers who are dejected [and] discouraged." During the 1975 Holy Year, Pope Paul devoted to joy his Apostolic Exhortation *Gaudete in Domino* (9 May 1975): AAS 67 (1975), 289–322.

104. *Precautions*, 15.

105. John Paul II, Apostolic Exhortation *Vita Consecrata* (25 March 1996), 42: AAS 88 (1996), 416.

106. *Confessiones*, IX, 10, 23–25: PL 32, 773–75.

107. I think especially of the three key words "please," "thank you," and "sorry." "The right words, spoken at the right time, daily protect and nurture love": Post-Synodal Apostolic Exhortation *Amoris Laetitia* (19 March 2016), 133: AAS 108 (2016), 363.

108. Thérèse of the Child Jesus, Manuscript C, 29 v-30r.

109. *Degrees of Perfection*, 2.

110. ID., *Counsels to a Religious on How to Attain Perfection*, 9.

111. Autobiography, 8, 5.

112. John Paul II, Apostolic Letter *Orientale Lumen* (2 May 1995), 16: AAS 87 (1995), 762.

113. *Meeting with the Participants in the Fifth Convention of the Italian Church*, Florence, (10 November 2015): AAS 107 (2015), 1284.

114. Cf. Bernard of Clairvaux, *Sermones in Canticum Canticorum*, 61, 3–5: PL 183:1071–73.

115. *The Way of a Pilgrim*, New York, 1965, pp. 17, 105–6.

116. Cf. *Spiritual Exercises*, 230–37.

117. Letter to Henry de Castries, 14 August 1901.

118. Fifth General Conference of the Latin American and Caribbean Bishops, *Aparecida Document* (29 June 2007), 259.

119. Conference of Catholic Bishops of India, *Final Declaration of the Twenty-First Plenary Assembly*, 18 February 2009, 3.2.

120. Cf. *Homily at Mass in Casa Santa Marta*, 11 October 2013: *L'Osservatore Romano*, 12 October 2013, p. 2.

121. Cf. Paul VI, *Catechesis*, General Audience of 15 November 1972: *Insegnamenti* X (1972), pp. 1168–70: "One of our greatest needs is defense against that evil which we call the devil. . . . Evil is not simply a deficiency, it is an efficiency, a living spiritual being, perverted and perverting. A terrible reality, mysterious and frightful. They no longer remain within the framework of biblical and ecclesiastical teaching who refuse to recognize its existence, or who make of it an independent principle that does not have, like every creature, its origin in God, or explain it as a pseudo-reality, a conceptual and imaginative personification of the hidden causes of our misfortunes."

122. José Gabriel del Rosario Brochero, "Plática de las banderas," in Conferencia Episcopal Argentina, *El Cura Brochero. Cartas y sermones*, Buenos Aires, 1999, 71.

123. Apostolic Exhortation *Evangelii Gaudium* (24 November 2013), 85: AAS 105 (2013), 1056.

124. The tomb of Saint Ignatius of Loyola bears this thought-provoking inscription: *Non coerceri a maximo, conteneri tamen a minimo divinum est* ("Not to be confined by the greatest, yet to be contained within the smallest, is truly divine").

125. *Collationes in Hexaemeron*, 1, 30.

Christus Vivit

Christ Is Alive

Post-Synodal Apostolic Exhortation to Young People and to the Entire People of God

March 25, 2019

POST-SYNODAL APOSTOLIC EXHORTATION

CHRISTUS VIVIT

OF THE HOLY FATHER

FRANCIS

TO YOUNG PEOPLE AND TO THE ENTIRE PEOPLE OF GOD

1. Christ is alive! He is our hope, and in a wonderful way he brings youth to our world, and everything he touches becomes young, new, full of life. The very first words, then, that I would like to say to every young Christian are these: Christ is alive and he wants you to be alive!

2. He is in you, he is with you, and he never abandons you. However far you may wander, he is always there, the Risen One. He calls you and he waits for you to return to him and start over again. When you feel you are growing old out of sorrow, resentment or fear, doubt or failure, he will always be there to restore your strength and your hope.

3. With great affection, I address this Apostolic Exhortation to all Christian young people. It is meant to remind you of certain convictions born of our faith, and at the same time to encourage you to grow in holiness and in commitment to your personal vocation. But since it is also part of a synodal process, I am also addressing this message to the entire People of God, pastors and faithful alike, since all of us are challenged and urged to reflect both on the young and for the young. Consequently, I will speak to young people directly in some places, while in others I will propose some more general considerations for the Church's discernment.

4. I have let myself be inspired by the wealth of reflections and conversations that emerged from last year's Synod. I cannot include all those contributions here, but you can read them in the Final Document. In writing this letter, though, I have attempted to summarize those proposals I considered most significant. In this way, my words will echo the myriad voices of believers the world over who made their opinions known to the Synod. Those young people who are not believers, yet wished to share their thoughts, also raised issues that led me to ask new questions.

CHAPTER ONE

WHAT DOES THE WORD OF GOD HAVE TO SAY ABOUT YOUNG PEOPLE?

5. Let us draw upon some of the richness of the sacred Scriptures, since they often speak of young people and of how the Lord draws near to encounter them.

In the Old Testament

6. In an age when young people were not highly regarded, some texts show that God sees them differently. Joseph, for example, was one of the youngest of his family (cf. Gn 37:2–3), yet God showed him great things in dreams and when about twenty years old he outshone all his brothers in important affairs (cf. Gn 37–47).

7. In Gideon, we see the frankness of young people, who are not used to sugar-coating reality. When told that the Lord was with him, he responded: "But if the Lord is with us, why then have all these things happened to us?" (Jgs 6:13). God was not offended by that reproach, but went on to order him: "Go in this might of yours and deliver Israel!" (Jgs 6:14).

8. Samuel was still a young boy, yet the Lord spoke to him. Thanks to the advice of an adult, he opened his heart to hear God's call: "Speak, Lord, for your servant is listening" (1 Sm 3:9-10). As a result, he became a great prophet who intervened at critical moments in the history of his country. King Saul was also young when the Lord called him to undertake his mission (cf. 1 Sm 9:2).

9. King David was chosen while still a boy. When the prophet Samuel was seeking the future king of Israel, a man offered as candidates his sons who were older and more experienced. Yet the prophet said that the chosen one was the young David, who was out tending the flock (cf. 1 Sm 16:6-13), for "man looks on the outward appearance, but the Lord

looks on the heart" (v. 7). The glory of youth is in the heart, more than in physical strength or the impression given to others.

10. Solomon, when he had to succeed his father, felt lost and told God: "I am a mere youth, not knowing at all how to act" (1 Kg 3:7). Yet the audacity of youth moved him to ask God for wisdom and he devoted himself to his mission. Something similar happened to the prophet Jeremiah, called despite his youth to rouse his people. In his fear, he said: "Ah, Lord God! Truly I do not know how to speak, for I am only a youth" (Jer 1:6). But the Lord told him not to say that (cf. Jer 1:7), and added: "Do not be afraid of them, for I am with you to deliver you" (Jer 1:8). The devotion of the prophet Jeremiah to his mission shows what can happen when the brashness of youth is joined to the power of God.

11. A Jewish servant girl of the foreign commander Naaman intervened with faith and helped him to be cured of his illness (cf. 2 Kg 5:2–6). The young Ruth was a model of generosity in remaining beside her mother-in-law who had fallen on hard times (cf. Ru 1:1-18), yet she also showed boldness in getting ahead in life (cf. Ru 4:1–17).

In the New Testament

12. One of Jesus' parables (cf. Lk 15:11–32) relates that a "younger" son wanted to leave his father's home for a distant land (cf. vv. 12–13). Yet his thoughts of independence turned into dissolution and excess (cf. v. 13), and he came to experience the bitterness of loneliness and poverty (cf. vv. 14–16). Nonetheless, he found the strength to make a new start (cf. vv. 17–19) and determined to get up and return home (cf. v. 20). Young hearts are naturally ready to change, to turn back, get up, and learn from life. How could anyone fail to support that son in this new resolution? Yet his older brother already had a heart grown old; he let himself be possessed by greed, selfishness, and envy (Lk 15:28–30). Jesus praises the young sinner who returned to the right path over the brother who considered himself faithful, yet lacked the spirit of love and mercy.

13. Jesus, himself eternally young, wants to give us hearts that are ever young. God's word asks us to "cast out the old leaven that you may be fresh dough" (1 Cor 5:7). Saint Paul invites us to strip ourselves of the "old self" and to put on a "young" self (Col 3:9–10).[1] In explaining what it means to put on that youthfulness "which is being renewed" (v. 10), he mentions "compassion, kindness, humility, meekness and patience, bearing with one another and forgiving each other if anyone has a complaint against another" (Col 3:12–13). In a word, true youth means having a heart capable of loving, whereas everything that separates us from others makes the soul grow old. And so he concludes: "above all, clothe yourselves with love, which binds everything together in perfect harmony" (Col 3:14).

14. Let us also keep in mind that Jesus had no use for adults who looked down on the young or lorded it over them. On the contrary, he insisted that "the greatest among you must become like the youngest" (Lk 22:26). For him age did not establish privileges, and being young did not imply lesser worth or dignity.

15. The word of God says that young people should be treated "as brothers" (1 Tm 5:1), and warns parents not to "provoke your children, lest they become discouraged" (Col 3:21). Young people are not meant to become discouraged; they are meant to dream great things, to seek vast horizons, to aim higher, to take on the world, to accept challenges, and to offer the best of themselves to the building of something better. That is why I constantly urge young people not to let themselves be robbed of hope; to each of them I repeat: "Let no one despise your youth" (1 Tm 4:12).

16. Nonetheless, young people are also urged "to accept the authority of those who are older" (1 Pt 5:5). The Bible never ceases to insist that profound respect be shown to the elderly, since they have a wealth of experience; they have known success and failure, life's joys and afflictions, its dreams and disappointments. In the silence of their heart, they have

a store of experiences that can teach us not to make mistakes or be taken in by false promises. An ancient sage asks us to respect certain limits and to master our impulses: "Urge the younger men to be self-controlled" (Ti 2.6). It is unhelpful to buy into the cult of youth or foolishly to dismiss others simply because they are older or from another generation. Jesus tells us that the wise are able to bring forth from their store things both new and old (cf. Mt 13:52). A wise young person is open to the future, yet still capable of learning something from the experience of others.

17. In the Gospel of Mark, we find a man who, listening to Jesus speak of the commandments, says, "All these I have observed from my youth" (10:20). The Psalmist had already said the same thing: "You, O Lord, are my hope; my trust, O Lord, from my youth. . . . From my youth you have taught me, and I still proclaim your wondrous deeds" (Ps 71:5, 17). We should never repent of spending our youth being good, opening our heart to the Lord, and living differently. None of this takes away from our youth but instead strengthens and renews it: "Your youth is renewed like the eagle's" (Ps 103:5). For this reason, Saint Augustine could lament: "Late have I loved you, beauty ever ancient, ever new! Late have I loved you!"[2] Yet that rich man, who had been faithful to God in his youth, allowed the passing years to rob his dreams; he preferred to remain attached to his riches (cf. Mk 10:22).

18. On the other hand, in the Gospel of Matthew we find a young man (cf. 19:20–22) who approaches Jesus and asks if there is more that he can do (v. 20); in this, he demonstrates that youthful openness of spirit which seeks new horizons and great challenges. Yet his spirit was not really that young, for he had already become attached to riches and comforts. He said he wanted something more, but when Jesus asked him to be generous and distribute his goods, he realized that he could not let go of everything he had. In the end, "hearing these words, the young man went away sad" (v. 22). He had given up his youth.

19. The Gospel also speaks about a group of wise young women, who were ready and waiting, while others were distracted and slumbering (cf. Mt 25:1–13). We can, in fact, spend our youth being distracted, skimming the surface of life, half-asleep, incapable of cultivating meaningful relationships or experiencing the deeper things in life. In this way, we can store up a paltry and unsubstantial future. Or we can spend our youth aspiring to beautiful and great things, and thus store up a future full of life and interior richness.

20. If you have lost your inner vitality, your dreams, your enthusiasm, your optimism, and your generosity, Jesus stands before you as once he stood before the dead son of the widow, and with all the power of his resurrection he urges you: "Young man, I say to you, arise!" (Lk 7:14).

21. To be sure, many other passages of the word of God can shed light on this stage of your life. We will take up some of them in the following chapters.

CHAPTER TWO

JESUS, EVER YOUNG

22. Jesus is "young among the young in order to be an example for the young and to consecrate them to the Lord."[3] For this reason the Synod said that "youth is an original and stimulating stage of life, which Jesus himself experienced, thereby sanctifying it."[4]

Jesus' Youth

23. The Lord "gave up his spirit" (cf. Mt 27:50) on a cross when he was little more than thirty years of age (cf. Lk 3:23). It is important to realize that Jesus was a young person. He gave his life when he was, in today's terms, a young adult. He began his public mission in the prime of life, and thus "a light dawned" (Mt 4:16) that would shine most brightly when he gave his life to the very end. That ending was not something that simply happened; rather, his entire youth, at every moment, was a precious preparation for it. "Everything in Jesus's life was a sign of his mystery";[5] indeed, "Christ's whole life is a mystery of redemption."[6]

24. The Gospel tells us nothing of Jesus' childhood, but it does recount several events of his adolescence and youth. Matthew situates the time of the Lord's youth between two events: his family's return to Nazareth after their exile, and Jesus' baptism in the Jordan, the beginning of his public ministry. The last images we have of Jesus as a child are those of a tiny refugee in Egypt (cf. Mt 2:14–15) and repatriated in Nazareth (cf. Mt 2:19–23). Our first image of Jesus as a young adult shows him standing among the crowds on the banks of the Jordan river to be baptized by his kinsman John the Baptist, just like any other member of his people (cf. Mt 3:13–17).

25. Jesus' baptism was not like our own, which introduces us to the life of grace, but a consecration prior to his embarking on the great mission of his life. The Gospel says that at his baptism the Father rejoiced and

was well pleased: "You are my beloved Son" (Lk 3:22). Jesus immediately appeared filled with the Holy Spirit, and was led by the Spirit into the desert. There he prepared to go forth to preach and to work miracles, to bring freedom and healing (cf. Lk 4:1–14). Every young person who feels called to a mission in this world is invited to hear the Father speaking those same words within his or her heart: "You are my beloved child."

26. Between these two accounts, we find another, which shows Jesus as an adolescent, when he had returned with his parents to Nazareth, after being lost and found in the Temple (cf. Lk 2:41–51). There we read that "he was obedient to them" (cf. Lk 2:51); he did not disown his family. Luke then adds that Jesus "grew in wisdom, age and grace before God and men" (cf. Lk 2:52). In a word, this was a time of preparation, when Jesus grew in his relationship with the Father and with others. Saint John Paul II explained that he did not only grow physically, but that "there was also a spiritual growth in Jesus," because "the fullness of grace in Jesus was in proportion to his age: there was always a fullness, but a fullness which increased as he grew in age."[7]

27. From what the Gospel tells us, we can say that Jesus, in the years of his youth, was "training," being prepared to carry out the Father's plan. His adolescence and his youth set him on the path to that sublime mission.

28. In his adolescence and youth, Jesus' relationship with the Father was that of the beloved Son. Drawn to the Father, he grew up concerned for his affairs: "Did you not know that I must be about my Father's business?" (Lk 2:49). Still, it must not be thought that Jesus was a withdrawn adolescent or a self-absorbed youth. His relationships were those of a young person who shared fully in the life of his family and his people. He learned his father's trade and then replaced him as a carpenter. At one point in the Gospel he is called "the carpenter's son" (Mt 13:55) and another time simply "the carpenter" (Mk 6:3). This detail shows that he was just another young person of his town, who related normally to others. No one regarded him as unusual or set apart from others. For

this very reason, once Jesus began to preach, people could not imagine where he got this wisdom: "Is this not Joseph's son?" (Lk 4:22).

29. In fact, "Jesus did not grow up in a narrow and stifling relationship with Mary and Joseph, but readily interacted with the wider family, the relatives of his parents and their friends."[8] Hence we can understand why, when he returned from his pilgrimage to Jerusalem, his parents readily thought that, as a twelve-year-old boy (cf. Lk 2:42), he was wandering freely among the crowd, even though they did not see him for an entire day: "supposing him to be in the group of travelers, they went a day's journey" (Lk 2:44). Surely, they assumed, Jesus was there, mingling with the others, joking with other young people, listening to the adults tell stories, and sharing the joys and sorrows of the group. Indeed, the Greek word that Luke uses to describe the group—*synodía*—clearly evokes a larger "community on a journey" of which the Holy Family is a part. Thanks to the trust of his parents, Jesus can move freely and learn to journey with others.

His Youth Teaches Us

30. These aspects of Jesus' life can prove inspiring for all those young people who are developing and preparing to take up their mission in life. This involves growing in a relationship with the Father, in awareness of being part of a family and a people, and in openness to being filled with the Holy Spirit and led to carry out the mission God gives them, their personal vocation. None of this should be overlooked in pastoral work with young people, lest we create projects that isolate young people from their family and the larger community, or turn them into a select few, protected from all contamination. Rather, we need projects that can strengthen them, accompany them, and impel them to encounter others, to engage in generous service, in mission.

31. Jesus does not teach you, young people, from afar or from without, but from within your very youth, a youth he shares with you. It is very important for you to contemplate the young Jesus as presented in the

Gospels, for he was truly one of you, and shares many of the features of your young hearts. We see this, for example, in the following: "Jesus had unconditional trust in the Father; he maintained friendship with his disciples, and even in moments of crisis he remained faithful to them. He showed profound compassion for the weakest, especially the poor, the sick, sinners and the excluded. He had the courage to confront the religious and political authorities of his time; he knew what it was to feel misunderstood and rejected; he experienced the fear of suffering and he knew the frailty of the Passion. He turned his gaze to the future, entrusting himself into the Father's safe hands in the strength of the Spirit. In Jesus, all the young can see themselves."[9]

32. On the other hand, Jesus is risen, and he wants to make us sharers in the new life of the resurrection. He is the true youthfulness of a world grown old, the youthfulness of a universe waiting "in travail" (Rom 8:22) to be clothed with his light and to live his life. With him at our side, we can drink from the true wellspring that keeps alive all our dreams, our projects, our great ideals, while impelling us to proclaim what makes life truly worthwhile. Two curious details in the Gospel of Mark show how those risen with Christ are called to authentic youth. In the Lord's passion we see a young man who wanted to follow Jesus, but in fear ran away naked (cf. 14:51–52); he lacked the strength to stake everything on following the Lord. Yet at the empty tomb, we see another young person, "dressed in a white tunic" (16:5), who tells the women not to be afraid and proclaims the joy of the resurrection (cf. 16:6–7).

33. The Lord is calling us to enkindle stars in the night of other young people. He asks you to look to the true stars, all those varied signs he gives us to guide our way, and to imitate the farmer who watches the stars before going out to plough his field. God lights up stars to help us keep walking: "The stars shine in their watches, and are glad; he calls them and they say: 'Here we are!'" (Bar 3:34–35). Christ himself is our great light of hope and our guide in the night, for he is the "bright morning star" (Rv 22:16).

The Youth of the Church

34. Youth is more than simply a period of time; it is a state of mind. That is why an institution as ancient as the Church can experience renewal and a return to youth at different points in her age-old history. Indeed, at the most dramatic moments of her history, she feels called to return with all her heart to her first love. Recalling this truth, the Second Vatican Council noted that, "enriched by a long and living history, and advancing toward human perfection in time and the ultimate destinies of history and of life, the Church is the real youth of the world." In her, it is always possible to encounter Christ "the companion and friend of youth."[10]

A Church Open to Renewal

35. Let us ask the Lord to free the Church from those who would make her grow old, encase her in the past, hold her back, or keep her at a standstill. But let us also ask him to free her from another temptation: that of thinking she is young because she accepts everything the world offers her, thinking that she is renewed because she sets her message aside and acts like everybody else. No! The Church is young when she is herself, when she receives ever anew the strength born of God's word, the Eucharist, and the daily presence of Christ and the power of his Spirit in our lives. The Church is young when she shows herself capable of constantly returning to her source.

36. Certainly, as members of the Church, we should not stand apart from others. All should regard us as friends and neighbors, like the apostles, who "enjoyed the good will of all the people" (Acts 2:47; cf. 4:21, 33; 5:13). Yet at the same time we must dare to be different, to point to ideals other than those of this world, testifying to the beauty of generosity, service, purity, perseverance, forgiveness, fidelity to our personal vocation, prayer, the pursuit of justice and the common good, love for the poor, and social friendship.

37. Christ's Church can always yield to the temptation to lose enthusiasm because she no longer hears the Lord calling her to take the risk of faith, to give her all without counting the dangers; she can be tempted to revert to seeking a false, worldly form of security. Young people can help keep her young. They can stop her from becoming corrupt; they can keep her moving forward, prevent her from being proud and sectarian, help her to be poorer and to bear better witness, to take the side of the poor and the outcast, to fight for justice, and humbly to let herself be challenged. Young people can offer the Church the beauty of youth by renewing her ability to "rejoice with new beginnings, to give unreservedly of herself, to be renewed and to set out for ever greater accomplishments."[11]

38. Those of us who are no longer young need to find ways of keeping close to the voices and concerns of young people. "Drawing together creates the conditions for the Church to become a place of dialogue and a witness to life-giving fraternity."[12] We need to make more room for the voices of young people to be heard: "Listening makes possible an exchange of gifts in a context of empathy. . . . At the same time, it sets the conditions for a preaching of the Gospel that can touch the heart truly, decisively and fruitfully."[13]

A Church Attentive to the Signs of the Times

39. "Even though to many young people, God, religion and the Church seem empty words, they are sensitive to the figure of Jesus when he is presented in an attractive and effective way."[14] Consequently, the Church should not be excessively caught up in herself but instead, and above all, reflect Jesus Christ. This means humbly acknowledging that some things concretely need to change, and if that is to happen, she needs to appreciate the vision but also the criticisms of young people.

40. The Synod recognized that "a substantial number of young people, for all sorts of reasons, do not ask the Church for anything because they do not see her as significant for their lives. Some even ask expressly to be left alone, as they find the presence of the Church a nuisance, even an

irritant. This request does not always stem from uncritical or impulsive contempt. It can also have serious and understandable reasons: sexual and financial scandals; a clergy ill-prepared to engage effectively with the sensitivities of the young; lack of care in homily preparation and the presentation of the word of God; the passive role assigned to the young within the Christian community; the Church's difficulty in explaining her doctrine and ethical positions to contemporary society."[15]

41. Although many young people are happy to see a Church that is humble yet confident in her gifts and capable of offering fair and fraternal criticism, others want a Church that listens more, that does more than simply condemn the world. They do not want to see a Church that is silent and afraid to speak, but neither one that is always battling obsessively over two or three issues. To be credible to young people, there are times when she needs to regain her humility and simply listen, recognizing that what others have to say can provide some light to help her better understand the Gospel. A Church always on the defensive, which loses her humility and stops listening to others, which leaves no room for questions, loses her youth and turns into a museum. How, then, will she be able to respond to the dreams of young people? Even if she possesses the truth of the Gospel, this does not mean that she has completely understood it; rather, she is called to keep growing in her grasp of that inexhaustible treasure.[16]

42. For example, a Church that is overly fearful and tied to its structures can be invariably critical of efforts to defend the rights of women, and constantly point out the risks and the potential errors of those demands. Instead, a living Church can react by being attentive to the legitimate claims of those women who seek greater justice and equality. A living Church can look back on history and acknowledge a fair share of male authoritarianism, domination, various forms of enslavement, abuse, and sexist violence. With this outlook, she can support the call to respect women's rights, and offer convinced support for greater reciprocity between males and females, while not agreeing with everything

some feminist groups propose. Along these lines, the Synod sought to renew the Church's commitment "against all discrimination and violence on sexual grounds."[17] That is the response of a Church that stays young and lets herself be challenged and spurred on by the sensitivities of young people.

Mary, the Young Woman of Nazareth

43. In the heart of the Church, Mary shines forth. She is the supreme model for a youthful Church that seeks to follow Christ with enthusiasm and docility. While still very young, she accepted the message of the angel, yet she was not afraid to ask questions (cf. Lk 1:34). With open heart and soul, she replied, "Behold, I am the handmaid of the Lord" (Lk 1:38).

44. "We are always struck by the strength of the young Mary's 'yes,' the strength in those words 'be it done' that she spoke to the angel. This was no merely passive or resigned acceptance, or a faint 'yes,' as if to say, 'Well, let's give it a try and see what happens.' Mary did not know the words, 'Let's see what happens.' She was determined; she knew what was at stake and she said 'yes' without thinking twice. Hers was the 'yes' of someone prepared to be committed, someone willing to take a risk, ready to stake everything she had, with no more security than the certainty of knowing that she was the bearer of a promise. So I ask each one of you: do you see yourselves as the bearers of a promise? What promise is present in my heart that I can take up? Mary's mission would undoubtedly be difficult, but the challenges that lay ahead were no reason to say 'no.' Things would get complicated, of course, but not in the same way as happens when cowardice paralyzes us because things are not clear or sure in advance. Mary did not take out an insurance policy! She took the risk, and for this reason she is strong, she is an 'influencer,' the 'influencer' of God. Her 'yes and her desire to serve were stronger than any doubts or difficulties.'"[18]

45. Without yielding to evasions or illusions, "she accompanied the suffering of her Son; she supported him by her gaze and protected him with her heart. She shared his suffering, yet was not overwhelmed by it. She was the woman of strength who uttered her 'yes,' who supports and accompanies, protects and embraces. She is the great guardian of hope. . . . From her, we learn how to say 'yes' to the stubborn endurance and creativity of those who, undaunted, are ever ready to start over again."[19]

46. Mary was a young woman whose heart overflowed with joy (cf. Lk 1:47), whose eyes, reflecting the light of the Holy Spirit, looked at life with faith and treasured all things in her youthful heart (cf. Lk 2:19–51). She was energetic, ready to set out immediately once she knew that her cousin needed her. She did not think about her own plans, but went "with haste" to the hill country (Lk 1:39).

47. When her young son needed protection, Mary set out with Joseph to a distant land (cf. Mt 2:13–14). She also joined the disciples in awaiting the outpouring of the Holy Spirit (cf. Acts 1:14). In her presence, a young Church was born, as the apostles went forth to give birth to a new world (cf. Acts 2:4–11).

48. Today, Mary is the Mother who watches over us, her children, on our journey through life, often weary and in need, anxious that the light of hope not fail. For that is our desire: that the light of hope never fail. Mary our Mother looks to this pilgrim people: a youthful people whom she loves, and who seek her in the silence of their hearts amid all the noise, the chatter, and the distractions of the journey. Under the gaze of our Mother, there is room only for the silence of hope. Thus Mary illumines anew our youth.

Young Saints

49. The heart of the Church is also full of young saints who devoted their lives to Christ, many of them even to dying a martyr's death. They were precious reflections of the young Christ; their radiant witness encourages

us and awakens us from our lethargy. The Synod pointed out that "many young saints have allowed the features of youth to shine forth in all their beauty, and in their day they have been real prophets of change. Their example shows what the young are capable of, when they open themselves up to encounter Christ."[20]

50. "Through the holiness of the young, the Church can renew her spiritual ardor and her apostolic vigor. The balm of holiness generated by the good lives of so many young people can heal the wounds of the Church and of the world, bringing us back to that fullness of love to which we have always been called: young saints inspire us to return to our first love (cf. Rv 2:4)."[21] Some saints never reached adulthood, yet they showed us that there is another way to spend our youth. Let us recall at least some of them who, each in his or her own way, and at different periods of history, lived lives of holiness.

51. In the third century, Saint Sebastian was a young captain of the Praetorian Guard. It is said that he spoke constantly of Christ and tried to convert his companions, to the point that he was ordered to renounce his faith. Since he refused, he was shot with arrows, yet he survived and continued to proclaim Christ fearlessly. In the end, Sebastian was flogged to death.

52. Saint Francis of Assisi, while very young and full of great dreams, heard Jesus' call to become poor like him and to rebuild the Church by his witness. He joyfully renounced everything he had and is now the saint of universal fraternity, the brother of all. He praised the Lord for his creatures. Francis died in 1226.

53. Saint Joan of Arc was born in 1412. She was a young peasant girl who, despite her tender years, fought to defend France from invaders. Misunderstood for her demeanor, her actions, and her way of living the faith, Joan was burned at the stake.

54. Blessed Andrew Phû Yên was a young Vietnamese man of the seventeenth century. He was a catechist and assisted the missionaries. He

was imprisoned for his faith, and since he refused to renounce it, he was killed. Andrew died uttering the name of Jesus.

55. In that same century, Saint Kateri Tekakwitha, a young native of North America, was persecuted for her faith and, to escape, walked over three hundred kilometers in the wilderness. Kateri consecrated herself to God and died saying: "Jesus, I love you!"

56. Saint Dominic Savio offered all his sufferings to Mary. When Saint John Bosco taught him that holiness involves being constantly joyful, he opened his heart to a contagious joy. He wanted to be close to the most abandoned and infirm of his fellow young people. Dominic died in 1857 at fourteen years of age, saying: "What a wondrous thing I am experiencing!"

57. Saint Thérèse of the Child Jesus was born in 1873. At fifteen years of age, having overcome many difficulties, she succeeded in entering the Carmelite convent. Thérèse lived the little way of complete trust in the Lord's love and determined to fan with her prayers the fire of love burning in the heart of the Church.

58. Blessed Ceferino Namuncurá was a young Argentinian, the son of the chief of a remote tribe of indigenous peoples. He became a Salesian seminarian, filled with the desire to return to his tribe, bringing Jesus Christ to them. Ceferino died in 1905.

59. Blessed Isidore Bakanja was a layman from the Congo who bore witness to his faith. He was tortured at length for having proposed Christianity to other young people. Forgiving his executioner, Isidore died in 1909.

60. Blessed Pier Giorgio Frassati, who died in 1925, "was a young man filled with a joy that swept everything along with it, a joy that also overcame many difficulties in his life."[22] Pier Giorgio said that he wanted to return the love of Jesus that he received in Holy Communion by visiting and helping the poor.

61. Blessed Marcel Callo was a young French man who died in 1945. Marcel was imprisoned in a concentration camp in Austria, where he strengthened his fellow prisoners in faith amid harsh labors.

62. The young Blessed Chiara Badano, who died in 1990, "experienced how pain could be transfigured by love. . . . The key to her peace and joy was her complete trust in the Lord and the acceptance of her illness as a mysterious expression of his will for her sake and that of others."[23]

63. May these and so many other young people who perhaps in silence and hiddenness lived the Gospel to the full, intercede for the Church, so that she may be full of joyous, courageous, and committed young people who can offer the world new testimonies of holiness.

CHAPTER THREE

YOU ARE THE "NOW" OF GOD

64. After this brief look at the word of God, we cannot just say that young people are the future of our world. They are its present; even now, they are helping to enrich it. Young people are no longer children. They are at a time of life when they begin to assume a number of responsibilities, sharing alongside adults in the growth of the family, society, and the Church. Yet the times are changing, leading us to ask: What are today's young people really like? What is going on in their lives?

In Positive Terms

65. The Synod recognized that the members of the Church do not always take the approach of Jesus. Rather than listening to young people attentively, "all too often, there is a tendency to provide prepackaged answers and ready-made solutions, without allowing their real questions to emerge and facing the challenges they pose."[24] Yet once the Church sets aside narrow preconceptions and listens carefully to the young, this empathy enriches her, for "it allows young people to make their own contribution to the community, helping it to appreciate new sensitivities and to consider new questions."[25]

66. We adults can often be tempted to list all the problems and failings of today's young people. Perhaps some will find it praiseworthy that we seem so expert in discerning difficulties and dangers. But what would be the result of such an attitude? Greater distance, less closeness, less mutual assistance.

67. Anyone called to be a parent, pastor, or guide to young people must have the farsightedness to appreciate the little flame that continues to burn, the fragile reed that is shaken but not broken (cf. Is 42:3). The ability to discern pathways where others only see walls, to recognize potential where others see only peril. That is how God the Father sees things; he

knows how to cherish and nurture the seeds of goodness sown in the hearts of the young. Each young person's heart should thus be considered "holy ground," a bearer of seeds of divine life, before which we must "take off our shoes" in order to draw near and enter more deeply into the Mystery.

Many Ways of Being Young

68. We might attempt to draw a picture of young people today, but first I would echo the Synod Fathers, who noted that "the makeup of the Synod brought out the presence and contribution of many different regions of the world, and highlighted the beauty of our being a universal Church. In a context of growing globalization, the Synod Fathers wanted the many differences of contexts and cultures, even within individual countries, to be duly emphasized. The worlds of today's 'youth' are so many that in some countries one tends to speak of 'young people' in the plural. The age group considered by the Synod (16–29 years) does not represent a homogeneous category, but is composed of distinct groups, each with its own life experience."[26]

69. From a demographic standpoint too, some countries have many young people, whereas others have a very low birth rate. "A further differentiating factor is historical: there are countries and continents of ancient Christian tradition, whose culture is indelibly marked by a memory that cannot be lightly dismissed, while other countries and continents are characterized by other religious traditions, where Christianity is a minority presence—and at times a recent one. In other places still, Christian communities, and young people who belong to them, experience persecution."[27] There is also a need to distinguish young people "with access to the growing opportunities offered by globalization from those who live on the fringes of society or in rural areas, and find themselves excluded or discarded."[28]

70. There are many more differences, which it would be difficult to examine here. In any event, I see no need for a detailed analysis of today's

young people, their lives, and their experiences. At the same time, since I do not want to neglect that reality, I will briefly summarize some contributions received before the Synod and others that I heard in the course of our meetings.

Some Experiences of Young People

71. Youth is not something to be analyzed in the abstract. Indeed, "youth" does not exist: there exist only young people, each with the reality of his or her own life. In today's rapidly changing world, many of those lives are exposed to suffering and manipulation.

Living in a World in Crisis

72. The Synod Fathers acknowledged with sorrow that "many young people today live in war zones and experience violence in countless different forms: kidnapping, extortion, organized crime, human trafficking, slavery and sexual exploitation, wartime rape, and so forth. Other young people, because of their faith, struggle to find their place in society and endure various kinds of persecution, even murder. Many young people, whether by force or lack of alternatives, live by committing crimes and acts of violence: child soldiers, armed criminal gangs, drug trafficking, terrorism, and so on. This violence destroys many young lives. Abuse and addiction, together with violence and wrongdoing, are some of the reasons that send young people to prison, with a higher incidence in certain ethnic and social groups."[29]

73. Many young people are taken in by ideologies, used and exploited as cannon fodder or a strike force to destroy, terrify, or ridicule others. Worse yet, many of them end up as individualists, hostile and distrustful of others; in this way, they become an easy target for the brutal and destructive strategies of political groups or economic powers.

74. "Even more numerous in the world are young people who suffer forms of marginalization and social exclusion for religious, ethnic or economic reasons. Let us not forget the difficult situation of adolescents and

young people who become pregnant, the scourge of abortion, the spread of HIV, various forms of addiction (drugs, gambling, pornography and so forth), and the plight of street children without homes, families or economic resources."[30] In the case of women, these situations are doubly painful and difficult.

75. As a Church, may we never fail to weep before these tragedies of our young. May we never become inured to them, for anyone incapable of tears cannot be a mother. We want to weep so that society itself can be more of a mother, so that in place of killing it can learn to give birth, to become a promise of life. We weep when we think of all those young people who have already lost their lives due to poverty and violence, and we ask society to learn to be a caring mother. None of this pain goes away; it stays with us, because the harsh reality can no longer be concealed. The worst thing we can do is adopt that worldly spirit whose solution is simply to anaesthetize young people with other messages, with other distractions, with trivial pursuits.

76. Perhaps "those of us who have a reasonably comfortable life don't know how to weep. Some realities in life are only seen with eyes cleansed by tears. I would like each of you to ask yourself this question: Can I weep? Can I weep when I see a child who is starving, on drugs or on the street, homeless, abandoned, mistreated or exploited as a slave by society? Or is my weeping only the self-centered whining of those who cry because they want something else?"[31] Try to learn to weep for all those young people less fortunate than yourselves. Weeping is also an expression of mercy and compassion. If tears do not come, ask the Lord to give you the grace to weep for the sufferings of others. Once you can weep, then you will be able to help others from the heart.

77. At times, the hurt felt by some young people is heart-rending, a pain too deep for words. They can only tell God how much they are suffering, and how hard it is for them to keep going, since they no longer believe in anyone. Yet in that sorrowful plea, the words of Jesus make themselves

heard: "Blessed are those who mourn, for they shall be comforted" (Mt 5:4). Some young men and women were able to move forward because they heard that divine promise. May all young people who are suffering feel the closeness of a Christian community that can reflect those words by its actions, its embrace, and its concrete help.

78. It is true that people in power offer some assistance, but often it comes at a high price. In many poor countries, economic aid provided by some richer countries or international agencies is usually tied to the acceptance of Western views of sexuality, marriage, life, or social justice. This ideological colonization is especially harmful to the young. We also see how a certain kind of advertising teaches young people to be perpetually dissatisfied and contributes to the throwaway culture, in which young people themselves end up being discarded.

79. Our present-day culture exploits the image of the young. Beauty is associated with a youthful appearance, cosmetic treatments that hide the traces of time. Young bodies are constantly advertised as a means of selling products. The ideal of beauty is youth, but we need to realize that this has very little to do with young people. It only means that adults want to snatch youth for themselves, not that they respect, love, and care for young people.

80. Some young people "find family traditions oppressive and they flee from them under the impulse of a globalized culture that at times leaves them without points of reference. In other parts of the world, even more than generational conflict between young people and adults, there is mutual estrangement. Sometimes adults fail, or do not even try, to hand on the basic values of life, or they try to imitate young people, thus inverting the relationship between generations. The relationship between young people and adults thus risks remaining on the affective level, leaving its educational and cultural aspects untouched."[32] What harm this does to young people, even though some do not notice it! Young people themselves have remarked how enormously difficult this makes the

transmission of the faith "in some countries without freedom of speech, where young people are prevented from attending Church."[33]

Desires, Hurts, and Longings

81. Young people are aware that the body and sexuality have an essential importance for their lives and for their process of growth in identity. Yet in a world that constantly exalts sexuality, maintaining a healthy relationship with one's body and a serene affective life is not easy. For this and other reasons, sexual morality often tends to be a source of "incomprehension and alienation from the Church, inasmuch as she is viewed as a place of judgment and condemnation." Nonetheless, young people also express "an explicit desire to discuss questions concerning the difference between male and female identity, reciprocity between men and women, and homosexuality."[34]

82. In our times, "advances in the sciences and in biomedical technologies have powerfully influenced perceptions about the body, leading to the idea that it is open to unlimited modification. The capacity to intervene in DNA, the possibility of inserting artificial elements into organisms (cyborgs) and the development of the neurosciences represent a great resource, but at the same time they raise serious anthropological and ethical questions."[35] They can make us forget that life is a gift, and that we are creatures with innate limits, open to exploitation by those who wield technological power.[36] "Moreover, in some youth circles, there is a growing fascination with risk-taking behavior as a means of self-exploration, seeking powerful emotions and gaining attention. . . . These realities, to which young generations are exposed, are an obstacle to their serene growth in maturity."[37]

83. Young people also experience setbacks, disappointments, and profoundly painful memories. Often they feel "the hurt of past failures, frustrated desires, experiences of discrimination and injustice, of feeling unloved and unaccepted." Then too "there are moral wounds, the burden of past errors, a sense of guilt for having made mistakes."[38] Jesus makes

his presence felt amid these crosses borne by young people; he offers them his friendship, his consolation, and his healing companionship. The Church wants to be his instrument on this path to interior healing and peace of heart.

84. In some young people, we can see a desire for God, albeit still vague and far from knowledge of the God of revelation. In others, we can glimpse an ideal of human fraternity, which is no small thing. Many have a genuine desire to develop their talents in order to offer something to our world. In some, we see a special artistic sensitivity, or a yearning for harmony with nature. In others, perhaps, a great need to communicate. In many of them, we encounter a deep desire to live life differently. In all of this, we can find real starting points, inner resources open to a word of incentive, wisdom, and encouragement.

85. The Synod dealt in particular with three areas of utmost importance. Here I would like to quote its conclusions, while recognizing that they call for greater analysis and the development of a more adequate and effective ability to respond.

The Digital Environment

86. "The digital environment is characteristic of the contemporary world. Broad swathes of humanity are immersed in it in an ordinary and continuous manner. It is no longer merely a question of 'using' instruments of communication, but of living in a highly digitalized culture that has had a profound impact on ideas of time and space, on our self-understanding, our understanding of others and the world, and our ability to communicate, learn, be informed and enter into relationship with others. An approach to reality that privileges images over listening and reading has influenced the way people learn and the development of their critical sense."[39]

87. The web and social networks have created a new way to communicate and bond. They are "a public square where the young spend much of

their time and meet one another easily, even though not all have equal access to it, particularly in some regions of the world. They provide an extraordinary opportunity for dialogue, encounter and exchange between persons, as well as access to information and knowledge. Moreover, the digital world is one of social and political engagement and active citizenship, and it can facilitate the circulation of independent information providing effective protection for the most vulnerable and publicizing violations of their rights. In many countries, the internet and social networks already represent a firmly established forum for reaching and involving young people, not least in pastoral initiatives and activities."[40]

88. Yet to understand this phenomenon as a whole, we need to realize that, like every human reality, it has its share of limitations and deficiencies. It is not healthy to confuse communication with mere virtual contact. Indeed, "the digital environment is also one of loneliness, manipulation, exploitation and violence, even to the extreme case of the 'dark web.' Digital media can expose people to the risk of addiction, isolation and gradual loss of contact with concrete reality, blocking the development of authentic interpersonal relationships. New forms of violence are spreading through social media, for example cyberbullying. The internet is also a channel for spreading pornography and the exploitation of persons for sexual purposes or through gambling."[41]

89. It should not be forgotten that "there are huge economic interests operating in the digital world, capable of exercising forms of control as subtle as they are invasive, creating mechanisms for the manipulation of consciences and of the democratic process. The way many platforms work often ends up favoring encounter between persons who think alike, shielding them from debate. These closed circuits facilitate the spread of fake news and false information, fomenting prejudice and hate. The proliferation of fake news is the expression of a culture that has lost its sense of truth and bends the facts to suit particular interests. The reputation of

individuals is put in jeopardy through summary trials conducted online. The Church and her pastors are not exempt from this phenomenon."[42]

90. A document prepared on the eve of the Synod by three hundred young people worldwide pointed out that "online relationships can become inhuman. Digital spaces blind us to the vulnerability of another human being and prevent us from our own self-reflection. Problems like pornography distort a young person's perception of human sexuality. Technology used in this way creates a delusional parallel reality that ignores human dignity."[43] For many people, immersion in the virtual world has brought about a kind of "digital migration," involving withdrawal from their families and their cultural and religious values, and entrance into a world of loneliness and of self-invention, with the result that they feel rootless even while remaining physically in one place. The fresh and exuberant lives of young people who want to affirm their personality today confront a new challenge: that of interacting with a real and virtual world that they enter alone, as if setting foot on an undiscovered global continent. Young people today are the first to have to effect this synthesis between what is personal, what is distinctive to their respective cultures, and what is global. This means that they must find ways to pass from virtual contact to good and healthy communication.

Migrants as an Epitome of Our Time

91. How can we fail to think of all those young people affected by movements of migration? "Migration, considered globally, is a structural phenomenon, and not a passing emergency. It may occur within one country or between different countries. The Church's concern is focused especially on those fleeing from war, violence, political or religious persecution, from natural disasters including those caused by climate change, and from extreme poverty. Many of them are young. In general, they are seeking opportunities for themselves and their families. They dream of a better future and they want to create the conditions for achieving it."[44]

Migrants "remind us of a basic aspect of our faith, that we are 'strangers and exiles on the earth' (Heb 11:13)."[45]

92. Other migrants are "attracted by Western culture, sometimes with unrealistic expectations that expose them to grave disappointments. Unscrupulous traffickers, frequently linked to drug cartels or arms cartels, exploit the weakness of migrants, who too often experience violence, trafficking, psychological and physical abuse and untold sufferings on their journey. Nor must we overlook the particular vulnerability of migrants who are unaccompanied minors, or the situation of those compelled to spend many years in refugee camps, or of those who remain trapped for a long time in transit countries, without being able to pursue a course of studies or to use their talents. In some host countries, migration causes fear and alarm, often fomented and exploited for political ends. This can lead to a xenophobic mentality, as people close in on themselves, and this needs to be addressed decisively."[46]

93. "Young migrants experience separation from their place of origin, and often a cultural and religious uprooting as well. Fragmentation is also felt by the communities they leave behind, which lose their most vigorous and enterprising elements, and by families, especially when one or both of the parents migrates, leaving the children in the country of origin. The Church has an important role as a point of reference for the young members of these divided families. However, the stories of migrants are also stories of encounter between individuals and between cultures. For the communities and societies to which they come, migrants bring an opportunity for enrichment and the integral human development of all. Initiatives of welcome involving the Church have an important role from this perspective; they can bring new life to the communities capable of undertaking them."[47]

94. "Given the varied backgrounds of the Synod Fathers, the discussion of migrants benefited from a great variety of approaches, particularly from countries of departure and countries of arrival. Grave concern was

also expressed by Churches whose members feel forced to escape war and persecution and by others who see in these forced migrations a threat to their survival. The very fact that the Church can embrace all these varied perspectives allows her to play a prophetic role in society with regard to the issue of migration."[48] In a special way, I urge young people not to play into the hands of those who would set them against other young people, newly arrived in their countries, and who would encourage them to view the latter as a threat, and not possessed of the same inalienable dignity as every other human being.

Ending Every Form of Abuse

95. Recently, urgent appeals have been made for us to hear the cry of the victims of different kinds of abuse perpetrated by some bishops, priests, religious, and laypersons. These sins cause their victims "sufferings that can last a lifetime and that no repentance can remedy. This phenomenon is widespread in society and it also affects the Church and represents a serious obstacle to her mission."[49]

96. It is true that "the scourge of the sexual abuse of minors is, and historically has been, a widespread phenomenon in all cultures and societies," especially within families and in various institutions; its extent has become known primarily "thanks to changes in public opinion." Even so, this problem, while it is universal and "gravely affects our societies as a whole . . . is in no way less monstrous when it takes place within the Church." Indeed, "in people's justified anger, the Church sees the reflection of the wrath of God, betrayed and insulted."[50]

97. "The Synod reaffirms the firm commitment made to adopting rigorous preventative measures intended to avoid the recurrence [of these crimes], starting with the selection and formation of those to whom tasks of responsibility and education will be entrusted."[51] At the same time, the determination to apply the "actions and sanctions that are so necessary" must be reiterated.[52] And all this with the grace of Christ. There can be no turning back.

98. "Abuse exists in various forms: the abuse of power, the abuse of conscience, sexual and financial abuse. Clearly, the ways of exercising authority that make all this possible have to be eradicated, and the irresponsibility and lack of transparency with which so many cases have been handled have to be challenged. The desire to dominate, lack of dialogue and transparency, forms of double life, spiritual emptiness, as well as psychological weaknesses, are the terrain on which corruption thrives."[53] Clericalism is a constant temptation on the part of priests who see "the ministry they have received as a power to be exercised, rather than a free and generous service to be offered. It makes us think that we belong to a group that has all the answers and no longer needs to listen or has anything to learn."[54] Doubtless, such clericalism can make consecrated persons lose respect for the sacred and inalienable worth of each person and of his or her freedom.

99. Together with the Synod Fathers, I wish to thank, with gratitude and affection, "those who had the courage to report the evil they experienced: they help the Church to acknowledge what happened and the need to respond decisively."[55] Particular gratitude is also due for "the generous commitment of countless lay persons, priests, consecrated men and women, and bishops who daily devote themselves with integrity and dedication to the service of the young. Their efforts are like a great forest that quietly grows. Many of the young people present at the Synod also expressed gratitude to those who have accompanied them and they emphasized the great need for adults who can serve as points of reference."[56]

100. Thank God, those who committed these horrible crimes are not the majority of priests, who carry out their ministry with fidelity and generosity. I ask young people to let themselves be inspired by this vast majority. And if you see a priest at risk, because he has lost the joy of his ministry, or seeks affective compensation, or is taking the wrong path, remind him of his commitment to God and his people, remind him of the Gospel, and urge him to hold to his course. In this way, you will

contribute greatly to something fundamental: preventing these atrocities from being repeated. This dark cloud also challenges all young people who love Jesus Christ and his Church: they can be a source of great healing if they employ their great capacity to bring about renewal, to urge and demand consistent witness, to keep dreaming and coming up with new ideas.

101. Nor is this the only sin of the members of the Church; her long history is not without its shadows. Our sins are before the eyes of everyone; they appear all too clearly in the lines on the age-old face of the Church, our Mother and Teacher. For two thousand years she has advanced on her pilgrim way, sharing "the joys and the hopes, the grief and anguish"[57] of all humanity. She has made this journey as she is, without cosmetic surgery of any kind. She is not afraid to reveal the sins of her members, which some try at times to hide, before the burning light of the word of the Gospel, which cleanses and purifies. Nor does she stop reciting each day, in shame: "Have mercy on me, Lord, in your kindness . . . my sin is always before me" (Ps 51:3, 5). Still, let us never forget that we must not abandon our Mother when she is wounded, but stand beside her, so that she can summon up all her strength and all her ability to begin ever anew.

102. In the midst of this tragedy, which rightly pains us, "the Lord Jesus, who never abandons his Church, offers her the strength and the means to set out on a new path."[58] This dark moment, "not without the valuable help of the young, can truly be an opportunity for a reform of epoch-making significance,"[59] opening us to a new Pentecost and inaugurating a new stage of purification and change capable of renewing the Church's youth. Young people will be all the more helpful if they feel fully a part of the "holy and patient, faithful People of God, borne up and enlivened by the Holy Spirit," for "it will be precisely this holy People of God to liberate us from the plague of clericalism, which is the fertile ground for all these disgraces."[60]

A Way Out

103. In this chapter, I have taken time to look at the reality of young people in today's world. Some other aspects will be dealt with in the following chapters. As I have said, I do not claim to be exhaustive in this analysis. I encourage communities to examine, respectfully and seriously, the situation of their young people, in order to find the most fitting ways of providing them with pastoral care. At the same time, I do not want to end this chapter without addressing some words to each of you.

104. I remind you of the good news we received as a gift on the morning of the resurrection: that in all the dark or painful situations that we mentioned, there is a way out. For example, it is true that the digital world can expose you to the risk of self-absorption, isolation, and empty pleasure. But don't forget that there are young people even there who show creativity and even genius. That was the case with the Venerable Carlo Acutis.

105. Carlo was well aware that the whole apparatus of communications, advertising, and social networking can be used to lull us, to make us addicted to consumerism and buying the latest thing on the market, obsessed with our free time, caught up in negativity. Yet he knew how to use the new communications technology to transmit the Gospel, to communicate values and beauty.

106. Carlo didn't fall into the trap. He saw that many young people, wanting to be different, really end up being like everyone else, running after whatever the powerful set before them with the mechanisms of consumerism and distraction. In this way they do not bring forth the gifts the Lord has given them; they do not offer the world those unique personal talents that God has given to each of them. As a result, Carlo said, "everyone is born as an original, but many people end up dying as photocopies." Don't let that happen to you!

107. Don't let them rob you of hope and joy, or drug you into becoming a slave to their interests. Dare to be more, because who you are is more important than any possession. What good are possessions or

appearances? You can become what God your Creator knows you are, if only you realize that you are called to something greater. Ask the help of the Holy Spirit and confidently aim for the great goal of holiness. In this way, you will not be a photocopy. You will be fully yourself.

108. If this is to happen, you need to realize one basic truth: being young is not only about pursuing fleeting pleasures and superficial achievements. If the years of your youth are to serve their purpose in life, they must be a time of generous commitment, whole-hearted dedication, and sacrifices that are difficult but ultimately fruitful. As a great poet put it:

> "If to regain what I regained,
> I first had to lose what I lost;
> If to achieve what I achieved,
> I had to endure what I endured;
> If to be in love now
> First I had to be hurt,
> I consider what I suffered well suffered,
> I consider what I wept for as well wept for.
> Because in the end I came to see
> That we do not really enjoy what we enjoyed
> Unless we have suffered for it.
> For in the end I realized
> That the blossoms on the tree
> Draw life from what lies buried beneath."[61]

109. If you are young in years, but feel weak, weary, or disillusioned, ask Jesus to renew you. With him, hope never fails. You can do the same if you feel overwhelmed by vices, bad habits, selfishness, or unhealthy pastimes. Jesus, brimming with life, wants to help you make your youth worthwhile. In this way, you will not deprive the world of the contribution that you alone can make, in all your uniqueness and originality.

110. Yet let me also remind you that, "when we live apart from others, it is very difficult to fight against concupiscence, the snares and temptations

of the devil, and the selfishness of the world. Bombarded as we are by so many enticements, we can grow too isolated, lose our sense of reality and inner clarity, and easily succumb."[62] This is especially the case with young people, for whenever you are united, you have marvelous strength. Whenever you are enthused about life in common, you are capable of great sacrifices for others and for the community. Isolation, on the other hand, saps our strength and exposes us to the worst evils of our time.

CHAPTER FOUR

A GREAT MESSAGE FOR ALL YOUNG PEOPLE

111. Putting all else aside, I now wish to speak to young people about what is essential, the one thing we should never keep quiet about. It is a message containing three great truths that all of us need constantly to keep hearing.

A God Who Is Love

112. The very first truth I would tell each of you is this: "God loves you." It makes no difference whether you have already heard it or not. I want to remind you of it. God loves you. Never doubt this, whatever may happen to you in life. At every moment, you are infinitely loved.

113. Perhaps your experience of fatherhood has not been the best. Your earthly father may have been distant or absent, or harsh and domineering. Or maybe he was just not the father you needed. I don't know. But what I can tell you, with absolute certainty, is that you can find security in the embrace of your heavenly Father, of the God who first gave you life and continues to give it to you at every moment. He will be your firm support, but you will also realize that he fully respects your freedom.

114. In God's word, we find many expressions of his love. It is as if he tried to find different ways of showing that love, so that, with one of them at least, he could touch your heart. For example, there are times when God speaks of himself as an affectionate father who plays with his children: "I led them with cords of compassion, with bands of love. I was to them like those who lift infants to their cheeks" (Hos 11:4).

At other times, he speaks of himself as filled with the love of a mother whose visceral love for her children makes it impossible for her to neglect or abandon them: "Can a woman forget her nursing child, or show no compassion for the child of her womb? Even these may forget, yet I will not forget you" (Is 49:15).

He even compares himself to a lover who goes so far as to write his beloved on the palm of his hands, to keep her face always before him: "See, I have inscribed you on the palms of my hands!" (Is 49:6).

At other times, he emphasizes the strength and steadfastness of his invincible love: "For the mountains may depart, and the hills be shaken, but my steadfast love shall not depart from you, and my covenant of peace shall not be shaken" (Is 54:10).

Or he tells us that we have been awaited from eternity, for it was not by chance that we came into this world: "I have loved you with an everlasting love; therefore I have continued my faithfulness to you" (Jer 31:3).

Or he lets us know that he sees in us a beauty that no one else can see: "For you are precious in my sight, and honored, and I love you" (Is 43:4).

Or he makes us realize that his love is not cheerless, but pure joy, welling up whenever we allow ourselves to be loved by him: "The Lord, your God, is in your midst, a warrior who gives victory. He will rejoice over you with gladness, he will renew you in his love; he will exult over you with loud singing" (Zep 3:17).

115. For him, you have worth; you are not insignificant. You are important to him, for you are the work of his hands. That is why he is concerned about you and looks to you with affection. "Trust the memory of God: his memory is not a 'hard disk' that 'saves' and 'archives' all our data. His memory is a heart filled with tender compassion, one that finds joy in 'deleting' from us every trace of evil."[63] He does not keep track of your failings and he always helps you learn something even from your mistakes. Because he loves you. Try to keep still for a moment and let yourself feel his love. Try to silence all the noise within, and rest for a second in his loving embrace.

116. His is "a love that does not overwhelm or oppress, cast aside or reduce to silence, humiliate or domineer. It is the love of the Lord, a daily,

discreet and respectful love; a love that is free and freeing, a love that heals and raises up. The love of the Lord has to do more with raising up than knocking down, with reconciling than forbidding, with offering new changes than condemning, with the future than the past."[64]

117. When he asks something of you, or simply makes you face life's challenges, he is hoping that you will make room for him to push you, to help you grow. He does not get upset if you share your questions with him. He is concerned when you *don't* talk to him, when you are not open to dialogue with him. The Bible tells us that Jacob fought with God (cf. Gn 32:25–31), but that did not keep him from persevering in his journey. The Lord himself urges us: "Come, let us argue it out" (Is 1:18). His love is so real, so true, so concrete, that it invites us to a relationship of openness and fruitful dialogue. Seek the closeness of our heavenly Father in the loving face of his courageous witnesses on earth!

Christ Saves You

118. The second great truth is that Christ, out of love, sacrificed himself completely in order to save you. His outstretched arms on the cross are the most telling sign that he is a friend who is willing to stop at nothing: "Having loved his own who were in the world, he loved them to the end" (Jn 13:1).

Saint Paul said that his life was one of complete trust in that self-sacrificing love: "I now live by faith in the Son of God who loved me, and gave himself for me" (Gal 2:20).

119. The same Christ who, by his cross, saved us from our sins, today continues to save and redeem us by the power of his total self-surrender. Look to his cross, cling to him, let him save you, for "those who accept his offer of salvation are set free from sin, sorrow, inner emptiness and loneliness."[65] And if you sin and stray far from him, he will come to lift you up by the power of his cross. Never forget that "he forgives us seventy times seven. Time and time again, he bears us on his shoulders. No

one can strip us of the dignity bestowed upon us by this boundless and unfailing love. With a tenderness that never disappoints but is always capable of restoring our joy, he makes it possible for us to lift up our heads and to start anew."[66]

120. "We are saved by Jesus because he loves us and cannot go against his nature. We can do any number of things against him, yet he loves us and he saves us. For only what is loved can be saved. Only what is embraced can be transformed. The Lord's love is greater than all our problems, frailties and flaws. Yet it is precisely through our problems, frailties and flaws that he wants to write this love story. He embraced the prodigal son, he embraced Peter after his denials, and he always, always, always embraces us after every fall, helping us to rise and get back on our feet. Because the worst fall, and pay attention to this, *the worst fall, the one that can ruin our lives, is when we stay down and do not allow ourselves to be helped up.*"[67]

121. His forgiveness and salvation are not something we can buy, or that we have to acquire by our own works or efforts. He forgives us and sets us free without cost. His self-sacrifice on the cross is so great that we can never repay it, but only receive it with immense gratitude and with the joy of being more greatly loved than we could ever imagine: "He loved us first" (1 Jn 4:19).

122. Young people, beloved of the Lord, how valuable must you be if you were redeemed by the precious blood of Christ! Dear young people, "you are priceless! You are not up for sale! Please, do not let yourselves be bought. Do not let yourselves be seduced. Do not let yourselves be enslaved by forms of ideological colonization that put ideas in your heads, with the result that you end up becoming slaves, addicts, failures in life. You are priceless. You must repeat this always: I am not up for sale; I do not have a price. I am free! Fall in love with this freedom, which is what Jesus offers."[68]

123. Keep your eyes fixed on the outstretched arms of Christ crucified, let yourself be saved over and over again. And when you go to confess your sins, believe firmly in his mercy which frees you of your guilt. Contemplate his blood poured out with such great love, and let yourself be cleansed by it. In this way, you can be reborn ever anew.

He Is Alive!

124. Finally, there is a third truth, inseparable from the second: Christ is alive! We need to keep reminding ourselves of this, because we can risk seeing Jesus Christ simply as a fine model from the distant past, as a memory, as someone who saved us two thousand years ago. But that would be of no use to us: it would leave us unchanged, it would not set us free. The one who fills us with his grace, the one who liberates us, transforms us, heals and consoles us is someone fully alive. He is the Christ, risen from the dead, filled with supernatural life and energy, and robed in boundless light. That is why Saint Paul could say: "If Christ has not been raised, your faith is futile" (1 Cor 15:7).

125. Alive, he can be present in your life at every moment, to fill it with light and to take away all sorrow and solitude. Even if all others depart, he will remain, as he promised: "I am with you always, to the end of the age" (Mt 28:20). He fills your life with his unseen presence; wherever you go, he will be waiting there for you. Because he did not only come in the past, but he comes to you today and every day, inviting you to set out toward ever new horizons.

126. See Jesus as happy, overflowing with joy. Rejoice with him as with a friend who has triumphed. They killed him, the holy one, the just one, the innocent one, but he triumphed in the end. Evil does not have the last word. Nor will it have the last word in your life, for you have a friend who loves you and wants to triumph in you. Your Savior lives.

127. Because he lives, there can be no doubt that goodness will have the upper hand in your life and that all our struggles will prove worthwhile.

If this is the case, we can stop complaining and look to the future, for with him this is always possible. That is the certainty we have. Jesus is eternally alive. If we hold fast to him, we will have life, and be protected from the threats of death and violence that may assail us in life.

128. Every other solution will prove inadequate and temporary. It may be helpful for a time, but once again we will find ourselves exposed and abandoned before the storms of life. With Jesus, on the other hand, our hearts experience a security that is firmly rooted and enduring. Saint Paul says that he wishes to be one with Christ in order "to know him and the power of his resurrection" (Phil 3:10). That power will constantly be revealed in your lives too, for he came to give you life, "and life in abundance" (Jn 10:10).

129. If in your heart you can learn to appreciate the beauty of this message, if you are willing to encounter the Lord, if you are willing to let him love you and save you, if you can make friends with him and start to talk to him, the living Christ, about the realities of your life, then you will have a profound experience capable of sustaining your entire Christian life. You will also be able to share that experience with other young people. For "being a Christian is not the result of an ethical choice or a lofty idea, but the encounter with an event, a person, which gives life a new horizon and a decisive direction."[69]

The Spirit Gives Life

130. In these three truths—God loves you; Christ is your Savior; he is alive—we see God the Father and Jesus. Wherever the Father and the Son are, there too is the Holy Spirit. He is the one who quietly opens hearts to receive that message. He keeps alive our hope of salvation, and he will help you grow in joy if you are open to his working. The Holy Spirit fills the heart of the risen Christ and then flows over into your lives. When you receive the Spirit, he draws you ever more deeply into the heart of Christ, so that you can grow in his love, his life, and his power.

131. Ask the Holy Spirit each day to help you experience anew the great message. Why not? You have nothing to lose, and he can change your life, fill it with light, and lead it along a better path. He takes nothing away from you, but instead helps you to find all that you need, and in the best possible way. Do you need love? You will not find it in dissipation, using other people, or trying to be possessive or domineering. You will find it in a way that will make you genuinely happy. Are you seeking powerful emotions? You will not experience them by accumulating material objects, spending money, chasing desperately after the things of this world. They will come, and in a much more beautiful and meaningful way, if you let yourself be prompted by the Holy Spirit.

132. Are you looking for passion? As that beautiful poem says: "Fall in love!" (or "let yourself be loved!"), because "nothing is more practical than finding God, than falling in love in a quite absolute, final way. What you are in love with, what seizes your imagination, will affect everything. It will decide what will get you out of bed in the morning, what you do with your evenings, how you spend your weekends, what you read, whom you know, what breaks your heart, and what amazes you with joy and gratitude. Fall in love, stay in love, and it will decide everything."[70] This love for God, that can approach everything in life with passion, is possible thanks to the Spirit, for "God's love has been poured into our hearts through the Holy Spirit who has been given to us" (Rom 5:5).

133. He is the source of youth at its best. For those who trust in the Lord are "like a tree planted by water sending out its roots by the stream; it shall not fear when heat comes, and its leaves shall stay green" (Jer 17:8). While "youths shall faint and be weary" (Is 40:30), those who wait for the Lord "shall renew their strength, they shall mount up with wings like eagles, they shall run and not be weary, they shall walk and not faint" (Is 40:31).

CHAPTER FIVE

PATHS OF YOUTH

134. What does it mean to live the years of our youth in the transforming light of the Gospel? We need to raise this question, because youth, more than a source of pride, is a gift of God: "To be young is a grace, a blessing."[71] It is a gift that we can squander meaninglessly, or receive with gratitude and live to the full.

135. God is the giver of youth and he is at work in the life of each young person. Youth is a blessed time for the young and a grace for the Church and for the world. It is joy, a song of hope, and a blessing. Making the most of our youthful years entails seeing this season of life as worthwhile in itself, and not simply as a brief prelude to adulthood.

A Time of Dreams and Decisions

136. In Jesus' day, the passage from childhood was a significant step in life, one joyfully celebrated. When Jesus restored life to a man's daughter, he first called her a "child" (Mk 5:39), but then addressed her as a "young girl" (Mk 5:41). By saying to her: "Young girl, get up (*talitha cum*)," he made her more responsible for her life, opening before her the door to youth.

137. "Youth, as a phase in the development of the personality, is marked by dreams which gather momentum, by relationships which acquire more and more consistency and balance, by trials and experiments, and by choices which gradually build a life project. At this stage in life, the young are called to move forward without cutting themselves off from their roots, to build autonomy but not in solitude."[72]

138. The love of God and our relationship with the living Christ do not hold us back from dreaming; they do not require us to narrow our horizons. On the contrary, that love elevates us, encourages us, and inspires us to a better and more beautiful life. Much of the longing present in the

hearts of young people can be summed up in the word *restlessness*. As Saint Paul VI said, "In the very discontent that you often feel . . . a ray of light is present."[73] Restless discontent, combined with exhilaration before the opening up of new horizons, generates a boldness that leads you to stand up and take responsibility for a mission. This healthy restlessness typical of youth continues to dwell in every heart that remains young, open, and generous. True inner peace coexists with that profound discontent. As Saint Augustine said: "You have created us for yourself, Lord, and our hearts are restless until they find their rest in you."[74]

139. Sometime ago, a friend asked me what I see in a young person. My response was that "I see someone who is searching for his or her own path, who wants to fly on their two feet, who faces the world and looks at the horizon with eyes full of the future, full of hope as well as illusions. A young person stands on two feet as adults do, but unlike adults, whose feet are parallel, he always has one foot forward, ready to set out, to spring ahead. Always racing onward. To talk about young people is to talk about promise and to talk about joy. Young people have so much strength; they are able to look ahead with hope. A young person is a promise of life that implies a certain degree of tenacity. He is foolish enough to delude himself, and resilient enough to recover from that delusion."[75]

140. Some young people might hate this stage of life, because they want to continue being children or indefinitely prolong their adolescence and put off having to make decisions. "Fear of the definitive thus generates a kind of paralysis of decision-making. Yet youth cannot remain on hold. It is the age of choices and herein lies its fascination and its greatest responsibility. Young people make decisions in professional, social and political fields, and in other more radical ways that determine the shape of their lives."[76] They also make decisions about love, choosing a spouse, and starting a family. We will look at these issues more closely in the final chapters, when dealing with individual vocations and their discernment.

141. But opposed to these hopes and dreams that generate decisions, there is always the temptation to complain or give up. "We can leave that to those who worship the 'goddess of lament.' . . . She is a false goddess: she makes you take the wrong road. When everything seems to be standing still and stagnant, when our personal issues trouble us, and social problems do not meet with the right responses, it does no good to give up. Jesus is the way: welcome him into your 'boat' and put out into the deep! He is the Lord! He changes the way we see life. Faith in Jesus leads to greater hope, to a certainty based not on our qualities and skills, but on the word of God, on the invitation that comes from him. Without making too many human calculations, and without worrying about things that challenge your security, put out into the deep. Go out of yourselves."[77]

142. Keep following your hopes and dreams. But be careful about one temptation that can hold us back. It is anxiety. Anxiety can work against us by making us give up whenever we do not see instant results. Our best dreams are only attained through hope, patience, and commitment, and not in haste. At the same time, we should not be hesitant, afraid to take chances or make mistakes. Avoid the paralysis of the living dead, who have no life because they are afraid to take risks, to make mistakes, or to persevere in their commitments. Even if you make mistakes, you can always get up and start over, for no one has the right to rob you of hope.

143. Dear young people, make the most of these years of your youth. Don't observe life from a balcony. Don't confuse happiness with an armchair, or live your life behind a screen. Whatever you do, do not become the sorry sight of an abandoned vehicle! Don't be parked cars, but dream freely and make good decisions. Take risks, even if it means making mistakes. Don't go through life anaesthetized or approach the world like tourists. Make a ruckus! Cast out the fears that paralyze you, so that you don't become young mummies. Live! Give yourselves over to the best of life! Open the door of the cage, go out, and fly! Please, don't take early retirement.

A Thirst for Life and Experience

144. While drawn toward the future and its promise, young people also have a powerful desire to experience the present moment, to make the most of the opportunities life offers. Our world is filled with beauty! How can we look down upon God's many gifts?

145. Contrary to what many people think, the Lord does not want to stifle these desires for a fulfilling life. We do well to remember the words of an Old Testament sage: "My child, treat yourself well, according to your means, and present your offerings to the Lord; do not deprive yourself of a day's enjoyment, do not let your share of desired good pass by" (Sir 14:11, 14). The true God, who loves you, wants you to be happy. For this reason, the Bible also contains this piece of advice to young people: "Rejoice, young man, while you are young, and let your heart cheer you in the days of your youth . . . banish anxiety from your mind" (Eccl 11:9–10). For God "richly provides us with everything for our enjoyment" (1 Tm 6:17).

146. How could God take pleasure in someone incapable of enjoying his small everyday blessings, someone blind to the simple pleasures we find all around us? "No one is worse than one who is grudging to himself" (Sir 14:6). Far from obsessively seeking new pleasures, which would keep us from making the most of the present moment, we are asked to open our eyes and take a moment to experience fully and with gratitude every one of life's little gifts.

147. Clearly, God's word asks you to enjoy the present, not simply to prepare for the future: "Do not worry about tomorrow, for tomorrow will bring worries of its own; today's trouble is enough for today" (Mt 6:34). But this is not the same as embarking irresponsibly on a life of dissipation that can only leave us empty and perpetually dissatisfied. Rather, it is about living the present to the full, spending our energies on good things, cultivating fraternity, following Jesus, and making the most of life's little joys as gifts of God's love.

148. Cardinal Francis Xavier Nguyên Van Thuân, when imprisoned in a concentration camp, refused to do nothing but await the day when he would be set free. He chose "to live the present moment, filling it to the brim with love." He decided: "I will seize the occasions that present themselves every day; I will accomplish ordinary actions in an extraordinary way."[78] As you work to achieve your dreams, make the most of each day and do your best to let each moment brim with love. This youthful day may well be your last, and so it is worth the effort to live it as enthusiastically and fully as possible.

149. This can also be applied to times of difficulty, that have to be fully experienced if we are to learn the message they can teach us. In the words of the Swiss Bishops: "God is there where we thought he had abandoned us and there was no further hope of salvation. It is a paradox, but for many Christians, suffering and darkness have become . . . places of encounter with God."[79] The desire to live fully and experience new things is also felt by many young people with physical, mental, and sensory disabilities. Even though they may not always be able to have the same experiences as others, they possess amazing resources and abilities that are often far above average. The Lord Jesus grants them other gifts, which the community is called to recognize and appreciate, so that they can discover his plan of love for each of them.

In Friendship with Christ

150. No matter how much you live the experience of these years of your youth, you will never know their deepest and fullest meaning unless you encounter each day your best friend, the friend who is Jesus.

151. Friendship is one of life's gifts and a grace from God. Through our friends, the Lord refines us and leads us to maturity. Faithful friends, who stand at our side in times of difficulty, are also a reflection of the Lord's love, his gentle and consoling presence in our lives. The experience of friendship teaches us to be open, understanding, and caring toward others, to come out of our own comfortable isolation and to share our lives

with others. For this reason, "there is nothing so precious as a faithful friend" (Sir 6:15).

152. Friendship is no fleeting or temporary relationship, but one that is stable, firm, and faithful, and matures with the passage of time. A relationship of affection that brings us together and a generous love that makes us seek the good of our friend. Friends may be quite different from one another, but they always have things in common that draw them closer in mutual openness and trust.[80]

153. Friendship is so important that Jesus calls himself a friend: "I do not call you servants any longer, but I call you friends" (Jn 15:15). By the gift of his grace, we are elevated in such a way that we truly become his friends. With the same love that Christ pours out on us, we can love him in turn and share his love with others, in the hope that they too will take their place in the community of friendship he established. And even as he enjoys the complete bliss of the life of the resurrection, we, for our part, can work generously to help him build his kingdom in this world, by bringing his message, his light, and above all his love, to others (cf. Jn 15:16). The disciples heard Jesus calling them to be his friends. It was an invitation that did not pressure them, but gently appealed to their freedom. "Come and see," Jesus told them; so "they came and saw where he was staying, and they remained with him that day" (Jn 1:39). After that unexpected and moving encounter, they left everything and followed him.

154. Friendship with Jesus cannot be broken. He never leaves us, even though at times it appears that he keeps silent. When we need him, he makes himself known to us (cf. Jer 29:14); he remains at our side wherever we go (cf. Jos 1:9). He never breaks his covenant. He simply asks that we not abandon him: "Abide in me" (Jn 15:4). But even if we stray from him, "he remains faithful, for he cannot deny himself" (2 Tm 2:13).

155. With a friend, we can speak and share our deepest secrets. With Jesus too, we can always have a conversation. Prayer is both a challenge

and an adventure. And what an adventure it is! Gradually Jesus makes us appreciate his grandeur and draw nearer to him. Prayer enables us to share with him every aspect of our lives and to rest confidently in his embrace. At the same time, it gives us a share in his own life and love. When we pray, "we open everything we do" to him, and we give him room "so that he can act, enter and claim victory."[81]

156. In this way, we can experience a constant closeness to him, greater than anything we can experience with another person: "It is no longer I who live, but it is Christ who lives in me" (Gal 2:20). Do not deprive your youth of this friendship. You will be able to feel him at your side not only when you pray, but at every moment. Try to look for him, and you will have the beautiful experience of seeing that he is always at your side. That is what the disciples of Emmaus experienced when, as they walked along dejectedly, Jesus "drew near and walked with them" (Lk 24:15). In the words of a saint, "Christianity is not a collection of truths to be believed, rules to be followed, or prohibitions. Seen that way, it puts us off. Christianity is a person who loved me immensely, who demands and claims my love. Christianity is Christ."[82]

157. Jesus can bring all the young people of the Church together in a single dream, "a great dream, a dream with a place for everyone. The dream for which Jesus gave his life on the cross, for which the Holy Spirit was poured out on the day of Pentecost and brought fire to the heart of every man and woman, to your heart and mine. To your heart too, he brought that fire, in the hope of finding room for it to grow and flourish. A dream whose name is Jesus, planted by the Father in the confidence that it would grow and live in every heart. A concrete dream who is a person, running through our veins, thrilling our hearts and making them dance."[83]

Growth in Maturity

158. Many young people are concerned about their bodies, trying to build up physical strength or improve their appearance. Others work

to develop their talents and knowledge, so as to feel more sure of themselves. Some aim higher, seeking to become more involved and to grow spiritually. Saint John said: "I write to you, young people, because you are strong and the word of God abides in you" (1 Jn 2:14). Seeking the Lord, keeping his word, entrusting our life to him, and growing in the virtues: all these things make young hearts strong. That is why you need to stay connected to Jesus, to "remain online" with him, since you will not grow happy and holy by your own efforts and intelligence alone. Just as you try not to lose your connection to the internet, make sure that you stay connected to the Lord. That means not cutting off dialogue, listening to him, sharing your life with him, and, whenever you aren't sure what you should do, asking him: "Jesus, what would you do in my place?"[84]

159. I hope that you will be serious enough about yourselves to make an effort to grow spiritually. Along with all the other exciting things about youth, there is also the beauty of seeking "righteousness, faith, love and peace" (2 Tm 2:22). This does not involve losing anything of your spontaneity, boldness, enthusiasm, and tenderness. Becoming an adult does not mean you have to abandon what is best about this stage of your lives. If you do, the Lord may one day reproach you: "I remember the devotion of your youth, your love as a bride, and how you followed me in the wilderness" (Jer 2:2).

160. Adults, too, have to mature without losing the values of youth. Every stage of life is a permanent grace, with its own enduring value. The experience of a youth well lived always remains in our heart. It continues to grow and bear fruit throughout adulthood. Young people are naturally attracted by an infinite horizon opening up before them.[85] Adult life, with its securities and comforts, can risk shrinking that horizon and losing that youthful excitement. The very opposite should happen: as we mature, grow older, and structure our lives, we should never lose that enthusiasm and openness to an ever greater reality. At every moment in life, we can renew our youthfulness. When I began my ministry as Pope, the Lord broadened my horizons and granted me renewed youth. The

same thing can happen to a couple married for many years, or to a monk in his monastery. There are things we need to "let go of" as the years pass, but growth in maturity can coexist with a fire constantly rekindled, with a heart ever young.

161. Growing older means preserving and cherishing the most precious things about our youth, but it also involves having to purify those things that are not good and receiving new gifts from God so we can develop the things that really matter. At times, a certain inferiority complex can make you overlook your flaws and weaknesses, but that can hold you back from growth in maturity. Instead, let yourself be loved by God, for he loves you just as you are. He values and respects you, but he also keeps offering you more: more of his friendship, more fervor in prayer, more hunger for his word, more longing to receive Christ in the Eucharist, more desire to live by his Gospel, more inner strength, more peace and spiritual joy.

162. But I would also remind you that you won't become holy and find fulfillment by copying others. Imitating the Saints does not mean copying their lifestyle and their way of living holiness: "There are some testimonies that may prove helpful and inspiring, but that we are not meant to copy, for that could even lead us astray from the one specific path that the Lord has in mind for us."[86] You have to discover who you are and develop your own way of being holy, whatever others may say or think. Becoming a saint means becoming more fully yourself, becoming what the Lord wished to dream and create, and not a photocopy. Your life ought to be a prophetic stimulus to others and leave a mark on this world, the unique mark that only you can leave. Whereas if you simply copy someone else, you will deprive this earth, and heaven too, of something that no one else can offer. I think of Saint John of the Cross, who wrote in his *Spiritual Canticle* that everyone should benefit from his spiritual advice "in his or her own way,"[87] for the one God wishes to manifest his grace "to some in one way and to others in another."[88]

Paths of Fraternity

163. Your spiritual growth is expressed above all by your growth in fraternal, generous, and merciful love. Saint Paul prayed: "May the Lord make you increase and abound in love for one another and for all" (1 Thes 3:12). How wonderful it would be to experience this "ecstasy" of coming out of ourselves and seeking the good of others, even to the sacrifice of our lives.

164. When an encounter with God is called an "ecstasy," it is because it takes us out of ourselves, lifts us up, and overwhelms us with God's love and beauty. Yet we can also experience ecstasy when we recognize in others their hidden beauty, their dignity, and their grandeur as images of God and children of the Father. The Holy Spirit wants to make us come out of ourselves, to embrace others with love, and to seek their good. That is why it is always better to live the faith together and to show our love by living in community and sharing with other young people our affection, our time, our faith, and our troubles. The Church offers many different possibilities for living our faith in community, for everything is easier when we do it together.

165. Hurts you have experienced might tempt you to withdraw from others, to turn in on yourself, and to nurse feelings of anger, but never stop listening to God's call to forgiveness. The Bishops of Rwanda put it well: "In order to reconcile with another person, you must first of all be able to see the goodness in that person, the goodness God created him with. . . . This requires great effort to distinguish the offence from the offender; it means you hate the offence the person has committed, but you love the person despite his weakness, because in him you see the image of God."[89]

166. There are times when all our youthful energy, dreams, and enthusiasm can flag because we are tempted to dwell on ourselves and our problems, our hurt feelings, and our grievances. Don't let this happen to you! You will grow old before your time. Each age has its beauty, and

the years of our youth need to be marked by shared ideals, hopes, and dreams, great horizons that we can contemplate together.

167. God loves the joy of young people. He wants them especially to share in the joy of fraternal communion, the sublime joy felt by those who share with others, for "it is more blessed to give than to receive" (Acts 20:35). "God loves a cheerful giver" (2 Cor 9:7). Fraternal love multiplies our ability to experience joy, since it makes us rejoice in the good of others: "Rejoice with those who rejoice, weep with those who weep" (Rom 12:15). May your youthful spontaneity increasingly find expression in fraternal love and a constant readiness to forgive, to be generous, and to build community. As an African proverb says: "If you want to go fast, go alone. If you want to go far, go together." Let us not allow ourselves to be robbed of fraternity.

Young and Committed

168. At times, seeing a world so full of violence and selfishness, young people can be tempted to withdraw into small groups, shunning the challenges and issues posed by life in society and in the larger world. They may feel that they are experiencing fraternity and love, but their small group may in fact become nothing other than an extension of their own ego. This is even more serious if they think of the lay vocation simply as a form of service inside the Church: serving as lectors, acolytes, catechists, and so forth. They forget that the lay vocation is directed above all to charity within the family and to social and political charity. It is a concrete and faith-based commitment to the building of a new society. It involves living in the midst of society and the world in order to bring the Gospel everywhere, to work for the growth of peace, harmony, justice, human rights, and mercy, and thus for the extension of God's kingdom in this world.

169. I ask young people to go beyond their small groups and to build "social friendship, where everyone works for the common good. Social enmity, on the other hand, is destructive. Families are destroyed by

enmity. Countries are destroyed by enmity. The world is destroyed by enmity. And the greatest enmity of all is war. Today we see that the world is destroying itself by war. . . . So find ways of building social friendship."[90] It is not easy, it always means having to give something up and to negotiate, but if we do it for the sake of helping others, we can have the magnificent experience of setting our differences aside and working together for something greater. If, as a result of our own simple and at times costly efforts, we can find points of agreement amid conflict, build bridges, and make peace for the benefit of all, then we will experience the miracle of the culture of encounter. This is something which young people can dare to pursue with passion.

170. The Synod recognized that "albeit in a different way from earlier generations, social commitment is a specific feature of today's young people. Alongside some who are indifferent, there are many others who are ready to commit themselves to initiatives of volunteer work, active citizenship and social solidarity. They need to be accompanied and encouraged to use their talents and skills creatively, and to be encouraged to take up their responsibilities. Social engagement and direct contact with the poor remain fundamental ways of finding or deepening one's faith and the discernment of one's vocation. . . . It was also noted that the young are prepared to enter political life so as to build the common good."[91]

171. Today, thank God, many young people in parishes, schools, movements, and university groups often go out to spend time with the elderly and the infirm, or to visit poor neighborhoods, or to meet people's needs through "nights of charity." Very often, they come to realize that there they receive much more than what they give. We grow in wisdom and maturity when we take the time to touch the suffering of others. The poor have a hidden wisdom and, with a few simple words, they can help us discover unexpected values.

172. Other young people take part in social programs that build houses for the homeless, or reclaim contaminated areas, or offer various kinds of

assistance to the needy. It would be helpful if this shared energy could be channeled and organized in a more stable way and with clear goals, so as to be even more effective. University students can apply their knowledge in an interdisciplinary way, together with young people of other churches or religions, in order to propose solutions to social problems.

173. As in the miracle of Jesus, the bread and the fish provided by young people can multiply (cf. Jn 6:4–13). As in the parable, the small seeds sown by young people can yield a rich harvest (cf. Mt 13:23, 31–32). All of this has its living source in the Eucharist, in which our bread and our wine are transformed to grant us eternal life. Young people face immense and difficult challenges. With faith in the risen Lord, they can confront them with creativity and hope, ever ready to be of service, like the servants at the wedding feast, who unknowingly cooperated in Jesus' first miracle. They did nothing more than follow the order of his Mother: "Do whatever he tells you" (Jn 2:5). Mercy, creativity, and hope make life grow.

174. I want to encourage all of you in this effort, because I know that "your young hearts want to build a better world. I have been following news reports of the many young people throughout the world who have taken to the streets to express the desire for a more just and fraternal society. Young people taking to the streets! The young want to be protagonists of change. Please, do not leave it to others to be protagonists of change. You are the ones who hold the future! Through you, the future enters into the world. I ask you also to be protagonists of this transformation. You are the ones who hold the key to the future! Continue to fight apathy and to offer a Christian response to the social and political troubles emerging in different parts of the world. I ask you to build the future, to work for a better world. Dear young people, please, do not be bystanders in life. Get involved! Jesus was not a bystander. He got involved. Don't stand aloof, but immerse yourselves in the reality of life, as Jesus did."[92] Above all, in one way or another, fight for the common good, serve the poor, be protagonists of the revolution of charity and

service, capable of resisting the pathologies of consumerism and superficial individualism.

Courageous Missionaries

175. Filled with the love of Christ, young people are called to be witnesses of the Gospel wherever they find themselves, by the way they live. Saint Alberto Hurtado once said that "being an apostle does not mean wearing a lapel pin; it is not about speaking about the truth but living it, embodying it, being transformed in Christ. Being an apostle does not mean carrying a torch in hand, possessing the light, but being that light. . . . The Gospel, more than a lesson, is an example. A message that becomes a life fully lived."[93]

176. The importance of witness does not mean that we should be silent about the word. Why should we not speak of Jesus, why should we not tell others that he gives us strength in life, that we enjoy talking with him, that we benefit from meditating on his words? Young people, do not let the world draw you only into things that are wrong and superficial. Learn to swim against the tide, learn how to share Jesus and the faith he has given you. May you be moved by that same irresistible impulse that led Saint Paul to say: "Woe to me if I do not proclaim the Gospel" (1 Cor 9:16)!

177. "Where does Jesus send us? There are no borders, no limits: he sends us everywhere. The Gospel is for everyone, not just for some. It is not only for those who seem closer to us, more receptive, more welcoming. It is for everyone. Do not be afraid to go and bring Christ into every area of life, to the fringes of society, even to those who seem farthest away and most indifferent. The Lord seeks all; he wants everyone to feel the warmth of his mercy and his love."[94] He invites us to be fearless missionaries wherever we are and in whatever company we find ourselves: in our neighborhoods, in school or sports or social life, in volunteer service or in the workplace. Wherever we are, we always have an opportunity to share the joy of the Gospel. That is how the Lord goes out to meet

everyone. He loves you, dear young people, for you are the means by which he can spread his light and hope. He is counting on your courage, your boldness, and your enthusiasm.

178. Don't think that this mission is soft and easy. Some young people have given their lives for the sake of missionary outreach. As the Korean bishops put it: "We hope that we can be grains of wheat and instruments for the salvation of humanity, following upon the example of the martyrs. Though our faith is as small as a mustard seed, God will give it growth and use it as an instrument for his work of salvation."[95] Young friends, don't wait until tomorrow to contribute your energy, your audacity, and your creativity to changing our world. Your youth is not an "in-between time." You are the *now* of God, and he wants you to bear fruit.[96] For "it is in giving that we receive."[97] The best way to prepare a bright future is to experience the present as best we can, with commitment and generosity.

CHAPTER SIX

YOUNG PEOPLE WITH ROOTS

179. I have sometimes seen young and beautiful trees, their branches reaching to the sky, pushing ever higher, and they seemed a song of hope. Later, following a storm, I would find them fallen and lifeless. They lacked deep roots. They spread their branches without being firmly planted, and so they fell as soon as nature unleashed her power. That is why it pains me to see young people sometimes being encouraged to build a future without roots, as if the world were just starting now. For "it is impossible for us to grow unless we have strong roots to support us and to keep us firmly grounded. It is easy to drift off, when there is nothing to clutch onto, to hold onto."[98]

Don't Allow Yourselves to Be Uprooted

180. This is an important issue, and I want to spend a brief chapter discussing it. If we appreciate this issue, we can distinguish the joy of youth from a false cult of youth that can be used to seduce and manipulate young people.

181. Think about it: if someone tells young people to ignore their history, to reject the experiences of their elders, to look down on the past, and to look forward to a future that he holds out, doesn't it then become easy to draw them along so that they only do what he tells them? He needs the young to be shallow, uprooted, and distrustful, so that they can trust only in his promises and act according to his plans. That is how various ideologies operate: they destroy (or deconstruct) all differences so that they can reign unopposed. To do so, however, they need young people who have no use for history, who spurn the spiritual and human riches inherited from past generations, and are ignorant of everything that came before them.

182. These masters of manipulation also use another tactic: the cult of youth, which dismisses all that is not young as contemptible and outmoded. The youthful body becomes the symbol of this new cult; everything associated with that body is idolized and lusted after, while whatever is not young is despised. But this cult of youth is simply an expedient that ultimately proves degrading to the young; it strips them of any real value and uses them for personal, financial, or political profit.

183. Dear young friends, do not let them exploit your youth to promote a shallow life that confuses beauty with appearances. Realize that there is beauty in the laborer who returns home grimy and unkempt, but with the joy of having earned food for his family. There is extraordinary beauty in the fellowship of a family at table, generously sharing what food it has. There is beauty in the wife, slightly disheveled and no longer young, who continues to care for her sick husband despite her own failing health. Long after the springtime of their courtship has passed, there is beauty in the fidelity of those couples who still love one another in the autumn of life, those elderly people who still hold hands as they walk. There is also a beauty, unrelated to appearances or fashionable dress, in all those men and women who pursue their personal vocation with love, in selfless service of community or nation, in the hard work of building a happy family, in the selfless and demanding effort to advance social harmony. To find, to disclose, and to highlight this beauty, which is like that of Christ on the cross, is to lay the foundations of genuine social solidarity and the culture of encounter.

184. Along with the stratagems of a false cult of youth and appearance, we are also witnessing attempts to promote a spirituality without God, an affectivity without community or concern for those who suffer, a fear of the poor, viewed as dangerous, and a variety of claims to offer a future paradise that nonetheless seems increasingly distant. I do not want to offer you any such thing, and with great love I urge you not to let yourselves be taken in by this ideology. It will not make you any younger, but enslave you instead. I propose another way, one born of

freedom, enthusiasm, creativity, and new horizons, while at the same time cultivating the roots that nourish and sustain us.

185. In this regard, I would note that "many Synod Fathers coming from non-Western contexts pointed out that in their countries globalization is bringing with it forms of cultural colonization that sever young people from their cultural and religious roots. The Church needs to make a commitment to accompanying these young people, so that in the process they do not lose sight of the most precious features of their identity."[99]

186. Today, in fact, we see a tendency to "homogenize" young people, blurring what is distinctive about their origins and backgrounds, and turning them into a new line of malleable goods. This produces a cultural devastation that is just as serious as the disappearance of species of animals and plants.[100] For this reason, in addressing young indigenous people gathered in Panama, I encouraged them to "care for your roots, because from the roots comes the strength that is going to make you grow, flourish and bear fruit."[101]

Your Relationship with the Elderly

187. At the Synod, we heard that "the young are focused on the future and they face life with energy and dynamism. But they are also tempted . . . to give little attention to the memory of the past from which they come, in particular the many gifts transmitted to them by their parents, their grandparents and the cultural experience of the society in which they live. Helping the young to discover the living richness of the past, to treasure its memory and to make use of it for their choices and opportunities, is a genuine act of love toward them, for the sake of their growth and the decisions they are called to make."[102]

188. The word of God encourages us to remain close to the elderly, so that we can benefit from their experience: "Stand in the assembly of the elders. Who is wise? Cling to him. . . . If you see an intelligent man, visit him; let your foot wear out his doorstep" (Sir 6:34.36). In every case, the

long years they lived and all they have experienced in life should make us look to them with respect: "You shall rise up before the hoary head" (Lv 19:32). For "the glory of young men is their strength, but the beauty of old men is their grey hair" (Prv 20:29).

189. The Bible also tells us: "Listen to your father who begot you, and do not despise your mother when she is old" (Prv 23:22). The command to honor our father and mother "is the first commandment to carry a promise with it" (Eph 6:2, cf. Ex 20:12; Deut 5:16; Lev 19:3), and that promise is: "that it may be well with you and that you may live long on the earth" (Eph 6:3).

190. This does not mean having to agree with everything adults say or approving all their actions. A young person should always have a critical spirit. Saint Basil the Great encouraged the young to esteem the classical Greek authors, but to accept only whatever good they could teach.[103] It is really a matter of being open to receiving a wisdom passed down from generation to generation, a wisdom familiar with human weakness and not deserving to vanish before the novelties of consumer society and the market.

191. The world has never benefited, nor will it ever benefit, from a rupture between generations. That is the siren song of a future without roots and origins. It is the lie that would have you believe that only what is new is good and beautiful. When intergenerational relationships exist, a collective memory is present in communities, as each generation takes up the teachings of its predecessors and in turn bequeaths a legacy to its successors. In this way, they provide frames of reference for firmly establishing a new society. As the old saying goes: "If the young had knowledge and the old strength, there would be nothing they could not accomplish."

Dreams and Visions

192. The prophecy of Joel contains a verse that expresses this nicely: "I will pour out my Spirit upon all flesh, and your sons and your daughters shall prophesy, and your young men shall see visions, and your old men shall dream dreams" (3:1; cf. Acts 2:17). When young and old alike are open to the Holy Spirit, they make a wonderful combination. The old dream dreams, and the young see visions. How do the two complement one another?

193. The elderly have dreams built up of memories and images that bear the mark of their long experience. If young people sink roots in those dreams, they can peer into the future; they can have visions that broaden their horizons and show them new paths. But if the elderly do not dream, young people lose clear sight of the horizon.

194. Perhaps our parents have preserved a memory that can help us imagine the dream our grandparents dreamed for us. All of us, even before our birth, received, as a blessing from our grandparents, a dream filled with love and hope, the dream of a better life. Even if not our grandparents, surely some of our great-grandparents had that happy dream as they contemplated their children and then grandchildren in the cradle. The very first dream of all is the creative dream of God our Father, which precedes and accompanies the lives of all his children. The memory of this blessing that extends from generation to generation is a precious legacy that we should keep alive so that we too can pass it on.

195. That is why it is a good thing to let older people tell their long stories, which sometimes seem legendary or fanciful—they are the dreams of old people—yet are often full of rich experiences, of eloquent symbols, of hidden messages. These stories take time to tell, and we should be prepared to listen patiently and let them sink in, even though they are much longer than what we are used to in social media. We have to realize that the wisdom needed for life bursts the confines of our present-day media resources.

196. In the book *Sharing the Wisdom of Time,*[104] I expressed some thoughts in the form of questions. "What do I ask of the elders among whom I count myself? I call us to be memory keepers. We grandfathers and grandmothers need to form a choir. I envision elders as a permanent choir of a great spiritual sanctuary, where prayers of supplication and songs of praise support the larger community that works and struggles in the field of life."[105] It is a beautiful thing when "young men and maidens together, old men and children, praise the name of the Lord" (Ps 148:12–13).

197. What can we elderly persons give to the young? "We can remind today's young people, who have their own blend of heroic ambitions and insecurities, that a life without love is an arid life."[106] What can we tell them? "We can tell fearful young people that anxiety about the future can be overcome."[107] What can we teach them? "We can teach those young people, sometimes so focused on themselves, that there is more joy in giving than in receiving, and that love is not only shown in words, but also in actions."[108]

Taking Risks Together

198. A love that is generous and outgoing, that acts and takes risks, may at times make mistakes. Here we may find timely the witness of Maria Gabriella Perin, who lost her father shortly after her birth: she reflects on how this influenced her life, in a relationship that did not last but that left her a mother and now a grandmother. "What I know is that God makes stories. In his genius and mercy, he takes our triumphs and our failures and weaves beautiful tapestries that are full of irony. The reverse of the fabric may look messy with its tangled threads—the events of our life—and maybe this is the side we dwell on when we doubt. But the right side of the tapestry displays a magnificent story, and this is the side that God sees."[109] When older people look at life closely, often they instinctively know what lies behind the tangled threads, and they recognize what God can create even out of our mistakes.

199. If we journey together, young and old, we can be firmly rooted in the present, and from here, revisit the past and look to the future. To revisit the past in order to learn from history and heal old wounds that at times still trouble us. To look to the future in order to nourish our enthusiasm, cause dreams to emerge, awaken prophecies, and enable hope to blossom. Together, we can learn from one another, warm hearts, inspire minds with the light of the Gospel, and lend new strength to our hands.

200. Roots are not anchors chaining us to past times and preventing us from facing the present and creating something new. Instead, they are a fixed point from which we can grow and meet new challenges. It does us no good "to sit down and long for times past; we must meet our culture with realism and love and fill it with the Gospel. We are sent today to proclaim the Good News of Jesus to a new age. We need to love this time with all its opportunities and risks, its joys and sorrows, its riches and its limits, its successes and failures."[110]

201. During the Synod, one of the young auditors from the Samoan Islands spoke of the Church as a canoe, in which the elderly help to keep on course by judging the position of the stars, while the young keep rowing, imagining what waits for them ahead. Let us steer clear of young people who think that adults represent a meaningless past, and those adults who always think they know how young people should act. Instead, let us all climb aboard the same canoe and together seek a better world, with the constantly renewed momentum of the Holy Spirit.

CHAPTER SEVEN

YOUTH MINISTRY

202. Youth ministry, as traditionally carried out, has been significantly affected by social and cultural changes. Young people frequently fail to find in our usual programs a response to their concerns, their needs, their problems and issues. The proliferation and growth of groups and movements predominantly associated with the young can be considered the work of the Holy Spirit who constantly shows us new paths. Even so, there is a need to look at the ways such groups participate in the Church's overall pastoral care, as well as a need for greater communion among them and a better coordination of their activities. Although it is never easy to approach young people, two things have become increasingly evident: the realization that the entire community has to be involved in evangelizing them, and the urgent requirement that young people take on a greater role in pastoral outreach.

A Pastoral Care That Is Synodal

203. I want to state clearly that young people themselves are agents of youth ministry. Certainly they need to he helped and guided, but at the same time left free to develop new approaches, with creativity and a certain audacity. So I will not attempt here to propose a kind of manual of youth ministry or a practical pastoral guide. I am more concerned with helping young people to use their insight, ingenuity, and knowledge to address the issues and concerns of other young people in their own language.

204. The young make us see the need for new styles and new strategies. For example, while adults often worry about having everything properly planned, with regular meetings and fixed times, most young people today have little interest in this kind of pastoral approach. Youth ministry needs to become more flexible: inviting young people to events

or occasions that provide an opportunity not only for learning, but also for conversing, celebrating, singing, listening to real stories, and experiencing a shared encounter with the living God.

205. At the same time, we should take into greater consideration those practices that have shown their value—the methods, language, and aims that have proved truly effective in bringing young people to Christ and the Church. It does not matter where they are coming from or what labels they have received, whether "conservative" or "liberal," "traditional" or "progressive." What is important is that we make use of everything that has borne good fruit and effectively communicates the joy of the Gospel.

206. Youth ministry has to be synodal; it should involve a "journeying together" that values "the charisms that the Spirit bestows in accordance with the vocation and role of each of the Church's members, through a process of co-responsibility. . . . Motivated by this spirit, we can move toward a participatory and co-responsible Church, one capable of appreciating its own rich variety, gratefully accepting the contributions of the lay faithful, including young people and women, consecrated persons, as well as groups, associations, and movements. No one should be excluded or exclude themselves."[111]

207. In this way, by learning from one another, we can better reflect that wonderful multifaceted reality that Christ's Church is meant to be. She will be able to attract young people, for her unity is not monolithic, but rather a network of varied gifts that the Spirit ceaselessly pours out upon her, renewing her and lifting her up from her poverty.

208. In the Synod, many concrete proposals emerged for renewing youth ministry and freeing it from approaches that are no longer effective because they are incapable of entering into dialogue with contemporary youth culture. Naturally, I cannot list them all here. A number of them can be found in the Final Document of the Synod.

Main Courses of Action

209. I wish simply to emphasize that youth ministry involves two main courses of action. One is *outreach,* the way we attract new young people to an experience of the Lord. The other is *growth,* the way we help those who have already had that experience to mature in it.

210. As for *outreach,* I trust that young people themselves know how best to find appealing ways to come together. They know how to organize events, sports competitions, and ways to evangelize using social media, through text messages, songs, videos, and other ways. They only have to be encouraged and given the freedom to be enthused about evangelizing other young people wherever they are to be found. When the message is first brought up, whether at a youth retreat, in a conversation at a bar, on school holidays, or in any of God's mysterious ways, it can awaken a deep experience of faith. What is most important, though, is that each young person can be daring enough to sow the seed of the message on that fertile terrain that is the heart of another young person.

211. In this outreach, we need to use above all the language of closeness, the language of generous, relational, and existential love that touches the heart, impacts life, and awakens hope and desires. Young people need to be approached with the grammar of love, not by being preached at. The language that young people understand is spoken by those who radiate life, by those who are there for them and with them. And those who, for all their limitations and weaknesses, try to live their faith with integrity. We also have to give greater thought to ways of incarnating the *kerygma* in the language of today's youth.

212. As for *growth,* I would make one important point. In some places, it happens that young people are helped to have a powerful experience of God, an encounter with Jesus that touched their hearts. But the only follow-up to this is a series of "formation" meetings featuring talks about doctrinal and moral issues, the evils of today's world, the Church, her social doctrine, chastity, marriage, birth control, and so on. As a result,

many young people get bored, they lose the fire of their encounter with Christ and the joy of following him; many give up and others become downcast or negative. Rather than being too concerned with communicating a great deal of doctrine, let us first try to awaken and consolidate the great experiences that sustain the Christian life. In the words of Romano Guardini, "When we experience a great love . . . everything else becomes part of it."[112]

213. Any educational project or path of growth for young people must certainly include formation in Christian doctrine and morality. It is likewise important that it have two main goals. One is the development of the *kerygma*, the foundational experience of encounter with God through Christ's death and resurrection. The other is growth in fraternal love, community life, and service.

214. This was something I emphasized in *Evangelii Gaudium*, and I consider it worth repeating here. It would be a serious mistake to think that in youth ministry "the kerygma should give way to a supposedly more 'solid' formation. Nothing is more solid, profound, secure, meaningful and wisdom-filled than that initial proclamation. All Christian formation consists of entering more deeply into the kerygma"[113] and incarnating it ever more fully in our lives. Consequently, youth ministry should always include occasions for renewing and deepening our personal experience of the love of God and the living Christ. It can do this in a variety of ways: testimonies, songs, moments of adoration, times of spiritual reflection on the sacred Scriptures, and even an intelligent use of social networks. Yet this joyful experience of encounter with the Lord should never be replaced by a kind of "indoctrination."

215. On the other hand, any program of youth ministry should clearly incorporate various means and resources that can help young people grow in fraternity, to live as brothers and sisters, to help one another, to build community, to be of service to others, to be close to the poor. If fraternal love is the "new commandment" (Jn 13:34), "the fullness of the

Law" (Rom 13:10), and our best way of showing our love for God, then it has to have a primary place in every project of youth formation and growth to maturity.

Suitable Environments

216. We need to make all our institutions better equipped to be more welcoming to young people, since so many have a real sense of being orphaned. Here I am not referring to family problems but to something experienced by boys and girls, young people and adults, parents and children alike. To all these orphans—including perhaps ourselves—communities like a parish or school should offer possibilities for experiencing openness and love, affirmation and growth. Many young people today feel that they have inherited the failed dreams of their parents and grandparents, dreams betrayed by injustice, social violence, selfishness, and lack of concern for others. In a word, they feel uprooted. If the young grow up in a world in ashes, it will be hard for them to keep alive the flame of great dreams and projects. If they grow up in a desert devoid of meaning, where will they develop a desire to devote their lives to sowing seeds? The experience of discontinuity, uprootedness, and the collapse of fundamental certainties, fostered by today's media culture, creates a deep sense of orphanhood to which we must respond by creating an attractive and fraternal environment where others can live with a sense of purpose.

217. In a word, to create a "home" is to create "a family." "It is to learn to feel connected to others by more than merely utilitarian and practical bonds, to be united in such a way as to feel that our life is a bit more human. To create a home is to let prophecy take flesh and make our hours and days less cold, less indifferent and anonymous. It is to create bonds by simple, everyday acts that all of us can perform. A home, as we all know, demands that everyone work together. No one can be indifferent or stand apart, since each is a stone needed to build the home. This also involves asking the Lord to grant us the grace to learn how to be patient, to forgive one another, to start over each day. How many times should

I forgive and start over? Seventy times seven times, as many times as necessary. To create strong bonds requires confidence and trust nurtured daily by patience and forgiveness. And that is how the miracle takes place: we feel that here we are reborn, here we are all reborn, because we feel God's caress that enables us to dream of a more human world, and therefore of a world more divine."[114]

218. Along these lines, our institutions should provide young people with places they can make their own, where they can come and go freely, feel welcome, and readily meet other young people, whether at times of difficulty and frustration, or of joy and celebration. Some of this is already happening in oratories and other youth centers, which in many cases offer a friendly and relaxed setting where friendships can grow, where young men and women can meet one another, where they can share music, games, sports, but also reflection and prayer. In such places, much can be offered, without great expenditure of funds. Then too, the person-to-person contact indispensable for passing on the message can happen, something whose place cannot be taken by any pastoral resource or strategy.

219. "Friendship and discussion, often within more or less structured groups, offer the opportunity to strengthen social and relational skills in a context in which one is neither analyzed nor judged. Group experience is also a great resource for sharing the faith and for mutual help in bearing witness. The young are able to guide other young people and to exercise a genuine apostolate among their friends."[115]

220. This is not to say that they should become isolated and lose all contact with parish communities, movements, and other ecclesial institutions. But they will be better integrated into communities that are open, living their faith, eager to radiate Christ, joyful, free, fraternal, and committed. These communities can be settings where they feel that it is possible to cultivate precious relationships.

Youth Ministry in Educational Institutions

221. Schools are unquestionably a platform for drawing close to children and young people. Precisely because they are such privileged places of personal development, the Christian community has always been concerned to train teachers and administrators, and to found its own schools of various kinds and levels. In this field of educating the young, the Spirit has raised up countless charisms and examples of holiness. Yet schools are in urgent need of self-criticism, if we consider the results of their pastoral outreach, which in many cases focuses on a kind of religious instruction that proves often incapable of nurturing lasting experiences of faith. Some Catholic schools seem to be structured only for the sake of self-preservation. Fear of change makes them entrenched and defensive before the dangers, real or imagined, that any change might bring. A school that becomes a "bunker," protecting its students from errors "from without," is a caricature of this tendency. Yet this image reflects, in a chilling way, what many young people experience when they graduate from certain educational institutions: an insurmountable disconnect between what they were taught and the world in which they live. The way they were instructed in religious and moral values did not prepare them to uphold those values in a world that holds them up to ridicule, nor did they learn ways of praying and practicing the faith that can be easily sustained amid the fast pace of today's society. For one of the greatest joys that any educator can have is to see a student turn into a strong, well-integrated person, a leader, someone prepared to give.

222. Catholic schools remain essential places for the evangelization of the young. Account should be taken of a number of guiding principles set forth in *Veritatis Gaudium* for the renewal and revival of missionary outreach on the part of schools and universities. These include a fresh experience of the kerygma, wide-ranging dialogue, interdisciplinary and cross-disciplinary approaches, the promotion of a culture of encounter, the urgency of creating networks, and an option in favor of those who are

least, those whom society discards.[116] Similarly important is the ability to integrate the knowledge of head, heart, and hands.

223. On the other hand, we cannot separate spiritual from cultural formation. The Church has always sought to develop ways of providing the young with the best education possible. Nor should she stop now, for young people have a right to it. "Today, above all, the right to a good education means protecting wisdom, that is, knowledge that is human and humanizing. All too often we are conditioned by trivial and fleeting models of life that drive us to pursue success at a low price, discrediting sacrifice and inculcating the idea that education is not necessary unless it immediately provides concrete results. No, education makes us raise questions, keeps us from being anaesthetized by banality, and impels us to pursue meaning in life. We need to reclaim our right not to be sidetracked by the many sirens that nowadays distract from this pursuit. Ulysses, in order not to give in to the siren song that bewitched his sailors and made them crash against the rocks, tied himself to the mast of the ship and had his companions plug their ears. Orpheus, on the other hand, did something else to counter the siren song: he intoned an even more beautiful melody, which enchanted the sirens. This, then, is your great challenge: to respond to the crippling refrains of cultural consumerism with thoughtful and firm decisions, with research, knowledge and sharing."[117]

Areas Needing to Be Developed

224. Many young people have come to appreciate silence and closeness to God. Groups that gather to adore the Blessed Sacrament or to pray with the word of God have also increased. We should never underestimate the ability of young people to be open to contemplative prayer. We need only find the right ways and means to help them embark on this precious experience. When it comes to worship and prayer, "in many settings, young Catholics are asking for prayer opportunities and sacramental celebrations capable of speaking to their daily lives through a

fresh, authentic and joyful liturgy."[118] It is important to make the most of the great moments of the liturgical year, particularly Holy Week, Pentecost, and Christmas. But other festive occasions can provide a welcome break in their routine and help them experience the joy of faith.

225. Christian service represents a unique opportunity for growth and openness to God's gifts of faith and charity. Many young people are attracted by the possibility of helping others, especially children and the poor. Often this service is the first step to a discovery or rediscovery of life in Christ and the Church. Many young people grow weary of our programs of doctrinal and spiritual formation, and at times demand a chance to be active participants in activities that benefit others.

226. Nor can we overlook the importance of the arts, like theater, painting, and others. "Music is particularly important, representing as it does a real environment in which the young are constantly immersed, as well as a culture and a language capable of arousing emotion and shaping identity. The language of music also represents a pastoral resource with a particular bearing on the liturgy and its renewal."[119] Singing can be a great incentive to young people as they make their way through life. As Saint Augustine says: "Sing, but continue on your journey. Do not grow lazy, but sing to make the way more enjoyable. Sing, but keep going. . . . If you make progress, you will continue your journey, but be sure that your progress is in virtue, true faith and right living. Sing then, and keep walking."[120]

227. "Equally significant is the emphasis that young people place on sports; the Church should not underestimate the potential of sports for education and formation, but instead maintain a strong presence there. The world of sport needs to be helped to overcome some of its problematic aspects, such as the idolization of champions, subservience to commercial interests and the ideology of success at any cost."[121] At the heart of the experience of sport is "joy: the joy of exercising, of being together, of being alive and rejoicing in the gifts the Creator gives us each day."[122]

Some Fathers of the Church used the example of the training of athletes to encourage the young to develop their strength and to overcome idleness and boredom. Saint Basil the Great, writing to young people, used the effort demanded by athletics to illustrate the value of self-sacrifice as a means of growth in virtue: "These men endure sufferings beyond number, they use many means to build their strength, they sweat constantly as they train . . . in a word, they so discipline themselves that their whole life prior to the contest is but a preparation for it. . . . How then can we, who have been promised rewards so wondrous in number and in splendor that no tongue can recount them, even think of winning them if we do nothing other than spend our lives in leisure and make but half-hearted efforts?"[123]

228. Nature holds a special attraction for many adolescents and young people who recognize our need to care for the environment. Such is the case with the scouting movement and other groups that encourage closeness to nature, camping trips, hiking, expeditions, and campaigns to improve the environment. In the spirit of Saint Francis of Assisi, these experiences can be a real initiation into the school of universal fraternity and contemplative prayer.

229. These and various other opportunities for evangelizing the young should not make us forget that, despite the changing times and sensibilities of young people, there are gifts of God that never grow old, for they contain a power transcending all times and places. There is the word of the Lord, ever living and effective, the nourishing presence of Christ in the Eucharist, and the sacrament of Reconciliation, which brings us freedom and strength. We can also mention the inexhaustible spiritual riches preserved by the Church in the witness of her saints and the teaching of the great spiritual masters. Although we have to respect different stages of growth, and at times need to wait patiently for the right moment, we cannot fail to invite young people to drink from these wellsprings of new life. We have no right to deprive them of this great good.

A "Popular" Youth Ministry

230. In addition to the ordinary, well-planned pastoral ministry that parishes and movements carry out, it is also important to allow room for a "popular" youth ministry, with a different style, schedule, pace, and method. Broader and more flexible, it goes out to those places where real young people are active, and fosters the natural leadership qualities and the charisms sown by the Holy Spirit. It tries to avoid imposing obstacles, rules, controls, and obligatory structures on these young believers who are natural leaders in their neighborhoods and in other settings. We need only to accompany and encourage them, trusting a little more in the genius of the Holy Spirit, who acts as he wills.

231. We are speaking of truly "popular" leaders, not elitists or those closed off in small groups of select individuals. To be able to generate a "popular" ministry to youth, "they need to learn to listen to the sense of the people, to become their spokespersons and to work for their promotion."[124] When we speak of "the people," we are not speaking about the structures of society or the Church, but about all those persons who journey, not as individuals, but as a closely bound community of all and for all, one that refuses to leave the poor and the vulnerable behind. "The people wants everyone to share in the common good and thus agree to keep pace with its least members, so that all can arrive together."[125] "Popular" leaders, then, are those able to make everyone, including the poor, the vulnerable, the frail, and the wounded, part of the forward march of youth. They do not shun or fear those young people who have experienced hurt or borne the weight of the cross.

232. Similarly, especially in the case of young people who do not come from Christian families or institutions, and are slowly growing to maturity, we have to encourage all the good that we can.[126] Christ warned us not to see only the good grain (cf. Mt 13:24–30). At times, in the attempt to develop a pure and perfect youth ministry, marked by abstract ideas, protected from the world, and free of every flaw, we can turn the Gospel

into a dull, meaningless, and unattractive proposition. Such a youth ministry ends up completely removed from the world of young people and suited only to an elite Christian youth that sees itself as different, while living in an empty and unproductive isolation. In rejecting the weeds, we also uproot or choke any number of shoots trying to spring up in spite of their limitations.

233. Instead of "overwhelming young people with a body of rules that make Christianity seem reductive and moralistic, we are called to invest in their fearlessness and to train them to take up their responsibilities, in the sure knowledge that error, failure and crisis are experiences that can strengthen their humanity."[127]

234. The Synod called for the development of a youth ministry capable of being inclusive, with room for all kinds of young people, to show that we are a Church with open doors. Nor does one have to accept fully all the teachings of the Church to take part in certain of our activities for young people. It is enough to have an open mind toward all those who have the desire and willingness to be encountered by God's revealed truth. Some of our pastoral activities can assume that a journey of faith has already begun, but we need a "popular" youth ministry that can open doors and make room for everyone, with their doubts and frustrations, their problems and their efforts to find themselves, their past errors, their experiences of sin, and all their difficulties.

235. Room should also be made for "all those who have other visions of life, who belong to other religions or who distance themselves from religion altogether. All the young, without exception, are in God's heart and thus in the Church's heart. We recognize frankly that this statement on our lips does not always find real expression in our pastoral actions: often we remain closed in our environments, where their voice does not penetrate, or else we dedicate ourselves to less demanding and more enjoyable activities, suppressing that healthy pastoral restlessness that would urge us to move out from our supposed security. The Gospel also

asks us to be daring, and we want to be so, without presumption and without proselytizing, testifying to the love of the Lord and stretching out our hands to all the young people in the world."[128]

236. Youth ministry, when it ceases to be elitist and is willing to be "popular," is a process that is gradual, respectful, patient, hopeful, tireless, and compassionate. The Synod proposed the example of the disciples of Emmaus (cf. Lk 24:13–35) as a model of what happens in youth ministry.

237. "Jesus walks with two disciples who did not grasp the meaning of all that happened to him, and are leaving Jerusalem and the community behind. Wanting to accompany them, he joins them on the way. He asks them questions and listens patiently to their version of events, and in this way he helps them *recognize* what they were experiencing. Then, with affection and power, he proclaims the word to them, leading them to *interpret* the events they had experienced in the light of the Scriptures. He accepts their invitation to stay with them as evening falls; he enters into their night. As they listen to him speak, their hearts burn within them and their minds are opened; they then recognize him in the breaking of the bread. They themselves *choose* to resume their journey at once in the opposite direction, to return to the community and to share the experience of their encounter with the risen Lord."[129]

238. Various manifestations of popular piety, especially pilgrimages, attract young people who do not readily feel at home in ecclesial structures, and represent a concrete sign of their trust in God. These ways of seeking God are seen particularly in young people who are poor, but also those in other sectors of society. They should not be looked down on, but encouraged and promoted. Popular piety "is a legitimate way of living the faith"[130] and "an expression of the spontaneous missionary activity of the People of God."[131]

Always Missionaries

239. Here I would point out that it doesn't take much to make young people missionaries. Even those who are most frail, limited, and troubled can be missionaries in their own way, for goodness can always be shared, even if it exists alongside many limitations. A young person who makes a pilgrimage to ask Our Lady for help, and invites a friend or companion along, by that single gesture is being a good missionary. Inseparable from a "popular" youth ministry is an irrepressible "popular" missionary activity that breaks through our customary models and ways of thinking. Let us accompany and encourage it, but not presume to overly regulate it.

240. If we can hear what the Spirit is saying to us, we have to realize that youth ministry is always missionary. Young people are greatly enriched when they overcome their reticence and dare to visit homes, and in this way make contact with people's lives. They learn how to look beyond their family and their group of friends, and they gain a broader vision of life. At the same time, their faith and their sense of being part of the Church grow stronger. Youth missions, which usually take place during school holidays after a period of preparation, can lead to a renewed experience of faith and even serious thoughts about a vocation.

241. Young people can find new fields for mission in the most varied settings. For example, since they are already so familiar with social networks, they should be encouraged to fill them with God, fraternity, and commitment.

Accompaniment by Adults

242. Young people need to have their freedom respected, yet they also need to be accompanied. The family should be the first place of accompaniment. Youth ministry can present the ideal of life in Christ as the process of building a house on rock (cf. Mt 7:24–25). For most young people, that house, their life, will be built on marriage and married love.

That is why youth ministry and the pastoral care of families should be coordinated and integrated, with the aim of ensuring a continuous and suitable accompaniment of the vocational process.

243. The community has an important role in the accompaniment of young people; it should feel collectively responsible for accepting, motivating, encouraging, and challenging them. All should regard young people with understanding, appreciation, and affection, and avoid constantly judging them or demanding of them a perfection beyond their years.

244. At the Synod, "many pointed to the shortage of qualified people devoted to accompaniment. Belief in the theological and pastoral value of listening entails rethinking and renewing the ways that priestly ministry is ordinarily exercised, and reviewing its priorities. The Synod also recognized the need to train consecrated persons and laypeople, male and female, to accompany young people. The charism of listening that the Holy Spirit calls forth within the communities might also receive institutional recognition as a form of ecclesial service."[132]

245. There is also a special need to accompany young men and women showing leadership potential, so that they can receive training and the necessary qualifications. The young people who met before the Synod called for "programs for the formation and continued development of young leaders. Some young women feel that there is a lack of leading female role models within the Church and they too wish to give their intellectual and professional gifts to the Church. We also believe that seminarians and religious should have an even greater ability to accompany young leaders."[133]

246. The same young people described to us the qualities they hope to find in a mentor, and they expressed this with much clarity. "The qualities of such a mentor include: being a faithful Christian who engages with the Church and the world; someone who constantly seeks holiness; someone who is a confidant without judging. Similarly, someone who actively listens to the needs of young people and responds in kind;

someone deeply loving and self-aware; someone who recognizes his or her limits and knows the joys and sorrows of the spiritual journey. An especially important quality in mentors is the acknowledgment of their own humanity—the fact that they are human beings who make mistakes: not perfect people but forgiven sinners. Sometimes mentors are put on a pedestal, and when they fall, it may have a devastating impact on young people's ability to continue to engage with the Church. Mentors should not lead young people as passive followers, but walk alongside them, allowing them to be active participants in the journey. They should respect the freedom that comes with a young person's process of discernment and equip them with tools to do so well. A mentor should believe wholeheartedly in a young person's ability to participate in the life of the Church. A mentor should therefore nurture the seeds of faith in young people, without expecting to immediately see the fruits of the work of the Holy Spirit. This role is not and cannot be limited to priests and consecrated life, but the laity should also be empowered to take on such a role. All such mentors should benefit from being well-formed, and engage in ongoing formation."[134]

247. The Church's educational institutions are undoubtedly a communal setting for accompaniment; they can offer guidance to many young people, especially when they "seek to welcome all young people, regardless of their religious choices, cultural origins and personal, family or social situations. In this way, the Church makes a fundamental contribution to the integral education of the young in various parts of the world."[135] They would curtail this role unduly were they to lay down rigid criteria for students to enter and remain in them, since they would deprive many young people of an accompaniment that could help enrich their lives.

CHAPTER EIGHT

VOCATION

248. The word *vocation* can be understood in a broad sense as a calling from God, including the call to life, the call to friendship with him, the call to holiness, and so forth. This is helpful, since it situates our whole life in relation to the God who loves us. It makes us realize that nothing is the result of pure chance but that everything in our lives can become a way of responding to the Lord, who has a wonderful plan for us.

249. In the Exhortation *Gaudete et Exsultate*, I spoke about the vocation of all to grow and mature for the glory of God; I wanted "to repropose the call to holiness in a practical way for our own time, with all its risks, challenges and opportunities."[136] The Second Vatican Council helped us to recognize anew this call addressed to each of us: "All the faithful, whatever their condition or state, are called by the Lord, each in his or her own way, to that perfect holiness by which the Father himself is perfect."[137]

God's Call to Friendship

250. The first thing we need to discern and discover is this: Jesus wants to be a friend to every young person. This discernment is the basis of all else. In the risen Lord's dialogue with Simon Peter, his great question was: "Simon, son of John, do you love me?" (Jn 21:16). In other words, do you love me as a friend? The mission that Peter received to shepherd Jesus' flock will always be linked to this gratuitous love, this love of friendship.

251. On the other hand, there was the unsuccessful encounter of Jesus and the rich young man, which clearly shows that the young man failed to perceive the Lord's loving gaze (cf. Mk 10:21). He went away sorrowful, despite his original good intentions, because he could not turn his back on his many possessions (cf. Mt 19:22). He missed the opportunity

of what surely would have been a great friendship. We will never know what that one young man, upon whom Jesus gazed with love and to whom he stretched out his hand, might have been for us, what he might have done for mankind.

252. "The life that Jesus gives us is a love story, a *life history* that wants to blend with ours and sink roots in the soil of our own lives. That life is not salvation up 'in the cloud' and waiting to be downloaded, a new 'app' to be discovered, or a technique of mental self-improvement. Still less is that life a 'tutorial' for finding out the latest news. The salvation that God offers us is *an invitation to be part of a love story* interwoven with our personal stories; it is alive and wants to be born in our midst so that we can bear fruit just as we are, wherever we are and with everyone all around us. The Lord comes there to sow and to be sown."[138]

Being There for Others

253. I would now like to speak of vocation in the strict sense, as a call to missionary service to others. The Lord calls us to share in his work of creation and to contribute to the common good by using the gifts we have received.

254. This missionary vocation thus has to do with service. For our life on earth reaches full stature when it becomes an offering. Here I would repeat that "the mission of being in the heart of the people is not just a part of my life or a badge I can take off; it is not an 'extra' or just another moment in life. Instead, it is something I cannot uproot from my being without destroying my very self. I am a mission on this earth; that is the reason why I am here in this world."[139] It follows that every form of pastoral activity, formation, and spirituality should be seen in the light of our Christian vocation.

255. Your own personal vocation does not consist only in the work you do, though that is an expression of it. Your vocation is something more: it is a path guiding your many efforts and actions toward service to others.

So in discerning your vocation, it is important to determine if you see in yourself the abilities needed to perform that specific service to society.

256. This gives greater value to everything you do. Your work stops being just about making money, keeping busy, or pleasing others. It becomes your vocation because you are called to it; it is something more than merely a pragmatic decision. In the end, it is a recognition of why I was made, why I am here on earth, and what the Lord's plan is for my life. He will not show me every place, time, and detail, since I will have to make my own prudent decisions about these. But he will show me a direction in life, for he is my Creator and I need to listen to his voice, so that, like clay in the hands of a potter, I can let myself be shaped and guided by him. Then I will become what I was meant to be, faithful to my own reality.

257. To respond to our vocation, we need to foster and develop all that we are. This has nothing to do with inventing ourselves or creating ourselves out of nothing. It has to do with finding our true selves in the light of God and letting our lives flourish and bear fruit. "In God's plan, every man and woman is meant to seek self-fulfillment, for every human life is called to some task by God."[140] Your vocation inspires you to bring out the best in yourself for the glory of God and the good of others. It is not simply a matter of doing things, but of doing them with meaning and direction. Saint Alberto Hurtado told young people to think very seriously about the direction their lives should take: "If the helmsman of a ship becomes careless, he is fired straightaway for not taking his sacred responsibility seriously. As for our lives, are we fully aware of the course they are taking? What course is your life taking? If it is necessary to give this more thought, I would beg each one of you to give it the highest consideration, because to get it right is tantamount to success; to err is quite simply to fail."[141]

258. In the life of each young person, this "being there for others" normally has to do with two basic issues: forming a new family and working. Surveys of young people repeatedly confirm that these are the two major

issues worrying them and, at the same time, exciting them. Both must be the object of particular discernment. Let us look briefly at each of them.

Love and Family

259. Young people intensely feel the call to love; they dream of meeting the right person with whom they can form a family and build a life together. This is undoubtedly a vocation which God himself makes known to them through their feelings, desires, and dreams. I dwelt more fully on this theme in the Apostolic Exhortation *Amoris Laetitia*. I would encourage all young people to read especially the fourth and fifth chapters of that Exhortation.

260. I like to think that "two Christians who marry have recognized the call of the Lord in their own love story, the vocation to form one flesh and one life from two, male and female. The Sacrament of Holy Matrimony envelops this love in the grace of God; it roots it in God himself. By this gift, and by the certainty of this call, you can go forward with assurance; you have nothing to fear; you can face everything together!"[142]

261. Here, we need to remember that God created us as sexual beings. He himself "created sexuality, which is a marvelous gift to his creatures."[143] Within the vocation to marriage we should acknowledge and appreciate that "sexuality, sex, is a gift from God. It is not taboo. It is a gift from God, a gift the Lord gives us. It has two purposes: to love and to generate life. It is passion, passionate love. True love is passionate. Love between a man and a woman, when it is passionate, always leads to giving life. Always. To give life with body and soul."[144]

262. The Synod insisted that "the family continues to be the principal point of reference for young people. Children appreciate the love and care of their parents, they give importance to family bonds, and they hope to succeed in forming a family when it is their time. Without doubt, the increase of separation, divorce, second unions and single-parent families can cause great suffering and a crisis of identity in young people.

Sometimes they must take on responsibilities that are not proportioned to their age and that force them to become adults before their time. Often, grandparents are a crucial aid in affection and religious education: with their wisdom they are a vital link in the relationship between generations."[145]

263. It is true that the difficulties they experience in their own family can lead many young people to ask whether it is worthwhile to start a new family, to be faithful, to be generous. I can tell you that it certainly is. It is worth your every effort to invest in the family; there you will find the best incentives to mature and the greatest joys to experience and share. Don't let yourselves be robbed of a great love. Don't let yourselves be led astray by those who propose a life of rampant individualism that in the end leads to isolation and the worst sort of loneliness.

264. Today, a culture of the ephemeral dominates, but it is an illusion. To think that nothing can be definitive is a deceptive lie. "Today, there are those who say that marriage is out of fashion. . . . In a culture of relativism and the ephemeral, many preach the importance of 'enjoying' the present moment. They say that it is not worth making a lifelong commitment, making a definitive decision. . . . I ask you, instead, to be revolutionaries, I ask you to swim against the tide; yes, I am asking you to rebel against this culture that sees everything as temporary and that ultimately believes you are incapable of responsibility, incapable of true love."[146] I have great confidence in you, and for this very reason, I urge you to opt for marriage.

265. Marriage requires preparation, and this calls for growing in self-knowledge, developing the greater virtues, particularly love, patience, openness to dialogue, and helping others. It also involves maturing in your own sexuality, so that it can become less and less a means of using others, and increasingly a capacity to entrust yourself fully to another person in an exclusive and generous way.

266. As the bishops of Colombia have taught, "Christ knows that spouses are not perfect and that they need to overcome their weakness and lack of constancy so that their love can grow and endure. For this reason, he grants spouses his grace, which is at once light and the strength enabling them to achieve progressively their ideal of married life in accordance with God's plan."[147]

267. For those who are not called to marriage or the consecrated life, it must always be remembered that the first and most important vocation is the vocation we have received in baptism. Those who are single, even if not by their own choice, can offer a particular witness to that vocation through their own path of personal growth.

Work

268. The bishops of the United States have pointed out that "young adulthood often signals a person's entrance into the world of work. 'What do you do for a living?' is a constant topic of conversation because work is a major part of their lives. For young adults, this experience is highly fluid because they move from job to job and even from career to career. Work can dictate their use of time and can determine what they can afford to do or buy. It can also determine the quality and quantity of leisure time. Work defines and influences a young adult's identity and self-concept and is a prime place where friendships and other relationships develop because generally it is not done alone. Young men and women speak of work as fulfilling a function and providing meaning. Work allows young adults to meet their practical needs but even more importantly to seek meaning and fulfillment of their dreams and visions. Although work may not help achieve their dreams, it is important for young adults to nurture a vision, learn how to work in a truly personal and life-giving way, and to continue to discern God's call."[148]

269. I ask young people not to expect to live without working, depending on others for help. This is not good, because "work is a necessity, part of the meaning of life on this earth, a path to growth, human development

and personal fulfillment. In this sense, helping the poor financially must always be a provisional solution in the face of pressing needs."[149] Hence, "together with the awe-filled contemplation of creation which we find in Saint Francis of Assisi, the Christian spiritual tradition has also developed a rich and balanced understanding of the meaning of work, as, for example, in the life of Blessed Charles de Foucauld and his followers."[150]

270. The Synod noted that in the area of work, young people can "experience forms of exclusion and marginalization, of which the first and most serious is youth unemployment, which in some countries reaches exorbitant levels. Besides making them poor, the lack of work impacts negatively on young people's capacity to dream and to hope, and it deprives them of the possibility of contributing to the development of society. In many countries, this situation depends on the fact that some sectors of the young population lack adequate professional skills, perhaps because of deficiencies in the system of education and training. Often job insecurity among the young is linked to economic interests that exploit labor."[151]

271. This is a highly complex and sensitive issue that politics must make a priority, especially at present, when the speed of technological advances and the concern to reduce labor costs can lead quickly to the replacement of many jobs by machines. It is also a crucial societal issue because employment for a young person is not merely a means of making money. Work is an expression of human dignity, a path of development and of social inclusion. It is a constant stimulus to grow in responsibility and creativity, a protection against the tendency toward individualism and personal gratification. At the same time, it is an opportunity to give glory to God by developing one's abilities.

272. Young people do not always have the chance to decide what kind of work they will do, or how their energies and talents will be spent. Because, alongside their own aspirations, abilities, and choices, there is the harsh reality of the job market. It is true that you cannot live without

working, and that sometimes you have to accept whatever is available, but I ask you never to give up on your dreams, never completely bury a calling, and never accept defeat. Keep seeking at least partial or imperfect ways to live what you have discerned to be your real calling.

273. When we discover that God is calling us to something, that this or that is what we were made for—whether it be nursing, carpentry, communication, engineering, teaching, art, or any other kind of work—then we will be able to summon up our best capacities for sacrifice, generosity, and dedication. Knowing that we don't do things just for the sake of doing them, but rather we endow them with meaning, as a response to a call that resounds in the depth of our being to offer something to others: that is what makes these occupations bring a sense of deep fulfillment. As we read in the ancient biblical book of Ecclesiastes: "I saw that there is nothing better than that a man should enjoy his work" (3:22).

The Vocation to Special Consecration

274. If we are indeed convinced that the Holy Spirit continues to inspire vocations to the priesthood and the religious life, we can "once more cast out the nets" in the Lord's name, with complete confidence. We can dare, as we should, to tell each young person to ask whether this is the path that they are meant to follow.

275. Occasionally, I would bring this up with young people, and they would respond almost jokingly: "No, that's not for me!" Yet, a few years later, some of them were in the seminary. The Lord cannot fail in his promise to provide the Church with shepherds, for without them she would not be able to live and carry out her mission. If it is true that some priests do not give good witness, that does not mean that the Lord stops calling. On the contrary, he doubles the stakes, for he never ceases to care for his beloved Church.

276. In discerning your vocation, do not dismiss the possibility of devoting yourself to God in the priesthood, the religious life, or in other forms

of consecration. Why not? You can be sure that, if you do recognize and follow a call from God, there you will find complete fulfillment.

277. Jesus is walking in our midst, as he did in Galilee. He walks through our streets, and he quietly stops and looks into our eyes. His call is attractive and intriguing. Yet today the stress and quick pace of a world constantly bombarding us with stimuli can leave no room for that interior silence in which we can perceive Jesus' gaze and hear his call. In the meantime, many attractively packaged offers will come your way. They may seem appealing and exciting, although in time they will only leave you feeling empty, weary, and alone. Don't let this happen to you, because the maelstrom of this world can drive you to take a route without real meaning, without direction, without clear goals, and thus thwart many of your efforts. It is better to seek out that calm and quiet that enable you to reflect, pray, look more clearly at the world around you, and then, with Jesus, come to recognize the vocation that is yours in this world.

CHAPTER NINE

DISCERNMENT

278. In the Apostolic Exhortation *Gaudete et Exsultate,* I spoke in rather general terms about discernment. I would now like to take up some of those reflections and apply them to the way we discern our own vocation in the world.

279. I mentioned there that all of us, but "especially the young, are immersed in a culture of zapping. We can navigate simultaneously on two or more screens and interact at the same time with two or three virtual scenarios. Without the wisdom of discernment, we can easily become prey to every passing trend."[152] Indeed, "this is all the more important when some novelty presents itself in our lives. Then we have to decide whether it is new wine brought by God or an illusion created by the spirit of this world or the spirit of the devil."[153]

280. Such discernment, "even though it includes reason and prudence, goes beyond them, for it seeks a glimpse of that unique and mysterious plan that God has for each of us. . . . It has to do with the meaning of my life before the Father who knows and loves me, and with the real purpose of my life, which nobody knows better than he."[154]

281. Here we see the importance of the formation of conscience, which allows discernment to grow in depth and in fidelity to God: "Forming our conscience is the work of a lifetime, in which we learn to cultivate the very sentiments of Jesus Christ, adopting the criteria behind his choices and the intentions behind his actions (cf. Phil 2:5)."[155]

282. In this process of formation, we let ourselves be transformed by Christ, even as we develop "the habit of doing good, which also is a part of our examination of conscience. We do not simply identify sins, but also recognize God's work in our daily lives, in the events of our personal history and the world around us, and in the witness of all those men and

women who have gone before us or accompany us with their wisdom. This helps us to grow in the virtue of prudence and to give an overall direction to our life through concrete choices, in the serene awareness of both our gifts and our limitations."[156]

Discerning Your Vocation

283. A particular form of discernment involves the effort to discover our own vocation. Since this is a very personal decision that others cannot make for us, it requires a certain degree of solitude and silence. "The Lord speaks to us in a variety of ways, at work, through others and at every moment. Yet we simply cannot do without the silence of prolonged prayer, which enables us better to perceive God's language, to interpret the real meaning of the inspirations we believe we have received, to calm our anxieties and to see the whole of our existence afresh in his own light."[157]

284. Yet this silence does not make us close in on ourselves. "We must remember that prayerful discernment has to be born of an openness to listening—to the Lord and to others, and to reality itself, which always challenges us in new ways. Only if we are prepared to listen, do we have the freedom to set aside our own partial or insufficient ideas. . . . In this way, we become truly open to accepting a call that can shatter our security, but lead us to a better life. It is not enough that everything be calm and peaceful. God may be offering us something more, but in our comfortable inadvertence, we do not recognize it."[158]

285. When seeking to discern our own vocation, there are certain questions we ought to ask. We should not start with wondering where we could make more money, or achieve greater recognition and social status. Nor even by asking what kind of work would be most pleasing to us. If we are not to go astray, we need a different starting point. We need to ask: Do I know myself, quite apart from my illusions and emotions? Do I know what brings joy or sorrow to my heart? What are my strengths and weaknesses? These questions immediately give rise to others: How can I serve people better and prove most helpful to our world and to the

Church? What is my real place in this world? What can I offer to society? Even more realistic questions then follow: Do I have the abilities needed to offer this kind of service? Could I develop those abilities?

286. These questions should be centered less on ourselves and our own inclinations, but on others, so that our discernment leads us to see our life in relation to their lives. That is why I would remind you of the most important question of all. "So often in life, we waste time asking ourselves: 'Who am I?' You can keep asking, 'Who am I?' for the rest of your lives. But the real question is: 'For whom am I?'"[159] Of course, you are for God. But he has decided that you should also be for others, and he has given you many qualities, inclinations, gifts, and charisms that are not for you, but to share with those around you.

The Call of Jesus Our Friend

287. To discern our personal vocation, we have to realize that it is a calling from a friend, who is Jesus. When we give something to our friends, we give them the best we have. It will not necessarily be what is most expensive or hard to obtain, but what we know will make them happy. Friends are so sensitive to this that they can already imagine the smile on their friend's face when he or she opens that gift. This sort of discernment that takes place among friends is what I suggest you take as a model for trying to discover God's will for your lives.

288. I want you to know that, when the Lord thinks of each of you and what he wants to give you, he sees you as his close friend. And if he plans to grant you a grace, a charism that will help you live to the full and become someone who benefits others, someone who leaves a mark in life, it will surely be a gift that will bring you more joy and excitement than anything else in this world. Not because that gift will be rare or extraordinary, but because it will perfectly fit you. It will be a perfect fit for your entire life.

289. A vocation, while a gift, will undoubtedly also be demanding. God's gifts are interactive; to enjoy them we have to be ready to take risks. Yet

the demands they make are not an obligation imposed from without, but an incentive to let that gift grow and develop, and then become a gift for others. When the Lord awakens a vocation, he thinks not only of what you already are, but of what you will one day be, in his company and in that of others.

290. Sheer vitality and strength of personality combine in the hearts of young people to make them constantly aim higher. This exuberance will be tempered by time and painful experiences, but it is important for "this youthful and still untested yearning for the infinite"[160] to encounter the unconditional friendship that Jesus offers us. More than rules and obligations, the choice that Jesus sets before us is to follow him as friends follow one another, seeking each other's company and spending time together out of pure friendship. Everything else will come in time, and even failures in life can be an invaluable way of experiencing that friendship, which will never be lost.

Listening and Accompaniment

291. There are many priests, men and women religious, lay and professional persons, and indeed qualified young people, who can help the young with their vocational discernment. When we are called upon to help others discern their path in life, what is uppermost is the ability to listen. Listening calls for three distinct and complementary kinds of sensitivity.

292. The *first kind of sensitivity* is directed to *the individual*. It is a matter of listening to someone who is sharing his very self in what he says. A sign of this willingness to listen is the time we are ready to spare for others. More than the amount of time we spend, it is about making others feel that my time is their time, that they have all the time they need to say everything they want. The other person must sense that I am listening unconditionally, without being offended or shocked, tired, or bored. We see an example of this kind of listening in the Lord; he walks alongside the disciples on the way to Emmaus, even though they are going in the wrong direction (cf. Lk 24:13–35). When Jesus says he plans to go farther, they realize that he has given them the gift of his time, so they decide to give him theirs by

offering their hospitality. Attentive and selfless listening is a sign of our respect for others, whatever their ideas or their choices in life.

293. The *second kind of sensitivity* is marked by *discernment*. It tries to grasp exactly where grace or temptation is present, for sometimes the things that flit across our minds are mere temptations that can distract us from our true path. I need to ask myself what is it that the other person is trying to tell me, what they want me to realize is happening in their lives. Asking such questions helps me appreciate their thinking and the effects it has on their emotions. This kind of listening seeks to discern the salutary promptings of the good Spirit who proposes to us the Lord's truth, but also the traps laid by the evil spirit—his empty works and promises. It takes courage, warmth, and tact to help others distinguish the truth from illusions or excuses.

294. The *third kind of sensitivity* is the ability to *perceive what is driving* the other person. This calls for a deeper kind of listening, one able to discern the direction in which that person truly wants to move. Apart from what they are feeling or thinking right now, and whatever has happened up to this point in their lives, the real issue is what they would like to be. This may demand that they look not to their own superficial wishes and desires, but rather to what is most pleasing to the Lord, to his plans for their life. And that is seen in a deeper inclination of the heart, beyond the surface level of their likes and feelings. This kind of listening seeks to discern their ultimate intention, the intention that definitively decides the meaning of their life. Jesus knows and appreciates this ultimate intention of the heart. He is always there, ready to help each of us to recognize it. We need but say to him: "Lord, save me! Have mercy on me!"

295. In this way, discernment becomes a genuine means of spiritual combat, helping us to follow the Lord more faithfully.[161] The desire to know our personal vocation thus takes on a supreme intensity, a different quality and higher level, one that better respects the dignity of our person and our life. In the end, good discernment is a path of freedom that brings to full fruit what is

unique in each person, something so personal that only God knows it. Others cannot fully understand or predict from the outside how it will develop.

296. When we listen to others in this way, at a certain moment we ourselves have to disappear in order to let the other person follow the path he or she has discovered. We have to vanish as the Lord did from the sight of his disciples in Emmaus, leaving them alone with burning hearts and an irresistible desire to set out immediately (cf. Lk 24:31–33). When they returned to the community, those disciples heard the good news that the Lord was indeed risen (cf. Lk 24:34).

297. Because "time is greater than space,"[162] we need to encourage and accompany processes, without imposing our own roadmaps. For those processes have to do with persons who remain always unique and free. There are no easy recipes, even when all the signs seem positive, since "positive factors themselves need to be subjected to a careful work of discernment, so that they do not become isolated and contradict one another, becoming absolutes and at odds with one another. The same is true for the negative factors, which are not to be rejected en bloc and without distinction, because in each one there may lie hidden some value which awaits liberation and restoration to its full truth."[163]

298. If you are to accompany others on this path, you must be the first to follow it, day in and day out. That is what Mary did, in her own youth, as she confronted her own questions and difficulties. May she renew your youthfulness by the power of her prayers and accompany you always by her maternal presence.

And to Conclude . . . a Wish

299. Dear young people, my joyful hope is to see you keep running the race before you, outstripping all those who are slow or fearful. Keep running, "attracted by the face of Christ, whom we love so much, whom we adore in the Holy Eucharist and acknowledge in the flesh of our suffering brothers and sisters. May the Holy Spirit urge you on as you run this

race. The Church needs your momentum, your intuitions, your faith. We need them! And when you arrive where we have not yet reached, have the patience to wait for us."[164]

Given in Loreto, at the Shrine of the Holy House, on 25 March, Solemnity of the Annunciation of the Lord, in the year 2019, the seventh of my Pontificate.

FRANCISCUS

Notes

1. The Greek word usually translated "new" can also mean "young."

2. *Confessions*, X, 27: PL 32, 795.

3. Saint Irenaeus, *Adversus Hæreses*, II, 22, 4: PG 7, 784.

4. *Final Document of the Fifteenth Ordinary General Assembly of the Synod of Bishops*, 60. Hereafter cited as FD. The document can be found at: http://www.vatican.va/roman_curia/synod/documents/rc_synod_doc_20181027_doc-final-instrumentum-xvassemblea-giovani_en.html.

5. *Catechism of the Catholic Church*, 515.

6. Ibid., 517.

7. Catechesis (27 June 1990), 2-3: *Insegnamenti* 13, 1 (1990), 1680–81.

8. Post-Synodal Apostolic Exhortation *Amoris Laetitia* (19 March 2016), 182: AAS 108 (2016), 384.

9. FD 63.

10. Second Vatican Ecumenical Council, *Message to Young Men and Women* (8 December 1965): AAS 58 (1966), 18.

11. Ibid.

12. FD 1.

13. Ibid., 8.

14. Ibid., 50.

15. Ibid., 53

16. Cf. Second Vatican Ecumenical Council, Dogmatic Constitution on Divine Revelation *Dei Verbum*, 8.

17. FD 150.

18. *Address at the Vigil with Young People, XXXIV World Youth Day in Panama* (26 January 2019): *L'Osservatore Romano*, 28–29 January 2019, 6.

19. *Prayer at the Conclusion of the Way of the Cross, XXXIV World Youth Day in Panama* (26 January 2019): *L'Osservatore Romano*, 27 January 2019, 12.

20. FD 65.

21. Ibid., 167.

22. Saint John Paul II, *Address to Young People in Turin* (13 April 1980), 4: *Insegnamenti* 3, 1 (1980), 905.

23. Benedict XVI, *Message for the XXVII World Youth Day* (15 March 2012): AAS 194 (2012), 359.

24. FD 8.

25. Ibid.

26. Ibid., 10.

27. Ibid., 11.

28. Ibid., 12.

29. Ibid., 41.

30. Ibid., 42.

31. *Address to Young People in Manila* (18 January 2015): *L'Osservatore Romano*, 19-20 January 2015, 7.

32. FD 34.

33. *Document of the Pre-Synodal Meeting in Preparation for the XV Ordinary General Assembly of the Synod of Bishops*, Rome (24 March 2018), I, 1.

34. FD 39.

35. Ibid., 37.

36. Cf. Encyclical Letter *Laudato Si'* (24 May 2015), 106: AAS 107 (2015), 889–90.

37. FD 37.

38. Ibid., 67.

39. Ibid., 21.

40. Ibid., 22.

41. Ibid., 23.

42. Ibid., 24.

43. *Document of the Pre-Synodal Meeting in Preparation for the XV Ordinary General Assembly of the Synod of Bishops*, Rome (24 March 2018), I, 4.

44. FD 25.

45. Ibid.

46. Ibid., 26.

47. Ibid., 27.

48. Ibid., 28.

49. Ibid., 29.

50. *Address at the Conclusion of the Meeting on the Protection of Minors in the Church* (24 February 2019): *L'Osservatore Romano*, 25–26 February 2019, 10.

51. FD 29.

52. *Letter to the People of God* (20 August 2018), 2: *L'Osservatore Romano*, 21–21 August 2018, 7.

53. FD 30.

54. *Address at the Opening of the XV Ordinary General Assembly of the Synod of Bishops* (3 October 2018): *L'Osservatore Romano*, 5 October 2018, 8.

55. FD 31.

56. Ibid.

57. Second Vatican Ecumenical Council, Pastoral Constitution on the Church in the Modern World *Gaudium et Spes*, 1.

58. FD 31.

59. Ibid.

60. *Address at the Conclusion of the Meeting on the Protection of Minors in the Church* (24 February 2019): *L'Osservatore Romano*, 25–26 February 2019, 11.

61. Francisco Luis Bernárdez, "Soneto," in *Cielo de tierra*, Buenos Aires, 1937.

62. Apostolic Exhortation *Gaudete et Exsultate* (19 March 2018), 140.

63. *Homily at Mass, XXXI World Youth Day in Krakow* (31 July 2016): AAS 108 (2016), 963.

64. *Address at the Opening of the XXXIV World Youth Day in Panama* (24 January 2019): *L'Osservatore Romano*, 26 January 2019, 12.

65. Apostolic Exhortation *Evangelii Gaudium* (24 November 2013), 1: AAS 105 (2013), 1019.

66. Ibid., 3: AAS 105 (2013), 1020.

67. *Address at the Vigil with Young People, XXXIV World Youth Day in Panama* (26 January 2019): *L'Osservatore Romano*, 28–29 January 2019, 6.

68. *Address at the Meeting with Young People during the Synod* (6 October 2018): *L'Osservatore Romano*, 8-9 October 2018, 7.

69. Benedict XVI, Encyclical Letter *Deus Caritas Est* (25 December 2005), 1: AAS 98 (2006), 217.

70. Pedro Arrupe, *Enamórate.*

71. Saint Paul VI, *Address for the Beatification of Nunzio Sulprizio* (1 December 1963): AAS 56 (1964), 28.

72. FD 65.

73. *Homily at Mass with Young People in Sydney* (2 December 1970): AAS 63 (1971), 64.

74. *Confessions*, I, 1, 1: PL 32, 661.

75. *God Is Young. A Conversation with Thomas Leoncini*, New York, Random House, 2018, 4.

76. FD 68.

77. *Meeting with Young People in Cagliari* (22 September 2013): AAS 105 (2013), 904–5.

78. *Five Loaves and Two Fish*, Pauline Books and Media, 2003, pp. 9, 13.

79. Conférence des Évêques Suisses, *Prendre le temps: pour toi, pour moi, pour nous*, 2 February 2018.

80. Cf. Saint Thomas Aquinas, *Summa Theologiae*, II-II, q. 23, art. 1.

81. *Address to the Volunteers of the XXXIV World Youth Day in Panama* (27 January 2019): *L'Osservatore Romano*, 28–29 January 2019, 11.

82. Saint Oscar Romero, *Homily* (6 November 1977), in *Su Pensamiento*, I-II, San Salvador, 2000, p. 312.

83. *Address at the Opening of the XXXIV World Youth Day in Panama* (24 January 2019): *L'Osservatore Romano*, 26 January 2019, 12.

84. Cf. *Meeting with Young People in the National Shrine of Maipú, Santiago de Chile* (17 January 2018): *L'Osservatore Romano*, 19 January 2018, 7.

85. Cf. Romano Guardini, *Die Lebensalter. Ihre ethische und pädagogische Bedeutung*, Würzburg, 3rd ed., 1955, 20.

86. Apostolic Exhortation *Gaudete et Exsultate* (19 March 2018), 11.

87. *Spiritual Canticle*, Red. B, Prologue, 2.

88. Ibid., XIV–XV, 2.

89. Episcopal Conference of Rowanda, *Letter of the Catholic Bishops of Rwanda for Christians in the Extraordinary Year of Reconciliation*, Kigali (18 January 2018), 17.

90. *Greeting to Young People of the Father Félix Varela Cultural Centre in Havana* (20 September 2015): *L'Osservatore Romano*, 21–22 September 2015, 6.

91. FD 46.

92. *Address at the Vigil of the XXVIII World Youth Day in Rio de Janeiro* (27 July 2013): AAS 105 (2013), 663.

93. *Ustedes son la luz del mundo*. Address in Cerro San Cristóbal, Chile, 1940. The text can be found at: https://www.padrealbertohurtado.cl/escritos-2/.

94. *Homily at Mass, XXVIII World Youth Day in Rio de Janeiro* (28 July 2013): AAS 105 (2013), 665.

95. Catholic Bishops' Conference of Korea, *Pastoral Letter on the occasion of the 150th Anniversary of the Martyrdom during the Byeong-in Persecution* (30 March 2016).

96. Cf. *Homily at Mass, XXXIV World Youth Day in Panama* (27 January 2018): *L'Osservatore Romano*, 28–29 January 2019, 12.

97. "Lord, make me a channel of your peace," prayer inspired by Saint Francis of Assisi.

98. *Address at the Vigil, XXIV World Youth Day in Panama*, (26 January 2019): *L'Osservatore Romano*, 28–29 January 2019, 6.

99. FD 14.

100. Cf. Encyclical Letter *Laudato Si'* (24 May 2015), 145: AAS 107 (2015), 906.

101. *Video Messsage for the World Meeting of Indigenous Youth in Panama* (17–21 January 2019): *L'Osservatore Romano*, 19 January 2019, 8.

102. FD 35.

103. Cf. *Ad Adolescentes*, I, 2: PG 31, 565.

104. Cf. Pope Francis and Friends, *Sharing the Wisdom of Time*, Chicago, Loyola Press, 2018.

105. Ibid., 12.

106. Ibid., 13.

107. Ibid.

109. Ibid., 162–63.

110. Eduardo Pironio, *Message to Young Argentinians at the National Youth Meeting in Cordoba*, (12–15 September 1985), 2.

111. FD 123.

112. *Das Wesen des Christentums. Die neue Wirklichkeit des Herrn*, Mainz, 7th ed., 1991, 14.

113. No. 165: AAS 105 (2013), 1089.

114. *Address at the Visit to the Good Samaritan Home, Panama*, (27 January 2019): *L'Osservatore Romano*, 28–29 January 2019, 10.

115. FD 36.

116. Cf. Apostolic Constitution *Veritatis Gaudium* (8 December 2017), 4: AAS 110 (2018), 7-8.

117. *Address at the Meeting with Students and Representatives of the Academic World in Piazza San Domenico, Bologna* (1 October 2017): AAS 109 (2017), 1115.

118. FD 51.

119. Ibid., 47.

120. *Sermo* 256, 3: PL 38, 1193.

121. FD 47.

122. *Address to a Delegation of the International Special Olympics* (16 February 2017): *L'Osservatore Romano*, 17 February 2017, 8.

123. *Ad Adolescentes*, VIII, 11–12: PG 31, 580.

124. Eiscopal Conference of Argentina, *Declaración de San Miguel*, Buenos Aires, 1969, X, 1.

125. Rafael Tello, *La nueva evangelización*, II (Appendices I and II), Buenos Aires, 2013, 111.

126. Cf. Apostolic Exhortation *Evangelii Gaudium* (24 November 2013), 44–45: *AAS* 105 (2013), 1038–39.

127. FD 70.

128. Ibid., 117.

129. Ibid., 4.

130. Apostolic Exhortation *Evangelii Gaudium* (24 November 2013), 124: AAS 105 (2013), 1072.

131. Ibid., No. 122, 1071.

132. FD 9.

133. *Document of the Pre-Synodal Meeting for the Preparation of the XV Ordinary Assembly of the Synod of Bishops*, Rome (24 March 2018), 12.

134. Ibid., 10.

135. FD 15.

136. Apostolic Exhortation *Gaudete et Exsultate* (19 March 2018), 2.

137. Dogmatic Constitution on the Church *Lumen Gentium*, 11.

138. *Address at the Vigil, XXXIV World Youth Day in Panama* (26 January 2019): *L'Osservatore Romano*, 28–29 January 2019, 6.

139. Apostolic Exhortation *Evangelii Gaudium* (24 November 2013), 273: AAS 105 (2013), 1130.

140. Saint Paul VI, Encyclical Letter *Populorum Progressio* (26 March 1967), 15: AAS 59 (1967), 265.

141. *Meditación de Semana Santa para jóvenes*, written aboard a cargo ship returning from the United States in 1946 (https://www.padrealbertohurtado.cl/escritos-2/).

142. *Meeting with the Young People of Umbria in Assisi* (4 October 2013): 105 (2013), 921.

143. Post-Synodal Apostolic Exhortation *Amoris Laetitia* (19 March 2016), 150: AAS 108 (2016), 369.

144. *Address to Young People from the Diocese of Grenoble-Vienne* (17 September 2018): *L'Osservatore Romano*, 19 September 2018, 8.

145. FD 32.

146. *Meeting with Volunteers, XXVIII World Youth Day in Rio de Janeiro* (28 July 2013): *Insegnamenti* 1, 2 (2013), 125.

147. Episcopal Conference of Colombia, *Mensaje Cristiano sobre el matrimonio* (14 May 1981).

148. United States Conference of Catholic Bishops, *Sons and Daughters of Light: A Pastoral Plan for Ministry with Young Adults,* November 12, 1996, Part One, 3.

149. Encyclical Letter *Laudato Si'* (24 May 2015), 128: AAS 107 (2015), 898.

150. Ibid., 125: AAS 107 (2015), 897.

151. FD 40.

152. Apostolic Exhortation *Gaudete et Exsultate* (19 March 2018), 167.

153. Ibid., 168.

154. Ibid., 170.

155. FD 108.

156. Ibid.

157. Apostolic Exhortation *Gaudete et Exsultate* (19 March 2018), 171.

158. Ibid., 172.

159. *Address of Pope Francis at the Prayer Vigil in Preparation for the XXXIV World Youth Day,* Papal Basilica of Saint Mary Major (8 April 2017): AAS 109 (2017), 447.

160. Romano Guardini, *Die Lebensalter. Ihre ethische und pädagogische Bedeutung,* Würzburg, 3rd ed., 1955, 20.

161. Cf. Apostolic Exhortation *Gaudete et Exsultate* (19 March 2018), 169.

162. Apostolic Exhortation *Evangelii Gaudium* (24 November 2013), 222: AAS 105 (2013), 1111.

163. Saint John Paul II, Post-Synodal Apostolic Exhortation *Pastores Dabo Vobis* (25 March 1992), 10: AAS 84 (1992), 672.

164. *Prayer Vigil with Young Italians at the Circus Maximus in Rome* (11 August 2018): *L'Osservatore Romano,* 13–14 August 2018, 6.

"Aperuit Illis"

Apostolic Letter Issued Motu Proprio
by the Supreme Pontiff Francis

Instituting the Sunday of the Word of God

September 30, 2019

APOSTOLIC LETTER
ISSUED "MOTU PROPRIO"
BY THE SUPREME PONTIFF
FRANCIS
"APERUIT ILLIS"
INSTITUTING THE
SUNDAY OF THE WORD OF GOD

1. "He opened their minds to understand the Scriptures" (Lk 24:45). This was one of the final acts of the risen Lord before his Ascension. Jesus appeared to the assembled disciples, broke bread with them, and opened their minds to the understanding of the sacred Scriptures. To them, amid their fear and bewilderment, he unveiled the meaning of the paschal mystery: that in accordance with the Father's eternal plan he had to suffer and rise from the dead, in order to bring repentance and the forgiveness of sins (cf. Lk 24:26, 46–47). He then promised to send the Holy Spirit, who would give them strength to be witnesses of this saving mystery (cf. Lk 24:49).

The relationship between the Risen Lord, the community of believers and sacred Scripture is essential to our identity as Christians. Without the Lord who opens our minds to them, it is impossible to understand the Scriptures in depth. Yet the contrary is equally true: without the Scriptures, the events of the mission of Jesus and of his Church in this world would remain incomprehensible. Hence, Saint Jerome could rightly claim: "Ignorance of the Scriptures is ignorance of Christ" (*Commentary on the Book of Isaiah*, Prologue: PL 24,17B).

2. At the conclusion of the Extraordinary Jubilee of Mercy, I proposed setting aside "a Sunday given over entirely to the word of God, so as to appreciate the inexhaustible riches contained in that constant dialogue between the Lord and his people" (*Misericordia et Misera*, 7). Devoting a specific Sunday of the liturgical year to the word of God can enable

the Church to experience anew how the risen Lord opens up for us the treasury of his word and enables us to proclaim its unfathomable riches before the world. Here, we are reminded of the teaching of Saint Ephrem: "Who is able to understand, Lord, all the richness of even one of your words? There is more that eludes us than what we can understand. We are like the thirsty drinking from a fountain. Your word has as many aspects as the perspectives of those who study it. The Lord has colored his word with diverse beauties, so that those who study it can contemplate what stirs them. He has hidden in his word all treasures, so that each of us may find a richness in what he or she contemplates" (*Commentary on the Diatessaron*, 1, 18).

With this Letter, I wish to respond to the many requests I have received from the people of God that the entire Church celebrate, in unity of purpose, a Sunday of the Word of God. It is now common for the Christian community to set aside moments to reflect on the great importance of the word of God for everyday living. The various local Churches have undertaken a wealth of initiatives to make the sacred Scripture more accessible to believers, to increase their gratitude for so great a gift, and to help them to strive daily to embody and bear witness to its teachings.

The Second Vatican Council gave great impulse to the rediscovery of the word of God, thanks to its Dogmatic Constitution *Dei Verbum*, a document that deserves to be read and appropriated ever anew. The Constitution clearly expounds the nature of sacred Scripture, its transmission from generation to generation (Chapter II), its divine inspiration (Chapter III) embracing the Old and New Testaments (Chapters IV and V), and the importance of Scripture for the life of the Church (Chapter VI). To advance this teaching, Pope Benedict XVI convoked an Assembly of the Synod of Bishops in 2008 on "The Word of God in the Life and Mission of the Church," and then issued the Apostolic Exhortation *Verbum Domini*, whose teaching remains fundamental for our communities.[1] That document emphasizes in particular the performative character of the Word of God, especially in the context of the liturgy, in which its distinctively sacramental character comes to the fore.[2]

It is fitting, then that the life of our people be constantly marked by this decisive relationship with the living word that the Lord never tires of speaking to his Bride, that she may grow in love and faithful witness.

3. Consequently, I hereby declare that the Third Sunday in Ordinary Time is to be devoted to the celebration, study, and dissemination of the word of God. This *Sunday of the Word of God* will thus be a fitting part of that time of the year when we are encouraged to strengthen our bonds with the Jewish people and to pray for Christian unity. This is more than a temporal coincidence: the celebration of the *Sunday of the Word of God* has ecumenical value, since the Scriptures point out, for those who listen, the path to authentic and firm unity.

The various communities will find their own ways to mark this *Sunday* with a certain solemnity. It is important, however, that in the Eucharistic celebration the sacred text be enthroned, in order to focus the attention of the assembly on the normative value of God's word. On this Sunday, it would be particularly appropriate to highlight the proclamation of the word of the Lord and to emphasize in the homily the honor that it is due. Bishops could celebrate the Rite of Installation of Lectors or a similar commissioning of readers, in order to bring out the importance of the proclamation of God's word in the liturgy. In this regard, renewed efforts should be made to provide members of the faithful with the training needed to be genuine proclaimers of the word, as is already the practice in the case of acolytes or extraordinary ministers of Holy Communion. Pastors can also find ways of giving a Bible, or one of its books, to the entire assembly as a way of showing the importance of learning how to read, appreciate, and pray daily with sacred Scripture, especially through the practice of *lectio divina*.

4. The return of the people of Israel to their homeland after the Babylonian exile was marked by the public reading of the book of the Law. In

the book of Nehemiah, the Bible gives us a moving description of that moment. The people assembled in Jerusalem, in the square before the Water Gate, to listen to the Law. They had been scattered in exile, but now they found themselves gathered "as one" around the sacred Scripture (Neh 8:1). The people lent "attentive ears" (Neh 8:3) to the reading of the sacred book, realizing that in its words they would discover the meaning of their lived experience. The reaction to the proclamation was one of great emotion and tears: "[The Levites] read from the book, from the law of God, clearly; and they gave the sense, so that the people understood the reading. And Nehemiah, who was the governor, and Ezra the priest and scribe, and the Levites who taught the people said to all the people, 'This day is holy to the Lord your God; do not mourn or weep.' For all the people wept when they heard the words of the law. Then he said to them, 'Go your way, eat the fat and drink sweet wine and send portions to him for whom nothing is prepared; for this day is holy to our Lord; and do not be grieved, for the joy of the Lord is your strength'" (Neh 8:8–10).

These words contain a great teaching. The Bible cannot be just the heritage of some, much less a collection of books for the benefit of a privileged few. It belongs above all to those called to hear its message and to recognize themselves in its words. At times, there can be a tendency to monopolize the sacred text by restricting it to certain circles or to select groups. It cannot be that way. The Bible is the book of the Lord's people, who, in listening to it, move from dispersion and division toward unity. The word of God unites believers and makes them one people.

5. In this unity born of listening, pastors are primarily responsible for explaining sacred Scripture and helping everyone to understand it. Since it is the people's book, those called to be ministers of the word must feel an urgent need to make it accessible to their community.

The homily, in particular, has a distinctive function, for it possesses "a quasi-sacramental character" (*Evangelii Gaudium*, 142). Helping people to enter more deeply into the word of God through simple and suitable language will allow priests themselves to discover the "beauty of the images used by the Lord to encourage the practice of the good" (ibid.). This is a pastoral opportunity that should not be wasted!

For many of our faithful, in fact, this is the only opportunity they have to grasp the beauty of God's word and to see it applied to their daily lives. Consequently, sufficient time must be devoted to the preparation of the homily. A commentary on the sacred readings cannot be improvised. Those of us who are preachers should not give long, pedantic homilies or wander off into unrelated topics. When we take time to pray and meditate on the sacred text, we can speak from the heart and thus reach the hearts of those who hear us, conveying what is essential and capable of bearing fruit. May we never tire of devoting time and prayer to Scripture, so that it may be received "not as a human word but as what it really is, the word of God" (1 Thes 2:13).

Catechists, too, in their ministry of helping people to grow in their faith, ought to feel an urgent need for personal renewal through familiarity with, and study of, the sacred Scriptures. This will help them foster in their hearers a true dialogue with the word of God.

6. Before encountering his disciples, gathered behind closed doors, and opening their minds to the understanding of the Scriptures (cf. Lk 24:44–45), the risen Lord appeared to two of them on the road to Emmaus from Jerusalem (cf. Lk 24:13–35). Saint Luke's account notes that this happened on the very day of his resurrection, a Sunday. The two disciples were discussing the recent events concerning Jesus' passion and death. Their journey was marked by sorrow and disappointment at his tragic death. They had hoped that he would be the Messiah who would set them free, but they found themselves instead confronted with the scandal of the cross. The risen Lord himself gently draws near and walks with them, yet they do not recognize him (cf. v. 16). Along the way, he questions them, and, seeing that they have not grasped the meaning of his passion and death, he exclaims: "O foolish men, and slow of heart" (v. 25). Then, "beginning with Moses and all the prophets, he interpreted to them the things about himself in all the Scriptures" (v. 27). Christ is the first

exegete! Not only did the Old Testament foretell what he would accomplish, but he himself wished to be faithful to its words, in order to make manifest the one history of salvation whose fulfillment is found in Christ.

7. The Bible, as sacred Scripture, thus speaks of Christ and proclaims him as the one who had to endure suffering and then enter into his glory (cf. v. 26). Not simply a part, but the whole of Scripture speaks of Christ. Apart from the Scriptures, his death and resurrection cannot be rightly understood. That is why one of the most ancient confessions of faith stressed that "Christ died for our sins in accordance with the Scriptures, that he was buried, that he was raised on the third day in accordance with the Scriptures, and that he appeared to Cephas" (1 Cor 15:3–5). Since the Scriptures everywhere speak of Christ, they enable us to believe that his death and resurrection are not myth but history, and are central to the faith of his disciples.

A profound bond links sacred Scripture and the faith of believers. Since faith comes from hearing, and what is heard is based on the word of Christ (cf. Rom 10:17), believers are bound to listen attentively to the word of the Lord, both in the celebration of the liturgy and in their personal prayer and reflection.

8. The journey that the Risen Lord makes with the disciples of Emmaus ended with a meal. The mysterious wayfarer accepts their insistent request: "Stay with us, for it is almost evening and the day is now far spent" (Lk 24:29). They sit down at table, and Jesus takes the bread, blesses it, breaks it, and offers it to them. At that moment, their eyes are opened, and they recognize him (cf. v. 31).

This scene clearly demonstrates the unbreakable bond between sacred Scripture and the Eucharist. As the Second Vatican Council teaches, "The Church has always venerated the divine Scriptures as she has venerated the Lord's body, in that she never ceases, above all in the sacred liturgy, to partake of the bread of life and to offer it to the faithful from the one table of the word of God and the body of Christ" (*Dei Verbum*, 21).

Regular reading of sacred Scripture and the celebration of the Eucharist make it possible for us to see ourselves as part of one another. As Christians, we are a single people, making our pilgrim way through history, sustained by the Lord, present in our midst, who speaks to us and nourishes us. A day devoted to the Bible should not be seen as a yearly event but rather a year-long event, for we urgently need to grow in our knowledge and love of the Scriptures and of the risen Lord, who continues to speak his word and to break bread in the community of believers. For this reason, we need to develop a closer relationship with sacred Scripture; otherwise, our hearts will remain cold and our eyes shut, struck as we are by so many forms of blindness.

Sacred Scripture and the sacraments are thus inseparable. When the sacraments are introduced and illumined by God's word, they become ever more clearly the goal of a process whereby Christ opens our minds and hearts to acknowledge his saving work. We should always keep in mind the teaching found in the Book of Revelation: the Lord is standing at the door and knocking. If anyone should hear his voice and open for him, he will come in and eat with them (cf. 3:20). Christ Jesus is knocking at our door in the words of sacred Scripture. If we hear his voice and open the doors of our minds and hearts, then he will enter our lives and remain ever with us.

9. In the Second Letter to Timothy, which is in some ways his spiritual testament, Saint Paul urges his faithful co-worker to have constant recourse to sacred Scripture. The Apostle is convinced that "all Scripture is inspired by God and profitable for teaching, for reproof, for correction, and for training in righteousness" (3:16). Paul's exhortation to Timothy is fundamental to the teaching of the conciliar Constitution *Dei Verbum* on the great theme of biblical inspiration, which emphasizes the Scriptures' *saving purpose, spiritual dimension,* and inherent *incarnational principle.*

First, recalling Paul's encouragement to Timothy, *Dei Verbum* stresses that "we must acknowledge that the books of Scripture firmly, faithfully and without error, teach that truth which God, for the sake of our salvation, wished to see confided to the sacred Scriptures" (No. 11). Since the Scriptures teach with a view to salvation through faith in Christ (cf. 2 Tm 3:15), the truths contained therein are profitable for our salvation. The Bible is not a collection of history books or a chronicle, but is aimed entirely at the integral salvation of the person. The evident historical setting of the books of the Bible should not make us overlook their primary goal, which is our salvation. Everything is directed to this purpose and essential to the very nature of the Bible, which takes shape as a history of salvation in which God speaks and acts in order to encounter all men and women and to save them from evil and death.

To achieve this saving purpose, sacred Scripture, by the working of the Holy Spirit, makes human words written in human fashion become the word of God (cf. *Dei Verbum*, 12). The role of the Holy Spirit in the Scriptures is primordial. Without the work of the Spirit, there would always be a risk of remaining limited to the written text alone. This would open the way to a fundamentalist reading, which needs to be avoided, lest we betray the inspired, dynamic, and spiritual character of the sacred text. As the Apostle reminds us: "The letter kills, but the Spirit gives life" (2 Cor 3:6). The Holy Spirit, then, makes sacred Scripture the living word of God, experienced and handed down in the faith of his holy people.

10. The work of the Holy Spirit has to do not only with the formation of sacred Scripture; it is also operative in those who hear the word of God. The words of the Council Fathers are instructive: sacred Scripture is to be "read and interpreted in the light of the same Spirit through whom it was written" (*Dei Verbum*, 12). God's revelation attains its completion and fullness in Jesus Christ; nonetheless, the Holy Spirit does not cease to act. It would be reductive indeed to restrict the working of the Spirit to the divine inspiration of sacred Scripture and its various human authors. We need to have confidence in the working of the Holy Spirit as he continues in his own way to provide "inspiration" whenever the Church teaches the sacred Scriptures, whenever the Magisterium authentically

interprets them (cf. ibid., 10), and whenever each believer makes them the norm of his or her spiritual life. In this sense, we can understand the words spoken by Jesus to his disciples when they told him that they now understood the meaning of his parables: "Every scribe who has been trained for the kingdom of heaven is like a householder who brings out of his treasure what is new and what is old" (Mt 13:52).

11. Finally, *Dei Verbum* makes clear that "the words of God, expressed in human language, are in every way like human speech, just as the Word of the eternal Father, in taking upon himself the weak flesh of human beings, also took on their likeness" (No. 13). We can say that the incarnation of the eternal Word gives shape and meaning to the relationship between God's word and our human language, in all its historical and cultural contingency. This event gives rise to Tradition, which is also God's word (cf. ibid., 9). We frequently risk separating sacred Scripture and sacred Tradition, without understanding that together they are the one source of Revelation. The written character of the former takes nothing away from its being fully a living word; in the same way, the Church's living Tradition, which continually hands that word down over the centuries from one generation to the next, possesses that sacred book as the "supreme rule of her faith" (ibid., 21). Moreover, before becoming a written text, sacred Scripture was handed down orally and kept alive by the faith of a people who, in the midst of many others, acknowledged it as their own history and the source of their identity. Biblical faith, then, is based on the living word, not on a book.

12. When sacred Scripture is read in the light of the same Spirit by whom it was written, it remains ever new. The Old Testament is never old once it is part of the New, since all has been transformed thanks to the one Spirit who inspired it. The sacred text as a whole serves a prophetic function regarding not the future but the present of whoever is nourished by this word. Jesus himself clearly stated this at the beginning of his ministry: "Today this Scripture has been fulfilled in your hearing" (Lk 4:21). Those who draw daily nourishment from God's word become, like

Jesus, a contemporary of all those whom they encounter: they are not tempted to fall into sterile nostalgia for the past, or to dream of ethereal utopias yet to come.

Sacred Scripture accomplishes its prophetic work above all in those who listen to it. It proves both sweet and bitter. We are reminded of the words of the prophet Ezekiel when, commanded by the Lord to eat the scroll of the book, he tells us: "It was in my mouth as sweet as honey" (3:3). John the Evangelist too, on the island of Patmos, echoes Ezekiel's experience of eating the scroll, but goes on to add: "It was sweet as honey in my mouth, but when I had eaten it my stomach was made bitter" (Rv 10:10).

The sweetness of God's word leads us to share it with all those whom we encounter in this life and to proclaim the sure hope that it contains (cf. 1 Pt 3:15–16). Its bitterness, in turn, often comes from our realization of how difficult it is to live that word consistently, or our personal experience of seeing it rejected as meaningless for life. We should never take God's word for granted, but instead let ourselves be nourished by it, in order to acknowledge and live fully our relationship with him and with our brothers and sisters.

13. Yet another challenge raised by sacred Scripture has to do with love. God's word constantly reminds us of the merciful love of the Father who calls his children to live in love. The life of Jesus is the full and perfect expression of this divine love, which holds nothing back but offers itself to all without reserve. In the parable of Lazarus, we find a valuable teaching. When both Lazarus and the rich man die, the latter, seeing the poor man Lazarus in Abraham's bosom, asks that Lazarus be sent to his brothers to warn them to love their neighbor, lest they also experience his torment. Abraham's answer is biting: "They have Moses and the prophets; let them hear them" (Lk 16:29). To listen to sacred Scripture and then to practice mercy: this is the great challenge before us in life. God's word has the power to open our eyes and to enable us to renounce

a stifling and barren individualism and instead to embark on a new path of sharing and solidarity.

14. One of the most significant moments in Jesus' relationship with his disciples is found in the account of the Transfiguration. He goes up the mountain with Peter, James, and John to pray. The evangelists tell us that as Jesus' face and clothing became dazzlingly white, two men conversed with him: Moses and Elijah, representing respectively the Law and the Prophets; in other words, sacred Scripture. Peter's reaction to this sight is one of amazement and joy: "Master, it is well that we are here; let us make three tents, one for you and one for Moses and one for Elijah" (Lk 9:33). At that moment a cloud overshadows them, and the disciples are struck with fear.

The Transfiguration reminds us of the Feast of Tabernacles, when Ezra and Nehemiah read the sacred text to the people after their return from exile. At the same time, it foreshadows Jesus' glory, as a way of preparing the disciples for the scandal of the Passion: that divine glory is also evoked by the cloud enveloping the disciples as a symbol of God's presence. A similar transfiguration takes place with sacred Scripture, which transcends itself whenever it nourishes the lives of believers. As the Apostolic Exhortation *Verbum Domini* reminds us: "In rediscovering the interplay between the different senses of Scripture it becomes essential to grasp the *passage from letter to spirit*. This is not an automatic, spontaneous passage; rather, the letter needs to be transcended" (No. 38).

15. Along our path of welcoming God's word into our hearts, the Mother of the Lord accompanies us. She is the one who was called blessed because she believed in the fulfillment of what the Lord had spoken to her (cf. Lk 1:45). Mary's own beatitude is prior to all the beatitudes proclaimed by Jesus about the poor and those who mourn, the meek, the peacemakers, and those who are persecuted, for it is the necessary condition for every other kind of beatitude. The poor are not blessed because they are poor; they become blessed if, like Mary, they believe

in the fulfillment of God's word. A great disciple and master of sacred Scripture, Saint Augustine, once wrote: "Someone in the midst of the crowd, seized with enthusiasm, cried out: 'Blessed is the womb that bore you,' and Jesus replied, 'Rather, blessed are they who hear the word of God and keep it.' As if to say: My mother, whom you call blessed, is indeed blessed, because she keeps the word of God. Not because in her the Word became flesh and dwelt among us, but because she keeps that same word of God by which she was made and which, in her womb, became flesh" (*Tractates on the Gospel of John*, 10, 3).

May the Sunday of the Word of God help his people to grow in religious and intimate familiarity with the sacred Scriptures. For as the sacred author taught of old: "This word is very near to you: it is in your mouth and in your heart for your observance" (Dt 30:14).

Given in Rome, at the Basilica of Saint John Lateran, on 30 September 2019, the liturgical Memorial of Saint Jerome, on the inauguration of the 1600th anniversary of his death.

FRANCISCUS

Notes

1. Cf. AAS 102 (2010), 692–787.

2. "The sacramentality of the word can thus be understood by analogy with the real presence of Christ under the appearances of the consecrated bread and wine. By approaching the altar and partaking in the Eucharistic banquet we truly share in the body and blood of Christ. The proclamation of God's word at the celebration entails an acknowledgment that Christ himself is present, that he speaks to us, and that he wishes to be heard" (*Verbum Domini*, 56).

Querida Amazonia
Beloved Amazon

Post-Synodal Apostolic Exhortation
to the People of God and to
All Persons of Good Will

February 12, 2020

POST-SYNODAL APOSTOLIC EXHORTATION
QUERIDA AMAZONIA
OF THE HOLY FATHER
FRANCIS
TO THE PEOPLE OF GOD
AND TO ALL PERSONS OF GOOD WILL

1. The beloved Amazon region stands before the world in all its splendor, its drama, and its mystery. God granted us the grace of focusing on that region during the Synod held in Rome from 6–27 October last, which concluded by issuing its Final Document, *The Amazon: New Paths for the Church and for an Integral Ecology.*

The Significance of This Exhortation

2. During the Synod, I listened to the presentations and read with interest the reports of the discussion groups. In this Exhortation, I wish to offer my own response to this process of dialogue and discernment. I will not go into all of the issues treated at length in the final document. Nor do I claim to replace that text or to duplicate it. I wish merely to propose a brief framework for reflection that can apply concretely to the life of the Amazon region a synthesis of some of the larger concerns that I have expressed in earlier documents, and that can help guide us to a harmonious, creative, and fruitful reception of the entire synodal process.

3. At the same time, I would like to officially present the Final Document, which sets forth the conclusions of the Synod, which profited from the participation of many people who know better than myself or the Roman Curia the problems and issues of the Amazon region, since they live there, they experience its suffering, and they love it passionately. I have preferred not to cite the Final Document in this Exhortation, because I would encourage everyone to read it in full.

4. May God grant that the entire Church be enriched and challenged by the work of the synodal assembly. May the pastors, consecrated men and women, and lay faithful of the Amazon region strive to apply it, and may it inspire in some way every person of good will.

Dreams for the Amazon Region

5. The Amazon region is a multinational and interconnected whole, a great biome shared by nine countries: Brazil, Bolivia, Colombia, Ecuador, Guyana, Peru, Surinam, Venezuela, and the territory of French Guiana. Yet I am addressing the present Exhortation to the whole world. I am doing so to help awaken their affection and concern for that land which is also "ours," and to invite them to value it and acknowledge it as a sacred mystery. But also because the Church's concern for the problems of this area obliges us to discuss, however briefly, a number of other important issues that can assist other areas of our world in confronting their own challenges.

6. Everything that the Church has to offer must become incarnate in a distinctive way in each part of the world, so that the Bride of Christ can take on a variety of faces that better manifest the inexhaustible riches of God's grace. Preaching must become incarnate, spirituality must become incarnate, ecclesial structures must become incarnate. For this reason, I humbly propose in this brief Exhortation to speak of four great dreams that the Amazon region inspires in me.

7. *I dream of an Amazon region that fights for the rights of the poor, the original peoples, and the least of our brothers and sisters, where their voices can be heard and their dignity advanced.*

I dream of an Amazon region that can preserve its distinctive cultural riches, where the beauty of our humanity shines forth in so many varied ways.

I dream of an Amazon region that can jealously preserve its overwhelming natural beauty and the superabundant life teeming in its rivers and forests.

I dream of Christian communities capable of generous commitment, incarnate in the Amazon region, and giving the Church new faces with Amazonian features.

CHAPTER ONE

A SOCIAL DREAM

8. Our dream is that of an Amazon region that can integrate and promote all its inhabitants, enabling them to enjoy "good living." But this calls for a prophetic plea and an arduous effort on behalf of the poor. For though it is true that the Amazon region is facing an ecological disaster, it also has to be made clear that "a true ecological approach always becomes a social approach; it must integrate questions of justice in debates on the environment, so as to hear both the cry of the earth and the cry of the poor."[1] We do not need an environmentalism "that is concerned for the biome but ignores the Amazonian peoples."[2]

Injustice and Crime

9. The colonizing interests that have continued to expand—legally and illegally—the timber and mining industries, and have expelled or marginalized the indigenous peoples, the river people, and those of African descent, are provoking a cry that rises up to heaven:

> "Many are the trees
> where torture dwelt,
> and vast are the forests purchased with a thousand deaths."[3]

> "The timber merchants have members of parliament,
> while our Amazonia has no one to defend her. . . .
> They exiled the parrots and the monkeys . . .
> the chestnut harvests will never be the same."[4]

10. This encouraged the more recent migrations of the indigenous peoples to the outskirts of the cities. There they find no real freedom from their troubles, but rather the worst forms of enslavement, subjection, and poverty. Those cities, marked by great inequality, where the majority of

the population of the Amazon region now live, are witnessing an increase of xenophobia, sexual exploitation, and human trafficking. The cry of the Amazon region does not rise up from the depths of the forests alone, but from the streets of its cities as well.

11. There is no need for me to repeat here the ample diagnoses presented before and during the Synod. Yet let us at least listen to one of the voices that was heard: "We are being affected by the timber merchants, ranchers and other third parties. Threatened by economic actors who import a model alien to our territories. The timber industries enter the territory in order to exploit the forest, whereas we protect the forest for the sake of our children, for there we have meat, fish, medicinal plants, fruit trees. . . . The construction of hydroelectric plants and the project of waterways has an impact on the river and on the land. . . . We are a region of stolen territories."[5]

12. My predecessor Benedict XVI condemned "the devastation of the environment and the Amazon basin, and the threats against the human dignity of the peoples living in that region."[6] I would add that many of these tragic situations were related to a false "mystique of the Amazon." It is well known that, ever since the final decades of the last century, the Amazon region has been presented as an enormous empty space to be filled, a source of raw resources to be developed, a wild expanse to be domesticated. None of this recognizes the rights of the original peoples; it simply ignores them as if they did not exist, or acts as if the lands on which they live do not belong to them. Even in the education of children and young people, the indigenous were viewed as intruders or usurpers. Their lives, their concerns, their ways of struggling to survive were of no interest. They were considered more an obstacle needing to be eliminated than as human beings with the same dignity as others and possessed of their own acquired rights.

13. Certain slogans contributed to this mistaken notion, including the slogan "Don't give it away!"[7] as if this sort of takeover could only come

from other countries, whereas in fact local powers, using the excuse of development, were also party to agreements aimed at razing the forest—together with the life forms that it shelters—with impunity and indiscriminately. The original peoples often witnessed helplessly the destruction of the natural surroundings that enabled them to be nourished and kept healthy, to survive and to preserve a way of life in a culture which gave them identity and meaning. The imbalance of power is enormous; the weak have no means of defending themselves, while the winners take it all, and "the needy nations grow more destitute, while the rich nations become even richer."[8]

14. The businesses, national or international, which harm the Amazon and fail to respect the right of the original peoples to the land and its boundaries, and to self-determination and prior consent, should be called for what they are: injustice and crime. When certain businesses out for quick profit appropriate lands and end up privatizing even potable water, or when local authorities give free access to the timber companies, mining or oil projects, and other businesses that raze the forests and pollute the environment, economic relationships are unduly altered and become an instrument of death. They frequently resort to utterly unethical means such as penalizing protests and even taking the lives of indigenous peoples who oppose projects, intentionally setting forest fires, and suborning politicians and the indigenous people themselves. All this accompanied by grave violations of human rights and new forms of slavery affecting women in particular, the scourge of drug trafficking used as a way of subjecting the indigenous peoples, or human trafficking that exploits those expelled from their cultural context. We cannot allow globalization to become "a new version of colonialism."[9]

To Feel Outrage and to Beg Forgiveness

15. We need to feel outrage,[10] as Moses did (cf. Ex 11:8), as Jesus did (cf. Mk 3:5), as God does in the face of injustice (cf. Am 2:4–8; 5:7–12; Ps 106:40). It is not good for us to become inured to evil; it is not good when

our social consciousness is dulled before "an exploitation that is leaving destruction and even death throughout our region . . . jeopardizing the lives of millions of people and especially the habitat of peasants and indigenous peoples."[11] The incidents of injustice and cruelty that took place in the Amazon region even in the last century ought to provoke profound abhorrence, but they should also make us more sensitive to the need to acknowledge current forms of human exploitation, abuse, and killing. With regard to the shameful past, let us listen, for example, to an account of the sufferings of the indigenous people during the "rubber age" in the Venezuelan Amazon region: "They gave no money to the indigenous people, but only merchandise, for which they charged dearly and the people never finished paying for it. . . . They would pay for it but they were told, 'You are racking up a debt' and the indigenous person would have to go back to work. . . . More than twenty ye'kuana towns were entirely razed to the ground. The ye'kuana women were raped and their breasts amputated, pregnant women had their children torn from the womb, men had their fingers or hands cut off so they could not sail . . . along with other scenes of the most absurd sadism."[12]

16. Such a history of suffering and contempt does not heal easily. Nor has colonization ended; in many places, it has been changed, disguised and concealed,[13] while losing none of its contempt for the life of the poor and the fragility of the environment. As the bishops of the Brazilian Amazon have noted, "The history of the Amazon region shows that it was always a minority that profited from the poverty of the majority and from the unscrupulous plundering of the region's natural riches, God's gift to the peoples who have lived there for millennia and to the immigrants who arrived in centuries past."[14]

17. Yet even as we feel this healthy sense of indignation, we are reminded that it is possible to overcome the various colonizing mentalities and to build networks of solidarity and development. "The challenge, in short, is to ensure a globalization in solidarity, a globalization without marginalization."[15] Alternatives can be sought for sustainable herding

and agriculture, sources of energy that do not pollute, dignified means of employment that do not entail the destruction of the natural environment and of cultures. At the same time, the indigenous peoples and the poor need to be given an education suited to developing their abilities and empowering them. These are the goals to which the genuine talent and shrewdness of political leaders should be directed. Not as a way of restoring to the dead the life taken from them, or even of compensating the survivors of that carnage, but at least today to be authentically human.

18. It is encouraging to remember that amid the grave excesses of the colonization of the Amazon region, so full of "contradictions and suffering,"[16] many missionaries came to bring the Gospel, leaving their homes and leading an austere and demanding life alongside those who were most defenseless. We know that not all of them were exemplary, yet the work of those who remained faithful to the Gospel also inspired "a legislation like the Laws of the Indies, which defended the dignity of the indigenous peoples from violence against their peoples and territories."[17] Since it was often the priests who protected the indigenous peoples from their plunderers and abusers, the missionaries recounted that "they begged insistently that we not abandon them and they extorted from us the promise that we would return."[18]

19. Today the Church can be no less committed. She is called to hear the plea of the Amazonian peoples and "to exercise with transparency her prophetic mission."[19] At the same time, since we cannot deny that the wheat was mixed with the tares, and that the missionaries did not always take the side of the oppressed, I express my shame and once more "I humbly ask forgiveness, not only for the offenses of the Church herself, but for the crimes committed against the native peoples during the so-called conquest of America"[20] as well as for the terrible crimes that followed throughout the history of the Amazon region. I thank the members of the original peoples and I repeat: "Your lives cry out. . . . You are living memory of the mission that God has entrusted to us all: the protection of our common home."[21]

A Sense of Community

20. Efforts to build a just society require a capacity for fraternity, a spirit of human fellowship. Hence, without diminishing the importance of personal freedom, it is clear that the original peoples of the Amazon region have a strong sense of community. It permeates "their work, their rest, their relationships, their rites and celebrations. Everything is shared; private areas—typical of modernity—are minimal. Life is a communal journey where tasks and responsibilities are apportioned and shared on the basis of the common good. There is no room for the notion of an individual detached from the community or from the land."[22] Their relationships are steeped in the surrounding nature, which they feel and think of as a reality that integrates society and culture, and a prolongation of their bodies, personal, familial and communal:

> "The morning star draws near,
> the wings of the hummingbirds flutter;
> my heart pounds louder than the cascade:
> with your lips I will water the land
> as the breeze softly blows among us."[23]

21. All this makes even more unsettling the sense of bewilderment and uprootedness felt by those indigenous people who feel forced to migrate to the cities, as they attempt to preserve their dignity amid more individualistic urban habitats and a hostile environment. How do we heal all these hurts, how do we bring serenity and meaning to these uprooted lives? Given situations like these, we ought to appreciate and accompany the efforts made by many of those groups to preserve their values and way of life, and to integrate in new situations without losing them, but instead offering them as their own contribution to the common good.

22. Christ redeemed the whole person, and he wishes to restore in each of us the capacity to enter into relationship with others. The Gospel proposes the divine charity welling up in the heart of Christ and generating a pursuit of justice that is at once a hymn of fraternity and of solidarity,

an impetus to the culture of encounter. The wisdom of the way of life of the original peoples—for all its limitations—encourages us to deepen this desire. In view of this, the bishops of Ecuador have appealed for "a new social and cultural system which privileges fraternal relations within a framework of acknowledgment and esteem for the different cultures and ecosystems, one capable of opposing every form of discrimination and oppression between human beings."[24]

Broken Institutions

23. In the Encyclical *Laudato Si'*, I noted that "if everything is related, then the health of the society's institutions has consequences for the environment and the quality of human life. . . . Within each social stratum, and between them, institutions develop to regulate human relationships. Anything which weakens those institutions has negative consequences, such as injustice, violence and loss of freedom. A number of countries have a relatively low level of institutional effectiveness, which results in greater problems for their people."[25]

24. Where do the institutions of civil society in the Amazon region stand? The Synod's *Instrumentum Laboris*, which synthesizes contributions made by numerous individuals and groups from the Amazon region, speaks of "a culture that poisons the state and its institutions, permeating all social strata, including the indigenous communities. We are talking about a true moral scourge; as a result, there is a loss of confidence in institutions and their representatives, which totally discredits politics and social organizations. The Amazonian peoples are not immune to corruption, and they end up being its principal victims."[26]

25. Nor can we exclude the possibility that members of the Church have been part of networks of corruption, at times to the point of agreeing to keep silent in exchange for economic assistance for ecclesial works. Precisely for this reason, proposals were made at the Synod to insist that "special attention be paid to the provenance of donations or other kinds

of benefits, as well as to investments made by ecclesiastical institutions or individual Christians."[27]

Social Dialogue

26. The Amazon region ought to be a place of social dialogue, especially between the various original peoples, for the sake of developing forms of fellowship and joint struggle. The rest of us are called to participate as "guests" and to seek out with great respect paths of encounter that can enrich the Amazon region. If we wish to dialogue, we should do this in the first place with the poor. They are not just another party to be won over, or merely another individual seated at a table of equals. They are our principal dialogue partners, those from whom we have the most to learn, to whom we need to listen out of a duty of justice, and from whom we must ask permission before presenting our proposals. Their words, their hopes, and their fears should be the most authoritative voice at any table of dialogue on the Amazon region. And the great question is: "What is their idea of 'good living' for themselves and for those who will come after them?"

27. Dialogue must not only favor the preferential option on behalf of the poor, the marginalized, and the excluded, but also respect them as having a leading role to play. Others must be acknowledged and esteemed precisely as others, each with his or her own feelings, choices, and ways of living and working. Otherwise, the result would be, once again, "a plan drawn up by the few for the few,"[28] if not "a consensus on paper or a transient peace for a contented minority."[29] Should this be the case, "a prophetic voice must be raised,"[30] and we as Christians are called to make it heard.

This gives rise to the following dream.

CHAPTER TWO

A CULTURAL DREAM

28. The important thing is to promote the Amazon region, but this does not imply colonizing it culturally but instead helping it to bring out the best of itself. That is in fact what education is meant to do: to cultivate without uprooting, to foster growth without weakening identity, to be supportive without being invasive. Just as there are potentialities in nature that could be lost forever, something similar could happen with cultures that have a message yet to be heard, but are now more than ever under threat.

The Amazonian Polyhedron

29. The Amazon region is host to many peoples and nationalities, and over 110 indigenous peoples in voluntary isolation (IPVI).[31] Their situation is very tenuous and many feel that they are the last bearers of a treasure doomed to disappear, allowed to survive only if they make no trouble, while the postmodern colonization advances. They should not be viewed as "uncivilized" savages. They are simply heirs to different cultures and other forms of civilization that in earlier times were quite developed.[32]

30. Prior to the colonial period, the population was concentrated on the shores of the rivers and lakes, but the advance of colonization drove the older inhabitants into the interior of the forest. Today, growing desertification once more drives many of them into the outskirts and sidewalks of the cities, at times in dire poverty but also in an inner fragmentation due to the loss of the values that had previously sustained them. There they usually lack the points of reference and the cultural roots that provided them with an identity and a sense of dignity, and they swell the ranks of the outcast. This disrupts the cultural transmission of a wisdom that had been passed down for centuries from generation to generation. Cities, which should be places of encounter, of mutual enrichment,

and of exchange between different cultures, become a tragic scenario of discarded lives.

31. Each of the peoples that has survived in the Amazon region possesses its own cultural identity and unique richness in our multicultural universe, thanks to the close relationship established by the inhabitants with their surroundings in a nondeterministic symbiosis which is hard to conceive using mental categories imported from without:

> "Once there was a countryside, with its river,
> its animals, its clouds and its trees.
> But sometimes, when the countryside, with its river and trees,
> was nowhere to be seen,
> those things had to spring up in the mind of a child."[33]

> "Make the river your blood. . . .
> Then plant yourself,
> blossom and grow:
> let your roots sink into the ground
> forever and ever,
> and then at last
> become a canoe,
> a skiff, a raft,
> soil, a jug,
> a farmhouse and a man."[34]

32. Human groupings, their lifestyles and their worldviews, are as varied as the land itself, since they have had to adapt themselves to geography and its possibilities. Fishers are not the same as hunters, and the gatherers of the interior are not the same as those who cultivate the flood lands. Even now, we see in the Amazon region thousands of indigenous communities, people of African descent, river people, and city dwellers, who differ from one another and embrace a great human diversity. In each land and its features, God manifests himself and reflects something of

his inexhaustible beauty. Each distinct group, then, in a vital synthesis with its surroundings, develops its own form of wisdom. Those of us who observe this from without should avoid unfair generalizations, simplistic arguments, and conclusions drawn only on the basis of our own mindsets and experiences.

Caring for Roots

33. Here I would like to point out that "a consumerist vision of human beings, encouraged by the mechanisms of today's globalized economy, has a leveling effect on cultures, diminishing the immense variety which is the heritage of all humanity."[35] This especially affects young people, for it has a tendency to "blur what is distinctive about their origins and backgrounds, and turn them into a new line of malleable goods."[36] In order to prevent this process of human impoverishment, there is a need to care lovingly for our roots, since they are "a fixed point from which we can grow and meet new challenges."[37] I urge the young people of the Amazon region, especially the indigenous peoples, to "take charge of your roots, because from the roots comes the strength that will make you grow, flourish and bear fruit."[38] For those of them who are baptized, these roots include the history of the people of Israel and the Church up to our own day. Knowledge of them can bring joy and, above all, a hope capable of inspiring noble and courageous actions.

34. For centuries, the Amazonian peoples passed down their cultural wisdom orally, with myths, legends, and tales, as in the case of "those primitive storytellers who traversed the forests bringing stories from town to town, keeping alive a community which, without the umbilical cord of those stories, distance and lack of communication would have fragmented and dissolved."[39] That is why it is important "to let older people tell their long stories"[40] and for young people to take the time to drink deeply from that source.

35. Although there is a growing risk that this cultural richness will be lost; thanks be to God, in recent years some peoples have taken to writing

down their stories and describing the meaning of their customs. In this way, they themselves can explicitly acknowledge that they possess something more than an ethnic identity and that they are bearers of precious personal, family, and collective memories. I am pleased to see that people who have lost contact with their roots are trying to recover their damaged memory. Then too, the professional sectors have seen a growing sense of Amazonian identity; even for people who are the descendants of immigrants, the Amazon region has become a source of artistic, literary, musical, and cultural inspiration. The various arts, and poetry in particular, have found inspiration in its water, its forests, its seething life, as well as its cultural diversity and its ecological and social challenges.

Intercultural Encounter

36. Like all cultural realities, the cultures of the interior Amazon region have their limits. Western urban cultures have them as well. Factors like consumerism, individualism, discrimination, inequality, and any number of others represent the weaker side of supposedly more developed cultures. The ethnic groups that, in interaction with nature, developed a cultural treasure marked by a strong sense of community, readily notice our darker aspects, which we do not recognize in the midst of our alleged progress. Consequently, it will prove beneficial to listen to their experience of life.

37. Starting from our roots, let us sit around the common table, a place of conversation and of shared hopes. In this way our differences, which could seem like a banner or a wall, can become a bridge. Identity and dialogue are not enemies. Our own cultural identity is strengthened and enriched as a result of dialogue with those unlike ourselves. Nor is our authentic identity preserved by an impoverished isolation. Far be it from me to propose a completely enclosed, a-historic, static "indigenism" that would reject any kind of blending (*mestizaje*). A culture can grow barren when it "becomes inward-looking, and tries to perpetuate obsolete ways of living by rejecting any exchange or debate with regard to

the truth about man."[41] That would be unrealistic, since it is not easy to protect oneself from cultural invasion. For this reason, interest and concern for the cultural values of the indigenous groups should be shared by everyone, for their richness is also our own. If we ourselves do not increase our sense of co-responsibility for the diversity that embellishes our humanity, we can hardly demand that the groups from the interior forest be uncritically open to "civilization."

38. In the Amazon region, even between the different original peoples, it is possible to develop "intercultural relations where diversity does not mean threat, and does not justify hierarchies of power of some over others, but dialogue between different cultural visions, of celebration, of interrelationship and of revival of hope."[42]

Endangered Cultures, Peoples at Risk

39. The globalized economy shamelessly damages human, social, and cultural richness. The disintegration of families that comes about as a result of forced migrations affects the transmission of values, for "the family is and has always been the social institution that has most contributed to keeping our cultures alive."[43] Furthermore, "faced with a colonizing invasion of means of mass communication," there is a need to promote for the original peoples "alternative forms of communication based on their own languages and cultures" and for "the indigenous subjects themselves [to] become present in already existing means of communication."[44]

40. In any project for the Amazon region, "there is a need to respect the rights of peoples and cultures and to appreciate that the development of a social group presupposes an historical process which takes place within a cultural context and demands the constant and active involvement of local people from within their own culture. Nor can the notion of the quality of life be imposed from without, for quality of life must be understood within the world of symbols and customs proper to each human group."[45] If the ancestral cultures of the original peoples

arose and developed in intimate contact with the natural environment, then it will be hard for them to remain unaffected once that environment is damaged.

This leads us to the next dream.

CHAPTER THREE

AN ECOLOGICAL DREAM

41. In a cultural reality like the Amazon region, where there is such a close relationship between human beings and nature, daily existence is always cosmic. Setting others free from their forms of bondage surely involves caring for the environment and defending it,[46] but, even more, helping the human heart to be open with trust to the God who not only has created all that exists, but has also given us himself in Jesus Christ. The Lord, who is the first to care for us, teaches us to care for our brothers and sisters and the environment which he daily gives us. This is the first ecology that that we need.

In the Amazon region, one better understands the words of Benedict XVI when he said that, "alongside the ecology of nature, there exists what can be called a 'human' ecology which in turn demands a 'social' ecology. All this means that humanity . . . must be increasingly conscious of the links between natural ecology, or respect for nature, and human ecology."[47] This insistence that "everything is connected"[48] is particularly true of a territory like the Amazon region.

42. If the care of people and the care of ecosystems are inseparable, this becomes especially important in places where "the forest is not a resource to be exploited; it is a being, or various beings, with which we have to relate."[49] The wisdom of the original peoples of the Amazon region "inspires care and respect for creation, with a clear consciousness of its limits, and prohibits its abuse. To abuse nature is to abuse our ancestors, our brothers and sisters, creation and the Creator, and to mortgage the future."[50] When the indigenous peoples "remain on their land, they themselves care for it best,"[51] provided that they do not let themselves be taken in by the siren songs and the self-serving proposals of power groups. The harm done to nature affects those peoples in a very direct and verifiable way, since, in their words, "we are water, air, earth and life of the

environment created by God. For this reason, we demand an end to the mistreatment and destruction of mother Earth. The land has blood, and it is bleeding; the multinationals have cut the veins of our mother Earth."[52]

This Dream Made of Water

43. In the Amazon region, water is queen; the rivers and streams are like veins, and water determines every form of life:

> "There, in the dead of summer, when the last gusts from the East subside in the still air, the hydrometer takes the place of the thermometer in determining the weather. Lives depend on a painful alternation of falls and rises in the level of the great rivers. These always swell in an impressive manner. The Amazonas overflows its bed and in just a few days raises the level of its waters. . . . The flooding puts a stop to everything. Caught in the dense foliage of the *igarapies*, man awaits with rare stoicism the inexorable end of that paradoxical winter of elevated temperatures. The receding of the waters is summer. It is the resurrection of the primitive activity of those who carry on with the only form of life compatible with the unequal extremes of nature that make the continuation of any effort impossible."[53]

44. The shimmering water of the great Amazon River collects and enlivens all its surroundings:

> "Amazonas,
> capital of the syllables of water,
> father and patriarch, you are
> the hidden eternity
> of the processes of fertilization;
> streams alight upon you like birds."[54]

45. The Amazon is also the spinal column that creates harmony and unity: "The river does not divide us. It unites us and helps us live together amid different cultures and languages."[55] While it is true that in these lands

there are many "Amazon regions," the principal axis is the great river, the offspring of many rivers:

> "From the high mountain range where the snows are eternal, the water descends and traces a shimmering line along the ancient skin of the rock: the Amazon is born. It is born every second. It descends slowly, a sinuous ray of light, and then swells in the lowland. Rushing upon green spaces, it invents its own path and expands. Underground waters well up to embrace the water that falls from the Andes. From the belly of the pure white clouds, swept by the wind, water falls from heaven. It collects and advances, multiplied in infinite pathways, bathing the immense plain. . . . This is the Great Amazonia, covering the humid tropic with its astonishingly thick forest, vast reaches untouched by man, pulsing with life threading through its deep waters. . . . From the time that men have lived there, there has arisen from the depths of its waters, and running through the heart of its forest, a terrible fear: that its life is slowly but surely coming to an end."[56]

46. Popular poets, enamored of its immense beauty, have tried to express the feelings this river evokes and the life that it bestows as it passes amid a dance of dolphins, anacondas, trees, and canoes. Yet they also lament the dangers that menace it. Those poets, contemplatives and prophets, help free us from the technocratic and consumerist paradigm that destroys nature and robs us of a truly dignified existence:

> "The world is suffering from its feet being turned into rubber, its legs into leather, its body into cloth and its head into steel. . . . The world is suffering from its trees being turned into rifles, its ploughshares into tanks, as the image of the sower scattering seed yields to the tank with its flamethrower, which sows only deserts. Only poetry, with its humble voice, will be able to save this world."[57]

The Cry of the Amazon Region

47. Poetry helps give voice to a painful sensation shared by many of us today. The inescapable truth is that, as things stand, this way of treating the Amazon territory spells the end for so much life, for so much beauty, even though people would like to keep thinking that nothing is happening:

> "Those who thought that the river was only a piece of rope,
> a plaything, were mistaken.
> The river is a thin vein on the face of the earth. . . .
> The river is a cord enclosing animals and trees.
> If pulled too tight, the river could burst.
> It could burst and spatter our faces with water and blood."[58]

48. The equilibrium of our planet also depends on the health of the Amazon region. Together with the biome of the Congo and Borneo, it contains a dazzling diversity of woodlands on which rain cycles, climate balance, and a great variety of living beings also depend. It serves as a great filter of carbon dioxide, which helps avoid the warming of the earth. For the most part, its surface is poor in topsoil, with the result that the forest "really grows on the soil and not from the soil."[59] When the forest is eliminated, it is not replaced, because all that is left is a terrain with few nutrients that then turns into a dry land or one poor in vegetation. This is quite serious, since the interior of the Amazonian forest contains countless resources that could prove essential for curing diseases. Its fish, fruit, and other abundant gifts provide rich nutrition for humanity. Furthermore, in an ecosystem like that of the Amazon region, each part is essential for the preservation of the whole. The lowlands and marine vegetation also need to be fertilized by the alluvium of the Amazon. The cry of the Amazon region reaches everyone because "the conquest and exploitation of resources . . . has today reached the point of threatening the environment's hospitable aspect: the environment as 'resource' risks

threatening the environment as 'home.'"[60] The interest of a few powerful industries should not be considered more important than the good of the Amazon region and of humanity as a whole.

49. It is not enough to be concerned about preserving the most visible species in danger of extinction. There is a crucial need to realize that "the good functioning of ecosystems also requires fungi, algae, worms, insects, reptiles and an innumerable variety of microorganisms. Some less numerous species, although generally unseen, nonetheless play a critical role in maintaining the equilibrium of a particular place."[61] This is easily overlooked when evaluating the environmental impact of economic projects of extraction, energy, timber, and other industries that destroy and pollute. So too, the water that abounds in the Amazon region is an essential good for human survival, yet the sources of pollution are increasing.[62]

50. Indeed, in addition to the economic interests of local business persons and politicians, there also exist "huge global economic interests."[63] The answer is not to be found, then, in "internationalizing" the Amazon region,[64] but rather in a greater sense of responsibility on the part of national governments. In this regard, "we cannot fail to praise the commitment of international agencies and civil society organizations which draw public attention to these issues and offer critical cooperation, employing legitimate means of pressure, to ensure that each government carries out its proper and inalienable responsibility to preserve its country's environment and natural resources, without capitulating to spurious local or international interests."[65]

51. To protect the Amazon region, it is good to combine ancestral wisdom with contemporary technical knowledge, always working for a sustainable management of the land while also preserving the lifestyle and value systems of those who live there.[66] They, particularly the original peoples, have a right to receive—in addition to basic education—thorough and straightforward information about projects, their extent and

their consequences and risks, in order to be able to relate that information to their own interests and their own knowledge of the place, and thus to give or withhold their consent, or to propose alternatives.[67]

52. The powerful are never satisfied with the profits they make, and the resources of economic power greatly increase as a result of scientific and technological advances. For this reason, all of us should insist on the urgent need to establish "a legal framework which can set clear boundaries and ensure the protection of ecosystems . . . otherwise, the new power structures based on the techno-economic paradigm may overwhelm not only our politics, but also freedom and justice."[68] If God calls us to listen both to the cry of the poor and that of the earth,[69] then for us, "the cry of the Amazon region to the Creator is similar to the cry of God's people in Egypt (cf. Ex 3:7). It is a cry of slavery and abandonment pleading for freedom."[70]

The prophecy of Contemplation

53. Frequently we let our consciences be deadened, since "distractions constantly dull our realization of just how limited and finite our world really is."[71] From a superficial standpoint, we might well think that "things do not look that serious, and the planet could continue as it is for some time. Such evasiveness serves as a license to carrying on with our present lifestyles and models of production and consumption. This is the way human beings contrive to feed their self-destructive vices: trying not to see them, trying not to acknowledge them, delaying the important decisions and pretending that nothing will happen."[72]

54. In addition, I would also observe that each distinct species has a value in itself, yet "each year sees the disappearance of thousands of plant and animal species which we will never know, which our children will never see, because they have been lost forever. The great majority become extinct for reasons related to human activity. Because of us, thousands of species will no longer give glory to God by their very existence, nor convey their message to us. We have no such right."[73]

55. From the original peoples, we can learn to *contemplate* the Amazon region and not simply analyze it, and thus appreciate this precious mystery that transcends us. We can love it, not simply use it, with the result that love can awaken a deep and sincere interest. Even more, we can *feel intimately a part of it* and not only defend it; then the Amazon region will once more become like a mother to us. For "we do not look at the world from without but from within, conscious of the bonds with which the Father has linked us to all beings."[74]

56. Let us awaken our God-given aesthetic and contemplative sense that so often we let languish. Let us remember that "if someone has not learned to stop and admire something beautiful, we should not be surprised if he or she treats everything as an object to be used and abused without scruple."[75] On the other hand, if we enter into communion with the forest, our voices will easily blend with its own and become a prayer: "as we rest in the shade of an ancient eucalyptus, our prayer for light joins in the song of the eternal foliage."[76] This interior conversion will enable us to weep for the Amazon region and to join in its cry to the Lord.

57. Jesus said: "Are not five sparrows sold for two pennies? Yet not one of them is forgotten in God's sight" (Lk 12:6). God our Father, who created each being in the universe with infinite love, calls us to be his means for hearing the cry of the Amazon region. If we respond to this heartrending plea, it will become clear that the creatures of the Amazon region are not forgotten by our heavenly Father. For Christians, Jesus himself cries out to us from their midst, "because the risen One is mysteriously holding them to himself and directing them toward fullness as their end. The very flowers of the field and the birds which his human eyes contemplated and admired are now imbued with his radiant presence."[77] For all these reasons, we believers encounter in the Amazon region a theological locus, a space where God himself reveals himself and summons his sons and daughters.

Ecological Education and Habits

58. In this regard, we can take one step further and note that an integral ecology cannot be content simply with fine-tuning technical questions or political, juridical, and social decisions. The best ecology always has an educational dimension that can encourage the development of new habits in individuals and groups. Sadly, many of those living in the Amazon region have acquired habits typical of the larger cities, where consumerism and the culture of waste are already deeply rooted. A sound and sustainable ecology, one capable of bringing about change, will not develop unless people are changed, unless they are encouraged to opt for another style of life, one less greedy and more serene, more respectful and less anxious, more fraternal.

59. Indeed, "the emptier a person's heart is, the more he or she needs things to buy, own and consume. It becomes almost impossible to accept the limits imposed by reality. . . . Our concern cannot be limited merely to the threat of extreme weather events, but must also extend to the catastrophic consequences of social unrest. Obsession with a consumerist lifestyle, above all when few people are capable of maintaining it, can only lead to violence and mutual destruction."[78]

60. The Church, with her broad spiritual experience, her renewed appreciation of the value of creation, her concern for justice, her option for the poor, her educational tradition, and her history of becoming incarnate in so many different cultures throughout the world, also desires to contribute to the protection and growth of the Amazon region.

This leads to the next dream, which I would like to share more directly with the Catholic pastors and faithful.

CHAPTER FOUR

AN ECCLESIAL DREAM

61. The Church is called to journey alongside the people of the Amazon region. In Latin America, this journey found privileged expression at the Bishops' Conference in Medellin (1968) and its application to the Amazon region at Santarem (1972),[79] followed by Puebla (1979), Santo Domingo (1992), and Aparecida (2007). The journey continues, and missionary efforts, if they are to develop a Church with an Amazonian face, need to grow in a culture of encounter toward "a multifaceted harmony."[80] But for this incarnation of the Church and the Gospel to be possible, the great missionary proclamation must continue to resound.

The Message That Needs to Be Heard in the Amazon Region

62. Recognizing the many problems and needs that cry out from the heart of the Amazon region, we can respond beginning with organizations, technical resources, opportunities for discussion, and political programs: all these can be part of the solution. Yet as Christians, we cannot set aside the call to faith that we have received from the Gospel. In our desire to struggle side by side with everyone, we are not ashamed of Jesus Christ. Those who have encountered him, those who live as his friends and identify with his message, must inevitably speak of him and bring to others his offer of new life: "Woe to me if I do not preach the Gospel!" (1 Cor 9:16).

63. An authentic option for the poor and the abandoned, while motivating us to liberate them from material poverty and to defend their rights, also involves inviting them to a friendship with the Lord that can elevate and dignify them. How sad it would be if they were to receive from us a body of teachings or a moral code, but not the great message of salvation, the missionary appeal that speaks to the heart and gives meaning to everything else in life. Nor can we be content with a social

message. If we devote our lives to their service, to working for the justice and dignity that they deserve, we cannot conceal the fact that we do so because we see Christ in them and because we acknowledge the immense dignity that they have received from God, the Father who loves them with boundless love.

64. They have a right to hear the Gospel, and above all that first proclamation, the *kerygma,* which is "the principal proclamation, the one which we must hear again and again in different ways, the one which we must announce one way or another."[81] It proclaims a God who infinitely loves every man and woman and has revealed this love fully in Jesus Christ, crucified for us and risen in our lives. I would ask that you re-read the brief summary of this "great message" found in Chapter Four of the Exhortation *Christus Vivit*. That message, expressed in a variety of ways, must constantly resound in the Amazon region. Without that impassioned proclamation, every ecclesial structure would become just another NGO and we would not follow the command given us by Christ: "Go into all the world and preach the Gospel to the whole creation" (Mk 16:15).

65. Any project for growth in the Christian life needs to be centered continually on this message, for "all Christian formation consists of entering more deeply into the kerygma."[82] The fundamental response to this message, when it leads to a personal encounter with the Lord, is fraternal charity, "the new commandment, the first and the greatest of the commandments, and the one that best identifies us as Christ's disciples."[83] Indeed, the kerygma and fraternal charity constitute the great synthesis of the whole content of the Gospel, to be proclaimed unceasingly in the Amazon region. That is what shaped the lives of the great evangelizers of Latin America, like Saint Turibius of Mongrovejo or Saint Joseph of Anchieta.

Inculturation

66. As she perseveres in the preaching of the kerygma, the Church also needs to grow in the Amazon region. In doing so, she constantly reshapes her identity through listening and dialogue with the people, the realities, and the history of the lands in which she finds herself. In this way, she is able to engage increasingly in a necessary process of inculturation that rejects nothing of the goodness that already exists in Amazonian cultures, but brings it to fulfillment in the light of the Gospel.[84] Nor does she scorn the richness of Christian wisdom handed down through the centuries, presuming to ignore the history in which God has worked in many ways. For the Church has a varied face, "not only in terms of space . . . but also of time."[85] Here we see the authentic Tradition of the Church, which is not a static deposit or a museum piece, but the root of a constantly growing tree.[86] This millennial Tradition bears witness to God's work in the midst of his people and "is called to keep the flame alive rather than to guard its ashes."[87]

67. Saint John Paul II taught that in proposing the Gospel message, "the Church does not intend to deny the autonomy of culture. On the contrary, she has the greatest respect for it," since culture "is not only an object of redemption and elevation but can also play a role of mediation and cooperation."[88] Addressing indigenous peoples of America, he reminded them that "a faith that does not become culture is a faith not fully accepted, not fully reflected upon, not faithfully lived."[89] Cultural challenges invite the Church to maintain "a watchful and critical attitude," while at the same time showing "confident attention."[90]

68. Here I would reiterate what I stated about inculturation in the Apostolic Exhortation *Evangelii Gaudium*, based on the conviction that "grace supposes culture, and God's gift becomes flesh in the culture of those who receive it."[91] We can see that it involves a double movement. On the one hand, a fruitful process takes place when the Gospel takes root in a given place, for "whenever a community receives the message of

salvation, the Holy Spirit enriches its culture with the transforming power of the Gospel."[92] On the other hand, the Church herself undergoes a process of reception that enriches her with the fruits of what the Spirit has already mysteriously sown in that culture. In this way, "the Holy Spirit adorns the Church, showing her new aspects of revelation and giving her a new face."[93] In the end, this means allowing and encouraging the inexhaustible riches of the Gospel to be preached "in categories proper to each culture, creating a new synthesis with that particular culture."[94]

69. "The history of the Church shows that Christianity does not have simply one cultural expression,"[95] and "we would not do justice to the logic of the incarnation if we thought of Christianity as monocultural and monotonous."[96] There is a risk that evangelizers who come to a particular area may think that they must not only communicate the Gospel but also the culture in which they grew up, failing to realize that it is not essential "to impose a specific cultural form, no matter how beautiful or ancient it may be."[97] What is needed is courageous openness to the novelty of the Spirit, who is always able to create something new with the inexhaustible riches of Jesus Christ. Indeed, "inculturation commits the Church to a difficult but necessary journey."[98] True, "this is always a slow process and that we can be overly fearful," ending up as "mere onlookers as the Church gradually stagnates."[99] But let us be fearless; let us not clip the wings of the Holy Spirit.

Paths of Inculturation in the Amazon Region

70. For the Church to achieve a renewed inculturation of the Gospel in the Amazon region, she needs to listen to its ancestral wisdom, listen once more to the voice of its elders, recognize the values present in the way of life of the original communities, and recover the rich stories of its peoples. In the Amazon region, we have inherited great riches from the pre-Columbian cultures. These include "openness to the action of God, a sense of gratitude for the fruits of the earth, the sacred character

of human life and esteem for the family, a sense of solidarity and shared responsibility in common work, the importance of worship, belief in a life beyond this earth, and many other values."[100]

71. In this regard, the indigenous peoples of the Amazon Region express the authentic quality of life as "good living." This involves personal, familial, communal, and cosmic harmony and finds expression in a communitarian approach to existence, the ability to find joy and fulfillment in an austere and simple life, and a responsible care of nature that preserves resources for future generations. The aboriginal peoples give us the example of a joyful sobriety and in this sense, "they have much to teach us."[101] They know how to be content with little; they enjoy God's little gifts without accumulating great possessions; they do not destroy things needlessly; they care for ecosystems and they recognize that the earth, while serving as a generous source of support for their life, also has a maternal dimension that evokes respect and tender love. All these things should be valued and taken up in the process of evangelization.[102]

72. While working for them and with them, we are called "to be their friends, to listen to them, to speak for them and to embrace the mysterious wisdom which God wishes to share with us through them."[103] Those who live in cities need to appreciate this wisdom and to allow themselves to be "re-educated" in the face of frenzied consumerism and urban isolation. The Church herself can be a means of assisting this cultural retrieval through a precious synthesis with the preaching of the Gospel. She can also become a sign and means of charity, inasmuch as urban communities must be missionary not only to those in their midst but also to the poor who, driven by dire need, arrive from the interior and are welcomed. In the same way, these communities can stay close to young migrants and help them integrate into the city without falling prey to its networks of depravity. All these forms of ecclesial outreach, born of love, are valuable contributions to a process of inculturation.

73. Inculturation elevates and fulfills. Certainly, we should esteem the indigenous mysticism that sees the interconnection and interdependence of the whole of creation, the mysticism of gratuitousness that loves life as a gift, the mysticism of a sacred wonder before nature and all its forms of life.

At the same time, though, we are called to turn this relationship with God present in the cosmos into an increasingly personal relationship with a "Thou" who sustains our lives and wants to give them a meaning, a "Thou" who knows us and loves us:

> "Shadows float from me, dead wood.
> But the star is born without reproach
> over the expert hands of this child,
> that conquer the waters and the night.
> It has to be enough for me to know
> that you know me
> completely, from before my days."[104]

74. Similarly, a relationship with Jesus Christ, true God and true man, liberator and redeemer, is not inimical to the markedly cosmic worldview that characterizes the indigenous peoples, since he is also the Risen Lord who permeates all things.[105] In Christian experience, "all the creatures of the material universe find their true meaning in the incarnate Word, for the Son of God has incorporated in his person part of the material world, planting in it a seed of definitive transformation."[106] He is present in a glorious and mysterious way in the river, the trees, the fish, and the wind, as the Lord who reigns in creation without ever losing his transfigured wounds, while in the Eucharist he takes up the elements of this world and confers on all things the meaning of the paschal gift.

Social and Spiritual Inculturation

75. Given the situation of poverty and neglect experienced by so many inhabitants of the Amazon region, inculturation will necessarily have a markedly social cast, accompanied by a resolute defense of human

rights; in this way it will reveal the face of Christ, who "wished with special tenderness to be identified with the weak and the poor."[107] Indeed, "from the heart of the Gospel we see the profound connection between evangelization and human advancement."[108] For Christian communities, this entails a clear commitment to the justice of God's kingdom through work for the advancement of those who have been "discarded." It follows that a suitable training of pastoral workers in the Church's social doctrine is most important.

76. At the same time, the inculturation of the Gospel in the Amazon region must better integrate the social and the spiritual, so that the poor do not have to look outside the Church for a spirituality that responds to their deepest yearnings. This does not mean an alienating and individualistic religiosity that would silence social demands for a more dignified life, but neither does it mean ignoring the transcendent and spiritual dimension, as if material development alone were sufficient for human beings. We are thus called not merely to join those two things, but to connect them at a deeper level. In this way, we will reveal the true beauty of the Gospel, which fully humanizes, integrally dignifies persons and peoples, and brings fulfillment to every heart and the whole of life.

Starting Points for an Amazonian Holiness

77. This will give rise to witnesses of holiness with an Amazonian face, not imitations of models imported from other places. A holiness born of encounter and engagement, contemplation and service, receptive solitude and life in community, cheerful sobriety and the struggle for justice. A holiness attained by "each individual in his or her own way,"[109] but also by peoples, where grace becomes incarnate and shines forth with distinctive features. Let us imagine a holiness with Amazonian features, called to challenge the universal Church.

78. A process of inculturation involving not only individuals but also peoples demands a respectful and understanding love for those peoples. This process has already begun in much of the Amazon region. More than

forty years ago, the bishops of the Peruvian Amazon pointed out that in many of the groups present in that region, those to be evangelized, shaped by a varied and changing culture, have been "initially evangelized." As a result, they possess "certain features of popular Catholicism that, perhaps originally introduced by pastoral workers, are now something that the people have made their own, even changing their meaning and handing them down from generation to generation."[110] Let us not be quick to describe as superstition or paganism certain religious practices that arise spontaneously from the life of peoples. Rather, we ought to know how to distinguish the wheat growing alongside the tares, for "popular piety can enable us to see how the faith, once received, becomes embodied in a culture and is constantly passed on."[111]

79. It is possible to take up an indigenous symbol in some way, without necessarily considering it as idolatry. A myth charged with spiritual meaning can be used to advantage and not always considered a pagan error. Some religious festivals have a sacred meaning and are occasions for gathering and fraternity, albeit in need of a gradual process of purification or maturation. A missionary of souls will try to discover the legitimate needs and concerns that seek an outlet in at times imperfect, partial, or mistaken religious expressions, and will attempt to respond to them with an inculturated spirituality.

80. Such a spirituality will certainly be centered on the one God and Lord, while at the same time in contact with the daily needs of people who strive for a dignified life, who want to enjoy life's blessings, to find peace and harmony, to resolve family problems, to care for their illnesses, and to see their children grow up happy. The greatest danger would be to prevent them from encountering Christ by presenting him as an enemy of joy or as someone indifferent to human questions and difficulties.[112] Nowadays, it is essential to show that holiness takes nothing away from our "energy, vitality or joy."[113]

The Inculturation of the Liturgy

81. The inculturation of Christian spirituality in the cultures of the original peoples can benefit in a particular way from the sacraments, since they unite the divine and the cosmic, grace and creation. In the Amazon region, the sacraments should not be viewed in discontinuity with creation. They "are a privileged way in which nature is taken up by God to become a means of mediating supernatural life."[114] They are the fulfillment of creation, in which nature is elevated to become a locus and instrument of grace, enabling us "to embrace the world on a different plane."[115]

82. In the Eucharist, God, "in the culmination of the mystery of the Incarnation, chose to reach our intimate depths through a fragment of matter." The Eucharist "joins heaven and earth; it embraces and penetrates all creation."[116] For this reason, it can be a "motivation for our concerns for the environment, directing us to be stewards of all creation."[117] In this sense, "encountering God does not mean fleeing from this world or turning our back on nature."[118] It means that we can take up into the liturgy many elements proper to the experience of indigenous peoples in their contact with nature, and respect native forms of expression in song, dance, rituals, gestures, and symbols. The Second Vatican Council called for this effort to inculturate the liturgy among indigenous peoples;[119] over fifty years have passed and we still have far to go along these lines.[120]

83. On Sunday, "Christian spirituality incorporates the value of relaxation and festivity. [Nowadays] we tend to demean contemplative rest as something unproductive and unnecessary, but this is to do away with the very thing which is most important about work: its meaning. We are called to include in our work a dimension of receptivity and gratuity."[121] Aboriginal peoples are familiar with this gratuity and this healthy contemplative leisure. Our celebrations should help them experience this in the Sunday liturgy and encounter the light of God's word and the Eucharist, which illumines our daily existence.

84. The sacraments reveal and communicate the God who is close and who comes with mercy to heal and strengthen his children. Consequently, they should be accessible, especially for the poor, and must never be refused for financial reasons. Nor is there room, in the presence of the poor and forgotten of the Amazon region, for a discipline that excludes and turns people away, for in that way they end up being discarded by a Church that has become a toll-house. Rather, "in such difficult situations of need, the Church must be particularly concerned to offer understanding, comfort and acceptance, rather than imposing straightaway a set of rules that only lead people to feel judged and abandoned by the very Mother called to show them God's mercy."[122] For the Church, mercy can become a mere sentimental catchword unless it finds concrete expression in her pastoral outreach.[123]

Inculturation of Forms of Ministry

85. Inculturation should also be increasingly reflected in an incarnate form of ecclesial organization and ministry. If we are to inculturate spirituality, holiness, and the Gospel itself, how can we not consider an inculturation of the ways we structure and carry out ecclesial ministries? The pastoral presence of the Church in the Amazon region is uneven, due in part to the vast expanse of the territory, its many remote places, its broad cultural diversity, its grave social problems, and the preference of some peoples to live in isolation. We cannot remain unconcerned; a specific and courageous response is required of the Church.

86. Efforts need to be made to configure ministry in such a way that it is at the service of a more frequent celebration of the Eucharist, even in the remotest and most isolated communities. At Aparecida, all were asked to heed the lament of the many Amazonian communities "deprived of the Sunday Eucharist for long periods of time."[124] There is also a need for ministers who can understand Amazonian sensibilities and cultures from within.

87. The way of shaping priestly life and ministry is not monolithic; it develops distinctive traits in different parts of the world. This is why it is important to determine what is most specific to a priest, what cannot be delegated. The answer lies in the sacrament of Holy Orders, which configures him to Christ the priest. The first conclusion, then, is that the exclusive character received in Holy Orders qualifies the priest alone to preside at the Eucharist.[125] That is his particular, principal, and non-delegable function. There are those who think that what distinguishes the priest is power, the fact that he is the highest authority in the community. Yet Saint John Paul II explained that, although the priesthood is considered "hierarchical," this function is not meant to be superior to the others, but rather is "totally ordered to the holiness of Christ's members."[126] When the priest is said to be a sign of "Christ the head," this refers principally to the fact that Christ is the source of all grace: he is the head of the Church because "he has the power of pouring out grace upon all the members of the Church."[127]

88. The priest is a sign of that head and wellspring of grace above all when he celebrates the Eucharist, the source and summit of the entire Christian life.[128] That is his great power, a power that can only be received in the sacrament of Holy Orders. For this reason, only the priest can say: "This is my body." There are other words too, that he alone can speak: "I absolve you from your sins." Because sacramental forgiveness is at the service of a worthy celebration of the Eucharist. These two sacraments lie at the heart of the priest's exclusive identity.[129]

89. In the specific circumstances of the Amazon region, particularly in its forests and more remote places, a way must be found to ensure this priestly ministry. The laity can proclaim God's word, teach, organize communities, celebrate certain sacraments, seek different ways to express popular devotion, and develop the multitude of gifts that the Spirit pours out in their midst. But they need the celebration of the Eucharist because it "makes the Church."[130] We can even say that "no Christian community is built up which does not grow from and hinge on the celebration of the

most holy Eucharist."[131] If we are truly convinced that this is the case, then every effort should be made to ensure that the Amazonian peoples do not lack this food of new life and the sacrament of forgiveness.

90. This urgent need leads me to urge all bishops, especially those in Latin America, not only to promote prayer for priestly vocations, but also to be more generous in encouraging those who display a missionary vocation to opt for the Amazon region.[132] At the same time, it is appropriate that the structure and content of both initial and ongoing priestly formation be thoroughly revised, so that priests can acquire the attitudes and abilities demanded by dialogue with Amazonian cultures. This formation must be preeminently pastoral and favor the development of priestly mercy.[133]

Communities Filled with Life

91. The Eucharist is also the great sacrament that signifies and realizes the Church's *unity*.[134] It is celebrated "so that from being strangers, dispersed and indifferent to each another, we may become united, equals and friends."[135] The one who presides at the Eucharist must foster communion, which is not just any unity, but one that welcomes the abundant variety of gifts and charisms that the Spirit pours out upon the community.

92. The Eucharist, then, as source and summit, requires the development of that rich variety. Priests are necessary, but this does not mean that permanent deacons (of whom there should be many more in the Amazon region), religious women, and lay persons cannot regularly assume important responsibilities for the growth of communities, and perform those functions ever more effectively with the aid of a suitable accompaniment.

93. Consequently, it is not simply a question of facilitating a greater presence of ordained ministers who can celebrate the Eucharist. That would be a very narrow aim, were we not also to strive to awaken new life in

communities. We need to promote an encounter with God's word and growth in holiness through various kinds of lay service that call for a process of education—biblical, doctrinal, spiritual, and practical—and a variety of programs of ongoing formation.

94. A Church of Amazonian features requires the stable presence of mature and lay leaders endowed with authority[136] and familiar with the languages, cultures, spiritual experience, and communal way of life in the different places, but also open to the multiplicity of gifts that the Holy Spirit bestows on every one. For wherever there is a particular need, he has already poured out the charisms that can meet it. This requires the Church to be open to the Spirit's boldness, to trust in, and concretely to permit, the growth of a specific ecclesial culture that is distinctively lay. The challenges in the Amazon region demand of the Church a special effort to be present at every level, and this can only be possible through the vigorous, broad, and active involvement of the laity.

95. Many consecrated persons have devoted their energies and a good part of their lives in service to the Kingdom of God in Amazonia. The consecrated life, as capable of dialogue, synthesis, incarnation, and prophecy, has a special place in this diverse and harmonious configuration of the Church in the Amazon region. But it needs a new impetus to inculturation, one that would combine creativity, missionary boldness, sensitivity, and the strength typical of community life.

96. Base communities, when able to combine the defense of social rights with missionary proclamation and spirituality, have been authentic experiences of synodality in the Church's journey of evangelization in the Amazon region. In many cases they "have helped form Christians committed to their faith, disciples and missionaries of the Lord, as is attested by the generous commitment of so many of their members, even to the point of shedding their blood."[137]

97. I encourage the growth of the collaborative efforts being made through the Pan Amazonian Ecclesial Network and other associations

to implement the proposal of Aparecida to "establish a collaborative ministry among the local churches of the various South American countries in the Amazon basin, with differentiated priorities."[138] This applies particularly to relations between Churches located on the borders between nations.

98. Finally, I would note that we cannot always plan projects with stable communities in mind, because the Amazonian region sees a great deal of internal mobility, constant and frequently pendular migration; "the region has effectively become a migration corridor."[139] "Transhumance in the Amazon has not been well understood or sufficiently examined from the pastoral standpoint."[140] Consequently, thought should be given to itinerant missionary teams and "support provided for the presence and mobility of consecrated men and women closest to those who are most impoverished and excluded."[141] This is also a challenge for our urban communities, which ought to come up with creative and generous ways, especially on the outskirts, to be close and welcoming to families and young people who arrive from the interior.

The Strength and Gift of Women

99. In the Amazon region, there are communities that have long preserved and handed on the faith even though no priest has come their way, even for decades. This could happen because of the presence of strong and generous women who, undoubtedly called and prompted by the Holy Spirit, baptized, catechized, prayed, and acted as missionaries. For centuries, women have kept the Church alive in those places through their remarkable devotion and deep faith. Some of them, speaking at the Synod, moved us profoundly by their testimony.

100. This summons us to broaden our vision, lest we restrict our understanding of the Church to her functional structures. Such a reductionism would lead us to believe that women would be granted a greater status and participation in the Church only if they were admitted to Holy Orders. But that approach would in fact narrow our vision; it would

lead us to clericalize women, diminish the great value of what they have already accomplished, and subtly make their indispensable contribution less effective.

101. Jesus Christ appears as the Spouse of the community that celebrates the Eucharist through the figure of a man who presides as a sign of the one Priest. This dialogue between the Spouse and his Bride, which arises in adoration and sanctifies the community, should not trap us in partial conceptions of power in the Church. The Lord chose to reveal his power and his love through two human faces: the face of his divine Son made man and the face of a creature, a woman, Mary. Women make their contribution to the Church in a way that is properly theirs, by making present the tender strength of Mary, the Mother. As a result, we do not limit ourselves to a functional approach, but enter instead into the inmost structure of the Church. In this way, we will fundamentally realize why, without women, the Church breaks down, and how many communities in the Amazon would have collapsed, had women not been there to sustain them, keep them together, and care for them. This shows the kind of power that is typically theirs.

102. We must keep encouraging those simple and straightforward gifts that enabled women in the Amazon region to play so active a role in society, even though communities now face many new and unprecedented threats. The present situation requires us to encourage the emergence of other forms of service and charisms that are proper to women and responsive to the specific needs of the peoples of the Amazon region at this moment in history.

103. In a synodal Church, those women who in fact have a central part to play in Amazonian communities should have access to positions, including ecclesial services, that do not entail Holy Orders and that can better signify the role that is theirs. Here it should be noted that these services entail stability, public recognition, and a commission from the bishop. This would also allow women to have a real and effective impact on the

organization, the most important decisions, and the direction of communities, while continuing to do so in a way that reflects their womanhood.

Expanding Horizons beyond Conflicts

104. It often happens that in particular places pastoral workers envisage very different solutions to the problems they face, and consequently propose apparently opposed forms of ecclesial organization. When this occurs, it is probable that the real response to the challenges of evangelization lies in transcending the two approaches and finding other, better ways, perhaps not yet even imagined. Conflict is overcome at a higher level, where each group can join the other in a new reality, while remaining faithful to itself. Everything is resolved "on a higher plane and preserves what is valid and useful on both sides."[142] Otherwise, conflict traps us; "we lose our perspective, our horizons shrink and reality itself begins to fall apart."[143]

105. In no way does this mean relativizing problems, fleeing from them, or letting things stay as they are. Authentic solutions are never found by dampening boldness, shirking concrete demands or assigning blame to others. On the contrary, solutions are found by "overflow," that is, by transcending the contraposition that limits our vision and recognizing a greater gift that God is offering. From that new gift, accepted with boldness and generosity, from that unexpected gift which awakens a new and greater creativity, there will pour forth as from an overflowing fountain the answers that contraposition did not allow us to see. In its earliest days, the Christian faith spread remarkably in accordance with this way of thinking, which enabled it, from its Jewish roots, to take shape in the Greco-Roman cultures, and in time to acquire distinctive forms. Similarly, in this historical moment, the Amazon region challenges us to transcend limited perspectives and "pragmatic" solutions mired in partial approaches, in order to seek paths of inculturation that are broader and bolder.

Ecumenical and Interreligious Coexistence

106. In an Amazonian region characterized by many religions, we believers need to find occasions to speak to one another and to act together for the common good and the promotion of the poor. This has nothing to do with watering down or concealing our deepest convictions when we encounter others who think differently than ourselves. If we believe that the Holy Spirit can work amid differences, then we will try to let ourselves be enriched by that insight, while embracing it from the core of our own convictions and our own identity. For the deeper, stronger, and richer that identity is, the more we will be capable of enriching others with our own proper contribution.

107. We Catholics possess in sacred Scripture a treasure that other religions do not accept, even though at times they may read it with interest and even esteem some of its teachings. We attempt to do something similar with the sacred texts of other religions and religious communities, which contain "precepts and doctrines that . . . often reflect a ray of that truth which enlightens all men and women."[144] We also possess a great treasure in the seven sacraments, which some Christian communities do not accept in their totality or in the same sense. At the same time that we believe firmly in Jesus as the sole Redeemer of the world, we cultivate a deep devotion to his Mother. Even though we know that this is not the case with all Christian confessions, we feel it our duty to share with the Amazon region the treasure of that warm, maternal love which we ourselves have received. In fact, I will conclude this Exhortation with a few words addressed to Mary.

108. None of this needs to create enmity between us. In a true spirit of dialogue, we grow in our ability to grasp the significance of what others say and do, even if we cannot accept it as our own conviction. In this way, it becomes possible to be frank and open about our beliefs, while continuing to discuss, to seek points of contact, and above all, to work and struggle together for the good of the Amazon region. The strength of what unites

all of us as Christians is supremely important. We can be so attentive to what divides us that at times we no longer appreciate or value what unites us. And what unites us is what lets us remain in this world without being swallowed up by its immanence, its spiritual emptiness, its complacent selfishness, its consumerist and self-destructive individualism.

109. All of us, as Christians, are united by faith in God, the Father who gives us life and loves us so greatly. We are united by faith in Jesus Christ, the one Savior, who set us free by his precious blood and his glorious resurrection. We are united by our desire for his word that guides our steps. We are united by the fire of the Spirit, who sends us forth on mission. We are united by the new commandment that Jesus left us, by the pursuit of the civilization of love, and by passion for the kingdom that the Lord calls us to build with him. We are united by the struggle for peace and justice. We are united by the conviction that not everything ends with this life, but that we are called to the heavenly banquet, where God will wipe away every tear and take up all that we did for those who suffer.

110. All this unites us. How can we not struggle together? How can we not pray and work together, side by side, to defend the poor of the Amazon region, to show the sacred countenance of the Lord, and to care for his work of creation?

CONCLUSION

MOTHER OF THE AMAZON REGION

111. After sharing a few of my dreams, I encourage everyone to advance along concrete paths that can allow the reality of the Amazon region to be transformed and set free from the evils that beset it. Let us now lift our gaze to Mary. The Mother whom Christ gave us is also the one Mother of all, who reveals herself in the Amazon region in distinct ways. We know that "the indigenous peoples have a vital encounter with Jesus Christ in many ways; but the path of Mary has contributed greatly to this encounter."[145] Faced with the marvel of the Amazon region, which we discovered ever more fully during the preparation and celebration of the Synod, I consider it best to conclude this Exhortation by turning to her:

Mother of life,
in your maternal womb Jesus took flesh,
the Lord of all that exists.
Risen, he transfigured you by his light
and made you the Queen of all creation.
For that reason, we ask you, Mary, to reign
in the beating heart of Amazonia.
Show yourself the Mother of all creatures,
in the beauty of the flowers, the rivers,
the great river that courses through it,
and all the life pulsing in its forests.
Tenderly care for this explosion of beauty.
Ask Jesus to pour out all his love
on the men and women who dwell there,
that they may know how to appreciate and care for it.
Bring your Son to birth in their hearts,
so that he can shine forth in the Amazon region,
in its peoples and in its cultures,

by the light of his word,
by his consoling love,
by his message of fraternity and justice.
And at every Eucharist,
may all this awe and wonder be lifted up
to the glory of the Father.
Mother, look upon the poor of the Amazon region,
for their home is being destroyed by petty interests.
How much pain and misery,
how much neglect and abuse there is
in this blessed land
overflowing with life!
Touch the hearts of the powerful,
for, even though we sense that the hour is late,
you call us to save what is still alive.
Mother whose heart is pierced,
who yourself suffer in your mistreated sons and daughters,
and in the wounds inflicted on nature,
reign in the Amazon, together with your Son.
Reign so that no one else can claim lordship
over the handiwork of God.
We trust in you, Mother of life.
Do not abandon us in this dark hour.
Amen.

Given in Rome, at the Cathedral of Saint John Lateran, on 2 February, the Feast of the Presentation of the Lord, in the year 2020, the seventh of my Pontificate.

FRANCISCUS

Notes

1. Encyclical Letter *Laudato Si'* (24 May 2015), 49: AAS 107 (2015), 866.
2. *Instrumentum Laboris,* 45.
3. Ana Varela Tafur, "Timareo," in *Lo que no veo en visiones,* Lima, 1992.
4. Jorge Vega Márquez, "Amazonia solitária," in *Poesía obrera,* Cobija-Pando-Bolivia, 2009, 39.
5. Red Eclesial Panamazónica (REPAM), Brazil, *Síntesis del aporte al Sínodo,* 120; cf. Instrumentum Laboris, 45.
6. Address to Young People, São Paulo, Brazil (10 May 2007), 2.
7. Cf. Alberto C. Araújo, "Imaginario amazónico," in *Amazonia real: amazoniareal.com.br* (29 January 2014).
8. Saint Paul VI, Encyclical Letter *Populorum Progressio* (26 March 1967), 57: AAS 59 (1967), 285.
9. Saint John Paul II, *Address to the Pontifical Academy of Social Sciences* (27 April 2001), 4: AAS 93 (2001), 600.
10. Cf. *Instrumentum Laboris,* 41.
11. Fifth General Conference of the Latin American and Caribbean Bishops, *Aparecida Document* (29 June 2007), 473.
12. Ramón Iribertegui, *Amazonas: El hombre y el caucho,* ed. Vicariato Apostólico de Puerto Ayacucho-Venezuela, Monografía n. 4, Caracas, 1987, 307ff.
13. Cf. "Amarílis Tupiassú," "Amazônia, das travessias lusitanas à literatura de até agora," in *Estudos Avançados* vol. 19, n. 53, São Paulo (Jan./Apr. 2005): "In effect, after the end of the first colonization, the Amazon region continued to be an area subject to age-old greed, now under new rhetorical guises . . . on the part of "civilizing" agents who did not even need to be personified in order to generate and multiply the new faces of the old decimation, now through a slow death."
14. Bishops of the Brazilian Amazon Region, *Carta al Pueblo de Dios,* Santarem-Brazil (6 July 2012).
15. Saint John Paul II, *Message for the 1998 World Day of Peace,* 3: AAS 90 (1998), 150.
16. Third General Conference of the Latin American and Caribbean Bishops, *Puebla Document* (23 March 1979), 6.
17. *Instrumentum Laboris,* 6. Pope Paul III, in his the Brief *Veritas Ipsa* (2 June 1537), condemned racist theses and recognized that the native peoples, whether Christian or not, possess the dignity of the human person, enjoy the right to their possessions, and may not be reduced to slavery. The Pope declared: "As truly men . . . are by no means to be deprived of their liberty or the possession of their property, even though they be outside the faith of Jesus Christ." This magisterial teaching was reaffirmed by Popes Gregory XIV, Bull *Cum Sicuti* (28 April 1591); Urban VIII, Bull *Commissum Nobis* (22 April 1639); Benedict XIV, Bull *Immensa Pastorum Principis* to the Bishops of Brazil (20 December 1741); Gregory XVI, Brief *In Supremo* (3 December 1839); Leo XIII, *Epistle to the Bishops of Brazil on Slavery* (15

May 1888); and Saint John Paul II, *Message to the Indigenous People of America*, Santo Domingo (12 October 1992), 2: *Insegnamenti* 15/2 (1982), 346.

18. Frederico Beníco de Sousa Costa, *Pastoral Letter* (1909). Ed. Imprenta del gobierno del estado de Amazonas, Manaus, 1994, 83.

19. *Instrumentum Laboris*, 7.

20. *Address at the Second World Meeting of Popular Movements*, Santa Cruz de la Sierra-Bolivia (9 July 2015).

21. *Address at the Meeting with Indigenous People of Amazonia*, Puerto Maldonado-Peru (19 January 2018): AAS 110 (2018), 300.

22. *Instrumentum Laboris*, 24.

23. Yana Lucila Lema, *Tamyahuan Shamakupani (Con la lluvia estoy viviendo)*, 1, at http://siwarmayu.com/es/yana-lucila-lema-6-poemas-de-tamyawan-shamukupani-con-la-lluvia-estoy-viviendo.

24. Bishops' Conference of Ecuador, *Cuidemos nuestro planeta* (20 April 2012), 3.

25. No. 142: AAS 107 (2015), 904–5.

26. No. 82.

27. Ibid., 83.

28. Apostolic Exhortation *Evangelii Gaudium* (24 November 2013), 239: AAS 105 (2013), 1116.

29. Ibid., 218: AAS 105 (2013), 1110.

30. Ibid.

31. Cf. *Instrumentum Laboris*, 57.

32. Cf. Evaristo Eduardo de Miranda, *Quando o Amazonas corria para o Pacifico*, Petrópolis, 2007, 83–93.

33. Juan Carlos Galeano, "Paisajes," in *Amazonia y otros poemas*, ed. Universidad Externado de Colombia, Bogotá, 2011, 31.

34. Javier Yglesias, "Llamado," in *Revista peruana de literatura*, n. 6 (June 2007), 31.

35. Encyclical Letter *Laudato Si'* (24 May 2015), 144: AAS 107 (2015) 905.

36. Post-Synodal Apostolic Exhortation *Christus Vivit* (25 March 2019), 186.

37. Ibid., 200.

38. Videomessage for the World Indigenous Youth Gathering, Soloy-Panama (18 January 2019).

39. Mario Vargas Llosa, Prologue to *El Hablador*, Madrid (8 October 2007).

40. Post-Synodal Apostolic Exhortation *Christus Vivit* (25 March 2019), 195.

41. Saint John Paul II, Encyclical Letter *Centesimus Annus* (1 May 1991), 50: AAS 83 (1991), 856.

42. Fifth General Conference of the Latin American and Caribbean Bishops, *Aparecida Document* (29 June 2007), 97.

43. *Address at the Meeting with Indigenous People of Amazonia*, Puerto Maldonado-Peru (19 January 2018): AAS 110 (2018), 301.

44. *Instrumentum Laboris*, 123, e.

45. Encyclical Letter *Laudato Si'* (24 May 2015), 144: AAS 107 (2015), 906.

46. Cf. Benedict XVI, Encyclical Letter *Caritas in veritate* (29 June 2009), 51: AAS 101 (2009), 687: "Nature, especially in our time, is so integrated into the dynamics of society and culture that by now it hardly constitutes an independent variable. Desertification and the decline in productivity in some agricultural areas are also the result of impoverishment and underdevelopment among their inhabitants."

47. Message for the 2007 World Day of Peace, 8: *Insegnamenti*, II/2 (2006), 776.

48. Encyclical Letter *Laudato Si'* (24 May 2015), 16, 91, 117, 138, 240: AAS 107 (2015), 854, 884, 894, 903, 941.

49. Document *Bolivia: informe país. Consulta pre sinodal*, 2019, p. 36; cf. *Instrumentum Laboris*, 23.

50. *Instrumentum Laboris*, 26.

51. Encyclical Letter *Laudato Si'* (24 May 2015), 146: AAS 107 (2015), 906.

52. *Documento con aportes al Sínodo de la Diócesis de San José del Guaviare y de la Arquidiócesis de Villavicencio y Granada* (Colombia); cf. *Instrumentum Laboris*, 17.

53. Euclides da Cunha, *Los Sertones (Os Sertões)*, Buenos Aires (1946), 65–66.

54. Pablo Neruda, "Amazonas" in *Canto General* (1938), I, IV.

55. REPAM, Document *Eje de Fronteras*. Preparación para el Sínodo de la Amazonia, Tabatinga-Brasil (3 February 2019), p. 3; cf. *Instrumentum Laboris*, 8.

56. Amadeu Thiago de Lello, *Amazonas, patria da agua*. Spanish translation by Jorge Timossi, in http://letras-uruguay.espaciolatino.com/aaa/mello_thiago/amazonas_patria_da_agua.htm.

57. Vinicius de Moraes, *Para vivir un gran amor*, Buenos Aires, 2013, 166.

58. Juan Carlos Galeano, "Los que creyeron," in *Amazonia y otros poemas*, ed. Universidad externado de Colombia, Bogotá, 2011, 44.

59. Harald Sioli, *A Amazônia*, Petropolis (1985), 60.

60. Saint John Paul II, *Address to an International Convention on "The Environment and Health"* (24 March 1997), 2.

61. Encyclical Letter *Laudato Si'* (24 May 2015), 34: AAS 107 (2015), 860.

62. Cf. ibid., 28–31: AAS 107 (2015), 858–59.

63. Ibid., 38: AAS 107 (2015), 862.

64. Cf. Fifth General Conference of the Latin American and Caribbean Bishops, *Aparecida Document* (29 June 2007), 86.

65. Encyclical Letter *Laudato Si'* (24 May 2015), 38: AAS 107 (2015), 862.

66. Cf. ibid, 144, 187: AAS 107 (2015), 905–6, 921.

67. Cf. ibid., 183: AAS 107 (2015), 920.

68. Ibid., 53: AAS 107 (2015), 868.

69. Cf. ibid., 49: AAS 107 (2015), 866.

70. Preparatory Document for the Synod on the Pan Amazon Region, 8.

71. Encyclical Letter *Laudato Si'* (24 May 2015), 56: AAS 107 (2015), 869.

72. Ibid., 59: AAS 107 (2015), 870.

73. Ibid., 33: AAS 107 (2015), 860.

74. Ibid, 220: AAS 107 (2015), 934.

75. Ibid., 215: AAS 107 (2015), 932.

76. Sui Yun, *Cantos para el mendigo y el rey*, Wiesbaden, 2000.

77. Encyclical Letter *Laudato Si'* (24 May 2015), 100: AAS 107 (2015), 887.

78. Ibid., 204: AAS 107 (2015), 928.

79. Cf. Documents of Santarem (1972) and Manaos (1997) in National Conference of the Bishops of Brazil, *Desafío missionário. Documentos da Igreja na Amazônia*, Brasilia, 2014, pp. 9–28 and 67–84.

80. Cf. Apostolic Exhortation *Evangelii Gaudium* (24 November 2013), 220: AAS 105 (2013), 1110.

81. Ibid., 164: AAS 105 (2013), 1088–89.

82. Ibid., 165: AAS 105 (2013), 1089.

83. Ibid., 161: AAS 105 (2013), 1087.

84. As the Second Vatican Council states in No. 44 of the Constitution *Gaudium et Spes*: "The Church learned early in her history to express the Christian message in the concepts and languages of different peoples and tried to clarify it in the light of the wisdom of their philosophers: it was an attempt to adapt the Gospel to the understanding of all and the requirements of the learned, insofar as this could be done. Indeed, this kind of adaptation and preaching of the revealed word must ever be the law of all evangelization. In this way it is possible to create in every country the possibility of expressing the message of Christ in suitable terms and to foster vital contact and exchange between the Church and different cultures."

85. *Letter to the Pilgrim People of God in Germany*, 29 June 2019, 9: *L'Osservatore Romano*, 1–2 July 2019, p. 9.

86. Cf. Saint Vincent of Lerins, *Commonitorium primum*, cap. 23: PL 50, 668: "Ut annis scilicet consolidetur, dilatetur tempore, sublimetur aetate."

87. *Letter to the Pilgrim People of God in Germany*, 29 June 2019, 9. Cf. the words attributed to Gustav Mahler: "Tradition ist nicht die Anbetung der Asche, sondern die Weitergabe des Feuers": "Tradition is not the worship of ashes but the passing on of the flame."

88. *Address to University Professors and Cultural Leaders*, Coimbra (15 May 1982): *Insegnamenti* 5/2 (1982), 1702–3.

89. *Message to the Indigenous Peoples of the American Continent*, Santo Domingo (12 October 1992), 6: *Insegnamenti* 15/2 (1992), 346; cf. *Address to Participants in the National Congress of the Ecclesial Movement of Cultural Commitment* (16 January 1982), 2: *Insegnamenti* 5/1 (1982), 131.

90. Saint John Paul II, Post-Synodal Apostolic Exhortation *Vita Consecrata* (15 March 1996), 98: AAS 88 (1996), 474–75.

91. No. 115: AAS 105 (2013), 1068.

92. Ibid., 116: AAS 105 (2013), 1068.

93. Ibid.

94. Ibid., 129: AAS 105 (2013), 1074.

95. Ibid., 116: AAS 105 (2013), 1068.

96. Ibid., 117: AAS 105 (2013), 1069.

97. Ibid.

98. Saint John Paul II, *Address to the Plenary Assembly of the Pontifical Council for Culture* (17 January 1987): *Insegnamenti* 10/1 (1987), 125.

99. Apostolic Exhortation *Evangelii Gaudium* (24 November 2013), 129: AAS 105 (2013), 1074.

100. Fourth General Meeting of the Latin American and Caribbean Episcopate, *Santo Domingo Document* (12–28 October 1992), 17.

101. Apostolic Exhortation *Evangelii Gaudium* (24 November 2013), 198: AAS 105 (2013), 1103.

102. Cf. Vittorio Messori-Joseph Ratzinger, *Rapporto sulla fede*, Cinisello Balsamo, 1985, 211–12.

103. Apostolic Exhortation *Evangelii Gaudium* (24 November 2013), 198: AAS 105 (2013), 1103.

104. Pedro Casaldáliga, "Carta de navegar (*Por el Tocantins amazónico*)" in *El tiempo y la espera*, Santander, 1986.

105. Saint Thomas Aquinas explains it in this way: "The threefold way that God is in things: one is common, by essence, presence and power; another by grace in his saints; a third in Christ, by union" (*Ad Colossenses*, II, 2).

106. Encyclical Letter *Laudato Si'* (24 May 2015), 235: AAS 107 (2015), 939.

107. Third General Meeting of the Latin American and Caribbean Episcopate, *Puebla Document* (23 March 1979), 196.

108. Apostolic Exhortation *Evangelii Gaudium* (24 November 2013), 178: AAS 105 (2013), 1094.

109. Second Vatican Ecumenical Council, Dogmatic Constitution on the Church *Lumen Gentium*, 11; cf. Apostolic Exhortation *Gaudete et Exsultate* (19 March 2018), 10–11.

110. Apostolic Vicariates of the Peruvian Amazon, "Segunda asamblea episcopal regional de la selva," San Ramón-Perú (5 October 1973), in *Éxodo de la Iglesia en la Amazonia. Documentos pastorales de la Iglesia en la Amazonia peruana*, Iquitos, 1976, 121.

111. Apostolic Exhortation *Evangelii Gaudium* (24 November 2013), 123: AAS 105 (2013), 1071.

112. Cf. Apostolic Exhortation *Gaudete et Exsultate* (19 March 2018), 126–27.

113. Ibid., 32.

114. Encyclical Letter *Laudato Si'* (24 May 2015), 235: AAS 107 (2015), 939.

115. Ibid.

116. Ibid., 236: AAS 107 (2015), 940.

117. Ibid.

118. Ibid., 235: AAS 107 (2015), 939.

119. Cf. Constitution on the Sacred Liturgy *Sacrosanctum Concilium*, 37–40, 65, 77, 81.

120. During the Synod, there was a proposal to develop an "Amazonian rite."

121. Encyclical Letter *Laudato Si'* (24 May 2015), 237: AAS 107 (2015), 940.

122. Apostolic Exhortation *Amoris Laetitia* (19 March 2016), 49: AAS 108 (2016), 331; cf. ibid. 305: AAS 108 (2016), 436–37.

123. Cf. ibid., 296, 308: AAS 108 (2016), 430–31, 438.

124. Fifth General Conference of the Latin American and Caribbean Bishops' Conferences, *Aparecida Document*, 29 June 2007, 100 e.

125. Cf. Congregation for the Doctrine of the Faith, Letter *Sacerdotium Ministeriale* to Bishops of the Catholic Church on certain questions concerning the minister of the Eucharist (6 August 1983): AAS 75 (1983), 1001–9.

126. Apostolic Letter *Mulieris Dignitatem* (15 August 1988), 27: AAS 80 (1988), 1718.

127. Saint Thomas Aquinas, *Summa Theologiae* III, q. 8, a.1, resp.

128. Cf. Second Vatican Ecumenical Council, Decree on the Ministry and Life of Priests *Presbyterorum Ordinis*, 5; Saint John Paul II, Encyclical Letter *Ecclesia de Eucharistia* (17 April 2003), 26: AAS 95 (2003), 448.

129. It is also proper to the priest to administer the Anointing of the Sick, because it is intimately linked to the forgiveness of sins: "And if he has committed sins, he will be forgiven" (Jas 5:15).

130. *Catechism of the Catholic Church*, 1396; Saint John Paul II, Encyclical Letter *Ecclesia de Eucharistia* (17 April 2003), 26: AAS 95 (2003), 451; cf. Henri de Lubac, *Meditation sur l'Église*, Paris (1968), 101.

131. Second Vatican Ecumenical Council, Decree on the Ministry and Life of Priests *Presbyterorum Ordinis*, 6.

132. It is noteworthy that, in some countries of the Amazon Basin, more missionaries go to Europe or the United States than remain to assist their own Vicariates in the Amazon region.

133. At the Synod, mention was also made of the lack of seminaries for the priestly formation of indigenous people.

134. Cf. Second Vatican Ecumenical Council, Dogmatic Constitution on the Church *Lumen Gentium*, 3.

135. Saint Paul VI, *Homily on the Solemnity of Corpus Christi*, 17 June 1965: *Insegnamenti* 3 (1965), 358.

136. It is possible that, due to a lack of priests, a bishop can entrust "participation in the exercise of the pastoral care of a parish . . . to a deacon, to another person who is not a priest, or to a community of persons" (*Code of Canon Law*, 517 §2).

137. Fifth General Conference of the Latin American and Caribbean Bishops' Conferences, *Aparecida Document*, 29 June 2007, 178.

138. Ibid., 475.

139. *Instrumentum Laboris*, 65.

140. Ibid., 63.

141. Ibid., 129, d, 2.

142. Apostolic Exhortation *Evangelii Gaudium* (24 November 2013), 228: AAS 105 (2013), 1113.

143. Ibid., 226: AAS 105 (2013), 1112.

144. Second Vatican Ecumenical Council, Declaration on the Relation of the Church to Non-Christian Religions *Nostra Aetate*, 2.

145. CELAM, *III Simposio latinoamericano sobre Teología India*, Ciudad de Guatemala (23-27 October 2006).

Fratelli Tutti
All Brothers and Sisters

Encyclical On Fraternity and Social Friendship

October 4, 2020

ENCYCLICAL LETTER

FRATELLI TUTTI

OF THE HOLY FATHER

FRANCIS

ON FRATERNITY AND SOCIAL FRIENDSHIP

1. *"Fratelli Tutti."*[1] With these words, Saint Francis of Assisi addressed his brothers and sisters and proposed to them a way of life marked by the flavor of the Gospel. Of the counsels Francis offered, I would like to select the one in which he calls for a love that transcends the barriers of geography and distance, and declares blessed all those who love their brother "as much when he is far away from him as when he is with him."[2] In his simple and direct way, Saint Francis expressed the essence of a fraternal openness that allows us to acknowledge, appreciate, and love each person, regardless of physical proximity, regardless of where he or she was born or lives.

2. This saint of fraternal love, simplicity, and joy, who inspired me to write the Encyclical *Laudato Si'*, prompts me once more to devote this new Encyclical to fraternity and social friendship. Francis felt himself a brother to the sun, the sea, and the wind, yet he knew that he was even closer to those of his own flesh. Wherever he went, he sowed seeds of peace and walked alongside the poor, the abandoned, the infirm, and the outcast, the least of his brothers and sisters.

Without Borders

3. There is an episode in the life of Saint Francis that shows his openness of heart, which knew no bounds and transcended differences of origin, nationality, color, or religion. It was his visit to Sultan Malik-el-Kamil, in Egypt, which entailed considerable hardship, given Francis's poverty, his scarce resources, the great distances to be traveled, and their differences of language, culture, and religion. That journey, undertaken at the time of the Crusades, further demonstrated the breadth and grandeur of his love, which sought to embrace everyone. Francis's fidelity to his Lord was

commensurate with his love for his brothers and sisters. Unconcerned for the hardships and dangers involved, Francis went to meet the Sultan with the same attitude that he instilled in his disciples: if they found themselves "among the Saracens and other nonbelievers," without renouncing their own identity they were not to "engage in arguments or disputes, but to be subject to every human creature for God's sake."[3] In the context of the times, this was an extraordinary recommendation. We are impressed that some eight hundred years ago Saint Francis urged that all forms of hostility or conflict be avoided and that a humble and fraternal "subjection" be shown to those who did not share his faith.

4. Francis did not wage a war of words aimed at imposing doctrines; he simply spread the love of God. He understood that "God is love and those who abide in love abide in God" (1 Jn 4:16). In this way, he became a father to all and inspired the vision of a fraternal society. Indeed, "only the man who approaches others, not to draw them into his own life, but to help them become ever more fully themselves, can truly be called a father."[4] In the world of that time, bristling with watchtowers and defensive walls, cities were a theater of brutal wars between powerful families, even as poverty was spreading through the countryside. Yet there Francis was able to welcome true peace into his heart and free himself of the desire to wield power over others. He became one of the poor and sought to live in harmony with all. Francis has inspired these pages.

5. Issues of human fraternity and social friendship have always been a concern of mine. In recent years, I have spoken of them repeatedly and in different settings. In this Encyclical, I have sought to bring together many of those statements and to situate them in a broader context of reflection. In the preparation of *Laudato Si'*, I had a source of inspiration in my brother Bartholomew, the Orthodox Patriarch, who has spoken forcefully of our need to care for creation. In this case, I have felt particularly encouraged by the Grand Imam Ahmad Al-Tayyeb, with whom I met in Abu Dhabi, where we declared that "God has created all human beings equal in rights, duties and dignity, and has called them to live

together as brothers and sisters."[5] This was no mere diplomatic gesture, but a reflection born of dialogue and common commitment. The present Encyclical takes up and develops some of the great themes raised in the Document that we both signed. I have also incorporated, along with my own thoughts, a number of letters, documents, and considerations that I have received from many individuals and groups throughout the world.

6. The following pages do not claim to offer a complete teaching on fraternal love, but rather to consider its universal scope, its openness to every man and woman. I offer this social Encyclical as a modest contribution to continued reflection, in the hope that in the face of present-day attempts to eliminate or ignore others, we may prove capable of responding with a new vision of fraternity and social friendship that will not remain at the level of words. Although I have written it from the Christian convictions that inspire and sustain me, I have sought to make this reflection an invitation to dialogue among all people of good will.

7. As I was writing this letter, the Covid-19 pandemic unexpectedly erupted, exposing our false securities. Aside from the different ways that various countries responded to the crisis, their inability to work together became quite evident. For all our hyper-connectivity, we witnessed a fragmentation that made it more difficult to resolve problems that affect us all. Anyone who thinks that the only lesson to be learned was the need to improve what we were already doing, or to refine existing systems and regulations, is denying reality.

8. It is my desire that, in this our time, by acknowledging the dignity of each human person, we can contribute to the rebirth of a universal aspiration to fraternity. Fraternity between all men and women. "Here we have a splendid secret that shows us how to dream and to turn our life into a wonderful adventure. No one can face life in isolation. . . . We need a community that supports and helps us, in which we can help one another to keep looking ahead. How important it is to dream together. . . . By ourselves, we risk seeing mirages, things that are not there. Dreams,

on the other hand, are built together."[6] Let us dream, then, as a single human family, as fellow travelers sharing the same flesh, as children of the same earth which is our common home, each of us bringing the richness of his or her beliefs and convictions, each of us with his or her own voice, brothers and sisters all.

CHAPTER ONE

DARK CLOUDS OVER A CLOSED WORLD

9. Without claiming to carry out an exhaustive analysis or to study every aspect of our present-day experience, I intend simply to consider certain trends in our world that hinder the development of universal fraternity.

Shattered Dreams

10. For decades, it seemed that the world had learned a lesson from its many wars and disasters, and was slowly moving toward various forms of integration. For example, there was the dream of a united Europe, capable of acknowledging its shared roots and rejoicing in its rich diversity. We think of "the firm conviction of the founders of the European Union, who envisioned a future based on the capacity to work together in bridging divisions and in fostering peace and fellowship between all the peoples of this continent."[7] There was also a growing desire for integration in Latin America, and several steps were taken in this direction. In some countries and regions, attempts at reconciliation and rapprochement proved fruitful, while others showed great promise.

11. Our own days, however, seem to be showing signs of a certain regression. Ancient conflicts thought long buried are breaking out anew, while instances of a myopic, extremist, resentful, and aggressive nationalism are on the rise. In some countries, a concept of popular and national unity influenced by various ideologies is creating new forms of selfishness and a loss of the social sense under the guise of defending national interests. Once more we are being reminded that "each new generation must take up the struggles and attainments of past generations, while setting its sights even higher. This is the path. Goodness, together with love, justice and solidarity, are not achieved once and for all; they have to be realized each day. It is not possible to settle for what was achieved in the past and complacently enjoy it, as if we could somehow disregard

the fact that many of our brothers and sisters still endure situations that cry out for our attention."[8]

12. "Opening up to the world" is an expression that has been co-opted by the economic and financial sector and is now used exclusively of openness to foreign interests or to the freedom of economic powers to invest without obstacles or complications in all countries. Local conflicts and disregard for the common good are exploited by the global economy in order to impose a single cultural model. This culture unifies the world, but divides persons and nations, for "as society becomes ever more globalized, it makes us neighbors, but does not make us brothers."[9] We are more alone than ever in an increasingly massified world that promotes individual interests and weakens the communitarian dimension of life. Indeed, there are markets where individuals become mere consumers or bystanders. As a rule, the advance of this kind of globalism strengthens the identity of the more powerful, who can protect themselves, but it tends to diminish the identity of the weaker and poorer regions, making them more vulnerable and dependent. In this way, political life becomes increasingly fragile in the face of transnational economic powers that operate with the principle of "divide and conquer."

The End of Historical Consciousness

13. As a result, there is a growing loss of the sense of history, which leads to even further breakup. A kind of "deconstructionism," whereby human freedom claims to create everything starting from zero, is making headway in today's culture. The one thing it leaves in its wake is the drive to limitless consumption and expressions of empty individualism. Concern about this led me to offer the young some advice. "If someone tells young people to ignore their history, to reject the experiences of their elders, to look down on the past and to look forward to a future that he himself holds out, doesn't it then become easy to draw them along so that they only do what he tells them? He needs the young to be shallow, uprooted and distrustful, so that they can trust only in his promises and

act according to his plans. That is how various ideologies operate: they destroy (or deconstruct) all differences so that they can reign unopposed. To do so, however, they need young people who have no use for history, who spurn the spiritual and human riches inherited from past generations, and are ignorant of everything that came before them."[10]

14. These are the new forms of cultural colonization. Let us not forget that "peoples that abandon their tradition and, either from a craze to mimic others or to foment violence, or from unpardonable negligence or apathy, allow others to rob their very soul, end up losing not only their spiritual identity but also their moral consistency and, in the end, their intellectual, economic and political independence."[11] One effective way to weaken historical consciousness, critical thinking, the struggle for justice, and the processes of integration is to empty great words of their meaning or to manipulate them. Nowadays, what do certain words like democracy, freedom, justice, or unity really mean? They have been bent and shaped to serve as tools for domination, as meaningless tags that can be used to justify any action.

Lacking a Plan for Everyone

15. The best way to dominate and gain control over people is to spread despair and discouragement, even under the guise of defending certain values. Today, in many countries, hyperbole, extremism, and polarization have become political tools. Employing a strategy of ridicule, suspicion, and relentless criticism, in a variety of ways one denies the right of others to exist or to have an opinion. Their share of the truth and their values are rejected and, as a result, the life of society is impoverished and subjected to the hubris of the powerful. Political life no longer has to do with healthy debates about long-term plans to improve people's lives and to advance the common good, but only with slick marketing techniques primarily aimed at discrediting others. In this craven exchange of charges and counter-charges, debate degenerates into a permanent state of disagreement and confrontation.

16. Amid the fray of conflicting interests, where victory consists in eliminating one's opponents, how is it possible to raise our sights to recognize our neighbors or to help those who have fallen along the way? A plan that would set great goals for the development of our entire human family nowadays sounds like madness. We are growing ever more distant from one another, while the slow and demanding march toward an increasingly united and just world is suffering a new and dramatic setback.

17. To care for the world in which we live means to care for ourselves. Yet we need to think of ourselves more and more as a single family dwelling in a common home. Such care does not interest those economic powers that demand quick profits. Often the voices raised in defense of the environment are silenced or ridiculed, using apparently reasonable arguments that are merely a screen for special interests. In this shallow, short-sighted culture that we have created, bereft of a shared vision, "it is foreseeable that, once certain resources have been depleted, the scene will be set for new wars, albeit under the guise of noble claims."[12]

A "Throwaway" World

18. Some parts of our human family, it appears, can be readily sacrificed for the sake of others considered worthy of a carefree existence. Ultimately, "persons are no longer seen as a paramount value to be cared for and respected, especially when they are poor and disabled, 'not yet useful'—like the unborn—or 'no longer needed'—like the elderly. We have grown indifferent to all kinds of wastefulness, starting with the waste of food, which is deplorable in the extreme."[13]

19. A decline in the birthrate, which leads to the aging of the population, together with the relegation of the elderly to a sad and lonely existence, is a subtle way of stating that it is all about us, that our individual concerns are the only thing that matters. In this way, "what is thrown away are not only food and dispensable objects, but often human beings themselves."[14] We have seen what happened with the elderly in certain places in our

world as a result of the coronavirus. They did not have to die that way. Yet something similar had long been occurring during heat waves and in other situations: older people found themselves cruelly abandoned. We fail to realize that, by isolating the elderly and leaving them in the care of others without the closeness and concern of family members, we disfigure and impoverish the family itself. We also end up depriving young people of a necessary connection to their roots and a wisdom that the young cannot achieve on their own.

20. This way of discarding others can take a variety of forms, such as an obsession with reducing labor costs with no concern for its grave consequences, since the unemployment that it directly generates leads to the expansion of poverty.[15] In addition, a readiness to discard others finds expression in vicious attitudes that we thought long past, such as racism, which retreats underground only to keep reemerging. Instances of racism continue to shame us, for they show that our supposed social progress is not as real or definitive as we think.

21. Some economic rules have proved effective for growth, but not for integral human development.[16] Wealth has increased, but together with inequality, with the result that "new forms of poverty are emerging."[17] The claim that the modern world has reduced poverty is made by measuring poverty with criteria from the past that do not correspond to present-day realities. In other times, for example, lack of access to electric energy was not considered a sign of poverty, nor was it a source of hardship. Poverty must always be understood and gauged in the context of the actual opportunities available in each concrete historical period.

Insufficiently Universal Human Rights

22. It frequently becomes clear that, in practice, human rights are not equal for all. Respect for those rights "is the preliminary condition for a country's social and economic development. When the dignity of the human person is respected, and his or her rights recognized and

guaranteed, creativity and interdependence thrive, and the creativity of the human personality is released through actions that further the common good."[18] Yet, "by closely observing our contemporary societies, we see numerous contradictions that lead us to wonder whether the equal dignity of all human beings, solemnly proclaimed seventy years ago, is truly recognized, respected, protected and promoted in every situation. In today's world, many forms of injustice persist, fed by reductive anthropological visions and by a profit-based economic model that does not hesitate to exploit, discard and even kill human beings. While one part of humanity lives in opulence, another part sees its own dignity denied, scorned or trampled upon, and its fundamental rights discarded or violated."[19] What does this tell us about the equality of rights grounded in innate human dignity?

23. Similarly, the organization of societies worldwide is still far from reflecting clearly that women possess the same dignity and identical rights as men. We say one thing with words, but our decisions and reality tell another story. Indeed, "doubly poor are those women who endure situations of exclusion, mistreatment and violence, since they are frequently less able to defend their rights."[20]

24. We should also recognize that "even though the international community has adopted numerous agreements aimed at ending slavery in all its forms, and has launched various strategies to combat this phenomenon, millions of people today—children, women and men of all ages—are deprived of freedom and forced to live in conditions akin to slavery. . . . Today, as in the past, slavery is rooted in a notion of the human person that allows him or her to be treated as an object. . . . Whether by coercion, or deception, or by physical or psychological duress, human persons created in the image and likeness of God are deprived of their freedom, sold and reduced to being the property of others. They are treated as means to an end. . . . [Criminal networks] are skilled in using modern means of communication as a way of luring young men and women in various parts of the world."[21] A perversion

that exceeds all limits when it subjugates women and then forces them to abort. An abomination that goes to the length of kidnapping persons for the sake of selling their organs. Trafficking in persons and other contemporary forms of enslavement are a worldwide problem that needs to be taken seriously by humanity as a whole: "since criminal organizations employ global networks to achieve their goals, efforts to eliminate this phenomenon also demand a common and, indeed, a global effort on the part of various sectors of society."[22]

Conflict and Fear

25. War, terrorist attacks, racial or religious persecution, and many other affronts to human dignity are judged differently, depending on how convenient it proves for certain, primarily economic, interests. What is true as long as it is convenient for someone in power stops being true once it becomes inconvenient. These situations of violence, sad to say, "have become so common as to constitute a real 'third world war' fought piecemeal."[23]

26. This should not be surprising, if we realize that we no longer have common horizons that unite us; indeed, the first victim of every war is "the human family's innate vocation to fraternity." As a result, "every threatening situation breeds mistrust and leads people to withdraw into their own safety zone."[24] Our world is trapped in a strange contradiction: we believe that we can "ensure stability and peace through a false sense of security sustained by a mentality of fear and mistrust."[25]

27. Paradoxically, we have certain ancestral fears that technological development has not succeeded in eliminating; indeed, those fears have been able to hide and spread behind new technologies. Today too, outside the ancient town walls lies the abyss, the territory of the unknown, the wilderness. Whatever comes from there cannot be trusted, for it is unknown, unfamiliar, not part of the village. It is the territory of the "barbarian," from whom we must defend ourselves at all costs. As a result, new walls are erected for self-preservation, the outside world ceases to exist and

leaves only "my" world, to the point that others, no longer considered human beings possessed of an inalienable dignity, become only "them." Once more, we encounter "the temptation to build a culture of walls, to raise walls, walls in the heart, walls on the land, in order to prevent this encounter with other cultures, with other people. And those who raise walls will end up as slaves within the very walls they have built. They are left without horizons, for they lack this interchange with others."[26]

28. The loneliness, fear, and insecurity experienced by those who feel abandoned by the system creates a fertile terrain for various "mafias." These flourish because they claim to be defenders of the forgotten, often by providing various forms of assistance even as they pursue their criminal interests. There also exists a typically "mafioso" pedagogy that, by appealing to a false communitarian mystique, creates bonds of dependency and fealty from which it is very difficult to break free.

Globalization and Progress without a Shared Roadmap

29. With the Grand Imam Ahmad Al-Tayyeb, we do not ignore the positive advances made in the areas of science, technology, medicine, industry, and welfare, above all in developed countries. Nonetheless, "we wish to emphasize that, together with these historical advances, great and valued as they are, there exists a moral deterioration that influences international action and a weakening of spiritual values and responsibility. This contributes to a general feeling of frustration, isolation and desperation." We see "outbreaks of tension and a buildup of arms and ammunition in a global context dominated by uncertainty, disillusionment, fear of the future, and controlled by narrow economic interests." We can also point to "major political crises, situations of injustice and the lack of an equitable distribution of natural resources. . . . In the face of such crises that result in the deaths of millions of children—emaciated from poverty and hunger—there is an unacceptable silence on the international level."[27] This panorama, for all its undeniable advances, does not appear to lead to a more humane future.

30. In today's world, the sense of belonging to a single human family is fading, and the dream of working together for justice and peace seems an outdated utopia. What reigns instead is a cool, comfortable, and globalized indifference, born of deep disillusionment concealed behind a deceptive illusion: thinking that we are all-powerful, while failing to realize that we are all in the same boat. This illusion, unmindful of the great fraternal values, leads to "a sort of cynicism. For that is the temptation we face if we go down the road of disenchantment and disappointment. . . . Isolation and withdrawal into one's own interests are never the way to restore hope and bring about renewal. Rather, it is closeness; it is the culture of encounter. Isolation, no; closeness, yes. Culture clash, no; culture of encounter, yes."[28]

31. In this world that races ahead, yet lacks a shared roadmap, we increasingly sense that "the gap between concern for one's personal well-being and the prosperity of the larger human family seems to be stretching to the point of complete division between individuals and human community. . . . It is one thing to feel forced to live together, but something entirely different to value the richness and beauty of those seeds of common life that need to be sought out and cultivated."[29] Technology is constantly advancing, yet "how wonderful it would be if the growth of scientific and technological innovation could come with more equality and social inclusion. How wonderful would it be, even as we discover faraway planets, to rediscover the needs of the brothers and sisters who orbit around us."[30]

Pandemics and Other Calamities in History

32. True, a worldwide tragedy like the Covid-19 pandemic momentarily revived the sense that we are a global community, all in the same boat, where one person's problems are the problems of all. Once more we realized that no one is saved alone; we can only be saved together. As I said in those days, "The storm has exposed our vulnerability and uncovered those false and superfluous certainties around which we constructed

our daily schedules, our projects, our habits and priorities. . . . Amid this storm, the façade of those stereotypes with which we camouflaged our egos, always worrying about appearances, has fallen away, revealing once more the ineluctable and blessed awareness that we are part of one another, that we are brothers and sisters of one another."[31]

33. The world was relentlessly moving toward an economy that, thanks to technological progress, sought to reduce "human costs"; there were those who would have had us believe that freedom of the market was sufficient to keep everything secure. Yet the brutal and unforeseen blow of this uncontrolled pandemic forced us to recover our concern for human beings, for everyone, rather than for the benefit of a few. Today we can recognize that "we fed ourselves on dreams of splendor and grandeur, and ended up consuming distraction, insularity and solitude. We gorged ourselves on networking, and lost the taste of fraternity. We looked for quick and safe results, only to find ourselves overwhelmed by impatience and anxiety. Prisoners of a virtual reality, we lost the taste and flavor of the truly real."[32] The pain, uncertainty, and fear, and the realization of our own limitations, brought on by the pandemic have only made it all the more urgent that we rethink our styles of life, our relationships, the organization of our societies, and, above all, the meaning of our existence.

34. If everything is connected, it is hard to imagine that this global disaster is unrelated to our way of approaching reality, our claim to be absolute masters of our own lives and of all that exists. I do not want to speak of divine retribution, nor would it be sufficient to say that the harm we do to nature is itself the punishment for our offences. The world is itself crying out in rebellion. We are reminded of the well-known verse of the poet Virgil that evokes the "tears of things," the misfortunes of life and history.[33]

35. All too quickly, however, we forget the lessons of history, "the teacher of life."[34] Once this health crisis passes, our worst response would be to plunge even more deeply into feverish consumerism and new forms of

egotistic self-preservation. God willing, after all this, we will think no longer in terms of "them" and "those," but only "us." If only this may prove not to be just another tragedy of history from which we learned nothing. If only we might keep in mind all those elderly persons who died for lack of respirators, partly as a result of the dismantling, year after year, of healthcare systems. If only this immense sorrow may not prove useless, but enable us to take a step forward toward a new style of life. If only we might rediscover once for all that we need one another, and that in this way our human family can experience a rebirth, with all its faces, all its hands, and all its voices, beyond the walls that we have erected.

36. Unless we recover the shared passion to create a community of belonging and solidarity worthy of our time, our energy, and our resources, the global illusion that misled us will collapse and leave many in the grip of anguish and emptiness. Nor should we naively refuse to recognize that "obsession with a consumerist lifestyle, above all when few people are capable of maintaining it, can only lead to violence and mutual destruction."[35] The notion of "every man for himself" will rapidly degenerate into a free-for-all that would prove worse than any pandemic.

An Absence of Human Dignity on the Borders

37. Certain populist political regimes, as well as certain liberal economic approaches, maintain that an influx of migrants is to be prevented at all costs. Arguments are also made for the propriety of limiting aid to poor countries, so that they can hit rock bottom and find themselves forced to take austerity measures. One fails to realize that behind such statements, abstract and hard to support, great numbers of lives are at stake. Many migrants have fled from war, persecution, and natural catastrophes. Others, rightly, "are seeking opportunities for themselves and their families. They dream of a better future and they want to create the conditions for achieving it."[36]

38. Sadly, some "are attracted by Western culture, sometimes with unrealistic expectations that expose them to grave disappointments.

Unscrupulous traffickers, frequently linked to drug cartels or arms cartels, exploit the weakness of migrants, who too often experience violence, trafficking, psychological and physical abuse and untold sufferings on their journey."[37] Those who emigrate "experience separation from their place of origin, and often a cultural and religious uprooting as well. Fragmentation is also felt by the communities they leave behind, which lose their most vigorous and enterprising elements, and by families, especially when one or both of the parents migrates, leaving the children in the country of origin."[38] For this reason, "there is also a need to reaffirm the right not to emigrate, that is, to remain in one's homeland."[39]

39. Then too, "in some host countries, migration causes fear and alarm, often fomented and exploited for political purposes. This can lead to a xenophobic mentality, as people close in on themselves, and it needs to be addressed decisively."[40] Migrants are not seen as entitled like others to participate in the life of society, and it is forgotten that they possess the same intrinsic dignity as any person. Hence they ought to be "agents in their own redemption."[41] No one will ever openly deny that they are human beings, yet in practice, by our decisions and the way we treat them, we can show that we consider them less worthy, less important, less human. For Christians, this way of thinking and acting is unacceptable, since it sets certain political preferences above deep convictions of our faith: the inalienable dignity of each human person regardless of origin, race, or religion, and the supreme law of fraternal love.

40. "Migrations, more than ever before, will play a pivotal role in the future of our world."[42] At present, however, migration is affected by the "loss of that sense of responsibility for our brothers and sisters on which every civil society is based."[43] Europe, for example, seriously risks taking this path. Nonetheless, "aided by its great cultural and religious heritage, it has the means to defend the centrality of the human person and to find the right balance between its twofold moral responsibility to protect the rights of its citizens and to assure assistance and acceptance to migrants."[44]

41. I realize that some people are hesitant and fearful with regard to migrants. I consider this part of our natural instinct of self-defense. Yet it is also true that an individual and a people are only fruitful and productive if they are able to develop a creative openness to others. I ask everyone to move beyond those primal reactions because "there is a problem when doubts and fears condition our way of thinking and acting to the point of making us intolerant, closed and perhaps even—without realizing it—racist. In this way, fear deprives us of the desire and the ability to encounter the other."[45]

The Illusion of Communication

42. Oddly enough, while closed and intolerant attitudes toward others are on the rise, distances are otherwise shrinking or disappearing to the point that the right to privacy scarcely exists. Everything has become a kind of spectacle to be examined and inspected, and people's lives are now under constant surveillance. Digital communication wants to bring everything out into the open; people's lives are combed over, laid bare, and bandied about, often anonymously. Respect for others disintegrates, and even as we dismiss, ignore, or keep others distant, we can shamelessly peer into every detail of their lives.

43. Digital campaigns of hatred and destruction, for their part, are not—as some would have us believe—a positive form of mutual support, but simply an association of individuals united against a perceived common enemy. "Digital media can also expose people to the risk of addiction, isolation, and a gradual loss of contact with concrete reality, blocking the development of authentic interpersonal relationships."[46] They lack the physical gestures, facial expressions, moments of silence, body language, and even the smells, the trembling of hands, the blushes, and perspiration that speak to us and are a part of human communication. Digital relationships, which do not demand the slow and gradual cultivation of friendships, stable interaction, or the building of a consensus that matures over time, have the appearance of sociability. Yet they do not

really build community; instead, they tend to disguise and expand the very individualism that finds expression in xenophobia and in contempt for the vulnerable. Digital connectivity is not enough to build bridges. It is not capable of uniting humanity.

Shameless Aggression

44. Even as individuals maintain their comfortable consumerist isolation, they can choose a form of constant and febrile bonding that encourages remarkable hostility, insults, abuse, defamation, and verbal violence destructive of others, and this with a lack of restraint that could not exist in physical contact without tearing us all apart. Social aggression has found unparalleled room for expansion through computers and mobile devices.

45. This has now given free rein to ideologies. Things that until a few years ago could not be said by anyone without risking the loss of universal respect can now be said with impunity, and in the crudest of terms, even by some political figures. Nor should we forget that "there are huge economic interests operating in the digital world, capable of exercising forms of control as subtle as they are invasive, creating mechanisms for the manipulation of consciences and of the democratic process. The way many platforms work often ends up favoring encounter between persons who think alike, shielding them from debate. These closed circuits facilitate the spread of fake news and false information, fomenting prejudice and hate."[47]

46. We should also recognize that destructive forms of fanaticism are at times found among religious believers, including Christians; they too "can be caught up in networks of verbal violence through the internet and the various forums of digital communication. Even in Catholic media, limits can be overstepped, defamation and slander can become commonplace, and all ethical standards and respect for the good name of others can be abandoned."[48] How can this contribute to the fraternity that our common Father asks of us?

Information without Wisdom

47. True wisdom demands an encounter with reality. Today, however, everything can be created, disguised, and altered. A direct encounter even with the fringes of reality can thus prove intolerable. A mechanism of selection then comes into play, whereby I can immediately separate likes from dislikes, what I consider attractive from what I deem distasteful. In the same way, we can choose the people with whom we wish to share our world. Persons or situations we find unpleasant or disagreeable are simply deleted in today's virtual networks; a virtual circle is then created, isolating us from the real world in which we are living.

48. The ability to sit down and listen to others, typical of interpersonal encounters, is paradigmatic of the welcoming attitude shown by those who transcend narcissism and accept others, caring for them and welcoming them into their lives. Yet "today's world is largely a deaf world. . . . At times, the frantic pace of the modern world prevents us from listening attentively to what another person is saying. Halfway through, we interrupt him and want to contradict what he has not even finished saying. We must not lose our ability to listen." Saint Francis "heard the voice of God, he heard the voice of the poor, he heard the voice of the infirm and he heard the voice of nature. He made of them a way of life. My desire is that the seed that Saint Francis planted may grow in the hearts of many."[49]

49. As silence and careful listening disappear, replaced by a frenzy of texting, this basic structure of sage human communication is at risk. A new lifestyle is emerging, where we create only what we want and exclude all that we cannot control or know instantly and superficially. This process, by its intrinsic logic, blocks the kind of serene reflection that could lead us to a shared wisdom.

50. Together, we can seek the truth in dialogue, in relaxed conversation, or in passionate debate. To do so calls for perseverance; it entails moments of silence and suffering, yet it can patiently embrace the

broader experience of individuals and peoples. The flood of information at our fingertips does not make for greater wisdom. Wisdom is not born of quick searches on the internet nor is it a mass of unverified data. That is not the way to mature in the encounter with truth. Conversations revolve only around the latest data; they become merely horizontal and cumulative. We fail to keep our attention focused, to penetrate to the heart of matters, and to recognize what is essential to give meaning to our lives. Freedom thus becomes an illusion that we are peddled, easily confused with the ability to navigate the internet. The process of building fraternity, be it local or universal, can only be undertaken by spirits that are free and open to authentic encounters.

Forms of Subjection and of Self-Contempt

51. Certain economically prosperous countries tend to be proposed as cultural models for less developed countries; instead, each of those countries should be helped to grow in its own distinct way and to develop its capacity for innovation while respecting the values of its proper culture. A shallow and pathetic desire to imitate others leads to copying and consuming in place of creating, and fosters low national self-esteem. In the affluent sectors of many poor countries, and at times in those who have recently emerged from poverty, there is a resistance to native ways of thinking and acting, and a tendency to look down on one's own cultural identity, as if it were the sole cause of every ill.

52. Destroying self-esteem is an easy way to dominate others. Behind these trends that tend to level our world, there flourish powerful interests that take advantage of such low self-esteem, while attempting, through the media and networks, to create a new culture in the service of the elite. This plays into the opportunism of financial speculators and raiders, and the poor always end up the losers. Then too, ignoring the culture of their people has led to the inability of many political leaders to devise an effective development plan that could be freely accepted and sustained over time.

53. We forget that "there is no worse form of alienation than to feel uprooted, belonging to no one. A land will be fruitful, and its people bear fruit and give birth to the future, only to the extent that it can foster a sense of belonging among its members, create bonds of integration between generations and different communities, and avoid all that makes us insensitive to others and leads to further alienation."[50]

Hope

54. Despite these dark clouds, which may not be ignored, I would like in the following pages to take up and discuss many new paths of hope. For God continues to sow abundant seeds of goodness in our human family. The recent pandemic enabled us to recognize and appreciate once more all those around us who, in the midst of fear, responded by putting their lives on the line. We began to realize that our lives are interwoven with and sustained by ordinary people valiantly shaping the decisive events of our shared history: doctors, nurses, pharmacists, storekeepers and supermarket workers, cleaning personnel, caretakers, transport workers, men and women working to provide essential services and public safety, volunteers, priests, and religious . . . They understood that no one is saved alone.[51]

55. I invite everyone to renewed hope, for hope "speaks to us of something deeply rooted in every human heart, independently of our circumstances and historical conditioning. Hope speaks to us of a thirst, an aspiration, a longing for a life of fulfillment, a desire to achieve great things, things that fill our heart and lift our spirit to lofty realities like truth, goodness and beauty, justice and love. . . . Hope is bold; it can look beyond personal convenience, the petty securities and compensations which limit our horizon, and it can open us up to grand ideals that make life more beautiful and worthwhile."[52] Let us continue, then, to advance along the paths of hope.

CHAPTER TWO

A STRANGER ON THE ROAD

56. The previous chapter should not be read as a cool and detached description of today's problems, for "the joys and hopes, the grief and anguish of the people of our time, especially of those who are poor or afflicted, are the joys and hopes, the grief and anguish of the followers of Christ as well. Nothing that is genuinely human fails to find an echo in their hearts."[53] In the attempt to search for a ray of light in the midst of what we are experiencing, and before proposing a few lines of action, I now wish to devote a chapter to a parable told by Jesus Christ two thousand years ago. Although this Letter is addressed to all people of good will, regardless of their religious convictions, the parable is one that any of us can relate to and find challenging.

> "Just then a lawyer stood up to test Jesus. 'Teacher,' he said, 'what must I do to inherit eternal life?' He said to him, 'What is written in the law? What do you read there?' He answered, 'You shall love the Lord your God with all your heart, and with all your soul, and with all your strength, and with all your mind; and your neighbor as yourself.' And he said to him, 'You have given the right answer; do this, and you will live.' But wanting to justify himself, he asked Jesus, 'And who is my neighbor?' Jesus replied, 'A man was going down from Jerusalem to Jericho, and fell into the hands of robbers, who stripped him, beat him, and went away, leaving him half dead. Now by chance a priest was going down that road; and when he saw him, he passed by on the other side. So likewise a Levite, when he came to the place and saw him, passed by on the other side. But a Samaritan while traveling came near him; and when he saw him, he was moved with pity. He went to him and bandaged his wounds, having

> poured oil and wine on them. Then he put him on his own animal, brought him to an inn, and took care of him. The next day he took out two denarii, gave them to the innkeeper, and said, 'Take care of him; and when I come back, I will repay you whatever more you spend.' Which of these three, do you think, was a neighbor to the man who fell into the hands of the robbers?" He said, 'The one who showed him mercy.' Jesus said to him, 'Go and do likewise.'" (Lk 10:25–37)

The Context

57. This parable has to do with an age-old problem. Shortly after its account of the creation of the world and of man, the Bible takes up the issue of human relationships. Cain kills his brother Abel and then hears God ask: "Where is your brother Abel?" (Gn 4:9). His answer is one that we ourselves all too often give: "Am I my brother's keeper?" (ibid.). By the very question he asks, God leaves no room for an appeal to determinism or fatalism as a justification for our own indifference. Instead, he encourages us to create a different culture, in which we resolve our conflicts and care for one another.

58. The Book of Job sees our origin in the one Creator as the basis of certain common rights: "Did not he who made me in the womb also make him? And did not the same one fashion us in the womb?" (Job 31:15). Many centuries later, Saint Irenaeus would use the image of a melody to make the same point: "One who seeks the truth should not concentrate on the differences between one note and another, thinking as if each was created separately and apart from the others; instead, he should realize that one and the same person composed the entire melody."[54]

59. In earlier Jewish traditions, the imperative to love and care for others appears to have been limited to relationships between members of the same nation. The ancient commandment to "love your neighbor as yourself" (Lv 19:18) was usually understood as referring to one's fellow

citizens, yet the boundaries gradually expanded, especially in the Judaism that developed outside of the land of Israel. We encounter the command not to do to others what you would not want them to do to you (cf. Tb 4:15). In the first century before Christ, Rabbi Hillel stated: "This is the entire Torah. Everything else is commentary."[55] The desire to imitate God's own way of acting gradually replaced the tendency to think only of those nearest us: "The compassion of man is for his neighbor, but the compassion of the Lord is for all living beings" (Sir 18:13).

60. In the New Testament, Hillel's precept was expressed in positive terms: "In everything, do to others as you would have them do to you; for this is the law and the prophets" (Mt 7:12). This command is universal in scope, embracing everyone on the basis of our shared humanity, since the heavenly Father "makes his sun rise on the evil and on the good" (Mt 5:45). Hence the summons to "be merciful, just as your Father is merciful" (Lk 6:36).

61. In the oldest texts of the Bible, we find a reason why our hearts should expand to embrace the foreigner. It derives from the enduring memory of the Jewish people that they themselves had once lived as foreigners in Egypt:

> "You shall not wrong or oppress a stranger, for you were strangers in the land of Egypt" (Ex 22:21).
>
> "You shall not oppress a stranger; you know the heart of a stranger, for you were strangers in the land of Egypt" (Ex 23:9).
>
> "When a stranger resides with you in your land, you shall not do him wrong. The stranger who resides with you shall be to you as the citizen among you; you shall love the stranger as yourself, for you were strangers in the land of Egypt" (Lv 19:33–34).

> "When you gather the grapes of your vineyard, do not glean what is left; it shall be for the sojourner, the orphan, and the widow. Remember that you were a slave in the land of Egypt" (Deut 24:21–22).

The call to fraternal love echoes throughout the New Testament:

> "For the whole law is summed up in a single commandment, 'You shall love your neighbor as yourself'" (Gal 5:14).

> "Whoever loves a brother or sister lives in the light, and in such a person there is no cause for stumbling. But whoever hates another believer is in the darkness" (1 Jn 2:10–11).

> "We know that we have passed from death to life because we love one another. Whoever does not love abides in death" (1 Jn 3:14).

> "Those who do not love a brother or sister whom they have seen, cannot love God whom they have not seen" (1 Jn 4:20).

62. Yet this call to love could be misunderstood. Saint Paul, recognizing the temptation of the earliest Christian communities to form closed and isolated groups, urged his disciples to abound in love "for one another and for all" (1 Thes 3:12). In the Johannine community, fellow Christians were to be welcomed, "even though they are strangers to you" (3 Jn 5). In this context, we can better understand the significance of the parable of the Good Samaritan: love does not care if a brother or sister in need comes from one place or another. For "love shatters the chains that keep us isolated and separate; in their place, it builds bridges. Love enables us to create one great family, where all of us can feel at home. . . . Love exudes compassion and dignity."[56]

Abandoned on the Wayside

63. Jesus tells the story of a man assaulted by thieves and lying injured on the wayside. Several persons passed him by, but failed to stop. These were people holding important social positions, yet lacking in real concern for the common good. They would not waste a couple of minutes caring for the injured man, or even in calling for help. Only one person stopped, approached the man, and cared for him personally, even spending his own money to provide for his needs. He also gave him something that in our frenetic world we cling to tightly: he gave him his time. Certainly, he had his own plans for that day, his own needs, commitments, and desires. Yet he was able to put all that aside when confronted with someone in need. Without even knowing the injured man, he saw him as deserving of his time and attention.

64. Which of these persons do you identify with? This question, blunt as it is, is direct and incisive. Which of these characters do you resemble? We need to acknowledge that we are constantly tempted to ignore others, especially the weak. Let us admit that, for all the progress we have made, we are still "illiterate" when it comes to accompanying, caring for, and supporting the most frail and vulnerable members of our developed societies. We have become accustomed to looking the other way, passing by, ignoring situations until they affect us directly.

65. Someone is assaulted on our streets, and many hurry off as if they did not notice. People hit someone with their car and then flee the scene. Their only desire is to avoid problems; it does not matter that, through their fault, another person could die. All these are signs of an approach to life that is spreading in various and subtle ways. What is more, caught up as we are with our own needs, the sight of a person who is suffering disturbs us. It makes us uneasy, since we have no time to waste on other people's problems. These are symptoms of an unhealthy society. A society that seeks prosperity but turns its back on suffering.

66. May we not sink to such depths! Let us look to the example of the Good Samaritan. Jesus' parable summons us to rediscover our vocation as citizens of our respective nations and of the entire world, builders of a new social bond. This summons is ever new, yet it is grounded in a fundamental law of our being: we are called to direct society to the pursuit of the common good and, with this purpose in mind, to persevere in consolidating its political and social order, its fabric of relations, its human goals. By his actions, the Good Samaritan showed that "the existence of each and every individual is deeply tied to that of others: life is not simply time that passes; life is a time for interactions."[57]

67. The parable eloquently presents the basic decision we need to make in order to rebuild our wounded world. In the face of so much pain and suffering, our only course is to imitate the Good Samaritan. Any other decision would make us either one of the robbers or one of those who walked by without showing compassion for the sufferings of the man on the roadside. The parable shows us how a community can be rebuilt by men and women who identify with the vulnerability of others, who reject the creation of a society of exclusion, and act instead as neighbors, lifting up and rehabilitating the fallen for the sake of the common good. At the same time, it warns us about the attitude of those who think only of themselves and fail to shoulder the inevitable responsibilities of life as it is.

68. The parable clearly does not indulge in abstract moralizing, nor is its message merely social and ethical. It speaks to us of an essential and often forgotten aspect of our common humanity: we were created for a fulfillment that can only be found in love. We cannot be indifferent to suffering; we cannot allow anyone to go through life as an outcast. Instead, we should feel indignant, challenged to emerge from our comfortable isolation and to be changed by our contact with human suffering. That is the meaning of dignity.

A Story Constantly Retold

69. The parable is clear and straightforward, yet it also evokes the interior struggle that each of us experiences as we gradually come to know ourselves through our relationships with our brothers and sisters. Sooner or later, we will all encounter a person who is suffering. Today there are more and more of them. The decision to include or exclude those lying wounded along the roadside can serve as a criterion for judging every economic, political, social, and religious project. Each day we have to decide whether to be Good Samaritans or indifferent bystanders. And if we extend our gaze to the history of our own lives and that of the entire world, all of us are, or have been, like each of the characters in the parable. All of us have in ourselves something of the wounded man, something of the robber, something of the passers-by, and something of the Good Samaritan.

70. It is remarkable how the various characters in the story change, once confronted by the painful sight of the poor man on the roadside. The distinctions between Judean and Samaritan, priest and merchant, fade into insignificance. Now there are only two kinds of people: those who care for someone who is hurting and those who pass by; those who bend down to help and those who look the other way and hurry off. Here, all our distinctions, labels, and masks fall away: it is the moment of truth. Will we bend down to touch and heal the wounds of others? Will we bend down and help another to get up? This is today's challenge, and we should not be afraid to face it. In moments of crisis, decisions become urgent. It could be said that, here and now, anyone who is neither a robber nor a passer-by is either injured himself or bearing an injured person on his shoulders.

71. The story of the Good Samaritan is constantly being repeated. We can see this clearly as social and political inertia is turning many parts of our world into a desolate byway, even as domestic and international disputes and the robbing of opportunities are leaving great numbers of

the marginalized stranded on the roadside. In his parable, Jesus does not offer alternatives; he does not ask what might have happened had the injured man or the one who helped him yielded to anger or a thirst for revenge. Jesus trusts in the best of the human spirit; with this parable, he encourages us to persevere in love, to restore dignity to the suffering, and to build a society worthy of the name.

The Characters of the Story

72. The parable begins with the robbers. Jesus chose to start when the robbery has already taken place, lest we dwell on the crime itself or the thieves who committed it. Yet we know them well. We have seen, descending on our world, the dark shadows of neglect and violence in the service of petty interests of power, gain, and division. The real question is this: will we abandon the injured man and run to take refuge from the violence, or will we pursue the thieves? Will the wounded man end up being the justification for our irreconcilable divisions, our cruel indifference, our intestine conflicts?

73. The parable then asks us to take a closer look at the passers-by. The nervous indifference that makes them pass to the other side of the road—whether innocently or not, whether the result of disdain or mere distraction—makes the priest and the Levite a sad reflection of the growing gulf between ourselves and the world around us. There are many ways to pass by at a safe distance: we can retreat inward, ignore others, or be indifferent to their plight. Or simply look elsewhere, as in some countries, or certain sectors of them, where contempt is shown for the poor and their culture, and one looks the other way, as if a development plan imported from without could edge them out. This is how some justify their indifference: the poor, whose pleas for help might touch their hearts, simply do not exist. The poor are beyond the scope of their interest.

74. One detail about the passers-by does stand out: they were religious, devoted to the worship of God: a priest and a Levite. This detail should not be overlooked. It shows that belief in God and the worship of God

are not enough to ensure that we are actually living in a way pleasing to God. A believer may be untrue to everything that his faith demands of him, and yet think he is close to God and better than others. The guarantee of an authentic openness to God, on the other hand, is a way of practicing the faith that helps open our hearts to our brothers and sisters. Saint John Chrysostom expressed this pointedly when he challenged his Christian hearers: "Do you wish to honor the body of the Savior? Do not despise it when it is naked. Do not honor it in church with silk vestments while outside it is naked and numb with cold."[58] Paradoxically, those who claim to be unbelievers can sometimes put God's will into practice better than believers.

75. "Robbers" usually find secret allies in those who "pass by and look the other way." There is a certain interplay between those who manipulate and cheat society, and those who, while claiming to be detached and impartial critics, live off that system and its benefits. There is a sad hypocrisy when the impunity of crime, the use of institutions for personal or corporate gain, and other evils apparently impossible to eradicate, are accompanied by a relentless criticism of everything, a constant sowing of suspicion that results in distrust and confusion. The complaint that "everything is broken" is answered by the claim that "it can't be fixed," or "what can I do?" This feeds into disillusionment and despair, and hardly encourages a spirit of solidarity and generosity. Plunging people into despair closes a perfectly perverse circle: such is the agenda of the invisible dictatorship of hidden interests that have gained mastery over both resources and the possibility of thinking and expressing opinions.

76. Let us turn at last to the injured man. There are times when we feel like him, badly hurt and left on side of the road. We can also feel helpless because our institutions are neglected and lack resources, or simply serve the interests of a few, without and within. Indeed, "globalized society often has an elegant way of shifting its gaze. Under the guise of being politically correct or ideologically fashionable, we look at those who

suffer without touching them. We televise live pictures of them, even speaking about them with euphemisms and with apparent tolerance."[59]

Starting Anew

77. Each day offers us a new opportunity, a new possibility. We should not expect everything from those who govern us, for that would be childish. We have the space we need for co-responsibility in creating and putting into place new processes and changes. Let us take an active part in renewing and supporting our troubled societies. Today we have a great opportunity to express our innate sense of fraternity, to be Good Samaritans who bear the pain of other people's troubles rather than fomenting greater hatred and resentment. Like the chance traveler in the parable, we need only have a pure and simple desire to be a people, a community, constant and tireless in the effort to include, integrate, and lift up the fallen. We may often find ourselves succumbing to the mentality of the violent, the blindly ambitious, those who spread mistrust and lies. Others may continue to view politics or the economy as an arena for their own power plays. For our part, let us foster what is good and place ourselves at its service.

78. We can start from below and, case by case, act at the most concrete and local levels, and then expand to the farthest reaches of our countries and our world, with the same care and concern that the Samaritan showed for each of the wounded man's injuries. Let us seek out others and embrace the world as it is, without fear of pain or a sense of inadequacy, because there we will discover all the goodness that God has planted in human hearts. Difficulties that seem overwhelming are opportunities for growth, not excuses for a glum resignation that can lead only to acquiescence. Yet let us not do this alone, as individuals. The Samaritan discovered an innkeeper who would care for the man; we too are called to unite as a family that is stronger than the sum of small individual members. For "the whole is greater than the part, but it is also greater than the sum of its parts."[60] Let us renounce the pettiness and resentment of useless

in-fighting and constant confrontation. Let us stop feeling sorry for ourselves and acknowledge our crimes, our apathy, our lies. Reparation and reconciliation will give us new life and set us all free from fear.

79. The Samaritan who stopped along the way departed without expecting any recognition or gratitude. His effort to assist another person gave him great satisfaction in life and before his God, and thus became a duty. All of us have a responsibility for the wounded, those of our own people and all the peoples of the earth. Let us care for the needs of every man and woman, young and old, with the same fraternal spirit of care and closeness that marked the Good Samaritan.

Neighbors without Borders

80. Jesus told the parable of the Good Samaritan in answer to the question: Who is my neighbor? The word *neighbor*, in the society of Jesus' time, usually meant those nearest us. It was felt that help should be given primarily to those of one's own group and race. For some Jews of that time, Samaritans were looked down upon, considered impure. They were not among those to be helped. Jesus, himself a Jew, completely transforms this approach. He asks us not to decide who is close enough to be our neighbor, but rather that we ourselves become neighbors to all.

81. Jesus asks us to be present to those in need of help, regardless of whether or not they belong to our social group. In this case, the Samaritan became a neighbor to the wounded Judean. By approaching and making himself present, he crossed all cultural and historical barriers. Jesus concludes the parable by saying: "Go and do likewise" (Lk 10:37). In other words, he challenges us to put aside all differences and, in the face of suffering, to draw near to others with no questions asked. I should no longer say that I have neighbors to help, but that I must myself be a neighbor to others.

82. The parable, though, is troubling, for Jesus says that the wounded man was a Judean, while the one who stopped and helped him was a

Samaritan. This detail is quite significant for our reflection on a love that includes everyone. The Samaritans lived in a region where pagan rites were practiced. For the Jews, this made them impure, detestable, dangerous. In fact, one ancient Jewish text referring to nations that were hated, speaks of Samaria as "not even a people" (Sir 50:25); it also refers to "the foolish people that live in Shechem" (50:26).

83. This explains why a Samaritan woman, when asked by Jesus for a drink, answered curtly: "How is it that you, a Jew, ask a drink of me, a woman of Samaria?" (Jn 4:9). The most offensive charge that those who sought to discredit Jesus could bring was that he was "possessed" and "a Samaritan" (Jn 8:48). So this encounter of mercy between a Samaritan and a Jew is highly provocative; it leaves no room for ideological manipulation and challenges us to expand our frontiers. It gives a universal dimension to our call to love, one that transcends all prejudices, all historical and cultural barriers, all petty interests.

The Plea of the Stranger

84. Finally, I would note that in another passage of the Gospel Jesus says: "I was a stranger and you welcomed me" (Mt 25:35). Jesus could speak those words because he had an open heart, sensitive to the difficulties of others. Saint Paul urges us to "rejoice with those who rejoice, weep with those who weep" (Rom 12:15). When our hearts do this, they are capable of identifying with others without worrying about where they were born or come from. In the process, we come to experience others as our "own flesh" (Is 58:7).

85. For Christians, the words of Jesus have an even deeper meaning. They compel us to recognize Christ himself in each of our abandoned or excluded brothers and sisters (cf. Mt 25:40, 45). Faith has untold power to inspire and sustain our respect for others, for believers come to know that God loves every man and woman with infinite love and "thereby confers infinite dignity" upon all humanity.[61] We likewise believe that Christ shed his blood for each of us and that no one is beyond the scope

of his universal love. If we go to the ultimate source of that love which is the very life of the triune God, we encounter in the community of the three divine Persons the origin and perfect model of all life in society. Theology continues to be enriched by its reflection on this great truth.

86. I sometimes wonder why, in light of this, it took so long for the Church unequivocally to condemn slavery and various forms of violence. Today, with our developed spirituality and theology, we have no excuses. Still, there are those who appear to feel encouraged or at least permitted by their faith to support varieties of narrow and violent nationalism, xenophobia and contempt, and even the mistreatment of those who are different. Faith, and the humanism it inspires, must maintain a critical sense in the face of these tendencies, and prompt an immediate response whenever they rear their head. For this reason, it is important that catechesis and preaching speak more directly and clearly about the social meaning of existence, the fraternal dimension of spirituality, our conviction of the inalienable dignity of each person, and our reasons for loving and accepting all our brothers and sisters.

CHAPTER THREE

ENVISAGING AND ENGENDERING AN OPEN WORLD

87. Human beings are so made that they cannot live, develop, and find fulfillment except "in the sincere gift of self to others."[62] Nor can they fully know themselves apart from an encounter with other persons: "I communicate effectively with myself only insofar as I communicate with others."[63] No one can experience the true beauty of life without relating to others, without having real faces to love. This is part of the mystery of authentic human existence. "Life exists where there is bonding, communion, fraternity; and life is stronger than death when it is built on true relationships and bonds of fidelity. On the contrary, there is no life when we claim to be self-sufficient and live as islands: in these attitudes, death prevails."[64]

Moving beyond Ourselves

88. In the depths of every heart, love creates bonds and expands existence, for it draws people out of themselves and toward others.[65] Since we were made for love, in each one of us "a law of *ekstasis*" seems to operate: "the lover 'goes outside' the self to find a fuller existence in another."[66] For this reason, "man always has to take up the challenge of moving beyond himself."[67]

89. Nor can I reduce my life to relationships with a small group, even my own family; I cannot know myself apart from a broader network of relationships, including those that have preceded me and shaped my entire life. My relationship with those whom I respect has to take account of the fact that they do not live only for me, nor do I live only for them. Our relationships, if healthy and authentic, open us to others who expand and enrich us. Nowadays, our noblest social instincts can easily be thwarted by self-centered chats that give the impression of being deep relationships. On the contrary, authentic and mature love

and true friendship can only take root in hearts open to growth through relationships with others. As couples or friends, we find that our hearts expand as we step out of ourselves and embrace others. Closed groups and self-absorbed couples that define themselves in opposition to others tend to be expressions of selfishness and mere self-preservation.

90. Significantly, many small communities living in desert areas developed a remarkable system of welcoming pilgrims as an exercise of the sacred duty of hospitality. The medieval monastic communities did likewise, as we see from the Rule of Saint Benedict. While acknowledging that it might detract from the discipline and silence of monasteries, Benedict nonetheless insisted that "the poor and pilgrims be treated with the utmost care and attention."[68] Hospitality was one specific way of rising to the challenge and the gift present in an encounter with those outside one's own circle. The monks realized that the values they sought to cultivate had to be accompanied by a readiness to move beyond themselves in openness to others.

The Unique Value of Love

91. People can develop certain habits that might appear as moral values: fortitude, sobriety, hard work, and similar virtues. Yet if the acts of the various moral virtues are to be rightly directed, one needs to take into account the extent to which they foster openness and union with others. That is made possible by the charity that God infuses. Without charity, we may perhaps possess only apparent virtues, incapable of sustaining life in common. Thus, Saint Thomas Aquinas could say—quoting Saint Augustine—that the temperance of a greedy person is in no way virtuous.[69] Saint Bonaventure, for his part, explained that the other virtues, without charity, strictly speaking do not fulfill the commandments "the way God wants them to be fulfilled."[70]

92. The spiritual stature of a person's life is measured by love, which in the end remains "the criterion for the definitive decision about a human life's worth or lack thereof."[71] Yet some believers think that it consists in

the imposition of their own ideologies upon everyone else, or in a violent defense of the truth, or in impressive demonstrations of strength. All of us, as believers, need to recognize that love takes first place: love must never be put at risk, and the greatest danger lies in failing to love (cf. 1 Cor 13:1–13).

93. Saint Thomas Aquinas sought to describe the love made possible by God's grace as a movement outward toward another, whereby we consider "the beloved as somehow united to ourselves."[72] Our affection for others makes us freely desire to seek their good. All this originates in a sense of esteem, an appreciation of the value of the other. This is ultimately the idea behind the word *charity*: those who are loved are "dear" to me; "they are considered of great value."[73] And "the love whereby someone becomes pleasing (*grata*) to another is the reason why the latter bestows something on him freely (*gratis*)."[74]

94. Love, then, is more than just a series of benevolent actions. Those actions have their source in a union increasingly directed toward others, considering them of value, worthy, pleasing, and beautiful apart from their physical or moral appearances. Our love for others, for who they are, moves us to seek the best for their lives. Only by cultivating this way of relating to one another will we make possible a social friendship that excludes no one and a fraternity that is open to all.

A Love Ever More Open

95. Love also impels us toward universal communion. No one can mature or find fulfillment by withdrawing from others. By its very nature, love calls for growth in openness and the ability to accept others as part of a continuing adventure that makes every periphery converge in a greater sense of mutual belonging. As Jesus told us: "You are all brothers" (Mt 23:8).

96. This need to transcend our own limitations also applies to different regions and countries. Indeed, "the ever-increasing number of

interconnections and communications in today's world makes us powerfully aware of the unity and common destiny of the nations. In the dynamics of history, and in the diversity of ethnic groups, societies and cultures, we see the seeds of a vocation to form a community composed of brothers and sisters who accept and care for one another."[75]

Open Societies That Integrate Everyone

97. Some peripheries are close to us, in city centers or within our families. Hence there is an aspect of universal openness in love that is existential rather than geographical. It has to do with our daily efforts to expand our circle of friends, to reach those who, even though they are close to me, I do not naturally consider a part of my circle of interests. Every brother or sister in need, when abandoned or ignored by the society in which I live, becomes an existential foreigner, even though born in the same country. They may be citizens with full rights, yet they are treated like foreigners in their own country. Racism is a virus that quickly mutates and, instead of disappearing, goes into hiding, and lurks in waiting.

98. I would like to mention some of those "hidden exiles" who are treated as foreign bodies in society.[76] Many persons with disabilities "feel that they exist without belonging and without participating." Much still prevents them from being fully enfranchised. Our concern should be not only to care for them but to ensure their "active participation in the civil and ecclesial community. That is a demanding and even tiring process, yet one that will gradually contribute to the formation of consciences capable of acknowledging each individual as a unique and unrepeatable person." I think, too, of "the elderly who, also due to their disability, are sometimes considered a burden." Yet each of them is able to offer "a unique contribution to the common good through their remarkable life stories." Let me repeat: we need to have "the courage to give a voice to those who are discriminated against due to their disability, because sadly, in some countries even today, people find it hard to acknowledge them as persons of equal dignity."[77]

Inadequate Understandings of Universal Love

99. A love capable of transcending borders is the basis of what in every city and country can be called "social friendship." Genuine social friendship within a society makes true universal openness possible. This is a far cry from the false universalism of those who constantly travel abroad because they cannot tolerate or love their own people. Those who look down on their own people tend to create within society categories of first and second class, people of greater or lesser dignity, people enjoying greater or fewer rights. In this way, they deny that there is room for everybody.

100. I am certainly not proposing an authoritarian and abstract universalism, devised or planned by a small group and presented as an ideal for the sake of leveling, dominating, and plundering. One model of globalization in fact "consciously aims at a one-dimensional uniformity and seeks to eliminate all differences and traditions in a superficial quest for unity. . . . If a certain kind of globalization claims to make everyone uniform, to level everyone out, that globalization destroys the rich gifts and uniqueness of each person and each people."[78] This false universalism ends up depriving the world of its various colors, its beauty, and, ultimately, its humanity. For "the future is not monochrome; if we are courageous, we can contemplate it in all the variety and diversity of what each individual person has to offer. How much our human family needs to learn to live together in harmony and peace, without all of us having to be the same!"[79]

Beyond a World of "Associates"

101. Let us now return to the parable of the Good Samaritan, for it still has much to say to us. An injured man lay on the roadside. The people walking by him did not heed their interior summons to act as neighbors; they were concerned with their duties, their social status, their professional position within society. They considered themselves important for the society of the time, and were anxious to play their proper part. The man on the roadside, bruised and abandoned, was a distraction, an

interruption from all that; in any event, he was hardly important. He was a "nobody," undistinguished, irrelevant to their plans for the future. The Good Samaritan transcended these narrow classifications. He himself did not fit into any of those categories; he was simply a foreigner without a place in society. Free of every label and position, he was able to interrupt his journey, change his plans, and unexpectedly come to the aid of an injured person who needed his help.

102. What would be the reaction to that same story nowadays, in a world that constantly witnesses the emergence and growth of social groups clinging to an identity that separates them from others? How would it affect those who organize themselves in a way that prevents any foreign presence that might threaten their identity and their closed and self-referential structures? There, even the possibility of acting as a neighbor is excluded; one is a neighbor only to those who serve their purpose. The word *neighbor* loses all meaning; there can only be "associates," partners in the pursuit of particular interests.[80]

Liberty, Equality, and Fraternity

103. Fraternity is born not only of a climate of respect for individual liberties, or even of a certain administratively guaranteed equality. Fraternity necessarily calls for something greater, which in turn enhances freedom and equality. What happens when fraternity is not consciously cultivated, when there is a lack of political will to promote it through education in fraternity, through dialogue, and through the recognition of the values of reciprocity and mutual enrichment? Liberty becomes nothing more than a condition for living as we will, completely free to choose to whom or what we will belong, or simply to possess or exploit. This shallow understanding has little to do with the richness of a liberty directed above all to love.

104. Nor is equality achieved by an abstract proclamation that "all men and women are equal." Instead, it is the result of the conscious and careful cultivation of fraternity. Those capable only of being "associates"

create closed worlds. Within that framework, what place is there for those who are not part of one's group of associates, yet long for a better life for themselves and their families?

105. Individualism does not make us more free, more equal, more fraternal. The mere sum of individual interests is not capable of generating a better world for the whole human family. Nor can it save us from the many ills that are now increasingly globalized. Radical individualism is a virus that is extremely difficult to eliminate, for it is clever. It makes us believe that everything consists in giving free rein to our own ambitions, as if by pursuing ever greater ambitions and creating safety nets we would somehow be serving the common good.

A Universal Love That Promotes Persons

106. Social friendship and universal fraternity necessarily call for an acknowledgment of the worth of every human person, always and everywhere. If each individual is of such great worth, it must be stated clearly and firmly that "the mere fact that some people are born in places with fewer resources or less development does not justify the fact that they are living with less dignity."[81] This is a basic principle of social life that tends to be ignored in a variety of ways by those who sense that it does not fit into their worldview or serve their purposes.

107. Every human being has the right to live with dignity and to develop integrally; this fundamental right cannot be denied by any country. People have this right even if they are unproductive, or were born with or developed limitations. This does not detract from their great dignity as human persons, a dignity based not on circumstances but on the intrinsic worth of their being. Unless this basic principle is upheld, there will be no future either for fraternity or for the survival of humanity.

108. Some societies accept this principle in part. They agree that opportunities should be available to everyone, but then go on to say that everything depends on the individual. From this skewed perspective, it

would be pointless "to favor an investment in efforts to help the slow, the weak or the less talented to find opportunities in life."[82] Investments in assistance to the vulnerable could prove unprofitable; they might make things less efficient. No. What we need in fact are states and civil institutions that are present and active, that look beyond the free and efficient working of certain economic, political or ideological systems, and are primarily concerned with individuals and the common good.

109. Some people are born into economically stable families, receive a fine education, grow up well nourished, or naturally possess great talent. They will certainly not need a proactive state; they need only claim their freedom. Yet the same rule clearly does not apply to a disabled person, to someone born in dire poverty, to those lacking a good education and with little access to adequate health care. If a society is governed primarily by the criteria of market freedom and efficiency, there is no place for such persons, and fraternity will remain just another vague ideal.

110. Indeed, "to claim economic freedom while real conditions bar many people from actual access to it, and while possibilities for employment continue to shrink, is to practice doublespeak."[83] Words like *freedom*, *democracy*, or *fraternity* prove meaningless, for the fact is that "only when our economic and social system no longer produces even a single victim, a single person cast aside, will we be able to celebrate the feast of universal fraternity."[84] A truly human and fraternal society will be capable of ensuring in an efficient and stable way that each of its members is accompanied at every stage of life. Not only by providing for their basic needs, but by enabling them to give the best of themselves, even though their performance may be less than optimum, their pace slow or their efficiency limited.

111. The human person, with his or her inalienable rights, is by nature open to relationship. Implanted deep within us is the call to transcend ourselves through an encounter with others. For this reason, "care must be taken not to fall into certain errors which can arise from

a misunderstanding of the concept of human rights and from its misuse. Today there is a tendency to claim ever broader individual—I am tempted to say individualistic—rights. Underlying this is a conception of the human person as detached from all social and anthropological contexts, as if the person were a "monad" (*monás*), increasingly unconcerned with others. . . . Unless the rights of each individual are harmoniously ordered to the greater good, those rights will end up being considered limitless and consequently will become a source of conflicts and violence."[85]

Promoting the Moral Good

112. Nor can we fail to mention that seeking and pursuing the good of others and of the entire human family also implies helping individuals and societies to mature in the moral values that foster integral human development. The New Testament describes one fruit of the Holy Spirit (cf. Gal 5:22) as *agathosyne*; the Greek word expresses attachment to the good, pursuit of the good. Even more, it suggests a striving for excellence and what is best for others, their growth in maturity and health, the cultivation of values, and not simply material wellbeing. A similar expression exists in Latin: *benevolentia*. This is an attitude that "wills the good" of others; it bespeaks a yearning for goodness, an inclination toward all that is fine and excellent, a desire to fill the lives of others with what is beautiful, sublime, and edifying.

113. Here, regrettably, I feel bound to reiterate that "we have had enough of immorality and the mockery of ethics, goodness, faith and honesty. It is time to acknowledge that light-hearted superficiality has done us no good. Once the foundations of social life are corroded, what ensues are battles over conflicting interests."[86] Let us return to promoting the good, for ourselves and for the whole human family, and thus advance together toward an authentic and integral growth. Every society needs to ensure that values are passed on; otherwise, what is handed down are selfishness,

violence, corruption in its various forms, indifference, and, ultimately, a life closed to transcendence and entrenched in individual interests.

The Value of Solidarity

114. I would like especially to mention solidarity, which, "as a moral virtue and social attitude born of personal conversion, calls for commitment on the part of those responsible for education and formation. I think first of families, called to a primary and vital mission of education. Families are the first place where the values of love and fraternity, togetherness and sharing, concern and care for others are lived out and handed on. They are also the privileged milieu for transmitting the faith, beginning with those first simple gestures of devotion which mothers teach their children. Teachers, who have the challenging task of training children and youth in schools or other settings, should be conscious that their responsibility extends also to the moral, spiritual and social aspects of life. The values of freedom, mutual respect and solidarity can be handed on from a tender age. . . . Communicators also have a responsibility for education and formation, especially nowadays, when the means of information and communication are so widespread."[87]

115. At a time when everything seems to disintegrate and lose consistency, it is good for us to appeal to the "solidity"[88] born of the consciousness that we are responsible for the fragility of others as we strive to build a common future. Solidarity finds concrete expression in service, which can take a variety of forms in an effort to care for others. And service in great part means "caring for vulnerability, for the vulnerable members of our families, our society, our people." In offering such service, individuals learn to "set aside their own wishes and desires, their pursuit of power, before the concrete gaze of those who are most vulnerable . . . Service always looks to their faces, touches their flesh, senses their closeness and even, in some cases, 'suffers' that closeness and tries to help them. Service is never ideological, for we do not serve ideas, we serve people."[89]

116. The needy generally "practice the special solidarity that exists among those who are poor and suffering, and which our civilization seems to have forgotten or would prefer in fact to forget. *Solidarity* is a word that is not always well received; in certain situations, it has become a dirty word, a word that dare not be said. Solidarity means much more than engaging in sporadic acts of generosity. It means thinking and acting in terms of community. It means that the lives of all are prior to the appropriation of goods by a few. It also means combatting the structural causes of poverty, inequality, the lack of work, land and housing, the denial of social and labor rights. It means confronting the destructive effects of the empire of money. . . . Solidarity, understood in its most profound meaning, is a way of making history, and this is what popular movements are doing."[90]

117. When we speak of the need to care for our common home, our planet, we appeal to that spark of universal consciousness and mutual concern that may still be present in people's hearts. Those who enjoy a surplus of water yet choose to conserve it for the sake of the greater human family have attained a moral stature that allows them to look beyond themselves and the group to which they belong. How marvelously human! The same attitude is demanded if we are to recognize the rights of all people, even those born beyond our own borders.

Re-envisaging the Social Role of Property

118. The world exists for everyone, because all of us were born with the same dignity. Differences of color, religion, talent, place of birth, or residence, and so many others, cannot be used to justify the privileges of some over the rights of all. As a community, we have an obligation to ensure that every person lives with dignity and has sufficient opportunities for his or her integral development.

119. In the first Christian centuries, a number of thinkers developed a universal vision in their reflections on the common destination of created goods.[91] This led them to realize that if one person lacks what is necessary

to live with dignity, it is because another person is detaining it. Saint John Chrysostom summarizes it in this way: "Not to share our wealth with the poor is to rob them and take away their livelihood. The riches we possess are not our own, but theirs as well."[92] In the words of Saint Gregory the Great, "When we provide the needy with their basic needs, we are giving them what belongs to them, not to us."[93]

120. Once more, I would like to echo a statement of Saint John Paul II whose forcefulness has perhaps been insufficiently recognized: "God gave the earth to the whole human race for the sustenance of all its members, without excluding or favoring anyone."[94] For my part, I would observe that "the Christian tradition has never recognized the right to private property as absolute or inviolable, and has stressed the social purpose of all forms of private property."[95] The principle of the common use of created goods is the "first principle of the whole ethical and social order";[96] it is a natural and inherent right that takes priority over others.[97] All other rights having to do with the goods necessary for the integral fulfillment of persons, including that of private property or any other type of property, should—in the words of Saint Paul VI—"in no way hinder [this right], but should actively facilitate its implementation."[98] The right to private property can only be considered a secondary natural right, derived from the principle of the universal destination of created goods. This has concrete consequences that ought to be reflected in the workings of society. Yet it often happens that secondary rights displace primary and overriding rights, in practice making them irrelevant.

Rights without Borders

121. No one, then, can remain excluded because of his or her place of birth, much less because of privileges enjoyed by others who were born in lands of greater opportunity. The limits and borders of individual states cannot stand in the way of this. As it is unacceptable that some have fewer rights by virtue of being women, it is likewise unacceptable

that the mere place of one's birth or residence should result in his or her possessing fewer opportunities for a developed and dignified life.

122. Development must not aim at the amassing of wealth by a few, but must ensure "human rights—personal and social, economic and political, including the rights of nations and of peoples."[99] The right of some to free enterprise or market freedom cannot supersede the rights of peoples and the dignity of the poor, or, for that matter, respect for the natural environment, for "if we make something our own, it is only to administer it for the good of all."[100]

123. Business activity is essentially "a noble vocation, directed to producing wealth and improving our world."[101] God encourages us to develop the talents he gave us, and he has made our universe one of immense potential. In God's plan, each individual is called to promote his or her own development,[102] and this includes finding the best economic and technological means of multiplying goods and increasing wealth. Business abilities, which are a gift from God, should always be clearly directed to the development of others and to eliminating poverty, especially through the creation of diversified work opportunities. The right to private property is always accompanied by the primary and prior principle of the subordination of all private property to the universal destination of the earth's goods, and thus the right of all to their use.[103]

The Rights of Peoples

124. Nowadays, a firm belief in the common destination of the earth's goods requires that this principle also be applied to nations, their territories, and their resources. Seen from the standpoint not only of the legitimacy of private property and the rights of its citizens, but also of the first principle of the common destination of goods, we can then say that each country also belongs to the foreigner, inasmuch as a territory's goods must not be denied to a needy person coming from elsewhere. As the Bishops of the United States have taught, there are fundamental rights

that "precede any society because they flow from the dignity granted to each person as created by God."[104]

125. This presupposes a different way of understanding relations and exchanges between countries. If every human being possesses an inalienable dignity, if all people are my brothers and sisters, and if the world truly belongs to everyone, then it matters little whether my neighbor was born in my country or elsewhere. My own country also shares responsibility for his or her development, although it can fulfill that responsibility in a variety of ways. It can offer a generous welcome to those in urgent need, or work to improve living conditions in their native lands by refusing to exploit those countries or to drain them of natural resources, backing corrupt systems that hinder the dignified development of their peoples. What applies to nations is true also for different regions within each country, since there too great inequalities often exist. At times, the inability to recognize equal human dignity leads the more developed regions in some countries to think that they can jettison the "dead weight" of poorer regions and so increase their level of consumption.

126. We are really speaking about a new network of international relations, since there is no way to resolve the serious problems of our world if we continue to think only in terms of mutual assistance between individuals or small groups. Nor should we forget that "inequity affects not only individuals but entire countries; it compels us to consider an ethics of international relations."[105] Indeed, justice requires recognizing and respecting not only the rights of individuals, but also social rights and the rights of peoples.[106] This means finding a way to ensure "the fundamental right of peoples to subsistence and progress,"[107] a right which is at times severely restricted by the pressure created by foreign debt. In many instances, debt repayment not only fails to promote development but gravely limits and conditions it. While respecting the principle that all legitimately acquired debt must be repaid, the way in which many poor countries fulfill this obligation should not end up compromising their very existence and growth.

127. Certainly, all this calls for an alternative way of thinking. Without an attempt to enter into that way of thinking, what I am saying here will sound wildly unrealistic. On the other hand, if we accept the great principle that there are rights born of our inalienable human dignity, we can rise to the challenge of envisaging a new humanity. We can aspire to a world that provides land, housing, and work for all. This is the true path of peace, not the senseless and myopic strategy of sowing fear and mistrust in the face of outside threats. For a real and lasting peace will only be possible "on the basis of a global ethic of solidarity and cooperation in the service of a future shaped by interdependence and shared responsibility in the whole human family."[108]

CHAPTER FOUR

A HEART OPEN TO THE WHOLE WORLD

128. If the conviction that all human beings are brothers and sisters is not to remain an abstract idea but to find concrete embodiment, then numerous related issues emerge, forcing us to see things in a new light and to develop new responses.

Borders and Their Limits

129. Complex challenges arise when our neighbor happens to be an immigrant.[109] Ideally, unnecessary migration ought to be avoided; this entails creating in countries of origin the conditions needed for a dignified life and integral development. Yet until substantial progress is made in achieving this goal, we are obliged to respect the right of all individuals to find a place that meets their basic needs and those of their families, and where they can find personal fulfillment. Our response to the arrival of migrating persons can be summarized by four words: welcome, protect, promote, and integrate. For "it is not a case of implementing welfare programs from the top down, but rather of undertaking a journey together, through these four actions, in order to build cities and countries that, while preserving their respective cultural and religious identity, are open to differences and know how to promote them in the spirit of human fraternity."[110]

130. This implies taking certain indispensable steps, especially in response to those who are fleeing grave humanitarian crises. As examples, we may cite: increasing and simplifying the granting of visas; adopting programs of individual and community sponsorship; opening humanitarian corridors for the most vulnerable refugees; providing suitable and dignified housing; guaranteeing personal security and access to basic services; ensuring adequate consular assistance and the right to retain personal identity documents; equitable access to the justice system; the possibility

of opening bank accounts and the guarantee of the minimum needed to survive; freedom of movement and the possibility of employment; protecting minors and ensuring their regular access to education; providing for programs of temporary guardianship or shelter; guaranteeing religious freedom; promoting integration into society; supporting the reuniting of families; and preparing local communities for the process of integration.[111]

131. For those who are not recent arrivals and already participate in the fabric of society, it is important to apply the concept of "citizenship," which "is based on the equality of rights and duties, under which all enjoy justice. It is therefore crucial to establish in our societies the concept of *full citizenship* and to reject the discriminatory use of the term *minorities,* which engenders feelings of isolation and inferiority. Its misuse paves the way for hostility and discord; it undoes any successes and takes away the religious and civil rights of some citizens who are thus discriminated against."[112]

132. Even when they take such essential steps, states are not able, on their own, to implement adequate solutions, "since the consequences of the decisions made by each inevitably have repercussions on the entire international community." As a result, "our response can only be the fruit of a common effort"[113] to develop a form of global governance with regard to movements of migration. Thus, there is "a need for mid-term and long-term planning which is not limited to emergency responses. Such planning should include effective assistance for integrating migrants in their receiving countries, while also promoting the development of their countries of origin through policies inspired by solidarity, yet not linking assistance to ideological strategies and practices alien or contrary to the cultures of the peoples being assisted."[114]

Reciprocal Gifts

133. The arrival of those who are different, coming from other ways of life and cultures, can be a gift, for "the stories of migrants are always

stories of an encounter between individuals and between cultures. For the communities and societies to which they come, migrants bring an opportunity for enrichment and the integral human development of all."[115] For this reason, "I especially urge young people not to play into the hands of those who would set them against other young people, newly arrived in their countries, and who would encourage them to view the latter as a threat, and not possessed of the same inalienable dignity as every other human being."[116]

134. Indeed, when we open our hearts to those who are different, this enables them, while continuing to be themselves, to develop in new ways. The different cultures that have flourished over the centuries need to be preserved, lest our world be impoverished. At the same time, those cultures should be encouraged to be open to new experiences through their encounter with other realities, for the risk of succumbing to cultural sclerosis is always present. That is why "we need to communicate with each other, to discover the gifts of each person, to promote that which unites us, and to regard our differences as an opportunity to grow in mutual respect. Patience and trust are called for in such dialogue, permitting individuals, families, and communities to hand on the values of their own culture and welcome the good that comes from others' experiences."[117]

135. Here I would mention some examples that I have used in the past. Latino culture is "a ferment of values and possibilities that can greatly enrich the United States," for "intense immigration always ends up influencing and transforming the culture of a place. . . . In Argentina, intense immigration from Italy has left a mark on the culture of the society, and the presence of some 200,000 Jews has a great effect on the cultural 'style' of Buenos Aires. Immigrants, if they are helped to integrate, are a blessing, a source of enrichment and new gift that encourages a society to grow."[118]

136. On an even broader scale, Grand Imam Ahmad Al-Tayyeb and I have observed that "good relations between East and West are indisputably necessary for both. They must not be neglected, so that each can be enriched by the other's culture through fruitful exchange and dialogue. The West can discover in the East remedies for those spiritual and religious maladies that are caused by a prevailing materialism. And the East can find in the West many elements that can help free it from weakness, division, conflict and scientific, technical and cultural decline. It is important to pay attention to religious, cultural and historical differences that are a vital component in shaping the character, culture and civilization of the East. It is likewise important to reinforce the bond of fundamental human rights in order to help ensure a dignified life for all the men and women of East and West, avoiding the politics of double standards."[119]

A Fruitful Exchange

137. Mutual assistance between countries proves enriching for each. A country that moves forward while remaining solidly grounded in its original cultural substratum is a treasure for the whole of humanity. We need to develop the awareness that nowadays we are either all saved together or no one is saved. Poverty, decadence, and suffering in one part of the earth are a silent breeding ground for problems that will end up affecting the entire planet. If we are troubled by the extinction of certain species, we should be all the more troubled that in some parts of our world individuals or peoples are prevented from developing their potential and beauty by poverty or other structural limitations. In the end, this will impoverish us all.

138. Although this has always been true, never has it been more evident than in our own day, when the world is interconnected by globalization. We need to attain a global juridical, political, and economic order "which can increase and give direction to international cooperation for the development of all peoples in solidarity."[120] Ultimately, this will benefit the

entire world, since "development aid for poor countries" implies "creating wealth for all."[121] From the standpoint of integral development, this presupposes "giving poorer nations an effective voice in shared decision-making"[122] and the capacity to "facilitate access to the international market on the part of countries suffering from poverty and underdevelopment."[123]

A Gratuitousness Open to Others

139. Even so, I do not wish to limit this presentation to a kind of utilitarian approach. There is always the factor of "gratuitousness": the ability to do some things simply because they are good in themselves, without concern for personal gain or recompense. Gratuitousness makes it possible for us to welcome the stranger, even though this brings us no immediate tangible benefit. Some countries, though, presume to accept only scientists or investors.

140. Life without fraternal gratuitousness becomes a form of frenetic commerce, in which we are constantly weighing up what we give and what we get back in return. God, on the other hand, gives freely, to the point of helping even those who are unfaithful; he "makes his sun rise on the evil and on the good" (Mt 5:45). There is a reason why Jesus told us: "When you give alms, do not let your right hand know what your left hand is doing, so that your alms may be in secret" (Mt 6:3–4). We received life freely; we paid nothing for it. Consequently, all of us are able to give without expecting anything in return, to do good to others without demanding that they treat us well in return. As Jesus told his disciples: "Without cost you have received, without cost you are to give" (Mt 10:8).

141. The true worth of the different countries of our world is measured by their ability to think not simply as a country but also as part of the larger human family. This is seen especially in times of crisis. Narrow forms of nationalism are an extreme expression of an inability to grasp the meaning of this gratuitousness. They err in thinking that they can develop on their own, heedless of the ruin of others, that by closing

their doors to others they will be better protected. Immigrants are seen as usurpers who have nothing to offer. This leads to the simplistic belief that the poor are dangerous and useless, while the powerful are generous benefactors. Only a social and political culture that readily and "gratuitously" welcomes others will have a future.

Local and Universal

142. It should be kept in mind that "an innate tension exists between globalization and localization. We need to pay attention to the global so as to avoid narrowness and banality. Yet we also need to look to the local, which keeps our feet on the ground. Together, the two prevent us from falling into one of two extremes. In the first, people get caught up in an abstract, globalized universe. . . . In the other, they turn into a museum of local folklore, a world apart, doomed to doing the same things over and over, incapable of being challenged by novelty or appreciating the beauty which God bestows beyond their borders."[124] We need to have a global outlook to save ourselves from petty provincialism. When our house stops being a home and starts to become an enclosure, a cell, then the global comes to our rescue, like a "final cause" that draws us toward our fulfillment. At the same time, though, the local has to be eagerly embraced, for it possesses something that the global does not: it is capable of being a leaven, of bringing enrichment, of sparking mechanisms of subsidiarity. Universal fraternity and social friendship are thus two inseparable and equally vital poles in every society. To separate them would be to disfigure each and to create a dangerous polarization.

Local Flavor

143. The solution is not an openness that spurns its own richness. Just as there can be no dialogue with "others" without a sense of our own identity, so there can be no openness between peoples except on the basis of love for one's own land, one's own people, one's own cultural roots. I cannot truly encounter another unless I stand on firm foundations, for it is on the basis of these that I can accept the gift the other brings and

in turn offer an authentic gift of my own. I can welcome others who are different, and value the unique contribution they have to make, only if I am firmly rooted in my own people and culture. Everyone loves and cares for his or her native land and village, just as they love and care for their home and are personally responsible for its upkeep. The common good likewise requires that we protect and love our native land. Otherwise, the consequences of a disaster in one country will end up affecting the entire planet. All this brings out the positive meaning of the right to property: I care for and cultivate something that I possess, in such a way that it can contribute to the good of all.

144. It also gives rise to healthy and enriching exchanges. The experience of being raised in a particular place and sharing in a particular culture gives us insight into aspects of reality that others cannot so easily perceive. Universal does not necessarily mean bland, uniform, and standardized, based on a single prevailing cultural model, for this will ultimately lead to the loss of a rich palette of shades and colors, and result in utter monotony. Such was the temptation referred to in the ancient account of the Tower of Babel. The attempt to build a tower that would reach to heaven was not an expression of unity between various peoples speaking to one another from their diversity. Instead, it was a misguided attempt, born of pride and ambition, to create a unity other than that willed by God in his providential plan for the nations (cf. Gn 11:1–9).

145. There can be a false openness to the universal, born of the shallowness of those lacking insight into the genius of their native land or harboring unresolved resentment toward their own people. Whatever the case, "we constantly have to broaden our horizons and see the greater good which will benefit us all. But this has to be done without evasion or uprooting. We need to sink our roots deeper into the fertile soil and history of our native place, which is a gift of God. We can work on a small scale, in our own neighborhood, but with a larger perspective. . . . The global need not stifle, nor the particular prove barren";[125] our model must be that of a polyhedron, in which the value of each individual is

respected, where "the whole is greater than the part, but it is also greater than the sum of its parts."[126]

A Universal Horizon

146. There is a kind of "local" narcissism unrelated to a healthy love of one's own people and culture. It is born of a certain insecurity and fear of the other that leads to rejection and the desire to erect walls for self-defense. Yet it is impossible to be "local" in a healthy way without being sincerely open to the universal, without feeling challenged by what is happening in other places, without openness to enrichment by other cultures, and without solidarity and concern for the tragedies affecting other peoples. A "local narcissism" instead frets over a limited number of ideas, customs, and forms of security; incapable of admiring the vast potential and beauty offered by the larger world, it lacks an authentic and generous spirit of solidarity. Life on the local level thus becomes less and less welcoming, people less open to complementarity. Its possibilities for development narrow; it grows weary and infirm. A healthy culture, on the other hand, is open and welcoming by its very nature; indeed, "a culture without universal values is not truly a culture."[127]

147. Let us realize that as our minds and hearts narrow, the less capable we become of understanding the world around us. Without encountering and relating to differences, it is hard to achieve a clear and complete understanding even of ourselves and of our native land. Other cultures are not "enemies" from which we need to protect ourselves, but differing reflections of the inexhaustible richness of human life. Seeing ourselves from the perspective of another, of one who is different, we can better recognize our own unique features and those of our culture: its richness, its possibilities, and its limitations. Our local experience needs to develop "in contrast to" and "in harmony with" the experiences of others living in diverse cultural contexts.[128]

148. In fact, a healthy openness never threatens one's own identity. A living culture, enriched by elements from other places, does not import a

mere carbon copy of those new elements, but integrates them in its own unique way. The result is a new synthesis that is ultimately beneficial to all, since the original culture itself ends up being nourished. That is why I have urged indigenous peoples to cherish their roots and their ancestral cultures. At the same time, though, I have wanted to stress that I have no intention of proposing "a completely enclosed, a-historic, static 'indigenism' that would reject any kind of blending (*mestizaje*)." For "our own cultural identity is strengthened and enriched as a result of dialogue with those unlike ourselves. Nor is our authentic identity preserved by an impoverished isolation."[129] The world grows and is filled with new beauty, thanks to the successive syntheses produced between cultures that are open and free of any form of cultural imposition.

149. For a healthy relationship between love of one's native land and a sound sense of belonging to our larger human family, it is helpful to keep in mind that global society is not the sum total of different countries, but rather the communion that exists among them. The mutual sense of belonging is prior to the emergence of individual groups. Each particular group becomes part of the fabric of universal communion and there discovers its own beauty. All individuals, whatever their origin, know that they are part of the greater human family, without which they will not be able to understand themselves fully.

150. To see things in this way brings the joyful realization that no one people, culture, or individual can achieve everything on its own: to attain fulfillment in life we need others. An awareness of our own limitations and incompleteness, far from being a threat, becomes the key to envisaging and pursuing a common project. For "man is a limited being who is himself limitless."[130]

Starting with Our Own Region

151. Thanks to regional exchanges, by which poorer countries become open to the wider world, universality does not necessarily water down their distinct features. An appropriate and authentic openness to the

world presupposes the capacity to be open to one's neighbor within a family of nations. Cultural, economic, and political integration with neighboring peoples should therefore be accompanied by a process of education that promotes the value of love for one's neighbor, the first indispensable step toward attaining a healthy universal integration.

152. In some areas of our cities, there is still a lively sense of neighborhood. Each person quite spontaneously perceives a duty to accompany and help his or her neighbor. In places where these community values are maintained, people experience a closeness marked by gratitude, solidarity, and reciprocity. The neighborhood gives them a sense of shared identity.[131] Would that neighboring countries were able to encourage a similar neighborly spirit between their peoples! Yet the spirit of individualism also affects relations between countries. The danger of thinking that we have to protect ourselves from one another, of viewing others as competitors or dangerous enemies, also affects relations between peoples in the same region. Perhaps we were trained in this kind of fear and mistrust.

153. There are powerful countries and large businesses that profit from this isolation and prefer to negotiate with each country separately. On the other hand, small or poor countries can sign agreements with their regional neighbors that will allow them to negotiate as a bloc and thus avoid being cut off, isolated, and dependent on the great powers. Today, no state can ensure the common good of its population if it remains isolated.

CHAPTER FIVE

A BETTER KIND OF POLITICS

154. The development of a global community of fraternity based on the practice of social friendship on the part of peoples and nations calls for a better kind of politics, one truly at the service of the common good. Sadly, politics today often takes forms that hinder progress toward a different world.

Forms of Populism and Liberalism

155. Lack of concern for the vulnerable can hide behind a populism that exploits them demagogically for its own purposes, or a liberalism that serves the economic interests of the powerful. In both cases, it becomes difficult to envisage an open world that makes room for everyone, including the most vulnerable, and shows respect for different cultures.

Popular vs. Populist

156. In recent years, the words *populism* and *populist* have invaded the communications media and everyday conversation. As a result, they have lost whatever value they might have had, and have become another source of polarization in an already divided society. Efforts are made to classify entire peoples, groups, societies, and governments as "populist" or not. Nowadays it has become impossible for someone to express a view on any subject without being categorized one way or the other, either to be unfairly discredited or to be praised to the skies.

157. The attempt to see populism as a key for interpreting social reality is problematic in another way: it disregards the legitimate meaning of the word *people*. Any effort to remove this concept from common parlance could lead to the elimination of the very notion of democracy as "government by the people." If we wish to maintain that society is more than a mere aggregate of individuals, the term *people* proves necessary. There

are social phenomena that create majorities, as well as megatrends and communitarian aspirations. Men and women are capable of coming up with shared goals that transcend their differences and can thus engage in a common endeavor. Then too, it is extremely difficult to carry out a long-term project unless it becomes a collective aspiration. All these factors lie behind our use of the words *people* and *popular*. Unless they are taken into account—together with a sound critique of demagoguery—a fundamental aspect of social reality would be overlooked.

158. Here, there can be a misunderstanding. "'People' is not a logical category, nor is it a mystical category, if by that we mean that everything the people does is good, or that the people is an 'angelic' reality. Rather, it is a mythic category. . . . When you have to explain what you mean by people, you use logical categories for the sake of explanation, and necessarily so. Yet in that way you cannot explain what it means to belong to a people. The word 'people' has a deeper meaning that cannot be set forth in purely logical terms. To be part of a people is to be part of a shared identity arising from social and cultural bonds. And that is not something automatic, but rather a slow, difficult process . . . of advancing toward a common project."[132]

159. "Popular" leaders, those capable of interpreting the feelings and cultural dynamics of a people, and significant trends in society, do exist. The service they provide by their efforts to unite and lead can become the basis of an enduring vision of transformation and growth that would also include making room for others in the pursuit of the common good. But this can degenerate into an unhealthy "populism" when individuals are able to exploit politically a people's culture, under whatever ideological banner, for their own personal advantage or continuing grip on power. Or when, at other times, they seek popularity by appealing to the basest and most selfish inclinations of certain sectors of the population. This becomes all the more serious when, whether in cruder or more subtle forms, it leads to the usurpation of institutions and laws.

160. Closed populist groups distort the word *people*, since they are not talking about a true people. The concept of "people" is in fact open-ended. A living and dynamic people, a people with a future, is one constantly open to a new synthesis through its ability to welcome differences. In this way, it does not deny its proper identity, but is open to being mobilized, challenged, broadened, and enriched by others, and thus to further growth and development.

161. Another sign of the decline of popular leadership is concern for short-term advantage. One meets popular demands for the sake of gaining votes or support, but without advancing in an arduous and constant effort to generate the resources people need to develop and earn a living by their own efforts and creativity. In this regard, I have made it clear that "I have no intention of proposing an irresponsible populism."[133] Eliminating inequality requires an economic growth that can help to tap each region's potential and thus guarantee a sustainable equality.[134] At the same time, it follows that "welfare projects, which meet certain urgent needs, should be considered merely temporary responses."[135]

162. The biggest issue is employment. The truly "popular" thing—since it promotes the good of the people—is to provide everyone with the opportunity to nurture the seeds that God has planted in each of us: our talents, our initiative, and our innate resources. This is the finest help we can give to the poor, the best path to a life of dignity. Hence my insistence that "helping the poor financially must always be a provisional solution in the face of pressing needs. The broader objective should always be to allow them a dignified life through work."[136] Since production systems may change, political systems must keep working to structure society in such a way that everyone has a chance to contribute his or her own talents and efforts. For "there is no poverty worse than that which takes away work and the dignity of work."[137] In a genuinely developed society, work is an essential dimension of social life, for it is not only a means of earning one's daily bread, but also of personal growth, the building of healthy relationships, self-expression, and the exchange of gifts.

Work gives us a sense of shared responsibility for the development of the world, and ultimately, for our life as a people.

The Benefits and Limits of Liberal Approaches

163. The concept of a "people," which naturally entails a positive view of community and cultural bonds, is usually rejected by individualistic liberal approaches, which view society as merely the sum of coexisting interests. One speaks of respect for freedom, but without roots in a shared narrative; in certain contexts, those who defend the rights of the most vulnerable members of society tend to be criticized as populists. The notion of a people is considered an abstract construct, something that does not really exist. But this is to create a needless dichotomy. Neither the notion of "people" nor that of "neighbor" can be considered purely abstract or romantic, in such a way that social organization, science, and civic institutions can be rejected or treated with contempt.[138]

164. Charity, on the other hand, unites both dimensions—the abstract and the institutional—since it calls for an effective process of historical change that embraces everything: institutions, law, technology, experience, professional expertise, scientific analysis, administrative procedures, and so forth. For that matter, "private life cannot exist unless it is protected by public order. A domestic hearth has no real warmth unless it is safeguarded by law, by a state of tranquility founded on law, and enjoys a minimum of wellbeing ensured by the division of labor, commercial exchange, social justice and political citizenship."[139]

165. True charity is capable of incorporating all these elements in its concern for others. In the case of personal encounters, including those involving a distant or forgotten brother or sister, it can do so by employing all the resources that the institutions of an organized, free, and creative society are capable of generating. Even the Good Samaritan, for example, needed to have a nearby inn that could provide the help that he was personally unable to offer. Love of neighbor is concrete and squanders none of the resources needed to bring about historical change that

can benefit the poor and disadvantaged. At times, however, leftist ideologies or social doctrines linked to individualistic ways of acting and ineffective procedures affect only a few, while the majority of those left behind remain dependent on the goodwill of others. This demonstrates the need for a greater spirit of fraternity, but also a more efficient worldwide organization to help resolve the problems plaguing the abandoned who are suffering and dying in poor countries. It also shows that there is no one solution, no single acceptable methodology, no economic recipe that can be applied indiscriminately to all. Even the most rigorous scientific studies can propose different courses of action.

166. Everything, then, depends on our ability to see the need for a change of heart, attitudes, and lifestyles. Otherwise, political propaganda, the media, and the shapers of public opinion will continue to promote an individualistic and uncritical culture subservient to unregulated economic interests and societal institutions at the service of those who already enjoy too much power. My criticism of the technocratic paradigm involves more than simply thinking that if we control its excesses everything will be fine. The bigger risk does not come from specific objects, material realities, or institutions, but from the way that they are used. It has to do with human weakness, the proclivity to selfishness that is part of what the Christian tradition refers to as "concupiscence": the human inclination to be concerned only with myself, my group, my own petty interests. Concupiscence is not a flaw limited to our own day. It has been present from the beginning of humanity, and has simply changed and taken on different forms down the ages, using whatever means each moment of history can provide. Concupiscence, however, can be overcome with the help of God.

167. Education and upbringing, concern for others, a well-integrated view of life and spiritual growth: all these are essential for quality human relationships and for enabling society itself to react against injustices, aberrations, and abuses of economic, technological, political, and media power. Some liberal approaches ignore this factor of human

weakness; they envisage a world that follows a determined order and is capable by itself of ensuring a bright future and providing solutions for every problem.

168. The marketplace, by itself, cannot resolve every problem, however much we are asked to believe this dogma of neoliberal faith. Whatever the challenge, this impoverished and repetitive school of thought always offers the same recipes. Neoliberalism simply reproduces itself by resorting to the magic theories of "spillover" or "trickle"—without using the name—as the only solution to societal problems. There is little appreciation of the fact that the alleged "spillover" does not resolve the inequality that gives rise to new forms of violence threatening the fabric of society. It is imperative to have a proactive economic policy directed at "promoting an economy that favors productive diversity and business creativity"[140] and makes it possible for jobs to be created and not cut. Financial speculation fundamentally aimed at quick profit continues to wreak havoc. Indeed, "without internal forms of solidarity and mutual trust, the market cannot completely fulfill its proper economic function. And today this trust has ceased to exist."[141] The story did not end the way it was meant to, and the dogmatic formulae of prevailing economic theory proved not to be infallible. The fragility of world systems in the face of the pandemic has demonstrated that not everything can be resolved by market freedom. It has also shown that, in addition to recovering a sound political life that is not subject to the dictates of finance, "we must put human dignity back at the center and on that pillar build the alternative social structures we need."[142]

169. In some closed and monochrome economic approaches, for example, there seems to be no place for popular movements that unite the unemployed, temporary, and informal workers and many others who do not easily find a place in existing structures. Yet those movements manage various forms of popular economy and of community production. What is needed is a model of social, political, and economic participation "that can include popular movements and invigorate local, national and

international governing structures with that torrent of moral energy that springs from including the excluded in the building of a common destiny," while also ensuring that "these experiences of solidarity which grow up from below, from the subsoil of the planet—can come together, be more coordinated, keep on meeting one another."[143] This, however, must happen in a way that will not betray their distinctive way of acting as "sowers of change, promoters of a process involving millions of actions, great and small, creatively intertwined like words in a poem."[144] In that sense, such movements are "social poets" that, in their own way, work, propose, promote, and liberate. They help make possible an integral human development that goes beyond "the idea of social policies being a policy for the poor, but never with the poor and never of the poor, much less part of a project that reunites peoples."[145] They may be troublesome, and certain "theorists" may find it hard to classify them, yet we must find the courage to acknowledge that, without them, "democracy atrophies, turns into a mere word, a formality; it loses its representative character and becomes disembodied, since it leaves out the people in their daily struggle for dignity, in the building of their future."[146]

International Power

170. I would once more observe that "the financial crisis of 2007–08 provided an opportunity to develop a new economy, more attentive to ethical principles, and new ways of regulating speculative financial practices and virtual wealth. But the response to the crisis did not include rethinking the outdated criteria which continue to rule the world."[147] Indeed, it appears that the actual strategies developed worldwide in the wake of the crisis fostered greater individualism, less integration, and increased freedom for the truly powerful, who always find a way to escape unscathed.

171. I would also insist that "to give to each his own—to cite the classic definition of justice—means that no human individual or group can consider itself absolute, entitled to bypass the dignity and the rights of

other individuals or their social groupings. The effective distribution of power (especially political, economic, defense-related, and technological power) among a plurality of subjects, and the creation of a juridical system for regulating claims and interests, are one concrete way of limiting power. Yet today's world presents us with many false rights and—at the same time—broad sectors which are vulnerable, victims of power badly exercised."[148]

172. The twenty-first century "is witnessing a weakening of the power of nation states, chiefly because the economic and financial sectors, being transnational, tend to prevail over the political. Given this situation, it is essential to devise stronger and more efficiently organized international institutions, with functionaries who are appointed fairly by agreement among national governments, and empowered to impose sanctions."[149] When we talk about the possibility of some form of world authority regulated by law,[150] we need not necessarily think of a personal authority. Still, such an authority ought at least to promote more effective world organizations, equipped with the power to provide for the global common good, the elimination of hunger and poverty, and the sure defense of fundamental human rights.

173. In this regard, I would also note the need for a reform of "the United Nations Organization, and likewise of economic institutions and international finance, so that the concept of the family of nations can acquire real teeth."[151] Needless to say, this calls for clear legal limits to avoid power being co-opted only by a few countries and to prevent cultural impositions or a restriction of the basic freedoms of weaker nations on the basis of ideological differences. For "the international community is a juridical community founded on the sovereignty of each member state, without bonds of subordination that deny or limit its independence."[152] At the same time, "the work of the United Nations, according to the principles set forth in the Preamble and the first Articles of its founding Charter, can be seen as the development and promotion of the rule of law, based on the realization that justice is an essential condition for achieving the ideal

of universal fraternity. . . . There is a need to ensure the uncontested rule of law and tireless recourse to negotiation, mediation and arbitration, as proposed by the Charter of the United Nations, which constitutes truly a fundamental juridical norm."[153] There is need to prevent this Organization from being delegitimized, since its problems and shortcomings are capable of being jointly addressed and resolved.

174. Courage and generosity are needed in order freely to establish shared goals and to ensure the worldwide observance of certain essential norms. For this to be truly useful, it is essential to uphold "the need to be faithful to agreements undertaken (*pacta sunt servanda*),"[154] and to avoid the "temptation to appeal to the law of force rather than to the force of law."[155] This means reinforcing the "normative instruments for the peaceful resolution of controversies . . . so as to strengthen their scope and binding force."[156] Among these normative instruments, preference should be given to multilateral agreements between states, because, more than bilateral agreements, they guarantee the promotion of a truly universal common good and the protection of weaker states.

175. Providentially, many groups and organizations within civil society help to compensate for the shortcomings of the international community, its lack of coordination in complex situations, its lack of attention to fundamental human rights and to the critical needs of certain groups. Here we can see a concrete application of the principle of subsidiarity, which justifies the participation and activity of communities and organizations on lower levels as a means of integrating and complementing the activity of the state. These groups and organizations often carry out commendable efforts in the service of the common good and their members at times show true heroism, revealing something of the grandeur of which our humanity is still capable.

Social and Political Charity

176. For many people today, politics is a distasteful word, often due to the mistakes, corruption, and inefficiency of some politicians. There are also

attempts to discredit politics, to replace it with economics, or to twist it to one ideology or another. Yet can our world function without politics? Can there be an effective process of growth toward universal fraternity and social peace without a sound political life?[157]

The Politics We Need

177. Here I would once more observe that "politics must not be subject to the economy, nor should the economy be subject to the dictates of an efficiency-driven paradigm of technocracy."[158] Although misuse of power, corruption, disregard for law, and inefficiency must clearly be rejected, "economics without politics cannot be justified, since this would make it impossible to favor other ways of handling the various aspects of the present crisis."[159] Instead, "what is needed is a politics which is far-sighted and capable of a new, integral and interdisciplinary approach to handling the different aspects of the crisis."[160] In other words, a "healthy politics . . . capable of reforming and coordinating institutions, promoting best practices and overcoming undue pressure and bureaucratic inertia."[161] We cannot expect economics to do this, nor can we allow economics to take over the real power of the state.

178. In the face of many petty forms of politics focused on immediate interests, I would repeat that "true statecraft is manifest when, in difficult times, we uphold high principles and think of the long-term common good. Political powers do not find it easy to assume this duty in the work of nation-building,"[162] much less in forging a common project for the human family, now and in the future. Thinking of those who will come after us does not serve electoral purposes, yet it is what authentic justice demands. As the Bishops of Portugal have taught, the earth "is lent to each generation, to be handed on to the generation that follows."[163]

179. Global society is suffering from grave structural deficiencies that cannot be resolved by piecemeal solutions or quick fixes. Much needs to change, through fundamental reform and major renewal. Only a healthy politics, involving the most diverse sectors and skills, is capable

of overseeing this process. An economy that is an integral part of a political, social, cultural, and popular program directed to the common good could pave the way for "different possibilities which do not involve stifling human creativity and its ideals of progress, but rather directing that energy along new channels."[164]

Political Love

180. Recognizing that all people are our brothers and sisters, and seeking forms of social friendship that include everyone, is not merely utopian. It demands a decisive commitment to devising effective means to this end. Any effort along these lines becomes a noble exercise of charity. For whereas individuals can help others in need, when they join together in initiating social processes of fraternity and justice for all, they enter the "field of charity at its most vast, namely political charity."[165] This entails working for a social and political order whose soul is social charity.[166] Once more, I appeal for a renewed appreciation of politics as "a lofty vocation and one of the highest forms of charity, inasmuch as it seeks the common good."[167]

181. Every commitment inspired by the Church's social doctrine is "derived from charity, which according to the teaching of Jesus is the synthesis of the entire Law (cf. Mt 22:36–40)."[168] This means acknowledging that "love, overflowing with small gestures of mutual care, is also civic and political, and it makes itself felt in every action that seeks to build a better world."[169] For this reason, charity finds expression not only in close and intimate relationships but also in "macro-relationships: social, economic and political."[170]

182. This political charity is born of a social awareness that transcends every individualistic mindset: "'Social charity makes us love the common good,' it makes us effectively seek the good of all people, considered not only as individuals or private persons, but also in the social dimension that unites them."[171] Each of us is fully a person when we are part of a people; at the same time, there are no peoples without respect for the

individuality of each person. *People* and *person* are correlative terms. Nonetheless, there are attempts nowadays to reduce persons to isolated individuals easily manipulated by powers pursuing spurious interests. Good politics will seek ways of building communities at every level of social life, in order to recalibrate and reorient globalization and thus avoid its disruptive effects.

Effective Love

183. "Social love"[172] makes it possible to advance toward a civilization of love, to which all of us can feel called. Charity, with its impulse to universality, is capable of building a new world.[173] No mere sentiment, it is the best means of discovering effective paths of development for everyone. Social love is a "force capable of inspiring new ways of approaching the problems of today's world, of profoundly renewing structures, social organizations and legal systems from within."[174]

184. Charity is at the heart of every healthy and open society, yet today "it is easily dismissed as irrelevant for interpreting and giving direction to moral responsibility."[175] Charity, when accompanied by a commitment to the truth, is much more than personal feeling, and consequently need not "fall prey to contingent subjective emotions and opinions."[176] Indeed its close relation to truth fosters its universality and preserves it from being "confined to a narrow field devoid of relationships."[177] Otherwise, it would be "excluded from the plans and processes of promoting human development of universal range, in dialogue between knowledge and praxis."[178] Without truth, emotion lacks relational and social content. Charity's openness to truth thus protects it from "a fideism that deprives it of its human and universal breadth."[179]

185. Charity needs the light of the truth that we constantly seek. "That light is both the light of reason and the light of faith,"[180] and does not admit any form of relativism. Yet it also respects the development of the sciences and their essential contribution to finding the surest and most practical means of achieving the desired results. For when the good of

others is at stake, good intentions are not enough. Concrete efforts must be made to bring about whatever they and their nations need for the sake of their development.

The Exercise of Political Love

186. There is a kind of love that is "elicited": its acts proceed directly from the virtue of charity and are directed to individuals and peoples. There is also a "commanded" love, expressed in those acts of charity that spur people to create more sound institutions, more just regulations, more supportive structures.[181] It follows that "it is an equally indispensable act of love to strive to organize and structure society so that one's neighbor will not find himself in poverty."[182] It is an act of charity to assist someone suffering, but it is also an act of charity, even if we do not know that person, to work to change the social conditions that caused his or her suffering. If someone helps an elderly person cross a river, that is a fine act of charity. The politician, on the other hand, builds a bridge, and that too is an act of charity. While one person can help another by providing something to eat, the politician creates a job for that other person, and thus practices a lofty form of charity that ennobles his or her political activity.

Sacrifices Born of Love

187. This charity, which is the spiritual heart of politics, is always a preferential love shown to those in greatest need; it undergirds everything we do on their behalf.[183] Only a gaze transformed by charity can enable the dignity of others to be recognized and, as a consequence, the poor to be acknowledged and valued in their dignity, respected in their identity and culture, and thus truly integrated into society. That gaze is at the heart of the authentic spirit of politics. It sees paths open up that are different from those of a soulless pragmatism. It makes us realize that "the scandal of poverty cannot be addressed by promoting strategies of containment that only tranquilize the poor and render them tame and inoffensive. How sad it is when we find, behind allegedly altruistic works, the other

being reduced to passivity."[184] What are needed are new pathways of self-expression and participation in society. Education serves these by making it possible for each human being to shape his or her own future. Here too we see the importance of the principle of subsidiarity, which is inseparable from the principle of solidarity.

188. These considerations help us recognize the urgent need to combat all that threatens or violates fundamental human rights. Politicians are called to "tend to the needs of individuals and peoples. To tend those in need takes strength and tenderness, effort and generosity in the midst of a functionalistic and privatized mindset that inexorably leads to a 'throwaway culture.' . . . It involves taking responsibility for the present with its situations of utter marginalization and anguish, and being capable of bestowing dignity upon it."[185] It will likewise inspire intense efforts to ensure that "everything be done to protect the status and dignity of the human person."[186] Politicians are doers, builders with ambitious goals, possessed of a broad, realistic, and pragmatic gaze that looks beyond their own borders. Their biggest concern should not be about a drop in the polls, but about finding effective solutions to "the phenomenon of social and economic exclusion, with its baneful consequences: human trafficking, the marketing of human organs and tissues, the sexual exploitation of boys and girls, slave labor, including prostitution, the drug and weapons trade, terrorism and international organized crime. Such is the magnitude of these situations, and their toll in innocent lives, that we must avoid every temptation to fall into a declarationist nominalism that would assuage our consciences. We need to ensure that our institutions are truly effective in the struggle against all these scourges."[187] This includes taking intelligent advantage of the immense resources offered by technological development.

189. We are still far from a globalization of the most basic of human rights. That is why world politics needs to make the effective elimination of hunger one of its foremost and imperative goals. Indeed, "when financial speculation manipulates the price of food, treating it as just

another commodity, millions of people suffer and die from hunger. At the same time, tons of food are thrown away. This constitutes a genuine scandal. Hunger is criminal; food is an inalienable right."[188] Often, as we carry on our semantic or ideological disputes, we allow our brothers and sisters to die of hunger and thirst, without shelter or access to health care. Alongside these basic needs that remain unmet, trafficking in persons represents another source of shame for humanity, one that international politics, moving beyond fine speeches and good intentions, must no longer tolerate. These things are essential; they can no longer be deferred.

A Love That Integrates and Unites

190. Political charity is also expressed in a spirit of openness to everyone. Government leaders should be the first to make the sacrifices that foster encounter and to seek convergence on at least some issues. They should be ready to listen to other points of view and to make room for everyone. Through sacrifice and patience, they can help to create a beautiful polyhedral reality in which everyone has a place. Here, economic negotiations do not work. Something else is required: an exchange of gifts for the common good. It may seem naïve and utopian, yet we cannot renounce this lofty aim.

191. At a time when various forms of fundamentalist intolerance are damaging relationships between individuals, groups, and peoples, let us be committed to living and teaching the value of respect for others, a love capable of welcoming differences, and the priority of the dignity of every human being over his or her ideas, opinions, practices, and even sins. Even as forms of fanaticism, closedmindedness, and social and cultural fragmentation proliferate in present-day society, a good politician will take the first step and insist that different voices be heard. Disagreements may well give rise to conflicts, but uniformity proves stifling and leads to cultural decay. May we not be content with being enclosed in one fragment of reality.

192. In this regard, Grand Imam Ahmad Al-Tayyeb and I have called upon "the architects of international policy and world economy to work strenuously to spread the culture of tolerance and of living together in peace; to intervene at the earliest opportunity to stop the shedding of innocent blood."[189] When a specific policy sows hatred and fear toward other nations in the name of its own country's welfare, there is need to be concerned, to react in time, and immediately to correct the course.

Fruitfulness over Results

193. Apart from their tireless activity, politicians are also men and women. They are called to practice love in their daily interpersonal relationships. As persons, they need to consider that "the modern world, with its technical advances, tends increasingly to functionalize the satisfaction of human desires, now classified and subdivided among different services. Less and less will people be called by name, less and less will this unique being be treated as a person with his or her own feelings, sufferings, problems, joys and family. Their illnesses will be known only in order to cure them, their financial needs only to provide for them, their lack of a home only to give them lodging, their desires for recreation and entertainment only to satisfy them." Yet it must never be forgotten that "loving the most insignificant of human beings as a brother, as if there were no one else in the world but him, cannot be considered a waste of time."[190]

194. Politics too must make room for a tender love of others. "What is tenderness? It is love that draws near and becomes real. A movement that starts from our heart and reaches the eyes, the ears and the hands . . . Tenderness is the path of choice for the strongest, most courageous men and women."[191] Amid the daily concerns of political life, "the smallest, the weakest, the poorest should touch our hearts: indeed, they have a 'right' to appeal to our heart and soul. They are our brothers and sisters, and as such we must love and care for them."[192]

195. All this can help us realize that what is important is not constantly achieving great results, since these are not always possible. In political

activity, we should remember that, "appearances notwithstanding, every person is immensely holy and deserves our love. Consequently, if I can help at least one person to have a better life, that already justifies the offering of my life. It is a wonderful thing to be God's faithful people. We achieve fulfillment when we break down walls and our hearts are filled with faces and names!"[193] The great goals of our dreams and plans may only be achieved in part. Yet beyond this, those who love, and who no longer view politics merely as a quest for power, "may be sure that none of our acts of love will be lost, nor any of our acts of sincere concern for others. No single act of love for God will be lost, no generous effort is meaningless, no painful endurance is wasted. All of these encircle our world like a vital force."[194]

196. For this reason, it is truly noble to place our hope in the hidden power of the seeds of goodness we sow, and thus to initiate processes whose fruits will be reaped by others. Good politics combines love with hope and with confidence in the reserves of goodness present in human hearts. Indeed, "authentic political life, built upon respect for law and frank dialogue between individuals, is constantly renewed whenever there is a realization that every woman and man, and every new generation, brings the promise of new relational, intellectual, cultural and spiritual energies."[195]

197. Viewed in this way, politics is something more noble than posturing, marketing, and media spin. These sow nothing but division, conflict, and a bleak cynicism incapable of mobilizing people to pursue a common goal. At times, in thinking of the future, we do well to ask ourselves, "Why I am doing this?" "What is my real aim?" For as time goes on, reflecting on the past, the questions will not be: "How many people endorsed me?" "How many voted for me?" "How many had a positive image of me?" The real, and potentially painful, questions will be, "How much love did I put into my work?" "What did I do for the progress of our people?" "What mark did I leave on the life of society?" "What real bonds did I create?" "What positive forces did I unleash?" "How much social peace did I sow?" "What good did I achieve in the position that was entrusted to me?"

CHAPTER SIX

DIALOGUE AND FRIENDSHIP IN SOCIETY

198. Approaching, speaking, listening, looking at, coming to know and understand one another, and to find common ground: all these things are summed up in the one word *dialogue*. If we want to encounter and help one another, we have to dialogue. There is no need for me to stress the benefits of dialogue. I have only to think of what our world would be like without the patient dialogue of the many generous persons who keep families and communities together. Unlike disagreement and conflict, persistent and courageous dialogue does not make headlines, but quietly helps the world to live much better than we imagine.

Social Dialogue for a New Culture

199. Some people attempt to flee from reality, taking refuge in their own little world; others react to it with destructive violence. Yet "between selfish indifference and violent protest there is always another possible option: that of dialogue. Dialogue between generations; dialogue among our people, for we are that people; readiness to give and receive, while remaining open to the truth. A country flourishes when constructive dialogue occurs between its many rich cultural components: popular culture, university culture, youth culture, artistic culture, technological culture, economic culture, family culture and media culture."[196]

200. Dialogue is often confused with something quite different: the feverish exchange of opinions on social networks, frequently based on media information that is not always reliable. These exchanges are merely parallel monologues. They may attract some attention by their sharp and aggressive tone. But monologues engage no one, and their content is frequently self-serving and contradictory.

201. Indeed, the media's noisy potpourri of facts and opinions is often an obstacle to dialogue, since it lets everyone cling stubbornly to his or

her own ideas, interests, and choices, with the excuse that everyone else is wrong. It becomes easier to discredit and insult opponents from the outset than to open a respectful dialogue aimed at achieving agreement on a deeper level. Worse, this kind of language, usually drawn from media coverage of political campaigns, has become so widespread as to be part of daily conversation. Discussion is often manipulated by powerful special interests that seek to tilt public opinion unfairly in their favor. This kind of manipulation can be exercised not only by governments, but also in economics, politics, communications, religion, and in other spheres. Attempts can be made to justify or excuse it when it tends to serve one's own economic or ideological interests, but sooner or later it turns against those very interests.

202. Lack of dialogue means that in these individual sectors people are concerned not for the common good, but for the benefits of power or, at best, for ways to impose their own ideas. Round tables thus become mere negotiating sessions, in which individuals attempt to seize every possible advantage, rather than cooperating in the pursuit of the common good. The heroes of the future will be those who can break with this unhealthy mindset and determine respectfully to promote truthfulness, aside from personal interest. God willing, such heroes are quietly emerging, even now, in the midst of our society.

Building Together

203. Authentic social dialogue involves the ability to respect the other's point of view and to admit that it may include legitimate convictions and concerns. Based on their identity and experience, others have a contribution to make, and it is desirable that they should articulate their positions for the sake of a more fruitful public debate. When individuals or groups are consistent in their thinking, defend their values and convictions, and develop their arguments, this surely benefits society. Yet, this can only occur to the extent that there is genuine dialogue and openness to others. Indeed, "in a true spirit of dialogue, we grow in our ability to grasp the

significance of what others say and do, even if we cannot accept it as our own conviction. In this way, it becomes possible to be frank and open about our beliefs, while continuing to discuss, to seek points of contact, and above all, to work and struggle together."[197] Public discussion, if it truly makes room for everyone and does not manipulate or conceal information, is a constant stimulus to a better grasp of the truth, or at least its more effective expression. It keeps different sectors from becoming complacent and self-centered in their outlook and their limited concerns. Let us not forget that "differences are creative; they create tension and in the resolution of tension lies humanity's progress."[198]

204. There is a growing conviction that, together with specialized scientific advances, we are in need of greater interdisciplinary communication. Although reality is one, it can be approached from various angles and with different methodologies. There is a risk that a single scientific advance will be seen as the only possible lens for viewing a particular aspect of life, society, and the world. Researchers who are expert in their own field, yet also familiar with the findings of other sciences and disciplines, are in a position to discern other aspects of the object of their study and thus to become open to a more comprehensive and integral knowledge of reality.

205. In today's globalized world, "the media can help us to feel closer to one another, creating a sense of the unity of the human family which in turn can inspire solidarity and serious efforts to ensure a more dignified life for all. . . . The media can help us greatly in this, especially nowadays, when the networks of human communication have made unprecedented advances. The internet, in particular, offers immense possibilities for encounter and solidarity. This is something truly good, a gift from God."[199] We need constantly to ensure that present-day forms of communication are in fact guiding us to generous encounter with others, to honest pursuit of the whole truth, to service, to closeness to the underprivileged and to the promotion of the common good. As the Bishops of Australia have pointed out, we cannot accept "a digital world designed to exploit our weaknesses and bring out the worst in people."[200]

The Basis of Consensus

206. The solution is not relativism. Under the guise of tolerance, relativism ultimately leaves the interpretation of moral values to those in power, to be defined as they see fit. "In the absence of objective truths or sound principles other than the satisfaction of our own desires and immediate needs . . . we should not think that political efforts or the force of law will be sufficient. . . . When the culture itself is corrupt, and objective truth and universally valid principles are no longer upheld, then laws can only be seen as arbitrary impositions or obstacles to be avoided."[201]

207. Is it possible to be concerned for truth, to seek the truth that responds to life's deepest meaning? What is law without the conviction, born of age-old reflection and great wisdom, that each human being is sacred and inviolable? If society is to have a future, it must respect the truth of our human dignity and submit to that truth. Murder is not wrong simply because it is socially unacceptable and punished by law, but because of a deeper conviction. This is a non-negotiable truth attained by the use of reason and accepted in conscience. A society is noble and decent not least for its support of the pursuit of truth and its adherence to the most basic of truths.

208. We need to learn how to unmask the various ways that the truth is manipulated, distorted, and concealed in public and private discourse. What we call "truth" is not only the reporting of facts and events, such as we find in the daily papers. It is primarily the search for the solid foundations sustaining our decisions and our laws. This calls for acknowledging that the human mind is capable of transcending immediate concerns and grasping certain truths that are unchanging, as true now as in the past. As it peers into human nature, reason discovers universal values derived from that same nature.

209. Otherwise, is it not conceivable that those fundamental human rights which we now consider unassailable will be denied by those in power, once they have gained the "consensus" of an apathetic or intimidated population? Nor would a mere consensus between different nations, itself equally open to manipulation, suffice to protect them. We have

ample evidence of the great good of which we are capable, yet we also have to acknowledge our inherent destructiveness. Is not the indifference and the heartless individualism into which we have fallen also a result of our sloth in pursuing higher values, values that transcend our immediate needs? Relativism always brings the risk that some or other alleged truth will be imposed by the powerful or the clever. Yet, "when it is a matter of the moral norms prohibiting intrinsic evil, there are no privileges or exceptions for anyone. It makes no difference whether one is the master of the world or the 'poorest of the poor' on the face of the earth. Before the demands of morality we are all absolutely equal."[202]

210. What is now happening, and drawing us into a perverse and barren way of thinking, is the reduction of ethics and politics to physics. Good and evil no longer exist in themselves; there is only a calculus of benefits and burdens. As a result of the displacement of moral reasoning, the law is no longer seen as reflecting a fundamental notion of justice but as mirroring notions currently in vogue. Breakdown ensues: everything is "leveled down" by a superficial bartered consensus. In the end, the law of the strongest prevails.

Consensus and Truth

211. In a pluralistic society, dialogue is the best way to realize what ought always to be affirmed and respected apart from any ephemeral consensus. Such dialogue needs to be enriched and illumined by clear thinking, rational arguments, a variety of perspectives, and the contribution of different fields of knowledge and points of view. Nor can it exclude the conviction that it is possible to arrive at certain fundamental truths always to be upheld. Acknowledging the existence of certain enduring values, however demanding it may be to discern them, makes for a robust and solid social ethics. Once those fundamental values are acknowledged and adopted through dialogue and consensus, we realize that they rise above consensus; they transcend our concrete situations and remain non-negotiable. Our understanding of their meaning and scope can increase—and

in that respect, consensus is a dynamic reality—but in themselves, they are held to be enduring by virtue of their inherent meaning.

212. If something always serves the good functioning of society, is it not because, lying beyond it, there is an enduring truth accessible to the intellect? Inherent in the nature of human beings and society there exist certain basic structures to support our development and survival. Certain requirements thus ensue, and these can be discovered through dialogue, even though, strictly speaking, they are not created by consensus. The fact that certain rules are indispensable for the very life of society is a sign that they are good in and of themselves. There is no need, then, to oppose the interests of society, consensus, and the reality of objective truth. These three realities can be harmonized whenever, through dialogue, people are unafraid to get to the heart of an issue.

213. The dignity of others is to be respected in all circumstances, not because that dignity is something we have invented or imagined, but because human beings possess an intrinsic worth superior to that of material objects and contingent situations. This requires that they be treated differently. That every human being possesses an inalienable dignity is a truth that corresponds to human nature apart from all cultural change. For this reason, human beings have the same inviolable dignity in every age of history and no one can consider himself or herself authorized by particular situations to deny this conviction or to act against it. The intellect can investigate the reality of things through reflection, experience, and dialogue, and come to recognize in that reality, which transcends it, the basis of certain universal moral demands.

214. To agnostics, this foundation could prove sufficient to confer a solid and stable universal validity on basic and non-negotiable ethical principles that could serve to prevent further catastrophes. As believers, we are convinced that human nature, as the source of ethical principles, was created by God, and that ultimately it is he who gives those principles their solid foundation.[203] This does not result in an ethical rigidity nor

does it lead to the imposition of any one moral system, since fundamental and universally valid moral principles can be embodied in different practical rules. Thus, room for dialogue will always exist.

A New Culture

215. "Life, for all its confrontations, is the art of encounter."[204] I have frequently called for the growth of a culture of encounter capable of transcending our differences and divisions. This means working to create a many-faceted polyhedron whose different sides form a variegated unity, in which "the whole is greater than the part."[205] The image of a polyhedron can represent a society where differences coexist, complementing, enriching, and reciprocally illuminating one another, even amid disagreements and reservations. Each of us can learn something from others. No one is useless and no one is expendable. This also means finding ways to include those on the peripheries of life. For they have another way of looking at things; they see aspects of reality that are invisible to the centers of power where weighty decisions are made.

Encounter That Becomes Culture

216. The word *culture* points to something deeply embedded within a people, its most cherished convictions and its way of life. A people's "culture" is more than an abstract idea. It has to do with their desires, their interests, and ultimately the way they live their lives. To speak of a "culture of encounter" means that we, as a people, should be passionate about meeting others, seeking points of contact, building bridges, planning a project that includes everyone. This becomes an aspiration and a style of life. The subject of this culture is the people, not simply one part of society that would pacify the rest with the help of professional and media resources.

217. Social peace demands hard work, craftsmanship. It would be easier to keep freedoms and differences in check with cleverness and a few resources. But such a peace would be superficial and fragile, not the fruit of a culture of encounter that brings enduring stability. Integrating

differences is a much more difficult and slow process, yet it is the guarantee of a genuine and lasting peace. That peace is not achieved by recourse only to those who are pure and untainted, since "even people who can be considered questionable on account of their errors have something to offer which must not be overlooked."[206] Nor does it come from ignoring social demands or quelling disturbances, since it is not "a consensus on paper or a transient peace for a contented minority."[207] What is important is to create processes of encounter, processes that build a people that can accept differences. Let us arm our children with the weapons of dialogue! Let us teach them to fight the good fight of the culture of encounter!

The Joy of Acknowledging Others

218. All this calls for the ability to recognize other people's right to be themselves and to be different. This recognition, as it becomes a culture, makes possible the creation of a social covenant. Without it, subtle ways can be found to make others insignificant, irrelevant, of no value to society. While rejecting certain visible forms of violence, another more insidious kind of violence can take root: the violence of those who despise people who are different, especially when their demands in any way compromise their own particular interests.

219. When one part of society exploits all that the world has to offer, acting as if the poor did not exist, there will eventually be consequences. Sooner or later, ignoring the existence and rights of others will erupt in some form of violence, often when least expected. Liberty, equality, and fraternity can remain lofty ideals unless they apply to everyone. Encounter cannot take place only between the holders of economic, political, or academic power. Genuine social encounter calls for a dialogue that engages the culture shared by the majority of the population. It often happens that good ideas are not accepted by the poorer sectors of society because they are presented in a cultural garb that is not their own and with which they cannot identify. A realistic and inclusive social covenant

must also be a "cultural covenant," one that respects and acknowledges the different worldviews, cultures, and lifestyles that coexist in society.

220. Indigenous peoples, for example, are not opposed to progress, yet theirs is a different notion of progress, often more humanistic than the modern culture of developed peoples. Theirs is not a culture meant to benefit the powerful, those driven to create for themselves a kind of earthly paradise. Intolerance and lack of respect for indigenous popular cultures is a form of violence grounded in a cold and judgmental way of viewing them. No authentic, profound, and enduring change is possible unless it starts from the different cultures, particularly those of the poor. A cultural covenant eschews a monolithic understanding of the identity of a particular place; it entails respect for diversity by offering opportunities for advancement and social integration to all.

221. Such a covenant also demands the realization that some things may have to be renounced for the common good. No one can possess the whole truth or satisfy his or her every desire, since that pretension would lead to nullifying others by denying their rights. A false notion of tolerance has to give way to a dialogic realism on the part of men and women who remain faithful to their own principles while recognizing that others also have the right to do likewise. This is the genuine acknowledgment of the other that is made possible by love alone. We have to stand in the place of others, if we are to discover what is genuine, or at least understandable, in their motivations and concerns.

Recovering Kindness

222. Consumerist individualism has led to great injustice. Other persons come to be viewed simply as obstacles to our own serene existence; we end up treating them as annoyances and we become increasingly aggressive. This is even more the case in times of crisis, catastrophe, and hardship, when we are tempted to think in terms of the old saying, "every man for himself." Yet even then, we can choose to cultivate kindness. Those who do so become stars shining in the midst of darkness.

223. Saint Paul describes kindness as a fruit of the Holy Spirit (Gal 5:22). He uses the Greek word *chrestótes*, which describes an attitude that is gentle, pleasant, and supportive, not rude or coarse. Individuals who possess this quality help make other people's lives more bearable, especially by sharing the weight of their problems, needs, and fears. This way of treating others can take different forms: an act of kindness, a concern not to offend by word or deed, a readiness to alleviate their burdens. It involves "speaking words of comfort, strength, consolation and encouragement" and not "words that demean, sadden, anger or show scorn."[208]

224. Kindness frees us from the cruelty that at times infects human relationships, from the anxiety that prevents us from thinking of others, from the frantic flurry of activity that forgets that others also have a right to be happy. Often nowadays we find neither the time nor the energy to stop and be kind to others, to say "excuse me," "pardon me," "thank you." Yet every now and then, miraculously, a kind person appears and is willing to set everything else aside in order to show interest, to give the gift of a smile, to speak a word of encouragement, to listen amid general indifference. If we make a daily effort to do exactly this, we can create a healthy social atmosphere in which misunderstandings can be overcome and conflict forestalled. Kindness ought to be cultivated; it is no superficial bourgeois virtue. Precisely because it entails esteem and respect for others, once kindness becomes a culture within society it transforms lifestyles, relationships, and the ways ideas are discussed and compared. Kindness facilitates the quest for consensus; it opens new paths where hostility and conflict would burn all bridges.

CHAPTER SEVEN

PATHS OF RENEWED ENCOUNTER

225. In many parts of the world, there is a need for paths of peace to heal open wounds. There is also a need for peacemakers, men and women prepared to work boldly and creatively to initiate processes of healing and renewed encounter.

Starting Anew from the Truth

226. Renewed encounter does not mean returning to a time prior to conflicts. All of us change over time. Pain and conflict transform us. We no longer have use for empty diplomacy, dissimulation, double-speak, hidden agendas, and good manners that mask reality. Those who were fierce enemies have to speak from the stark and clear truth. They have to learn how to cultivate a penitential memory, one that can accept the past in order not to cloud the future with their own regrets, problems, and plans. Only by basing themselves on the historical truth of events will they be able to make a broad and persevering effort to understand one another and to strive for a new synthesis for the good of all. Every "peace process requires enduring commitment. It is a patient effort to seek truth and justice, to honor the memory of victims and to open the way, step by step, to a shared hope stronger than the desire for vengeance."[209] As the Bishops of the Congo have said with regard to one recurring conflict: "Peace agreements on paper will not be enough. We will have to go further, by respecting the demands of truth regarding the origins of this recurring crisis. The people have the right to know what happened."[210]

227. "Truth, in fact, is an inseparable companion of justice and mercy. All three together are essential to building peace; each, moreover, prevents the other from being altered. . . . Truth should not lead to revenge, but rather to reconciliation and forgiveness. Truth means telling families torn apart by pain what happened to their missing relatives. Truth

means confessing what happened to minors recruited by cruel and violent people. Truth means recognizing the pain of women who are victims of violence and abuse . . . Every act of violence committed against a human being is a wound in humanity's flesh; every violent death diminishes us as people. . . . Violence leads to more violence, hatred to more hatred, death to more death. We must break this cycle which seems inescapable."[211]

The Art and Architecture of Peace

228. The path to peace does not mean making society blandly uniform, but getting people to work together, side-by-side, in pursuing goals that benefit everyone. A wide variety of practical proposals and diverse experiences can help achieve shared objectives and serve the common good. The problems that a society is experiencing need to be clearly identified, so that the existence of different ways of understanding and resolving them can be appreciated. The path to social unity always entails acknowledging the possibility that others have, at least in part, a legitimate point of view, something worthwhile to contribute, even if they were in error or acted badly. "We should never confine others to what they may have said or done, but value them for the promise that they embody,"[212] a promise that always brings with it a spark of new hope.

229. The Bishops of South Africa have pointed out that true reconciliation is achieved proactively, "by forming a new society, a society based on service to others, rather than the desire to dominate; a society based on sharing what one has with others, rather than the selfish scramble by each for as much wealth as possible; a society in which the value of being together as human beings is ultimately more important than any lesser group, whether it be family, nation, race or culture."[213] As the Bishops of South Korea have pointed out, true peace "can be achieved only when we strive for justice through dialogue, pursuing reconciliation and mutual development."[214]

230. Working to overcome our divisions without losing our identity as individuals presumes that a basic sense of belonging is present in everyone. Indeed, "society benefits when each person and social group feels truly at home. In a family, parents, grandparents and children all feel at home; no one is excluded. If someone has a problem, even a serious one, even if he brought it upon himself, the rest of the family comes to his assistance; they support him. His problems are theirs. . . . In families, everyone contributes to the common purpose; everyone works for the common good, not denying each person's individuality but encouraging and supporting it. They may quarrel, but there is something that does not change: the family bond. Family disputes are always resolved afterwards. The joys and sorrows of each of its members are felt by all. That is what it means to be a family! If only we could view our political opponents or neighbors in the same way that we view our children or our spouse, mother or father! How good would this be! Do we love our society or is it still something remote, something anonymous that does not involve us, something to which we are not committed?"[215]

231. Negotiation often becomes necessary for shaping concrete paths to peace. Yet the processes of change that lead to lasting peace are crafted above all by peoples; each individual can act as an effective leaven by the way he or she lives each day. Great changes are not produced behind desks or in offices. This means that "everyone has a fundamental role to play in a single great creative project: to write a new page of history, a page full of hope, peace and reconciliation."[216] There is an "architecture" of peace, to which different institutions of society contribute, each according to its own area of expertise, but there is also an "art" of peace that involves us all. From the various peace processes that have taken place in different parts of the world, "we have learned that these ways of making peace, of placing reason above revenge, of the delicate harmony between politics and law, cannot ignore the involvement of ordinary people. Peace is not achieved by normative frameworks and institutional arrangements between well-meaning political or economic groups. . . . It

is always helpful to incorporate into our peace processes the experience of those sectors that have often been overlooked, so that communities themselves can influence the development of a collective memory."[217]

232. There is no end to the building of a country's social peace; rather, it is "an open-ended endeavor, a never-ending task that demands the commitment of everyone and challenges us to work tirelessly to build the unity of the nation. Despite obstacles, differences and varying perspectives on the way to achieve peaceful coexistence, this task summons us to persevere in the struggle to promote a 'culture of encounter.' This requires us to place at the center of all political, social and economic activity the human person, who enjoys the highest dignity, and respect for the common good. May this determination help us flee from the temptation for revenge and the satisfaction of short-term partisan interests."[218] Violent public demonstrations, on one side or the other, do not help in finding solutions. Mainly because, as the Bishops of Colombia have rightly noted, the "origins and objectives of civil demonstrations are not always clear; certain forms of political manipulation are present and in some cases they have been exploited for partisan interests."[219]

Beginning with the Least

233. Building social friendship does not only call for rapprochement between groups who took different sides at some troubled period of history, but also for a renewed encounter with the most impoverished and vulnerable sectors of society. For peace "is not merely absence of war but a tireless commitment—especially on the part of those of us charged with greater responsibility—to recognize, protect and concretely restore the dignity, so often overlooked or ignored, of our brothers and sisters, so that they can see themselves as the principal protagonists of the destiny of their nation."[220]

234. Often, the more vulnerable members of society are the victims of unfair generalizations. If at times the poor and the dispossessed react with attitudes that appear antisocial, we should realize that in many

cases those reactions are born of a history of scorn and social exclusion. The Latin American Bishops have observed that "only the closeness that makes us friends can enable us to appreciate deeply the values of the poor today, their legitimate desires, and their own manner of living the faith. The option for the poor should lead us to friendship with the poor."[221]

235. Those who work for tranquil social coexistence should never forget that inequality and lack of integral human development make peace impossible. Indeed, "without equal opportunities, different forms of aggression and conflict will find a fertile terrain for growth and eventually explode. When a society—whether local, national or global—is willing to leave a part of itself on the fringes, no political programs or resources spent on law enforcement or surveillance systems can indefinitely guarantee tranquility."[222] If we have to begin anew, it must always be from the least of our brothers and sisters.

The Value and Meaning of Forgiveness

236. There are those who prefer not to talk of reconciliation, for they think that conflict, violence, and breakdown are part of the normal functioning of a society. In any human group there are always going to be more or less subtle power struggles between different parties. Others think that promoting forgiveness means yielding ground and influence to others. For this reason, they feel it is better to keep things as they are, maintaining a balance of power between differing groups. Still others believe that reconciliation is a sign of weakness; incapable of truly serious dialogue, they choose to avoid problems by ignoring injustices. Unable to deal with problems, they opt for an apparent peace.

Inevitable Conflict

237. Forgiveness and reconciliation are central themes in Christianity and, in various ways, in other religions. Yet there is a risk that an inadequate understanding and presentation of these profound convictions can lead to fatalism, apathy, and injustice, or even intolerance and violence.

238. Jesus never promoted violence or intolerance. He openly condemned the use of force to gain power over others: "You know that the rulers of the Gentiles lord it over them, and their great ones are tyrants over them. It will not be so among you" (Mt 20:25–26). Instead, the Gospel tells us to forgive "seventy times seven" (Mt 18:22) and offers the example of the unmerciful servant who was himself forgiven, yet unable to forgive others in turn (cf. Mt 18:23–35).

239. Reading other texts of the New Testament, we can see how the early Christian communities, living in a pagan world marked by widespread corruption and aberrations, sought to show unfailing patience, tolerance, and understanding. Some texts are very clear in this regard: we are told to admonish our opponents "with gentleness" (2 Tm 2:25) and encouraged "to speak evil of no one, to avoid quarreling, to be gentle, and to show every courtesy to everyone. For we ourselves were once foolish" (Ti 3:2–3). The Acts of the Apostles notes that the disciples, albeit persecuted by some of the authorities, "had favor with all the people" (2:47; cf. 4:21, 33; 5:13).

240. Yet when we reflect upon forgiveness, peace, and social harmony, we also encounter the jarring saying of Christ: "Do not think that I have come to bring peace to the earth; I have not come to bring peace, but a sword. For I have come to set a man against his father, and a daughter against her mother, and a daughter-in-law against her mother-in-law; and a man's foes will be members of his own household" (Mt 10:34–36). These words need to be understood in the context of the chapter in which they are found, where it is clear that Jesus is speaking of fidelity to our decision to follow him; we are not to be ashamed of that decision, even if it entails hardships of various sorts, and even our loved ones refuse to accept it. Christ's words do not encourage us to seek conflict, but simply to endure it when it inevitably comes, lest deference to others, for the sake of supposed peace in our families or society, should detract from our own fidelity. Saint John Paul II observed that the Church "does not intend to condemn every possible form of social conflict. The Church

is well aware that in the course of history conflicts of interest between different social groups inevitably arise, and that in the face of such conflicts Christians must often take a position, honestly and decisively."[223]

Legitimate Conflict and Forgiveness

241. Nor does this mean calling for forgiveness when it involves renouncing our own rights, confronting corrupt officials, criminals, or those who would debase our dignity. We are called to love everyone, without exception; at the same time, loving an oppressor does not mean allowing him to keep oppressing us, or letting him think that what he does is acceptable. On the contrary, true love for an oppressor means seeking ways to make him cease his oppression; it means stripping him of a power that he does not know how to use, and that diminishes his own humanity and that of others. Forgiveness does not entail allowing oppressors to keep trampling on their own dignity and that of others, or letting criminals continue their wrongdoing. Those who suffer injustice have to defend strenuously their own rights and those of their family, precisely because they must preserve the dignity they have received as a loving gift from God. If a criminal has harmed me or a loved one, no one can forbid me from demanding justice and ensuring that this person—or anyone else—will not harm me, or others, again. This is entirely just; forgiveness does not forbid it but actually demands it.

242. The important thing is not to fuel anger, which is unhealthy for our own soul and the soul of our people, or to become obsessed with taking revenge and destroying the other. No one achieves inner peace or returns to a normal life in that way. The truth is that "no family, no group of neighbors, no ethnic group, much less a nation, has a future if the force that unites them, brings them together and resolves their differences is vengeance and hatred. We cannot come to terms and unite for the sake of revenge, or treating others with the same violence with which they treated us, or plotting opportunities for retaliation under

apparently legal auspices."[224] Nothing is gained this way and, in the end, everything is lost.

243. To be sure, "it is no easy task to overcome the bitter legacy of injustices, hostility and mistrust left by conflict. It can only be done by overcoming evil with good (cf. Rom 12:21) and by cultivating those virtues which foster reconciliation, solidarity and peace."[225] In this way, "persons who nourish goodness in their heart find that such goodness leads to a peaceful conscience and to profound joy, even in the midst of difficulties and misunderstandings. Even when affronted, goodness is never weak but rather, shows its strength by refusing to take revenge."[226] Each of us should realize that "even the harsh judgment I hold in my heart against my brother or my sister, the open wound that was never cured, the offense that was never forgiven, the rancour that is only going to hurt me, are all instances of a struggle that I carry within me, a little flame deep in my heart that needs to be extinguished before it turns into a great blaze."[227]

The Best Way to Move On

244. When conflicts are not resolved but kept hidden or buried in the past, silence can lead to complicity in grave misdeeds and sins. Authentic reconciliation does not flee from conflict, but is achieved in conflict, resolving it through dialogue and open, honest, and patient negotiation. Conflict between different groups "if it abstains from enmities and mutual hatred, gradually changes into an honest discussion of differences founded on a desire for justice."[228]

245. On numerous occasions, I have spoken of "a principle indispensable to the building of friendship in society: namely, that unity is greater than conflict. . . . This is not to opt for a kind of syncretism, or for the absorption of one into the other, but rather for a resolution which takes place on a higher plane and preserves what is valid and useful on both sides."[229] All of us know that "when we, as individuals and communities, learn to look beyond ourselves and our particular interests, then understanding

and mutual commitment bear fruit . . . in a setting where conflicts, tensions and even groups once considered inimical can attain a multifaceted unity that gives rise to new life."[230]

Memory

246. Of those who have endured much unjust and cruel suffering, a sort of "social forgiveness" must not be demanded. Reconciliation is a personal act, and no one can impose it upon an entire society, however great the need to foster it. In a strictly personal way, someone, by a free and generous decision, can choose not to demand punishment (cf. Mt 5:44–46), even if it is quite legitimately demanded by society and its justice system. However, it is not possible to proclaim a "blanket reconciliation" in an effort to bind wounds by decree or to cover injustices in a cloak of oblivion. Who can claim the right to forgive in the name of others? It is moving to see forgiveness shown by those who are able to leave behind the harm they suffered, but it is also humanly understandable in the case of those who cannot. In any case, forgetting is never the answer.

247. The Shoah must not be forgotten. It is "the enduring symbol of the depths to which human evil can sink when, spurred by false ideologies, it fails to recognize the fundamental dignity of each person, which merits unconditional respect regardless of ethnic origin or religious belief."[231] As I think of it, I cannot help but repeat this prayer: "Lord, remember us in your mercy. Grant us the grace to be ashamed of what we men have done, to be ashamed of this massive idolatry, of having despised and destroyed our own flesh which you formed from the earth, to which you gave life with your own breath of life. Never again, Lord, never again!."[232]

248. Nor must we forget the atomic bombs dropped on Hiroshima and Nagasaki. Once again, "I pay homage to all the victims, and I bow before the strength and dignity of those who, having survived those first moments, for years afterward bore in the flesh immense suffering, and in their spirit seeds of death that drained their vital energy. . . . We cannot allow present and future generations to lose the memory of

what happened. It is a memory that ensures and encourages the building of a more fair and fraternal future."[233] Neither must we forget the persecutions, the slave trade, and the ethnic killings that continue in various countries, as well as the many other historical events that make us ashamed of our humanity. They need to be remembered, always and ever anew. We must never grow accustomed or inured to them.

249. Nowadays, it is easy to be tempted to turn the page, to say that all these things happened long ago and we should look to the future. For God's sake, no! We can never move forward without remembering the past; we do not progress without an honest and unclouded memory. We need to "keep alive the flame of collective conscience, bearing witness to succeeding generations to the horror of what happened," because that witness "awakens and preserves the memory of the victims, so that the conscience of humanity may rise up in the face of every desire for dominance and destruction."[234] The victims themselves—individuals, social groups, or nations—need to do so, lest they succumb to the mindset that leads to justifying reprisals and every kind of violence in the name of the great evil endured. For this reason, I think not only of the need to remember the atrocities, but also all those who, amid such great inhumanity and corruption, retained their dignity and, with gestures small or large, chose the part of solidarity, forgiveness, and fraternity. To remember goodness is also a healthy thing.

Forgiving but Not Forgetting

250. Forgiving does not mean forgetting. Or better, in the face of a reality that can in no way be denied, relativized, or concealed, forgiveness is still possible. In the face of an action that can never be tolerated, justified, or excused, we can still forgive. In the face of something that cannot be forgotten for any reason, we can still forgive. Free and heartfelt forgiveness is something noble, a reflection of God's own infinite ability to forgive. If forgiveness is gratuitous, then it can be shown even to someone who resists repentance and is unable to beg pardon.

251. Those who truly forgive do not forget. Instead, they choose not to yield to the same destructive force that caused them so much suffering. They break the vicious circle; they halt the advance of the forces of destruction. They choose not to spread in society the spirit of revenge that will sooner or later return to take its toll. Revenge never truly satisfies victims. Some crimes are so horrendous and cruel that the punishment of those who perpetrated them does not serve to repair the harm done. Even killing the criminal would not be enough, nor could any form of torture prove commensurate with the sufferings inflicted on the victim. Revenge resolves nothing.

252. This does not mean impunity. Justice is properly sought solely out of love of justice itself, out of respect for the victims, as a means of preventing new crimes and protecting the common good, not as an alleged outlet for personal anger. Forgiveness is precisely what enables us to pursue justice without falling into a spiral of revenge or the injustice of forgetting.

253. When injustices have occurred on both sides, it is important to take into clear account whether they were equally grave or in any way comparable. Violence perpetrated by the state, using its structures and power, is not on the same level as that perpetrated by particular groups. In any event, one cannot claim that the unjust sufferings of one side alone should be commemorated. The Bishops of Croatia have stated that "we owe equal respect to every innocent victim. There can be no racial, national, confessional or partisan differences."[235]

254. I ask God "to prepare our hearts to encounter our brothers and sisters, so that we may overcome our differences rooted in political thinking, language, culture and religion. Let us ask him to anoint our whole being with the balm of his mercy, which heals the injuries caused by mistakes, misunderstandings and disputes. And let us ask him for the grace to send us forth, in humility and meekness, along the demanding but enriching path of seeking peace."[236]

War and the Death Penalty

255. There are two extreme situations that may come to be seen as solutions in especially dramatic circumstances, without realizing that they are false answers that do not resolve the problems they are meant to solve and ultimately do no more than introduce new elements of destruction in the fabric of national and global society. These are war and the death penalty.

The Injustice of War

256. "Deceit is in the mind of those who plan evil, but those who counsel peace have joy" (Prv 12:20). Yet there are those who seek solutions in war, frequently fueled by a breakdown in relations, hegemonic ambitions, abuses of power, fear of others, and a tendency to see diversity as an obstacle.[237] War is not a ghost from the past but a constant threat. Our world is encountering growing difficulties on the slow path to peace upon which it had embarked and which had already begun to bear good fruit.

257. Since conditions that favor the outbreak of wars are once again increasing, I can only reiterate that "war is the negation of all rights and a dramatic assault on the environment. If we want true integral human development for all, we must work tirelessly to avoid war between nations and peoples. To this end, there is a need to ensure the uncontested rule of law and tireless recourse to negotiation, mediation and arbitration, as proposed by the Charter of the United Nations, which constitutes truly a fundamental juridical norm."[238] The seventy-five years since the establishment of the United Nations and the experience of the first twenty years of this millennium have shown that the full application of international norms proves truly effective, and that failure to comply with them is detrimental. The Charter of the United Nations, when observed and applied with transparency and sincerity, is an obligatory reference point of justice and a channel of peace. Here there can be no room for disguising false intentions or placing the partisan interests of

one country or group above the global common good. If rules are considered simply as means to be used whenever it proves advantageous, and to be ignored when it is not, uncontrollable forces are unleashed that cause grave harm to societies, to the poor and vulnerable, to fraternal relations, to the environment and to cultural treasures, with irretrievable losses for the global community.

258. War can easily be chosen by invoking all sorts of allegedly humanitarian, defensive, or precautionary excuses, and even resorting to the manipulation of information. In recent decades, every single war has been ostensibly "justified." The Catechism of the Catholic Church speaks of the possibility of legitimate defense by means of military force, which involves demonstrating that certain "rigorous conditions of moral legitimacy"[239] have been met. Yet it is easy to fall into an overly broad interpretation of this potential right. In this way, some would also wrongly justify even "preventive" attacks or acts of war that can hardly avoid entailing "evils and disorders graver than the evil to be eliminated."[240] At issue is whether the development of nuclear, chemical, and biological weapons, and the enormous and growing possibilities offered by new technologies, have granted war an uncontrollable destructive power over great numbers of innocent civilians. The truth is that "never has humanity had such power over itself, yet nothing ensures that it will be used wisely."[241] We can no longer think of war as a solution, because its risks will probably always be greater than its supposed benefits. In view of this, it is very difficult nowadays to invoke the rational criteria elaborated in earlier centuries to speak of the possibility of a "just war." Never again war![242]

259. It should be added that, with increased globalization, what might appear as an immediate or practical solution for one part of the world initiates a chain of violent and often latent effects that end up harming the entire planet and opening the way to new and worse wars in the future. In today's world, there are no longer just isolated outbreaks of war in one country or another; instead, we are experiencing a "world

war fought piecemeal," since the destinies of countries are so closely interconnected on the global scene.

260. In the words of Saint John XXIII, "it no longer makes sense to maintain that war is a fit instrument with which to repair the violation of justice."[243] In making this point amid great international tension, he voiced the growing desire for peace emerging in the Cold War period. He supported the conviction that the arguments for peace are stronger than any calculation of particular interests and confidence in the use of weaponry. The opportunities offered by the end of the Cold War were not, however, adequately seized due to a lack of a vision for the future and a shared consciousness of our common destiny. Instead, it proved easier to pursue partisan interests without upholding the universal common good. The dread specter of war thus began to gain new ground.

261. Every war leaves our world worse than it was before. War is a failure of politics and of humanity, a shameful capitulation, a stinging defeat before the forces of evil. Let us not remain mired in theoretical discussions, but touch the wounded flesh of the victims. Let us look once more at all those civilians whose killing was considered "collateral damage." Let us ask the victims themselves. Let us think of the refugees and displaced, those who suffered the effects of atomic radiation or chemical attacks, the mothers who lost their children, and the boys and girls maimed or deprived of their childhood. Let us hear the true stories of these victims of violence, look at reality through their eyes, and listen with an open heart to the stories they tell. In this way, we will be able to grasp the abyss of evil at the heart of war. Nor will it trouble us to be deemed naive for choosing peace.

262. Rules by themselves will not suffice if we continue to think that the solution to current problems is deterrence through fear or the threat of nuclear, chemical, or biological weapons. Indeed, "if we take into consideration the principal threats to peace and security with their many dimensions in this multipolar world of the twenty-first century as, for

example, terrorism, asymmetrical conflicts, cybersecurity, environmental problems, poverty, not a few doubts arise regarding the inadequacy of nuclear deterrence as an effective response to such challenges. These concerns are even greater when we consider the catastrophic humanitarian and environmental consequences that would follow from any use of nuclear weapons, with devastating, indiscriminate and uncontainable effects, over time and space. . . . We need also to ask ourselves how sustainable is a stability based on fear, when it actually increases fear and undermines relationships of trust between peoples. International peace and stability cannot be based on a false sense of security, on the threat of mutual destruction or total annihilation, or on simply maintaining a balance of power. . . . In this context, the ultimate goal of the total elimination of nuclear weapons becomes both a challenge and a moral and humanitarian imperative. . . . Growing interdependence and globalization mean that any response to the threat of nuclear weapons should be collective and concerted, based on mutual trust. This trust can be built only through dialogue that is truly directed to the common good and not to the protection of veiled or particular interests."[244] With the money spent on weapons and other military expenditures, let us establish a global fund[245] that can finally put an end to hunger and favor development in the most impoverished countries, so that their citizens will not resort to violent or illusory solutions, or have to leave their countries in order to seek a more dignified life.

The Death Penalty

263. There is yet another way to eliminate others, one aimed not at countries but at individuals. It is the death penalty. Saint John Paul II stated clearly and firmly that the death penalty is inadequate from a moral standpoint and no longer necessary from that of penal justice.[246] There can be no stepping back from this position. Today we state clearly that "the death penalty is inadmissible"[247] and the Church is firmly committed to calling for its abolition worldwide.[248]

264. In the New Testament, while individuals are asked not to take justice into their own hands (cf. Rom 12:17, 19), there is also a recognition of the need for authorities to impose penalties on evildoers (cf. Rom 13:4; 1 Pt 2:14). Indeed, "civic life, structured around an organized community, needs rules of coexistence, the willful violation of which demands appropriate redress."[249] This means that legitimate public authority can and must "inflict punishments according to the seriousness of the crimes"[250] and that judicial power be guaranteed a "necessary independence in the realm of law."[251]

265. From the earliest centuries of the Church, some were clearly opposed to capital punishment. Lactantius, for example, held that "there ought to be no exception at all; that it is always unlawful to put a man to death."[252] Pope Nicholas I urged that efforts be made "to free from the punishment of death not only each of the innocent, but all the guilty as well."[253] During the trial of the murderers of two priests, Saint Augustine asked the judge not to take the life of the assassins with this argument: "We do not object to your depriving these wicked men of the freedom to commit further crimes. Our desire is rather that justice be satisfied without the taking of their lives or the maiming of their bodies in any part. And, at the same time, that by the coercive measures provided by the law, they be turned from their irrational fury to the calmness of men of sound mind, and from their evil deeds to some useful employment. This too is considered a condemnation, but who does not see that, when savage violence is restrained and remedies meant to produce repentance are provided, it should be considered a benefit rather than a mere punitive measure. . . . Do not let the atrocity of their sins feed a desire for vengeance, but desire instead to heal the wounds which those deeds have inflicted on their souls."[254]

266. Fear and resentment can easily lead to viewing punishment in a vindictive and even cruel way, rather than as part of a process of healing and reintegration into society. Nowadays, "in some political sectors and certain media, public and private violence and revenge are incited, not only against those responsible for committing crimes, but also against those suspected, whether proven or not, of breaking the law. . . . There is at

times a tendency to deliberately fabricate enemies: stereotyped figures who represent all the characteristics that society perceives or interprets as threatening. The mechanisms that form these images are the same that allowed the spread of racist ideas in their time."[255] This has made all the more dangerous the growing practice in some countries of resorting to preventive custody, imprisonment without trial, and especially the death penalty.

267. Here I would stress that "it is impossible to imagine that states today have no other means than capital punishment to protect the lives of other people from the unjust aggressor." Particularly serious in this regard are so-called extrajudicial or extralegal executions, which are "homicides deliberately committed by certain states and by their agents, often passed off as clashes with criminals or presented as the unintended consequences of the reasonable, necessary and proportionate use of force in applying the law."[256]

268. "The arguments against the death penalty are numerous and well-known. The Church has rightly called attention to several of these, such as the possibility of judicial error and the use made of such punishment by totalitarian and dictatorial regimes as a means of suppressing political dissidence or persecuting religious and cultural minorities, all victims whom the legislation of those regimes consider 'delinquents.' All Christians and people of good will are today called to work not only for the abolition of the death penalty, legal or illegal, in all its forms, but also to work for the improvement of prison conditions, out of respect for the human dignity of persons deprived of their freedom. I would link this to life imprisonment. . . . A life sentence is a secret death penalty."[257]

269. Let us keep in mind that "not even a murderer loses his personal dignity, and God himself pledges to guarantee this."[258] The firm rejection of the death penalty shows to what extent it is possible to recognize the inalienable dignity of every human being and to accept that he or she has a place in this universe. If I do not deny that dignity to the worst of

criminals, I will not deny it to anyone. I will give everyone the possibility of sharing this planet with me, despite all our differences.

270. I ask Christians who remain hesitant on this point, and those tempted to yield to violence in any form, to keep in mind the words of the book of Isaiah: "They shall beat their swords into plowshares" (2:4). For us, this prophecy took flesh in Christ Jesus who, seeing a disciple tempted to violence, said firmly: "Put your sword back into its place; for all who take the sword will perish by the sword" (Mt 26:52). These words echoed the ancient warning: "I will require a reckoning for human life. Whoever sheds the blood of a man, by man shall his blood be shed" (Gn 9:5–6). Jesus' reaction, which sprang from his heart, bridges the gap of the centuries and reaches the present as an enduring appeal.

CHAPTER EIGHT

RELIGIONS AT THE SERVICE OF FRATERNITY IN OUR WORLD

271. The different religions, based on their respect for each human person as a creature called to be a child of God, contribute significantly to building fraternity and defending justice in society. Dialogue between the followers of different religions does not take place simply for the sake of diplomacy, consideration, or tolerance. In the words of the Bishops of India, "the goal of dialogue is to establish friendship, peace and harmony, and to share spiritual and moral values and experiences in a spirit of truth and love."[259]

The Ultimate Foundation

272. As believers, we are convinced that, without an openness to the Father of all, there will be no solid and stable reasons for an appeal to fraternity. We are certain that "only with this awareness that we are not orphans, but children, can we live in peace with one another."[260] For "reason, by itself, is capable of grasping the equality between men and of giving stability to their civic coexistence, but it cannot establish fraternity."[261]

273. In this regard, I wish to cite the following memorable statement: "If there is no transcendent truth, in obedience to which man achieves his full identity, then there is no sure principle for guaranteeing just relations between people. Their self-interest as a class, group or nation would inevitably set them in opposition to one another. If one does not acknowledge transcendent truth, then the force of power takes over, and each person tends to make full use of the means at his disposal in order to impose his own interests or his own opinion, with no regard for the rights of others. . . . The root of modern totalitarianism is to be found in the denial of the transcendent dignity of the human person who, as

the visible image of the invisible God, is therefore by his very nature the subject of rights that no one may violate—no individual, group, class, nation or state. Not even the majority of the social body may violate these rights, by going against the minority."[262]

274. From our faith experience and from the wisdom accumulated over centuries, but also from lessons learned from our many weaknesses and failures, we, the believers of the different religions, know that our witness to God benefits our societies. The effort to seek God with a sincere heart, provided it is never sullied by ideological or self-serving aims, helps us recognize one another as traveling companions, truly brothers and sisters. We are convinced that "when, in the name of an ideology, there is an attempt to remove God from a society, that society ends up adoring idols, and very soon men and women lose their way, their dignity is trampled and their rights violated. You know well how much suffering is caused by the denial of freedom of conscience and of religious freedom, and how that wound leaves a humanity which is impoverished, because it lacks hope and ideals to guide it."[263]

275. It should be acknowledged that "among the most important causes of the crises of the modern world are a desensitized human conscience, a distancing from religious values and the prevailing individualism accompanied by materialistic philosophies that deify the human person and introduce worldly and material values in place of supreme and transcendental principles."[264] It is wrong when the only voices to be heard in public debate are those of the powerful and "experts." Room needs to be made for reflections born of religious traditions that are the repository of centuries of experience and wisdom. For "religious classics can prove meaningful in every age; they have an enduring power [to open new horizons, to stimulate thought, to expand the mind and the heart]." Yet often they are viewed with disdain as a result of "the myopia of a certain rationalism."[265]

276. For these reasons, the Church, while respecting the autonomy of political life, does not restrict her mission to the private sphere. On the contrary, "she cannot and must not remain on the sidelines" in the building of a better world, or fail to "reawaken the spiritual energy" that can contribute to the betterment of society.[266] It is true that religious ministers must not engage in the party politics that are the proper domain of the laity, but neither can they renounce the political dimension of life itself,[267] which involves a constant attention to the common good and a concern for integral human development. The Church "has a public role over and above her charitable and educational activities." She works for "the advancement of humanity and of universal fraternity."[268] She does not claim to compete with earthly powers, but to offer herself as "a family among families, this is the Church, open to bearing witness in today's world, open to faith hope and love for the Lord and for those whom he loves with a preferential love. A home with open doors. The Church is a home with open doors, because she is a mother."[269] And in imitation of Mary, the Mother of Jesus, "we want to be a Church that serves, that leaves home and goes forth from its places of worship, goes forth from its sacristies, in order to accompany life, to sustain hope, to be the sign of unity . . . to build bridges, to break down walls, to sow seeds of reconciliation."[270]

Christian Identity

277. The Church esteems the ways in which God works in other religions, and "rejects nothing of what is true and holy in these religions. She has a high regard for their manner of life and conduct, their precepts and doctrines which . . . often reflect a ray of that truth which enlightens all men and women."[271] Yet we Christians are very much aware that "if the music of the Gospel ceases to resonate in our very being, we will lose the joy born of compassion, the tender love born of trust, the capacity for reconciliation that has its source in our knowledge that we have been forgiven and sent forth. If the music of the Gospel ceases to sound in our

homes, our public squares, our workplaces, our political and financial life, then we will no longer hear the strains that challenge us to defend the dignity of every man and woman."[272] Others drink from other sources. For us the wellspring of human dignity and fraternity is in the Gospel of Jesus Christ. From it, there arises, "for Christian thought and for the action of the Church, the primacy given to relationship, to the encounter with the sacred mystery of the other, to universal communion with the entire human family, as a vocation of all."[273]

278. Called to take root in every place, the Church has been present for centuries throughout the world, for that is what it means to be "catholic." She can thus understand, from her own experience of grace and sin, the beauty of the invitation to universal love. Indeed, "all things human are our concern . . . wherever the councils of nations come together to establish the rights and duties of man, we are honored to be permitted to take our place among them."[274] For many Christians, this journey of fraternity also has a Mother, whose name is Mary. Having received this universal motherhood at the foot of the cross (cf. Jn 19:26), she cares not only for Jesus but also for "the rest of her children" (cf. Rv 12:17). In the power of the risen Lord, she wants to give birth to a new world, where all of us are brothers and sisters, where there is room for all those whom our societies discard, where justice and peace are resplendent.

279. We Christians ask that, in those countries where we are a minority, we be guaranteed freedom, even as we ourselves promote that freedom for non-Christians in places where they are a minority. One fundamental human right must not be forgotten in the journey toward fraternity and peace. It is religious freedom for believers of all religions. That freedom proclaims that we can "build harmony and understanding between different cultures and religions. It also testifies to the fact that, since the important things we share are so many, it is possible to find a means of serene, ordered and peaceful coexistence, accepting our differences and rejoicing that, as children of the one God, we are all brothers and sisters."[275]

280. At the same time, we ask God to strengthen unity within the Church, a unity enriched by differences reconciled by the working of the Spirit. For "in the one Spirit we were all baptized into one body" (1 Cor 12:13), in which each member has his or her distinctive contribution to make. As Saint Augustine said, "the ear sees through the eye, and the eye hears through the ear."[276] It is also urgent to continue to bear witness to the journey of encounter between the different Christian confessions. We cannot forget Christ's desire "that they may all be one" (cf. Jn 17:21). Hearing his call, we recognize with sorrow that the process of globalization still lacks the prophetic and spiritual contribution of unity among Christians. This notwithstanding, "even as we make this journey toward full communion, we already have the duty to offer common witness to the love of God for all people by working together in the service of humanity."[277]

Religion and Violence

281. A journey of peace is possible between religions. Its point of departure must be God's way of seeing things. "God does not see with his eyes, God sees with his heart. And God's love is the same for everyone, regardless of religion. Even if they are atheists, his love is the same. When the last day comes, and there is sufficient light to see things as they really are, we are going to find ourselves quite surprised."[278]

282. It follows that "we believers need to find occasions to speak with one another and to act together for the common good and the promotion of the poor. This has nothing to do with watering down or concealing our deepest convictions when we encounter others who think differently than ourselves. . . . For the deeper, stronger and richer our own identity is, the more we will be capable of enriching others with our own proper contribution."[279] We believers are challenged to return to our sources, in order to concentrate on what is essential: worship of God and love for our neighbor, lest some of our teachings, taken out of context, end up feeding forms of contempt, hatred, xenophobia, or negation of others. The truth

is that violence has no basis in our fundamental religious convictions, but only in their distortion.

283. Sincere and humble worship of God "bears fruit not in discrimination, hatred and violence, but in respect for the sacredness of life, respect for the dignity and freedom of others, and loving commitment to the welfare of all."[280] Truly, "whoever does not love does not know God, for God is love" (1 Jn 4:8). For this reason, "terrorism is deplorable and threatens the security of people—be they in the East or the West, the North or the South—and disseminates panic, terror and pessimism, but this is not due to religion, even when terrorists instrumentalize it. It is due, rather, to an accumulation of incorrect interpretations of religious texts and to policies linked to hunger, poverty, injustice, oppression, and pride. That is why it is so necessary to stop supporting terrorist movements fueled by financing, the provision of weapons and strategy, and by attempts to justify these movements, even using the media. All these must be regarded as international crimes that threaten security and world peace. Such terrorism must be condemned in all its forms and expressions."[281] Religious convictions about the sacred meaning of human life permit us "to recognize the fundamental values of our common humanity, values in the name of which we can and must cooperate, build and dialogue, pardon and grow; this will allow different voices to unite in creating a melody of sublime nobility and beauty, instead of fanatical cries of hatred."[282]

284. At times fundamentalist violence is unleashed in some groups, of whatever religion, by the rashness of their leaders. Yet, "the commandment of peace is inscribed in the depths of the religious traditions that we represent. . . . As religious leaders, we are called to be true 'people of dialogue,' to cooperate in building peace not as intermediaries but as authentic mediators. Intermediaries seek to give everyone a discount, ultimately in order to gain something for themselves. The mediator, on the other hand, is one who retains nothing for himself, but rather spends himself generously until he is consumed, knowing that the only gain is peace. Each one of us is called to be an artisan of peace, by uniting and

not dividing, by extinguishing hatred and not holding on to it, by opening paths of dialogue and not by constructing new walls."[283]

An Appeal

285. In my fraternal meeting, which I gladly recall, with the Grand Imam Ahmad Al-Tayyeb, "we resolutely [declared] that religions must never incite war, hateful attitudes, hostility and extremism, nor must they incite violence or the shedding of blood. These tragic realities are the consequence of a deviation from religious teachings. They result from a political manipulation of religions and from interpretations made by religious groups who, in the course of history, have taken advantage of the power of religious sentiment in the hearts of men and women. . . . God, the Almighty, has no need to be defended by anyone and does not want his name to be used to terrorize people."[284] For this reason I would like to reiterate here the appeal for peace, justice, and fraternity that we made together:

> "In the name of God, who has created all human beings equal in rights, duties and dignity, and who has called them to live together as brothers and sisters, to fill the earth and make known the values of goodness, love and peace;
>
> "In the name of innocent human life that God has forbidden to kill, affirming that whoever kills a person is like one who kills the whole of humanity, and that whoever saves a person is like one who saves the whole of humanity;
>
> "In the name of the poor, the destitute, the marginalized and those most in need, whom God has commanded us to help as a duty required of all persons, especially the wealthy and those of means;
>
> "In the name of orphans, widows, refugees and those exiled from their homes and their countries; in the name of all victims of wars, persecution and injustice; in the name of the weak, those who live in fear, prisoners of

war and those tortured in any part of the world, without distinction;

"In the name of peoples who have lost their security, peace and the possibility of living together, becoming victims of destruction, calamity and war;

"In the name of *human fraternity*, that embraces all human beings, unites them and renders them equal;

"In the name of this *fraternity* torn apart by policies of extremism and division, by systems of unrestrained profit or by hateful ideological tendencies that manipulate the actions and the future of men and women;

"In the name of freedom, that God has given to all human beings, creating them free and setting them apart by this gift;

"In the name of justice and mercy, the foundations of prosperity and the cornerstone of faith;

"In the name of all persons of goodwill present in every part of the world;

"In the name of God and of everything stated thus far, [we] declare the adoption of a culture of dialogue as the path; mutual cooperation as the code of conduct; reciprocal understanding as the method and standard."[285]

•••

286. In these pages of reflection on universal fraternity, I felt inspired particularly by Saint Francis of Assisi, but also by others of our brothers and sisters who are not Catholics: Martin Luther King, Desmond Tutu, Mahatma Gandhi, and many more. Yet I would like to conclude by mentioning another person of deep faith who, drawing upon his intense experience of God, made a journey of transformation toward feeling a brother to all. I am speaking of Blessed Charles de Foucauld.

287. Blessed Charles directed his ideal of total surrender to God toward an identification with the poor, abandoned in the depths of the African desert. In that setting, he expressed his desire to feel himself a brother

to every human being,[286] and asked a friend to "pray to God that I truly be the brother of all."[287] He wanted to be, in the end, "the universal brother."[288] Yet only by identifying with the least did he come at last to be the brother of all. May God inspire that dream in each one of us. Amen.

A Prayer to the Creator

Lord, Father of our human family,
you created all human beings equal in dignity:
pour forth into our hearts a fraternal spirit
and inspire in us a dream of renewed encounter,
dialogue, justice, and peace.
Move us to create healthier societies
and a more dignified world,
a world without hunger, poverty, violence, and war.

May our hearts be open
to all the peoples and nations of the earth.
May we recognize the goodness and beauty
that you have sown in each of us,
and thus forge bonds of unity, common projects,
and shared dreams. Amen.

An Ecumenical Christian Prayer

O God, Trinity of love,
from the profound communion of your divine life,
pour out upon us a torrent of fraternal love.
Grant us the love reflected in the actions of Jesus,
in his family of Nazareth,
and in the early Christian community.

Grant that we Christians may live the Gospel,
discovering Christ in each human being,
recognizing him crucified
in the sufferings of the abandoned

and forgotten of our world,
and risen in each brother or sister
who makes a new start.

Come, Holy Spirit, show us your beauty,
reflected in all the peoples of the earth,
so that we may discover anew
that all are important and all are necessary,
different faces of the one humanity
that God so loves. Amen.

Given in Assisi, at the tomb of Saint Francis, on 3 October, Vigil of the Feast of the Saint, in the year 2020, the eighth of my Pontificate.

FRANCISCUS

Notes

1. *Admonitions*, 6, 1. English translation in *Francis of Assisi: Early Documents*, vol 1., New York, London, Manila (1999), 131.

2. Ibid., 25: op. cit., 136.

3. Saint Francis of Assisi, *Earlier Rule of the Friars Minor (Regula non bullata)*, 16: 3.6: op. cit. 74.

4. Eloi Leclerc, O.F.M., *Exil et tendresse*, Éd. Franciscaines, Paris, 1962, 205.

5. *Document on Human Fraternity for World Peace and Living Together*, Abu Dhabi (4 February 2019): *L'Osservatore Romano*, 4–5 February 2019, p. 6.

6. *Address at the Ecumenical and Interreligious Meeting with Young People*, Skopje, North Macedonia (7 May 2019): *L'Osservatore Romano*, 9 May 2019, p. 9.

7. *Address to the European Parliament*, Strasbourg (25 November 2014): AAS 106 (2014), 996.

8. *Meeting with Authorities, Civil Society and the Diplomatic Corps*, Santiago, Chile (16 January 2018): AAS 110 (2018), 256.

9. Benedict XVI, Encyclical Letter *Caritas in Veritate* (29 June 2009), 19: AAS 101 (2009), 655.

10. Post-Synodal Apostolic Exhortation *Christus Vivit* (25 March 2019), 181.

11. Cardinal Raúl Silva Henríquez, *Homily at the Te Deum*, Santiago de Chile (18 September 1974).

12. Encyclical Letter *Laudato Si'* (24 May 2015), 57: AAS 107 (2015), 869.

13. *Address to the Diplomatic Corps accredited to the Holy See* (11 January 2016): AAS 108 (2016), 120.

14. *Address to the Diplomatic Corps accredited to the Holy See* (13 January 2014): AAS 106 (2014), 83–84.

15. Cf. *Address to the "Centesimus Annus pro Pontifice" Foundation* (25 May 2013): *Insegnamenti* I, 1 (2013), 238.

16. Cf. Saint Paul VI, Encyclical Letter *Populorum Progressio* (26 March 1967): AAS 59 (1967), 264.

17. Benedict XVI, Encyclical Letter *Caritas in Veritate* (29 June 2009), 22: AAS 101 (2009), 657.

18. *Address to the Civil Authorities, Tirana, Albania* (21 September 2014): AAS 106 (2014), 773.

19. *Message to Participants in the International Conference "Human Rights in the Contemporary World: Achievements, Omissions, Negations"* (10 December 2018): *L'Osservatore Romano*, 10–11 December 2018, p. 8.

20. Apostolic Exhortation *Evangelii Gaudium* (24 November 2013), 212: AAS 105 (2013), 1108.

21. *Message for the 2015 World Day of Peace* (8 December 2014), 3–4: AAS 107 (2015), 69–71.

22. Ibid., 5: AAS 107 (2015), 72.

23. *Message for the 2016 World Day of Peace* (8 December 2015), 2: AAS 108 (2016), 49.

24. *Message for the 2020 World Day of Peace* (8 December 2019), 1: *L'Osservatore Romano*, 13 December 2019, p. 8.

25. *Address on Nuclear Weapons*, Nagasaki, Japan (24 November 2019): *L'Osservatore Romano*, 25–26 November 2019, p. 6.

26. *Dialogue with Students and Teachers of the San Carlo College in Milan* (6 April 2019): *L'Osservatore Romano*, 8–9 April 2019, p. 6.

27. *Document on Human Fraternity for World Peace and Living Together*, Abu Dhabi (4 February 2019): *L'Osservatore Romano*, 4–5 February 2019, p. 6.

28. *Address to the World of Culture*, Cagliari, Italy (22 September 2013): *L'Osservatore Romano*, 23–24 September 2013, p. 7.

29. *Humana Communitas*. Letter to the President of the Pontifical Academy for Life on the Twenty-fifth Anniversary of its Founding (6 January 2019), 2.6: *L'Osservatore Romano*, 16 January 2019, pp. 6–7.

30. *Video Message to the TED Conference in Vancouver* (26 April 2017): *L'Osservatore Romano*, 27 April 2017, p. 7.

31. *Extraordinary Moment of Prayer in Time of Epidemic* (27 March 2020): *L'Osservatore Romano*, 29 March 2020, p. 10.

32. *Homily* in Skopje, North Macedonia (7 May 2019): *L'Osservatore Romano*, 8 May 2019, p. 12.

33. Cf. *Aeneid* 1, 462: *"Sunt lacrimae rerum et mentem mortalia tangunt."*

34. *"Historia . . . magistra vitae"* (Cicero, *De Oratore*, 2, 6).

35. Encyclical Letter *Laudato Si'* (24 May 2015), 204: AAS 107 (2015), 928.

36. Post-Synodal Apostolic Exhortation *Christus Vivit* (25 March 2019), 91.

37. Ibid., 92.

38. Ibid., 93.

39. Benedict XVI, *Message for the 2013 World Day of Migrants and Refugees* (12 October 2012): AAS 104 (2012), 908.

40. Post-Synodal Apostolic Exhortation *Christus Vivit* (25 March 2019), 92.

41. *Message for the 2020 World Day of Migrants and Refugees* (13 May 2020): *L'Osservatore Romano*, 16 May 2020, p. 8.

42. *Address to the Diplomatic Corps accredited to the Holy See* (11 January 2016): AAS 108 (2016), 124.

43. *Address to the Diplomatic Corps accredited to the Holy See* (13 January 2014): AAS 106 (2014), 84.

44. *Address to the Diplomatic Corps accredited to the Holy See* (11 January 2016): AAS 108 (2016), 123.

45. *Message for the 2019 World Day of Migrants and Refugees* (27 May 2019): *L'Osservatore Romano*, 27–28 May 2019, p. 8.

46. Post-Synodal Apostolic Exhortation *Christus Vivit* (25 March 2019), 88.

47. Ibid., 89.

48. Apostolic Exhortation *Gaudete et Exsultate* (19 March 2018), 115.

49. From the film *Pope Francis: A Man of His Word*, by Wim Wenders (2018).

50. *Address to Authorities, Civil Society and the Diplomatic Corps*, Tallinn, Estonia (25 September 2018): *L'Osservatore Romano*, 27 September 2018, p. 7.

51. Cf. *Extraordinary Moment of Prayer in Time of Epidemic* (27 March 2020): *L'Osservatore Romano*, 29 March 2020, p. 10; *Message for the 2020 World Day of the Poor* (13 June 2020), 6: *L'Osservatore Romano*, 14 June 2020, p. 8.

52. *Greeting to Young People at the Padre Félix Varela Cultural Centre*, Havana, Cuba (20 September 2015): *L'Osservatore Romano*, 21–22 September 2015, p. 6.

53. Second Vatican Ecumenical Council, Pastoral Constitution on the Church in the Modern World *Gaudium et Spes*, 1.

54. Saint Irenaeus of Lyons, *Adversus Haereses*, II, 25, 2: PG 7/1, 798ff.

55. *Talmud Bavli* (Babylonian Talmud), *Shabbat*, 31a.

56. *Address to Those Assisted by the Charitable Works of the Church*, Tallinn, Estonia (25 September 2018): *L'Osservatore Romano*, 27 September 2018, p. 8.

57. *Video Message to the TED Conference in Vancouver* (26 April 2017): *L'Osservatore Romano*, 27 April 2017, p. 7.

58. *Homiliae in Matthaeum*, 50: 3–4: PG 58, 508.

59. *Message to the Meeting of Popular Movements*, Modesto, California, United States of America (10 February 2017): AAS 109 (2017), 291.

60. Apostolic Exhortation *Evangelii Gaudium* (24 November 2013), 235: AAS 105 (2013), 1115.

61. Saint John Paul II, *Message to the Handicapped, Angelus* in Osnabrück, Germany (16 November 1980): *Insegnamenti* III, 2 (1980), 1232.

62. Second Vatican Ecumenical Council, Pastoral Constitution on the Church in the Modern World *Gaudium et Spes*, 24.

63. Gabriel Marcel, *Du refus à l'invocation*, ed. NRF, Paris, 1940, 50.

64. *Angelus* (10 November 2019): *L'Osservatore Romano*, 11–12 November 2019, 8.

65. Cf. Saint Thomas Aquinas: *Scriptum super Sententiis*, lib. 3, dist. 27, q. 1, a. 1, ad 4: "Dicitur amor extasim facere et fervere, quia quod fervet extra se bullit et exhalat."

66. Karol Wojtyła, *Love and Responsibility*, London, 1982, 126.

67. Karl Rahner, *Kleines Kirchenjahr. Ein Gang durch den Festkreis*, Herderbücherei 901, Freiburg, 1981, 30.

68. *Regula*, 53, 15: *"Pauperum et peregrinorum maxime susceptioni cura sollicite exhibeatur."*

69. Cf. *Summa Theologiae*, II-II, q. 23, a. 7; Saint Augustine, Contra Julianum, 4, 18: PL 44, 748: "How many pleasures do misers forego, either to increase their treasures or for fear of seeing them diminish!."

70. *"Secundum acceptionem divinam"* (*Scriptum super Sententiis*, lib. 3, dist. 27, a. 1, q. 1, concl. 4).

71. Benedict XVI, Encyclical Letter *Deus Caritas Est* (25 December 2005), 15: AAS 98 (2006), 230.

72. *Summa Theologiae* II-II, q. 27, a. 2, resp.

73. Cf. ibid., I-II, q. 26, a. 3, resp.

74. Ibid., q. 110, a. 1, resp.

75. *Message for the 2014 World Day of Peace* (8 December 2013), 1: AAS 106 (2014), 22.

76. Cf. *Angelus* (29 December 2013): *L'Osservatore Romano*, 30–31 December 2013, p. 7; *Address to the Diplomatic Corps Accredited to the Holy See* (12 January 2015): AAS 107 (2015), 165.

77. *Message for the World Day of Persons with Disabilities* (3 December 2019): *L'Osservatore Romano*, 4 December 2019, 7.

78. *Address to the Meeting for Religious Liberty with the Hispanic Community and Immigrant Groups*, Philadelphia, Pennsylvania, United States of America (26 September 2015): AAS 107 (2015), 1050–51.

79. *Address to Young People*, Tokyo, Japan (25 November 2019): *L'Osservatore Romano*, 25–26 November 2019, 10.

80. In these considerations, I have been inspired by the thought of Paul Ricoeur, "Le socius et le prochain," in *Histoire et Verité*, ed. Le Seuil, Paris, 1967, 113–27.

81. Apostolic Exhortation *Evangelii Gaudium* (24 November 2013), 190: AAS 105 (2013), 1100.

82. Ibid., 209: AAS 105 (2013), 1107.

83. Encyclical Letter *Laudato Si'* (24 May 2015), 129: AAS 107 (2015), 899.

84. *Message for the "Economy of Francesco" Event* (1 May 2019): *L'Osservatore Romano*, 12 May 2019, 8.

85. *Address to the European Parliament*, Strasbourg (25 November 2014): AAS 106 (2014), 997.

86. Encyclical Letter *Laudato Si'* (24 May 2015), 229: AAS 107 (2015), 937.

87. *Message for the 2016 World Day of Peace* (8 December 2015), 6: AAS 108 (2016), 57–58.

88. Solidity is etymologically related to "solidarity." Solidarity, in the ethical-political meaning that it has taken on in the last two centuries, results in a secure and firm social compact.

89. *Homily*, Havana, Cuba (20 September 2015): *L'Osservatore Romano*, 21-22 September 2015, 8.

90. Address to Participants in the Meeting of Popular Movements (28 October 2014): AAS 106 (2014), 851-52.

91. Cf. Saint Basil, *Homilia XXI, Quod rebus mundanis adhaerendum non sit*, 3.5: PG 31, 545–49; *Regulae brevius tractatae*, 92: PG 31, 1145–48; Saint Peter Chrysologus, *Sermo* 123: PL 52, 536–40; Saint Ambrose, *De Nabuthe*, 27.52: PL 14, 738ff.; Saint Augustine, *In Iohannis Evangelium*, 6, 25: PL 35, 1436ff.

92. *De Lazaro Concio*, II, 6: PG 48, 992D.

93. *Regula Pastoralis*, III, 21: PL 77, 87.

94. Saint John Paul II, Encyclical Letter *Centesimus Annus* (1 May 1991), 31: AAS 83 (1991), 831.

95. Encyclical Letter *Laudato Si'* (24 May 2015), 93: AAS 107 (2015), 884.

96. Saint John Paul II, Encyclical Letter *Laborem Exercens* (14 September 1981), 19: AAS 73 (1981), 626.

97. Cf.Pontifical Council for Justice and Peace, *Compendium of the Social Doctrine of the Church*, 172.

98. Encyclical Letter *Populorum Progressio* (26 March 1967): AAS 59 (1967), 268.

99. Saint John Paul II, Encyclical Letter *Sollicitudo Rei Socialis* (30 December 1987), 33: AAS 80 (1988), 557.

100. Encyclical Letter *Laudato Si'* (24 May 2015), 95: AAS 107 (2015), 885.

101. Ibid., 129: AAS 107 (2015), 899.

102. Cf. Saint Paul VI, Encyclical Letter *Populorum Progressio* (26 March 1967): AAS 59 (1967), 265; Benedict XVI, Encyclical Letter *Caritas in Veritate* (29 June 2009), 16: AAS 101 (2009), 652.

103. Cf. Encyclical Letter *Laudato Si'* (24 May 2015), 93: AAS 107 (2015), 884–85; Apostolic Exhortation *Evangelii Gaudium* (24 November 2013), 189–90: AAS 105 (2013), 1099–100.

104. United States Conference of Catholic Bishops, Pastoral Letter Against Racism *Open Wide Our Hearts: The Enduring Call to Love* (November 2018).

105. Encyclical Letter *Laudato Si'* (24 May 2015), 51: AAS 107 (2015), 867.

106. Cf. Benedict XVI, Encyclical Letter *Caritas in Veritate* (29 June 2009), 6: AAS 101 (2009), 644.

107. Saint John Paul II, Encyclical Letter *Centesimus Annus* (1 May 1991), 35: AAS 83 (1991), 838.

108. *Address on Nuclear Weapons*, Nagasaki, Japan (24 November 2019): *L'Osservatore Romano*, 25–26 November 2019, 6.

109. Cf. Catholic Bishops of Mexico and the United States, *A Pastoral Letter Concerning Migration: "Strangers No Longer Together on the Journey of Hope"* (January 2003).

110. *General Audience* (3 April 2019): *L'Osservatore Romano*, 4 April 2019, p. 8.

111. Cf. *Message for the 2018 World Day of Migrants and Refugees* (14 January 2018): AAS 109 (2017), 918–23.

112. *Document on Human Fraternity for World Peace and Living Together*, Abu Dhabi (4 February 2019): *L'Osservatore Romano*, 4–5 February 2019, p. 7.

113. *Address to the Diplomatic Corps Accredited to the Holy See*, 11 January 2016: AAS 108 (2016), 124.

114. Ibid., 122.

115. Post-Synodal Apostolic Exhortation *Christus Vivit* (25 March 2019), 93.

116. Ibid., 94.

117. *Address to Authorities*, Sarajevo, Bosnia and Herzegovina (6 June 2015): *L'Osservatore Romano*, 7 June 2015, p. 7.

118. *Latinoamérica. Conversaciones con Hernán Reyes Alcaide*, ed. Planeta, Buenos Aires, 2017, 105.

119. *Document on Human Fraternity for World Peace and Living Together*, Abu Dhabi (4 February 2019): *L'Osservatore Romano*, 4–5 February 2019, p. 7.

120. Benedict XVI, Encyclical Letter *Caritas in Veritate* (29 June 2009), 67: AAS 101 (2009), 700.

121. Ibid., 60: AAS 101 (2009), 695.

122. Ibid., 67: AAS 101 (2009), 700.

123. Pontifical Council for Justice and Peace, *Compendium of the Social Doctrine of the Church*, 447.

124. Apostolic Exhortation *Evangelii Gaudium* (24 November 2013), 234: AAS 105 (2013), 1115.

125. Ibid., 235: AAS 105 (2013), 1115.

126. Ibid.

127. Saint John Paul II, *Address to Representatives of Argentinian Culture*, Buenos Aires, Argentina (12 April 1987), 4: *L'Osservatore Romano*, 14 April 1987, p. 7.

128. Cf. ID., *Address to the Roman Curia* (21 December 1984), 4: AAS 76 (1984), 506.

129. Post-Synodal Apostolic Exhortation *Querida Amazonia* (2 February 2020), 37.

130. Georg Simmel, *Brücke und Tür. Essays des Philosophen zur Geschichte, Religion, Kunst und Gesellschaft*, ed. Michael Landmann, Köhler-Verlag, Stuttgart, 1957, 6.

131. Cf. Jaime Hoyos-Vásquez, S.J., "Lógica de las relaciones sociales. Reflexión onto-lógica," *Revista Universitas Philosophica*, 15–16 (December 1990–June 1991), Bogotá, 95–106.

132. Antonio Spadaro, S.J., *Le orme di un pastore. Una conversazione con Papa Francesco*, in Jorge Mario Bergolio—Papa Francesco, *Nei tuoi occhi è la mia parola. Omelie e discorsi di Buenos Aires 1999–2013*, Rizzoli, Milan 2016, XVI; cf. Apostolic Exhortation Evangelii Gaudium (24 November 2013), 220–21: AAS 105 (2013), 1110–11.

133. Apostolic Exaltation *Evangelii Gaudium* (24 November 2013), 204: AAS 105 (2013), 1106.

134. Cf. ibid.: AAS 105 (2013), 1105–6.

135. Ibid., 202: AAS 105 (2013), 1105.

136. Encyclical Letter *Laudato Si'* (24 May 2015), 128: AAS 107 (2015), 898.

137. *Address to the Diplomatic Corps Accredited to the Holy See* (12 January 2015): AAS 107 (2015), 165; cf. *Address to Participants in the World Meeting of Popular Movements* (28 October 2014): AAS 106 (2014), 851–59.

138. A similar point could be made with regard to the biblical category of the Kingdom of God.

139. Paul Ricoeur, *Histoire et Verité*, ed. Le Seuil Paris, 1967, 122.

140. Encyclical Letter *Laudato Si'* (24 May 2015), 129: AAS 107 (2015), 899.

141. Benedict XVI, Encyclical Letter *Caritas in Veritate* (29 June 2009), 35: AAS 101 (2009), 670.

142. *Address to Participants in the World Meeting of Popular Movements* (28 October 2014): AAS 106 (2014), 858.

143. Ibid.

144. *Address to Participants in the World Meeting of Popular Movements* (5 November 2016): *L'Osservatore Romano*, 7–8 November 2016, pp. 4–5.

145. Ibid.

146. Ibid.

147. Encyclical Letter *Laudato Si'* (24 May 2015), 189: AAS 107 (2015), 922.

148. *Address to the Members of the General Assembly of the United Nations Organization*, New York (25 September 2015): AAS 107 (2015), 1037.

149. Encyclical Letter *Laudato Si'* (24 May 2015), 175: AAS 107 (2015), 916–17.

150. Cf. Benedict XVI, Encyclical Letter *Caritas in Veritate* (29 June 2009), 67: AAS 101 (2009), 700–701.

151. Ibid.: AAS 101 (2009), 700.

152. Pontifical Council for Justice and Peace, *Compendium of the Social Doctrine of the Church*, 434.

153. *Address to the Members of the General Assembly of the United Nations Organization*, New York (25 September 2015): AAS 107 (2015), 1037, 1041.

154. Pontifical Council for Justice and Peace, *Compendium of the Social Doctrine of the Church*, 437.

155. Saint John Paul II, *Message for the 2004 World Day of Peace*, 5: AAS 96 (2004), 117.

156. Pontifical Council for Justice and Peace, *Compendium of the Social Doctrine of the Church*, 439.

157. Cf. Social Commission of th Bishops of France, Declaration *Réhabiliter la Politique* (17 February 1999).

158. Encyclical Letter *Laudato Si'* (24 May 2015), 189: AAS 107 (2015), 922.

159. Ibid., 196: AAS 107 (2015), 925.

160. Ibid., 197: AAS 107 (2015), 925.

161. Ibid., 181: AAS 107 (2015), 919.

162. Ibid., 178: AAS 107 (2015), 918.

163. Portuguese Bishops' Conference, Pastoral Letter *Responsabilidade Solidária pelo Bem Comum* (15 September 2003), 20; cf. Encyclical Letter *Laudato Si'* (24 May 2015), 159: AAS 107 (2015), 911.

164. Encyclical Letter *Laudato Si'* (24 May 2015), 191: AAS 107 (2015), 923.

165. Pius XI, *Address to the Italian Catholic Federation of University Students* (18 December 1927): *L'Osservatore Romano*, 23 December 1927, p. 3.

166. Cf. ID., Encyclical Letter *Quadragesimo Anno* (15 May 1931): AAS 23 (1931), 206–7.

167. Apostolic Exhortation *Evangelii Gaudium* (24 November 2013), 205: AAS 105 (2013), 1106

168. Benedict XVI, Encyclical Letter *Caritas in Veritate* (29 June 2009), 2: AAS 101 (2009), 642.

169. Encyclical Letter *Laudato Si'* (24 May 2015), 231: AAS 107 (2015), 937.

170. Benedict XVI, Encyclical Letter *Caritas in Veritate* (29 June 2009), 2: AAS 101 (2009), 642.

171. Pontifical Council for Justice and Peace, *Compendium of the Social Doctrine of the Church*, 207.

172. Saint John Paul II, Encyclical Letter *Redemptor Hominis* (4 March 1979), 15: AAS 71 (1979), 288.

173. Cf. Saint Paul VI, Encyclical Letter *Populorum Progressio* (26 March 1967), 44: AAS 59 (1967), 279.

174. Pontifical Council for Justice and Peace, *Compendium of the Social Doctrine of the Church*, 207.

175. Benedict XVI, Encyclical Letter *Caritas in Veritate* (29 June 2009), 2: AAS 101 (2009), 642.

176. Ibid., 3: AAS 101 (2009), 643.

177. Ibid., 4: AAS 101 (2009), 643.

178. Ibid.

179. Ibid., 3: AAS 101 (2009), 643.

180. Ibid.: AAS 101 (2009), 642.

181. Catholic moral doctrine, following the teaching of Saint Thomas Aquinas, distinguishes between "elicited" and "commanded" acts; cf. *Summa Theologiae*, I-II, qq. 8–17; M. ZALBA, S.J., *Theologiae Moralis Summa. Theologia Moralis Fundamentalis. Tractatus de Virtutibus Theologicis*, ed. BAC, Madrid, 1952, vol. I, 69; A. Royo Marín, *Teología de la Perfección Cristiana*, ed. BAC, Madrid, 1962, 192–96.

182. Pontifical Council for Justice and Peace, *Compendium of the Social Doctrine of the Church*, 208.

183. Cf. Saint John Paul II, Encyclical Letter *Sollicitudo Rei Socialis* (30 December 1987), 42: AAS 80 (1988), 572–74; Encyclical Letter *Centesimus Annus* (1 May 1991), 11: AAS 83 (1991), 806–7.

184. *Address to Participants in the World Meeting of Popular Movements* (28 October 2014): AAS 106 (2014), 852.

185. *Address to the European Parliament*, Strasbourg (25 November 2014): AAS 106 (2014), 999.

186. *Address at the Meeting with Authorities and the Diplomatic Corps in the Central African Republic*, Bangui (29 November 2015): AAS 107 (2015), 1320.

187. *Address to the United Nations Organization*, New York (25 September 2015): AAS 107 (2015), 1039.

188. *Address to Participants in the World Meeting of Popular Movements* (28 October 2014): AAS 106 (2014), 853.

189. *Document on Human Fraternity for World Peace and Living Together*, Abu Dhabi (4 February 2019): *L'Osservatore Romano*, 4–5 February 2019, p. 6.

190. René Voillaume, *Frères de tous*, ed. Cerf, Paris, 1968, 12–13.

191. *Video Message to the TED Conference in Vancouver* (26 April 2017): *L'Osservatore Romano*, 27 April 2017, p. 7.

192. General Audience (18 February 2015): *L'Osservatore Romano*, 19 February 2015, p. 8.

193. Apostolic Exhortation *Evangelii Gaudium* (24 November 2013), 274: AAS 105 (2013), 1130.

194. Ibid., 279: AAS 105 (2013), 1132.

195. *Message for the 2019 World Day of Peace* (8 December 2018), 5: *L'Osservatore Romano*, 19 December 2018, p. 8.

196. *Meeting with Brazilian Political, Economic and Cultural Leaders*, Rio de Janeiro, Brazil (27 July 2013): AAS 105 (2013), 683–84.

197. Apostolic Exhortation *Querida Amazonia* (2 February 2020), 108.

198. From the film *Pope Francis: A Man of His Word*, by Wim Wenders (2018).

199. *Message for the 2014 World Communications Day* (24 January 2014): AAS 106 (2014), 113.

200. Australian Catholic Bishops' Conference, Commission for Social Justice, Mission and Service, *Making It Real: Genuine Human Encounter in Our Digital World* (November 2019).

201. Encyclical Letter *Laudato Si'* (24 May 2015), 123: AAS 107 (2015), 896.

202. Saint John Paul II, Encyclical Letter *Veritatis Splendor* (6 August 1993), 96: AAS 85 (1993), 1209.

203. As Christians, we also believe that God grants us his grace to enable us to act as brothers and sisters.

204. Vinicius de Moraes, *Samba da Benção, from the recording Um encontro no Au bon Gourmet*, Rio de Janeiro (2 August 1962).

205. Apostolic Exhortation *Evangelii Gaudium* (24 November 2013), 237: AAS 105 (2013), 1116.

206. Ibid., 236: AAS 105 (2013), 1115.

207. Ibid., 218: AAS 105 (2013), 1110.

208. Apostolic Exhortation *Amoris Laetitia* (19 March 2016), 100: AAS 108 (2016), 351.

209. *Message for the 2020 World Day of Peace* (8 December 2019), 2: *L'Osservatore Romano*, 13 December 2019, p. 8.

210. Episcopal Conference of the Congo, *Message au Peuple de Dieu et aux femmes et aux hommes de bonne volonté* (9 May 2018).

211. *Address at the National Reconciliation Encunter*, Villavicencio, Colombia (8 September 2017): AAS 109 (2017), 1063–64, 1066.

212. *Message for the 2020 World Day of Peace* (8 December 2019), 3: *L'Osservatore Romano*, 13 December 2019, p. 8.

213. Southern African Catholic Bishops' Conference, *Pastoral Letter on Christian Hope in the Current Crisis* (May 1986).

214. Catholic Bishops' Conference of Korea, *Appeal of the Catholic Church in Korea for Peace on the Korean Peninsula* (15 August 2017).

215. *Meeting with Political, Economic and Civic Leaders*, Quito, Ecuador (7 July 2015): *L'Osservatore Romano*, 9 July 2015, p. 9.

216. *Interreligious Meeting with Youth*, Maputo, Mozambique (5 September 2019): *L'Osservatore Romano*, 6 September 2019, p. 7.

217. *Homily*, Cartagena de Indias, Colombia (10 September 2017): AAS 109 (2017), 1086.

218. *Meeting with Authorities, the Diplomatic Corps and Representatives of Civil Society*, Bogotá, Colombia (7 September 2017): AAS 109 (2017), 1029.

219. Bishops' Conference of Colombia, *Por el bien de Colombia: diálogo, reconciliación y desarrollo integral* (26 November 2019), 4.

220. *Meeting with the Authorities, Civil Society and the Diplomatic Corps*, Maputo, Mozambique (5 September 2019): *L'Osservatore Romano*, 6 September 2019, p. 6.

221. Fifth General Conference of the Latin American and Caribbean Bishops, *Aparecida Document* (29 June 2007), 398.

222. Apostolic Exhortation *Evangelii Gaudium* (24 November 2013), 59: AAS 105 (2013), 1044.

223. Encyclical Letter *Centesimus Annus* (1 May 1991), 14: AAS 83 (1991), 810.

224. *Homily at Mass for the Progress of Peoples*, Maputo, Mozambique (6 September 2019): *L'Osservatore Romano*, 7 September 2019, p. 8.

225. *Arrival Ceremony*, Colombo, Sri Lanka (13 January 2015): *L'Osservatore Romano*, 14 January 2015, p. 7.

226. *Meeting with the Children of the "Bethany Centre" and Representatives of other Charitable Centres of Albania*, Tirana, Albania (21 September 2014): *Insegnamenti* II, 2 (2014), 288.

227. *Video Message to the TED Conference in Vancouver* (26 April 2017): *L'Osservatore Romano*, 27 April 2017, p. 7.

228. Pius XI, Encyclical Letter *Quadragesimo Anno* (15 May 1931): AAS 23 (1931), 213.

229. Apostolic Exhortation *Evangelii Gaudium* (24 November 2013), 228: AAS 105 (2013), 1113.

230. *Meeting with the Civil Authorities, Civil Society and the Diplomatic Corps*, Riga, Latvia (24 September 2018): *L'Osservatore Romano*, 24–25 September 2018, p. 7.

231. *Arrival Ceremony*, Tel Aviv, Israel (25 May 2014): *Insegnamenti* II, 1 (2014), 604.

232. *Visit to the Yad Vashem Memorial*, Jerusalem (26 May 2014): AAS 106 (2014), 228.

233. *Address at the Peace Memorial*, Hiroshima, Japan (24 November 2019): *L'Osservatore Romano*, 25–26 November 2019, p. 8.

234. *Message for the 2020 World Day of Peace* (8 December 2019), 2: *L'Osservatore Romano*, 13 December 2019, p. 8.

235. Croatian Bishops' Conference, *Letter on the Fiftieth Anniversary of the End of the Second World War* (1 May 1995).

236. *Homily*, Amman, Jordan (24 May 2014): *Insegnamenti* II, 1 (2014), 593.

237. Cf. *Message for the 2020 World Day of Peace* (8 December 2019), 1: *L'Osservatore Romano*, 13 December 2019, p. 8.

238. *Address to the Members of the General Assembly of the United Nations*, New York (25 September 2015): AAS 107 (2015), 1041–42.

239. No. 2309.

240. Ibid.

241. Encyclical Letter *Laudato Si'* (24 May 2015), 104: AAS 107 (2015), 888.

242. Saint Augustine, who forged a concept of "just war" that we no longer uphold in our own day, also said that "it is a higher glory still to stay war itself with a word, than to slay men with the sword, and to procure or maintain peace by peace, not by war" (*Epistola* 229, 2: PL 33, 1020).

243. Encyclical Letter *Pacem in Terris* (11 April 1963): AAS 55 (1963), 291.

244. *Message to the United Nations Conference to Negotiate a Legally Binding Instrument to Prohibit Nuclear Weapons* (23 March 2017): AAS 109 (2017), 394–96.

245. Cf. Saint Paul VI, Encyclical Letter *Populorum Progressio* (26 March 1967): AAS 59 (1967), 282.

246. Cf. Encyclical Letter *Evangelium Vitae* (25 March 1995), 56: AAS 87 (1995), 463-64.

247. *Address on the Twenty-fifth Anniversary of the Promulgation of the Catechism of the Catholic Church* (11 October 2017): AAS 109 (2017), 1196.

248. Cf. Congregation for the Doctrine of the Faith, *Letter to the Bishops Regarding the Revision of No. 2267 of the Catechism of the Catholic Church on the Death Penalty* (1 August 2018): *L'Osservatore Romano*, 3 August 2018, p. 8.

249. *Address to Delegates of the International Association of Penal Law* (23 October 2014): AAS 106 (2014), 840.

250. Pontifical Council for Justice and Peace, *Compendium of the Social Doctrine of the Church*, 402.

251. Saint John Paul II, *Address to the National Association of Magistrates* (31 March 2000), 4: AAS 92 (2000), 633.

252. *Divinae Institutiones* VI, 20, 17: PL 6, 708.

253. *Epistola 97 (Responsa ad consulta Bulgarorum)*, 25: PL 119, 991. "ipsi (Christo) non solum innoxios quosque, verum etiam et noxios a mortis exitio satagite cunctos eruere. . . ."

254. *Epistola ad Marcellinum* 133, 1.2: PL 33, 509.

255. *Address to Delegates of the International Association of Penal Law* (23 October 2014): AAS 106 (2014), 840–41.

256. Ibid., 842.

257. Ibid.

258. Saint John Paul II, Encyclical Letter *Evangelium Vitae* (25 March 1995), 9: AAS 87 (1995), 411.

259. Catholic Bishops' Conference of India, *Response of the Church in India to the Present-day Challenges* (9 March 2016).

260. *Homily at Mass in Domus Sanctae Marthae* (17 May 2020).

261. Benedict XVI, Encyclical Letter *Caritas in Veritate* (29 June 2009), 19: AAS 101 (2009), 655.

262. Saint John Paul II, Encyclical Letter *Centesimus Annus* (1 May 1991), 44: AAS 83 (1991), 849.

263. *Address to the Leaders of Other Religions and Other Christian Denominations*, Tirana, Albania (21 September 2014): *Insegnamenti* II, 2 (2014), 277.

264. *Document on Human Fraternity for World Peace and Living Together*, Abu Dhabi (4 February 2019): *L'Osservatore Romano*, 4–5 February 2019, p. 6.

265. Apostolic Exhortation *Evangelii Gaudium* (24 November 2013), 256: AAS 105 (2013), 1123.

266. Benedict XVI, Encyclical Letter *Deus Caritas Est* (25 December 2005), 28: AAS 98 (2006), 240.

267. "Man is a political animal," Aristotle, *Politics*, 1253a 1–3.

268. Benedict XVI, Encyclical Letter *Caritas in Veritate* (29 June 2009), 11: AAS 101 (2009), 648.

269. *Address to the Catholic Community*, Rakovski, Bulgaria (6 May 2019): *L'Osservatore Romano*, 8 May 2019, p. 9.

270. *Homily*, Santiago de Cuba (22 September 2015): AAS 107 (2015), 1005.

271. Second Vatican Ecumenical Council, Declaration on the Relation of the Church to Non-Christian Religions *Nostra Aetate*, 2.

272. *Ecumenical Prayer Service*, Riga, Latvia (24 September 2018): *L'Osservatore Romano*, 24–25 September 2018, p. 8.

273. *Lectio Divina*, Pontifical Lateran University, Rome (26 March 2019): *L'Osservatore Romano*, 27 March 2019, p. 10.

274. Saint Paul VI, Encyclical Letter *Ecclesiam Suam* (6 August 1964): AAS 56 (1964), 650.

275. *Address to the Civil Authorities*, Bethlehem, Palestine (25 May 2014): *Insegnamenti* II, 1 (2014), 597.

276. *Enarrationes in Psalmos*, 130, 6: PL 37, 1707.

277. *Common Declaration of Pope Francis and Ecumenical Patriarch Bartholomew*, Jerusalem (25 May 2014), 5: *L'Osservatore Romano*, 26–27 May 2014, p. 6.

278. From the film *Pope Francis: A Man of His Word*, by Wim Wenders (2018).

279. Post-Synodal Apostolic Exhortation *Querida Amazonia* (2 February 2020), 106.

280. *Homily*, Colombo, Sri Lanka (14 January 2015): AAS 107 (2015), 139.

281. *Document on Human Fraternity for World Peace and Living Together*, Abu Dhabi (4 February 2019): *L'Osservatore Romano*, 4–5 February 2019, p. 7.

282. *Address to Civil Authorities*, Sarajevo, Bosnia-Herzegovina (6 June 2015): *L'Osservatore Romano*, 7 June 2015, p. 7.

283. *Address to the International Meeting for Peace organized by the Community of Sant'Egidio* (30 September 2013): *Insegnamenti* I, 1 (2013), 301–2.

284. *Document on Human Fraternity for World Peace and Living Together*, Abu Dhabi (4 February 2019): *L'Osservatore Romano*, 4–5 February 2019, p. 6.

285. Ibid.

286. Cf. Charles de Foucauld, *Méditation sur le Notre Père* (23 January 1897).

287. *Letter to Henry de Castries* (29 November 1901).

288. *Letter to Madame de Bondy* (7 January 1902). Saint Paul VI used these words in praising his commitment: Encyclical Letter *Populorum Progressio* (26 March 1967): AAS 59 (1967), 263.

Patris Corde

With a Father's Heart

Apostolic Letter On the 150th Anniversary of the Proclamation of Saint Joseph as Patron of the Universal Church

December 8, 2020

APOSTOLIC LETTER
PATRIS CORDE
OF THE HOLY FATHER
FRANCIS
ON THE 150th ANNIVERSARY OF THE PROCLAMATION OF SAINT JOSEPH AS PATRON OF THE UNIVERSAL CHURCH

With a father's heart: that is how Joseph loved Jesus, whom all four Gospels refer to as *"the son of Joseph."*[1]

Matthew and Luke, the two Evangelists who speak most of Joseph, tell us very little, yet enough for us to appreciate what sort of father he was, and the mission entrusted to him by God's providence.

We know that Joseph was a lowly carpenter (cf. Mt 13:55), betrothed to Mary (cf. Mt 1:18; Lk 1:27). He was a "just man" (Mt 1:19), ever ready to carry out God's will as revealed to him in the Law (cf. Lk 2:22, 27, 39) and through four dreams (cf. Mt 1:20; 2:13, 19, 22). After a long and tiring journey from Nazareth to Bethlehem, he beheld the birth of the Messiah in a stable, since "there was no place for them" elsewhere (cf. Lk 2:7). He witnessed the adoration of the shepherds (cf. Lk 2:8–20) and the Magi (cf. Mt 2:1–12), who represented respectively the people of Israel and the pagan peoples.

Joseph had the courage to become the legal father of Jesus, to whom he gave the name revealed by the angel: "You shall call his name Jesus, for he will save his people from their sins" (Mt 1:21). As we know, for ancient peoples, to give a name to a person or to a thing, as Adam did in the account in the Book of Genesis (cf. 2:19–20), was to establish a relationship.

In the Temple, forty days after Jesus' birth, Joseph and Mary offered their child to the Lord and listened with amazement to Simeon's prophecy concerning Jesus and his Mother (cf. Lk 2:22–35). To protect

Jesus from Herod, Joseph dwelt as a foreigner in Egypt (cf. Mt 2:13–18). After returning to his own country, he led a hidden life in the tiny and obscure village of Nazareth in Galilee, far from Bethlehem, his ancestral town, and from Jerusalem and the Temple. Of Nazareth it was said, "No prophet is to rise" (cf. Jn 7:52) and indeed, "Can anything good come out of Nazareth?" (cf. Jn 1:46). When, during a pilgrimage to Jerusalem, Joseph and Mary lost track of the twelve-year-old Jesus, they anxiously sought him out and they found him in the Temple, in discussion with the doctors of the Law (cf. Lk 2:41–50).

After Mary, the Mother of God, no saint is mentioned more frequently in the papal magisterium than Joseph, her spouse. My Predecessors reflected on the message contained in the limited information handed down by the Gospels in order to appreciate more fully his central role in the history of salvation. Blessed Pius IX declared him "Patron of the Catholic Church,"[2] Venerable Pius XII proposed him as "Patron of Workers"[3] and Saint John Paul II as "Guardian of the Redeemer."[4] Saint Joseph is universally invoked as the "patron of a happy death."[5]

Now, one hundred and fifty years after his proclamation as *Patron of the Catholic Church* by Blessed Pius IX (8 December 1870), I would like to share some personal reflections on this extraordinary figure, so close to our own human experience. For, as Jesus says, "out of the abundance of the heart the mouth speaks" (Mt 12:34). My desire to do so increased during these months of pandemic, when we experienced, amid the crisis, how "our lives are woven together and sustained by ordinary people, people often overlooked. People who do not appear in newspaper and magazine headlines, or on the latest television show, yet in these very days are surely shaping the decisive events of our history. Doctors, nurses, storekeepers and supermarket workers, cleaning personnel, caregivers, transport workers, men and women working to provide essential services and public safety, volunteers, priests, men and women religious, and so very many others. They understood that no one is saved alone . . . How many people daily exercise patience and offer hope, taking care to spread not panic, but shared responsibility. How many fathers, mothers, grandparents and teachers are showing our children, in small everyday ways, how to accept and deal with a crisis by adjusting their routines, looking ahead and encouraging the practice of prayer. How many are praying, making sacrifices and interceding for the good of all."[6] Each of us can discover in Joseph—the man who goes unnoticed, a daily, discreet, and hidden presence—an intercessor, a support, and a guide in times of trouble. Saint Joseph reminds us that those who appear hidden or in the shadows can play an incomparable role in the history of salvation. A word of recognition and of gratitude is due to them all.

1. A Beloved Father

The greatness of Saint Joseph is that he was the spouse of Mary and the father of Jesus. In this way, he placed himself, in the words of Saint John Chrysostom, "at the service of the entire plan of salvation."[7]

Saint Paul VI pointed out that Joseph concretely expressed his fatherhood "by making his life a sacrificial service to the mystery of the incarnation and its redemptive purpose. He employed his legal authority over the Holy Family to devote himself completely to them in his life and work. He turned his human vocation to domestic love into a superhuman oblation of himself, his heart and all his abilities, a love placed at the service of the Messiah who was growing to maturity in his home."[8]

Thanks to his role in salvation history, Saint Joseph has always been venerated as a father by the Christian people. This is shown by the countless churches dedicated to him worldwide, the numerous religious Institutes, Confraternities, and ecclesial groups inspired by his spirituality and bearing his name, and the many traditional expressions of piety in his honor. Innumerable holy men and women were passionately devoted to him. Among them was Teresa of Avila, who chose him as her advocate and intercessor, had frequent recourse to him, and received whatever graces she asked of him. Encouraged by her own experience, Teresa persuaded others to cultivate devotion to Joseph.[9]

Every prayer book contains prayers to Saint Joseph. Special prayers are offered to him each Wednesday and especially during the month of March, which is traditionally dedicated to him.[10]

Popular trust in Saint Joseph is seen in the expression "Go to Joseph," which evokes the famine in Egypt, when the Egyptians begged Pharaoh for bread. He in turn replied: "Go to Joseph; what he says to you, do" (Gn 41:55). Pharaoh was referring to Joseph the son of Jacob, who was sold into slavery because of the jealousy of his brothers (cf. Gn 37:11–28) and who—according to the biblical account—subsequently became viceroy of Egypt (cf. Gn 41:41–44).

As a descendant of David (cf. Mt 1:16–20), from whose stock Jesus was to spring according to the promise made to David by the prophet Nathan (cf. 2 Sm 7), and as the spouse of Mary of Nazareth, Saint Joseph stands at the crossroads between the Old and New Testaments.

2. A Tender and Loving Father

Joseph saw Jesus grow daily "in wisdom and in years and in divine and human favor" (Lk 2:52). As the Lord had done with Israel, so Joseph did with Jesus: he taught him to walk, taking him by the hand; he was for him like a father who raises an infant to his cheeks, bending down to him and feeding him (cf. Hos 11:3–4).

In Joseph, Jesus saw the tender love of God: "As a father has compassion for his children, so the Lord has compassion for those who fear him" (Ps 103:13).

In the synagogue, during the praying of the Psalms, Joseph would surely have heard again and again that the God of Israel is a God of tender love,[11] who is good to all, whose "compassion is over all that he has made" (Ps 145:9).

The history of salvation is worked out "in hope against hope" (Rom 4:18), through our weaknesses. All too often, we think that God works only through our better parts, yet most of his plans are realized in and despite our frailty. Thus Saint Paul could say: "To keep me from being too elated, a thorn was given me in the flesh, a messenger of Satan to torment me, to keep me from being too elated. Three times I appealed to the Lord about this, that it would leave me, but he said to me: 'My grace is sufficient for you, for power is made perfect in weakness'" (2 Cor 12:7–9).

Since this is part of the entire economy of salvation, we must learn to look upon our weaknesses with tender mercy.[12]

The evil one makes us see and condemn our frailty, whereas the Spirit brings it to light with tender love. Tenderness is the best way to touch the frailty within us. Pointing fingers and judging others are frequently signs of an inability to accept our own weaknesses, our own frailty. Only tender love will save us from the snares of the accuser (cf. Rv 12:10). That is why it is so important to encounter God's mercy, especially in the Sacrament of Reconciliation, where we experience his truth and tenderness. Paradoxically, the evil one can also speak the truth to us, yet he does so only to condemn us. We know that God's truth does not condemn, but instead welcomes, embraces, sustains, and forgives us. That truth always presents itself to us like the merciful father in Jesus' parable (cf. Lk 15:11–32). It comes out to meet us, restores our dignity, sets us back on our feet, and rejoices for us, for, as the father says: "This my son was dead and is alive again; he was lost and is found" (v. 24).

Even through Joseph's fears, God's will, his history, and his plan were at work. Joseph, then, teaches us that faith in God includes believing that he can work even through our fears, our frailties, and our weaknesses. He also teaches us that amid the tempests of life, we must never be afraid to let the Lord steer our course. At times, we want to be in complete control, yet God always sees the bigger picture.

3. An Obedient Father

As he had done with Mary, God revealed his saving plan to Joseph. He did so by using dreams, which in the Bible and among all ancient peoples, were considered a way for him to make his will known.[13]

Joseph was deeply troubled by Mary's mysterious pregnancy. He did not want to "expose her to public disgrace,"[14] so he decided to "dismiss her quietly" (Mt 1:19).

In the first dream, an angel helps him resolve his grave dilemma: "Do not be afraid to take Mary as your wife, for the child conceived in her is from the Holy Spirit. She will bear a son, and you are to name him Jesus, for he will save his people from their sins" (Mt 1:20–21). Joseph's response was immediate: "When Joseph awoke from sleep, he did as the angel of the Lord commanded him" (Mt 1:24). Obedience made it possible for him to surmount his difficulties and spare Mary.

In the second dream, the angel tells Joseph: "Get up, take the child and his mother, and flee to Egypt, and remain there until I tell you; for Herod is about to search for the child, to destroy him" (Mt 2:13). Joseph did not hesitate to obey, regardless of the hardship involved: "He got up, took the child and his mother by night, and went to Egypt, and remained there until the death of Herod" (Mt 2:14–15).

In Egypt, Joseph awaited with patient trust the angel's notice that he could safely return home. In a third dream, the angel told him that those who sought to kill the child were dead and ordered him to rise, take the child and his mother, and return to the land of Israel (cf. Mt 2:19–20). Once again, Joseph promptly obeyed. "He got up, took the child and his mother, and went to the land of Israel" (Mt 2:21).

During the return journey, "when Joseph heard that Archelaus was ruling over Judea in place of his father Herod, he was afraid to go there. After being warned in a dream"—now for the fourth time—"he went away to the district of Galilee. There he made his home in a town called Nazareth" (Mt 2:22–23).

The evangelist Luke, for his part, tells us that Joseph undertook the long and difficult journey from Nazareth to Bethlehem to be registered in his family's town of origin in the census of the Emperor Caesar Augustus. There Jesus was born (cf. Lk 2:7) and his birth, like that of every other child, was recorded in the registry of the Empire. Saint Luke is especially concerned to tell us that Jesus' parents observed all the prescriptions of the Law: the rites of the circumcision of Jesus, the purification of Mary after childbirth, the offering of the firstborn to God (cf. 2:21–24).[15]

In every situation, Joseph declared his own "fiat," like those of Mary at the Annunciation and Jesus in the Garden of Gethsemane.

In his role as the head of a family, Joseph taught Jesus to be obedient to his parents (cf. Lk 2:51), in accordance with God's command (cf. Ex 20:12).

During the hidden years in Nazareth, Jesus learned at the school of Joseph to do the will of the Father. That will was to be his daily food (cf. Jn 4:34). Even at the most difficult moment of his life, in Gethsemane, Jesus chose to do the Father's will rather than his own,[16] becoming "obedient unto death, even death on a cross" (Phil 2:8). The author of the Letter to the Hebrews thus concludes that Jesus "learned obedience through what he suffered" (5:8).

All this makes it clear that "Saint Joseph was called by God to serve the person and mission of Jesus directly through the exercise of his fatherhood" and that in this way, "he cooperated in the fullness of time in the great mystery of salvation and is truly a minister of salvation."[17]

4. An Accepting Father

Joseph accepted Mary unconditionally. He trusted in the angel's words. "The nobility of Joseph's heart is such that what he learned from the law he made dependent on charity. Today, in our world where psychological, verbal and physical violence toward women is so evident, Joseph appears as the figure of a respectful and sensitive man. Even though he does not understand the bigger picture, he makes a decision to protect Mary's good name, her dignity, and her life. In his hesitation about how best to act, God helped him by enlightening his judgment."[18]

Often in life, things happen whose meaning we do not understand. Our first reaction is frequently one of disappointment and rebellion. Joseph set aside his own ideas in order to accept the course of events and, mysterious as they seemed, to embrace them, take responsibility for them, and make them part of his own history. Unless we are reconciled with our own history, we will be unable to take a single step forward, for we will always remain hostage to our expectations and the disappointments that follow.

The spiritual path that Joseph traces for us is not one that *explains*, but *accepts*. Only as a result of this acceptance, this reconciliation, can we begin to glimpse a broader history, a deeper meaning. We can almost hear an echo of the impassioned reply of Job to his wife, who had urged him to rebel against the evil he endured: "Shall we receive the good at the hand of God, and not receive the bad?" (Job 2:10).

Joseph is certainly not passively resigned, but courageously and firmly proactive. In our own lives, acceptance and welcome can be an expression of the Holy Spirit's gift of fortitude. Only the Lord can give us the strength needed to accept life as it is, with all its contradictions, frustrations, and disappointments.

Jesus' appearance in our midst is a gift from the Father, which makes it possible for each of us to be reconciled to the flesh of our own history, even when we fail to understand it completely.

Just as God told Joseph: "Son of David, do not be afraid!" (Mt 1:20), so he seems to tell us: "Do not be afraid!" We need to set aside all anger and disappointment, and to embrace the way things are, even when they do not turn out as we wish. Not with mere resignation but with hope and courage. In this way, we become open to a deeper meaning. Our lives can be miraculously reborn if we find the courage to live them in accordance with the Gospel. It does not matter if everything seems to have gone wrong or some things can no longer be fixed. God can make flowers spring up from stony ground. Even if our heart condemns us, "God is greater than our hearts, and he knows everything" (1 Jn 3:20).

Here, once again, we encounter that Christian realism which rejects nothing that exists. Reality, in its mysterious and irreducible complexity, is the bearer of existential meaning, with all its lights and shadows. Thus, the Apostle Paul can say: "We know that all things work together for good, for those who love God" (Rom 8:28). To which Saint Augustine adds, "even that which is called evil (*etiam illud quod malum dicitur*)."[19] In this greater perspective, faith gives meaning to every event, however happy or sad.

Nor should we ever think that believing means finding facile and comforting solutions. The faith Christ taught us is what we see in Saint Joseph. He did not look for shortcuts, but confronted reality with open eyes and accepted personal responsibility for it.

Joseph's attitude encourages us to accept and welcome others as they are, without exception, and to show special concern for the weak, for God chooses what is weak (cf. 1 Cor 1:27). He is the "Father of orphans and protector of widows" (Ps 68:6), who commands us to love the stranger in our midst.[20] I like to think that it was from Saint Joseph that Jesus drew inspiration for the parable of the prodigal son and the merciful father (cf. Lk 15:11–32).

5. A Creatively Courageous Father

If the first stage of all true interior healing is to accept our personal history and embrace even the things in life that we did not choose, we must now add another important element: creative courage. This emerges especially in the way we deal with difficulties. In the face of difficulty, we can either give up and walk away, or somehow engage with it. At times, difficulties bring out resources we did not even think we had.

As we read the infancy narratives, we may often wonder why God did not act in a more direct and clear way. Yet God acts through events and people. Joseph was the man chosen by God to guide the beginnings of the history of redemption. He was the true "miracle" by which God saves the child and his mother. God acted by trusting in Joseph's creative courage. Arriving in Bethlehem and finding no lodging where Mary could give birth, Joseph took a stable and, as best he could, turned it into a welcoming home for the Son of God come into the world (cf. Lk 2:6–7).

Faced with imminent danger from Herod, who wanted to kill the child, Joseph was warned once again in a dream to protect the child, and rose in the middle of the night to prepare the flight into Egypt (cf. Mt 2:13–14).

A superficial reading of these stories can often give the impression that the world is at the mercy of the strong and mighty, but the "good news" of the Gospel consists in showing that, for all the arrogance and violence of worldly powers, God always finds a way to carry out his saving plan. So too, our lives may at times seem to be at the mercy of the powerful, but the Gospel shows us what counts. God always finds a way to save us, provided we show the same creative courage as the carpenter of Nazareth, who was able to turn a problem into a possibility by trusting always in divine providence.

If at times God seems not to help us, surely this does not mean that we have been abandoned, but instead are being trusted to plan, to be creative, and to find solutions ourselves.

That kind of creative courage was shown by the friends of the paralytic, who lowered him from the roof in order to bring him to Jesus (cf. Lk 5:17–26). Difficulties did not stand in the way of those friends' boldness and persistence. They were convinced that Jesus could heal the man, and "finding no way to bring him in because of the crowd, they went up on the roof and let him down with his bed through the tiles into the middle of the crowd in front of Jesus. When he saw their faith, he said, 'Friend, your sins are forgiven you'" (vv. 19–20). Jesus recognized the creative faith with which they sought to bring their sick friend to him.

The Gospel does not tell us how long Mary, Joseph, and the child remained in Egypt. Yet they certainly needed to eat, to find a home and employment. It does not take much imagination to fill in those details. The Holy Family had to face concrete problems like every other family, like so many of our migrant brothers and sisters who, today too, risk their lives to escape misfortune and hunger. In this regard, I consider Saint Joseph the special patron of all those forced to leave their native lands because of war, hatred, persecution, and poverty.

At the end of every account in which Joseph plays a role, the Gospel tells us that he gets up, takes the child and his mother, and does what God commanded him (cf. Mt 1:24; 2:14.21). Indeed, Jesus and Mary his Mother are the most precious treasure of our faith.[21]

In the divine plan of salvation, the Son is inseparable from his Mother, from Mary, who "advanced in her pilgrimage of faith, and faithfully persevered in her union with her Son until she stood at the cross."[22]

We should always consider whether we ourselves are protecting Jesus and Mary, for they are also mysteriously entrusted to our own responsibility, care, and safekeeping. The Son of the Almighty came into our world in a state of great vulnerability. He needed to be defended, protected, cared for, and raised by Joseph. God trusted Joseph, as did Mary, who found in him someone who would not only save her life, but would always provide for her and her child. In this sense, Saint Joseph could not be other than the Guardian of the Church, for the Church is the continuation of the Body of Christ in history, even as Mary's motherhood is reflected in the motherhood of the Church.[23] In his continued protection of the Church, Joseph continues to protect *the child and his mother*, and we too, by our love for the Church, continue to love *the child and his mother*.

That child would go on to say: "As you did it to one of the least of these who are members of my family, you did it to me" (Mt 25:40). Consequently, every poor, needy, suffering, or dying person, every stranger, every prisoner, every infirm person is "the child" whom Joseph continues to protect. For this reason, Saint Joseph is invoked as protector of the unfortunate, the needy, exiles, the afflicted, the poor, and the dying. Consequently, the Church cannot fail to show a special love for the least of our brothers and sisters, for Jesus showed a particular concern for them and personally identified with them. From Saint Joseph, we must learn that same care and responsibility. We must learn to love the child and his mother, to love the sacraments and charity, to love the Church and the poor. Each of these realities is always *the child and his mother*.

6. A Working Father

An aspect of Saint Joseph that has been emphasized from the time of the first social Encyclical, Pope Leo XIII's *Rerum Novarum,* is his relation to work. Saint Joseph was a carpenter who earned an honest living to provide for his family. From him, Jesus learned the value, the dignity, and the joy of what it means to eat bread that is the fruit of one's own labor.

In our own day, when employment has once more become a burning social issue, and unemployment at times reaches record levels even in nations that for decades have enjoyed a certain degree of prosperity, there is a renewed need to appreciate the importance of dignified work, of which Saint Joseph is an exemplary patron.

Work is a means of participating in the work of salvation, an opportunity to hasten the coming of the Kingdom, to develop our talents and abilities, and to put them at the service of society and fraternal communion. It becomes an opportunity for the fulfillment not only of oneself, but also of that primary cell of society which is the family. A family without work is particularly vulnerable to difficulties, tensions, estrangement, and even break-up. How can we speak of human dignity without working to ensure that everyone is able to earn a decent living?

Working persons, whatever their job may be, are cooperating with God himself, and in some way become creators of the world around us. The crisis of our time, which is economic, social, cultural, and spiritual, can serve as a summons for all of us to rediscover the value, the importance, and necessity of work for bringing about a new "normal" from which no one is excluded. Saint Joseph's work reminds us that God himself, in becoming man, did not disdain work. The loss of employment that affects so many of our brothers and sisters, and has increased as a result of the Covid-19 pandemic, should serve as a summons to review our priorities. Let us implore Saint Joseph the Worker to help us find ways to express our firm conviction that no young person, no person at all, no family should be without work!

7. A Father in the Shadows

The Polish writer Jan Dobraczyński, in his book *The Shadow of the Father*,[24] tells the story of Saint Joseph's life in the form of a novel. He uses the evocative image of a shadow to define Joseph. In his relationship to Jesus, Joseph was the earthly shadow of the heavenly Father: he watched over him and protected him, never leaving him to go his own way. We can think of Moses' words to Israel: "In the wilderness . . . you saw how the Lord your God carried you, just as one carries a child, all the way that you traveled" (Deut 1:31). In a similar way, Joseph acted as a father for his whole life.[25]

Fathers are not born, but made. A man does not become a father simply by bringing a child into the world, but by taking up the responsibility to care for that child. Whenever a man accepts responsibility for the life of another, in some way he becomes a father to that person.

Children today often seem orphans, lacking fathers. The Church too needs fathers. Saint Paul's words to the Corinthians remain timely: "Though you have countless guides in Christ, you do not have many fathers" (1 Cor 4:15). Every priest or bishop should be able to add, with the Apostle: "I became your father in Christ Jesus through the Gospel" (ibid.). Paul likewise calls the Galatians: "My little children, with whom I am again in travail until Christ be formed in you!" (4:19).

Being a father entails introducing children to life and reality. Not holding them back, being overprotective or possessive, but rather making them capable of deciding for themselves, enjoying freedom and exploring new possibilities. Perhaps for this reason, Joseph is traditionally called a "most chaste" father. That title is not simply a sign of affection, but the summation of an attitude that is the opposite of possessiveness. Chastity is freedom from possessiveness in every sphere of one's life. Only when love is chaste, is it truly love. A possessive love ultimately becomes dangerous: it imprisons, constricts, and makes for misery. God himself loved humanity with a chaste love; he left us free even to go astray and set ourselves against him. The logic of love is always the logic of freedom, and Joseph knew how to love with extraordinary freedom. He never made himself the center of things. He did not think of himself, but focused instead on the lives of Mary and Jesus.

Joseph found happiness not in mere self-sacrifice but in self-gift. In him, we never see frustration but only trust. His patient silence was the prelude to concrete expressions of trust. Our world today needs fathers. It has no use for tyrants who would domineer others as a means of compensating for their own needs. It rejects those who confuse authority with authoritarianism, service with servility, discussion with oppression, charity with a welfare mentality, power with destruction. Every true vocation is born of the gift of oneself, which is the fruit of mature sacrifice. The priesthood and consecrated life likewise require this kind of maturity. Whatever our vocation, whether to marriage, celibacy, or virginity, our gift of self will not come to fulfillment if it stops at sacrifice; were that the case, instead of becoming a sign of the beauty and joy of love, the gift of self would risk being an expression of unhappiness, sadness, and frustration.

When fathers refuse to live the lives of their children for them, new and unexpected vistas open up. Every child is the bearer of a unique mystery that can only be brought to light with the help of a father who respects that child's freedom. A father who realizes that he is most a father and educator at the point when he becomes "useless," when he sees that his child has become independent and can walk the paths of life unaccompanied. When he becomes like Joseph, who always knew that his child was not his own but had merely been entrusted to his care. In the end, this is what Jesus would have us understand when he says: "Call no man your father on earth, for you have one Father, who is in heaven" (Mt 23:9).

In every exercise of our fatherhood, we should always keep in mind that it has nothing to do with possession, but is rather a "sign" pointing to a greater fatherhood. In a way, we are all like Joseph: a shadow of the heavenly Father, who "makes his sun rise on the evil and on the good, and sends rain on the just and on the unjust" (Mt 5:45). And a shadow that follows his Son.

•••

"Get up, take the child and his mother" (Mt 2:13), God told Saint Joseph.

The aim of this Apostolic Letter is to increase our love for this great saint, to encourage us to implore his intercession and to imitate his virtues and his zeal.

Indeed, the proper mission of the saints is not only to obtain miracles and graces, but to intercede for us before God, like Abraham[26] and Moses[27], and like Jesus, the "one mediator" (1 Tm 2:5), who is our "advocate" with the Father (1 Jn 2:1) and who "always lives to make intercession for [us" (Heb 7:25; cf. Rom 8:34).

The saints help all the faithful "to strive for the holiness and the perfection of their particular state of life."[28] Their lives are concrete proof that it is possible to put the Gospel into practice.

Jesus told us: "Learn from me, for I am gentle and lowly in heart" (Mt 11:29). The lives of the saints too are examples to be imitated. Saint Paul explicitly says this: "Be imitators of me!" (1 Cor 4:16).[29] By his eloquent silence, Saint Joseph says the same.

Before the example of so many holy men and women, Saint Augustine asked himself: "What they could do, can you not also do?" And so he drew closer to his definitive conversion, when he could exclaim: "Late have I loved you, Beauty ever ancient, ever new!"[30]

We need only ask Saint Joseph for the grace of graces: our conversion.

Let us now make our prayer to him:

Hail, Guardian of the Redeemer,
Spouse of the Blessed Virgin Mary.
To you God entrusted his only Son;
in you Mary placed her trust;
with you Christ became man.

Blessed Joseph, to us too,
show yourself a father
and guide us in the path of life.
Obtain for us grace, mercy and courage,
and defend us from every evil. Amen.

Given in Rome, at Saint John Lateran, on 8 December, Solemnity of the Immaculate Conception of the Blessed Virgin Mary, in the year 2020, the eighth of my Pontificate.

FRANCISCUS

Notes

1. Lk 4:22; Jn 6:42; cf. Mt 13:55; Mk 6:3.

2. S. Rituum Congregatio, *Quemadmodum Deus* (8 December 1870): ASS 6 (1870–71), 194.

3. Cf. *Address to ACLI on the Solemnity of Saint Joseph the Worker* (1 May 1955): AAS 47 (1955), 406.

4. Cf. Apostolic Exhortation *Redemptoris Custos* (15 August 1989): AAS 82 (1990), 5–34.

5. *Catechism of the Catholic Church*, 1014.

6. *Meditation in the Time of Pandemic* (27 March 2020): *L'Osservatore Romano*, 29 March 2020, p. 10.

7. *In Matthaeum Homiliae*, V, 3: PG 57, 58.

8. *Homily* (19 March 1966): *Insegnamenti di Paolo VI*, IV (1966), 110.

9. Cf. *Autobiography*, 6, 6–8.

10. Every day, for over forty years, following Lauds I have recited a prayer to Saint Joseph taken from a nineteenth-century French prayer book of the Congregation of the Sisters of Jesus and Mary. It expresses devotion and trust, and even poses a certain challenge to Saint Joseph: "Glorious Patriarch Saint Joseph, whose power makes the impossible possible, come to my aid in these times of anguish and difficulty. Take under your protection the serious and troubling situations that I commend to you, that they may have a happy outcome. My beloved father, all my trust is in you. Let it not be said that I invoked you in vain, and since you can do everything with Jesus and Mary, show me that your goodness is as great as your power. Amen."

11. Cf. Deut 4:31; Ps 69:16; 78:38; 86:5; 111:4; 116:5; Jer 31:20.

12. Cf. Apostolic Exhortation *Evangelii Gaudium* (24 November 2013), 88, 288: AAS 105 (2013), 1057, 1136–37.

13. Cf. Gn 20:3; 28:12; 31:11.24; 40:8; 41:1–32; Num 12:6; 1 Sm 3:3–10; Dan 2, 4; Job 33:15.

14. In such cases, provisions were made even for stoning (cf. Deut 22:20–21).

15. Cf. Lev 12:1–8; Ex 13:2.

16. Cf. Mt 26:39; Mk 14:36; Lk 22:42.

17. Saint John Paul II, Apostolic Exhortation *Redemptoris Custos* (15 August 1989), 8: AAS 82 (1990), 14.

18. *Homily at Mass and Beatifications*, Villavicencio, Colombia (8 September 2017): AAS 109 (2017), 1061.

19. *Enchiridion de fide, spe et caritate*, 3.11: PL 40, 236.

20. Cf. Deut 10:19; Ex 22:20–22; Lk 10:29–37.

21. Cf. S. Rituum Congregatio, *Quemadmodum Deus* (8 December 1870): ASS 6 (1870–71), 193; Blessed Pius IX, Apostolic Letter *Inclytum Patriarcham* (7 July 1871): l.c., 324–27.

22. Second Vatican Ecumenical Council, Dogmatic Constitution on the Church *Lumen Gentium*, 58.

23. *Catechism of the Catholic Church*, 963–70.

24. Original edition: *Cień Ojca*, Warsaw, 1977.

25. Cf. Saint John Paul II, Apostolic Exhortation *Redemptoris Custos*, 7–8: AAS 82 (1990), 12–16.

26. Cf. Gn 18:23–32.

27. Cf. Ex 17:8–13; 32:30–35.

28. Second Vatican Ecumenical Council, Dogmatic Constitution *Lumen Gentium*, 42.

29. Cf. 1 Cor 11:1; Phil 3:17; 1 Thes 1:6.

30. *Confessions*, VIII, 11, 27: PL 32, 761; X, 27, 38: PL 32, 795.

Appendix

Document on Human Fraternity for World Peace and Living Together

Apostolic Journey to the United Arab Emirates

February 4, 2019

A DOCUMENT ON HUMAN FRATERNITY FOR WORLD PEACE AND LIVING TOGETHER

Introduction

Faith leads a believer to see in the other a brother or sister to be supported and loved. Through faith in God, who has created the universe, creatures, and all human beings (equal on account of his mercy), believers are called to express this human fraternity by safeguarding creation and the entire universe and supporting all persons, especially the poorest and those most in need.

This transcendental value served as the starting point for several meetings characterized by a friendly and fraternal atmosphere where we shared the joys, sorrows, and problems of our contemporary world. We did this by considering scientific and technical progress, therapeutic achievements, the digital era, the mass media, and communications. We reflected also on the level of poverty, conflict, and suffering of so many brothers and sisters in different parts of the world as a consequence of the arms race, social injustice, corruption, inequality, moral decline, terrorism, discrimination, extremism, and many other causes.

From our fraternal and open discussions, and from the meeting that expressed profound hope in a bright future for all human beings, the idea of this Document on *Human Fraternity* was conceived. It is a text that has been given honest and serious thought so as to be a joint declaration of good and heartfelt aspirations. It is a document that invites all persons who have faith in God and faith in *human fraternity* to unite and work together so that it may serve as a guide for future generations to advance a culture of mutual respect in the awareness of the great divine grace that makes all human beings brothers and sisters.

Document

In the name of God who has created all human beings equal in rights, duties, and dignity, and who has called them to live together as brothers and sisters, to fill the earth and make known the values of goodness, love, and peace;

In the name of innocent human life that God has forbidden to kill, affirming that whoever kills a person is like one who kills the whole of humanity, and that whoever saves a person is like one who saves the whole of humanity;

In the name of the poor, the destitute, the marginalized, and those most in need whom God has commanded us to help as a duty required of all persons, especially the wealthy and of means;

In the name of orphans, widows, refugees, and those exiled from their homes and their countries; in the name of all victims of wars, persecution, and injustice; in the name of the weak, those who live in fear, prisoners of war, and those tortured in any part of the world, without distinction;

In the name of peoples who have lost their security, peace, and the possibility of living together, becoming victims of destruction, calamity, and war;

In the name of *human fraternity* that embraces all human beings, unites them, and renders them equal;

In the name of this *fraternity* torn apart by policies of extremism and division, by systems of unrestrained profit, or by hateful ideological tendencies that manipulate the actions and the future of men and women;

In the name of freedom, that God has given to all human beings creating them free and distinguishing them by this gift;

In the name of justice and mercy, the foundations of prosperity and the cornerstone of faith;

In the name of all persons of good will present in every part of the world;

In the name of God and of everything stated thus far; Al-Azhar al-Sharif and the Muslims of the East and West, together with the Catholic Church and the Catholics of the East and West, declare the adoption of a culture of dialogue as the path; mutual cooperation as the code of conduct; reciprocal understanding as the method and standard.

We, who believe in God and in the final meeting with Him and His judgment, on the basis of our religious and moral responsibility, and through this Document, call upon ourselves, upon the leaders of the world, as well as the architects of international policy and world economy, to work strenuously to spread the culture of tolerance and of living together in peace; to intervene at the earliest opportunity to stop the shedding of innocent blood and bring an end to wars, conflicts, environmental decay, and the moral and cultural decline that the world is presently experiencing.

We call upon intellectuals, philosophers, religious figures, artists, media professionals, and men and women of culture in every part of the world, to rediscover the values of peace, justice, goodness, beauty, human fraternity, and coexistence in order to confirm the importance of these values as anchors of salvation for all, and to promote them everywhere.

This Declaration, setting out from a profound consideration of our contemporary reality, valuing its successes, and in solidarity with its suffering, disasters, and calamities, believes firmly that among the most important causes of the crises of the modern world are a desensitized human conscience, a distancing from religious values, and a prevailing individualism accompanied by materialistic philosophies that deify the human person and introduce worldly and material values in place of supreme and transcendental principles.

While recognizing the positive steps taken by our modern civilization in the fields of science, technology, medicine, industry, and welfare, especially in developed countries, we wish to emphasize that, associated with such historic advancements, great and valued as they are, there exists both a moral deterioration that influences international action and a weakening of spiritual values and responsibility. All this contributes to a general feeling of frustration, isolation, and desperation leading many to fall either into a vortex of atheistic, agnostic, or religious extremism, or into blind and fanatic extremism, which ultimately encourage forms of dependency and individual or collective self-destruction.

History shows that religious extremism, national extremism, and also intolerance have produced in the world, be it in the East or West, what might be referred to as signs of a "third world war being fought piecemeal." In several parts of the world and in many tragic circumstances these signs have begun to be painfully apparent, as in those situations where the precise number of victims, widows, and orphans is unknown. We see, in addition, other regions preparing to become theaters of new conflicts, with outbreaks of tension and a build-up of arms and ammunition, and all this in a global context overshadowed by uncertainty, disillusionment, fear of the future, and controlled by narrow-minded economic interests.

We likewise affirm that major political crises, situations of injustice and lack of equitable distribution of natural resources—which only a rich minority benefit from, to the detriment of the majority of the peoples of the earth—have generated, and continue to generate, vast numbers of poor, infirm, and deceased persons. This leads to catastrophic crises that various countries have fallen victim to despite their natural resources and the resourcefulness of young people which characterize these nations. In the face of such crises that result in the deaths of millions of children—wasted away from poverty and hunger—there is an unacceptable silence on the international level.

It is clear in this context how the family as the fundamental nucleus of society and humanity is essential in bringing children into the world, raising them, educating them, and providing them with solid moral formation and domestic security. To attack the institution of the family, to regard it with contempt, or to doubt its important role, is one of the most threatening evils of our era.

We affirm also the importance of awakening religious awareness and the need to revive this awareness in the hearts of new generations through sound education and an adherence to moral values and upright religious teachings. In this way we can confront tendencies that are individualistic, selfish, conflicting, and also address radicalism and blind extremism in all its forms and expressions.

The first and most important aim of religions is to believe in God, to honor Him, and to invite all men and women to believe that this universe depends on a God who governs it. He is the Creator who has formed us with His divine wisdom and has granted us the gift of life to protect it. It is a gift that no one has the right to take away, threaten, or manipulate to suit oneself. Indeed, everyone must safeguard this gift of life from its beginning up to its natural end. We therefore condemn all those practices that are a threat to life such as genocide, acts of terrorism, forced displacement, human organ trafficking, abortion, and euthanasia. We likewise condemn the policies that promote these practices.

Moreover, we resolutely declare that religions must never incite war, hateful attitudes, hostility, and extremism, nor must they incite violence or the shedding of blood. These tragic realities are the consequence of a deviation from religious teachings. They result from a political manipulation of religions and from interpretations made by religious groups who, in the course of history, have taken advantage of the power of religious sentiment in the hearts of men and women in order to make them act in a way that has nothing to do with the truth of religion. This is done for the purpose of achieving objectives that are political, economic, worldly, and short-sighted. We thus call upon all concerned to stop using religions to incite hatred, violence, extremism, and blind fanaticism, and to refrain from using the name of God to justify acts of murder, exile, terrorism, and oppression. We ask this on the basis of our common belief in God who did not create men and women to be killed or to fight one another, nor to be tortured or humiliated in their lives and circumstances. God, the Almighty, has no need to be defended by anyone and does not want His name to be used to terrorize people.

This Document, in accordance with previous International Documents that have emphasized the importance of the role of religions in the construction of world peace, upholds the following:

- The firm conviction that authentic teachings of religions invite us to remain rooted in the values of peace; to defend the values of mutual understanding, *human fraternity*, and harmonious coexistence; to re-establish wisdom, justice, and love; and to reawaken religious awareness among young people so that future generations may be protected from the realm of materialistic thinking and from dangerous policies of unbridled greed and indifference that are based on the law of force and not on the force of law;
- Freedom is a right of every person: each individual enjoys the freedom of belief, thought, expression, and action. The pluralism and the diversity of religions, colour, sex, race, and language are willed by God in His wisdom, through which He created human beings. This divine wisdom is the source from which the right to freedom of belief and the freedom to be different derives. Therefore, the fact that people are forced to adhere to a certain religion or culture must be rejected, as too the imposition of a cultural way of life that others do not accept;
- Justice based on mercy is the path to follow in order to achieve a dignified life to which every human being has a right;
- Dialogue, understanding, and the widespread promotion of a culture of tolerance, acceptance of others and of living together peacefully would contribute significantly to reducing many economic, social, political, and environmental problems that weigh so heavily on a large part of humanity;
- Dialogue among believers means coming together in the vast space of spiritual, human, and shared social values and, from here, transmitting the highest moral virtues that religions aim for. It also means avoiding unproductive discussions;

- The protection of places of worship—synagogues, churches, and mosques—is a duty guaranteed by religions, human values, laws, and international agreements. Every attempt to attack places of worship or threaten them by violent assaults, bombings, or destruction, is a deviation from the teachings of religions as well as a clear violation of international law;
- Terrorism is deplorable and threatens the security of people, be they in the East or the West, the North or the South, and disseminates panic, terror, and pessimism, but this is not due to religion, even when terrorists instrumentalize it. It is due, rather, to an accumulation of incorrect interpretations of religious texts and to policies linked to hunger, poverty, injustice, oppression, and pride. This is why it is so necessary to stop supporting terrorist movements fuelled by financing, the provision of weapons and strategy, and by attempts to justify these movements even using the media. All these must be regarded as international crimes that threaten security and world peace. Such terrorism must be condemned in all its forms and expressions;
- The concept of *citizenship* is based on the equality of rights and duties, under which all enjoy justice. It is therefore crucial to establish in our societies the concept of *full citizenship* and reject the discriminatory use of the term *minorities* which engenders feelings of isolation and inferiority. Its misuse paves the way for hostility and discord; it undoes any successes and takes away the religious and civil rights of some citizens who are thus discriminated against;
- Good relations between East and West are indisputably necessary for both. They must not be neglected, so that each can be enriched by the other's culture through fruitful exchange and dialogue. The West can discover in the East remedies for those spiritual and religious maladies that are caused by a prevailing materialism. And the East can find in the West many elements that can help free it from weakness, division, conflict, and scientific, technical, and cultural decline. It is important to

pay attention to religious, cultural, and historical differences that are a vital component in shaping the character, culture, and civilization of the East. It is likewise important to reinforce the bond of fundamental human rights in order to help ensure a dignified life for all the men and women of East and West, avoiding the politics of double standards;

- It is an essential requirement to recognize the right of women to education and employment, and to recognize their freedom to exercise their own political rights. Moreover, efforts must be made to free women from historical and social conditioning that runs contrary to the principles of their faith and dignity. It is also necessary to protect women from sexual exploitation and from being treated as merchandise or objects of pleasure or financial gain. Accordingly, an end must be brought to all those inhuman and vulgar practices that denigrate the dignity of women. Efforts must be made to modify those laws that prevent women from fully enjoying their rights;
- The protection of the fundamental rights of children to grow up in a family environment, to receive nutrition, education, and support, are duties of the family and society. Such duties must be guaranteed and protected so that they are not overlooked or denied to any child in any part of the world. All those practices that violate the dignity and rights of children must be denounced. It is equally important to be vigilant against the dangers that they are exposed to, particularly in the digital world, and to consider as a crime the trafficking of their innocence and all violations of their youth;
- The protection of the rights of the elderly, the weak, the disabled, and the oppressed is a religious and social obligation that must be guaranteed and defended through strict legislation and the implementation of the relevant international agreements.

To this end, by mutual cooperation, the Catholic Church and Al-Azhar announce and pledge to convey this Document to authorities, influential leaders, persons of religion all over the world, appropriate regional and international organizations, organizations within civil society, religious institutions, and leading thinkers. They further pledge to make known the principles contained in this Declaration at all regional and international levels, while requesting that these principles be translated into policies, decisions, legislative texts, courses of study, and materials to be circulated.

Al-Azhar and the Catholic Church ask that this Document become the object of research and reflection in all schools, universities, and institutes of formation, thus helping to educate new generations to bring goodness and peace to others, and to be defenders everywhere of the rights of the oppressed and of the least of our brothers and sisters.

In conclusion, our aspiration is that:

this Declaration may constitute an invitation to reconciliation and fraternity among all believers, indeed among believers and non-believers, and among all people of good will;

this Declaration may be an appeal to every upright conscience that rejects deplorable violence and blind extremism; an appeal to those who cherish the values of tolerance and fraternity that are promoted and encouraged by religions;

this Declaration may be a witness to the greatness of faith in God that unites divided hearts and elevates the human soul;

this Declaration may be a sign of the closeness between East and West, between North and South, and between all who believe that God has created us to understand one another, cooperate with one another, and live as brothers and sisters who love one another.

This is what we hope and seek to achieve with the aim of finding a universal peace that all can enjoy in this life.

Abu Dhabi, 4 February 2019

His Holiness	The Grand Imam of Al-Azhar
Pope Francis	Ahmad Al-Tayyeb

Pope Francis was born Jorge Mario Bergoglio in Buenos Aires, Argentina, to parents of Italian descent. He was ordained a Jesuit priest in 1969, ordained auxiliary bishop of Buenos Aires in 1992, installed as bishop in 1998, and elevated to cardinal in 2001. He was elected by the College of Cardinals in March 2013 as the 266th pontiff of the Roman Catholic Church and took the name Francis for St. Francis of Assisi. He is the first Jesuit pope, the first pope from the Americas, and the first non-European pope in more than twelve centuries.